CHINA

An Introduction

CHINA
An Introduction
Third Edition

LUCIAN W. PYE
Massachusetts Institute of Technology

With the collaboration of Mary W. Pye

LITTLE, BROWN AND COMPANY
Boston Toronto

Library of Congress Cataloging in Publication Data

Pye, Lucian W., 1921–
China.

Bibliography: p.
Includes index.
1. China. I. Pye, Mary W. II. Title.
DS706.P9 1983 951.05 83-9864
ISBN 0-316-72412-2

Library of Congress Catalog Card No. 83-9864

ISBN 0-673-39470-0

9 8 7 6 5 4

HAL

Printed in the United States of America

The translation of the poem on page v is reprinted from Lin Yutang, *The Gay Genius* (New York: John Day, 1947), p. 171.

To A. Doak Barnett, Charles T. Cross, Harold R. Isaacs,
and to the memory of John M. H. Lindbeck
and Alexander Eckstein,
friends who have shared my China

The affairs of men are in a turmoil,
The lonely scholar's spirit is vexed.
Why should the melody of the lute
Be drowned in the noise of the kettle drum?
Three cups can drown ten thousand worries,
And after waking up my spirit is cleansed . . .

Su Tung-Po
A.D. 1036–1101

Preface to the Third Edition

Now is an appropriate time for a revised edition of *China: An Introduction.* The Mao Zedong era has ended, leaving a lasting mark on Chinese society; the struggle for succession between Deng Xiaoping and Hua Guofeng has been resolved in a victory for the former; and a phase of experimentation with modernization policies has gone on long enough for observers to arrive at preliminary judgments. The first edition of this book was written in the wake of the Cultural Revolution and completed at the time of President Richard Nixon's first visit to China; the second edition included revisions up to the death of Mao Zedong; and now in this third edition we have the added story of the ways in which Deng Xiaoping and his associates have changed China.

The need for revision is proof that China is a dynamic and restlessly changing society. Yet the more the changes, the greater the need for perspective. Hence the historical approach, adopted in the first edition, remains unchanged.

Those who wish to understand the current scene in China need, in addition to the information about present policies and practices, a dual historical perspective: first, that provided by an appreciation of the Confucian order of traditional China, and second, that offered by some knowledge of the roots of the Maoist revolutionary era, against which so many of Deng's policies are either calculated or reflex reactions.

The third edition is published at a time when tourism in China has become fashionable, and consequently more and more Americans are able to gain first-hand introduction to China. At the same time thousands of Chinese are coming to the United States for study. Such exchanges are to be welcomed, for they can provide the bases for better mutual understanding. Yet if the reactions to direct exposure are to significantly enhance relations between the two peoples, they need to be grounded in the kind of understanding that can only be derived from historical and cultural study. Moreover, such deeper understanding is essential to temper the shifts in the American mood from uncritical acceptance of all things Chinese, including their pretensions, to cynically dwelling on Chinese warts. Fortunately the mood is still substantially on the positive side, and it is hoped that the striving for balance and objectivity in this work will contribute to stabilizing attitudes in a constructive manner.

I am indebted to those who have made helpful suggestions in both the first and second editions. Mary Pye has assumed a heavy burden in our collaboration, especially as she has grappled with the frustrating task of making sure that we have made both appropriate and correct changes to the *pinyin* system. Lola Klein has typed and retyped the major additions.

Preface to the First Edition

I resolved to write this book after my colleague Harold R. Isaacs remarked to me that "what we really need is a simple, straightforward introduction to China." I have not sought to advance novel theses or excessively unconventional interpretations, for the rapid expansion in the numbers of monographs on China provides ample opportunities for these. Now, more than ever, there is a need for better understanding of China and its historical evolution. In international politics there is debate over whether it is possible to have "two Chinas," but in intellectual circles there has been for several years an ever growing number of Chinas as different kinds of specialists analyze China from their particular vantage points. Quite often specialists on contemporary Communist China have little feeling for the Confucian traditions, and, conversely, scholars of old China and even Republican China may have little understanding of Mao's China. Growth of knowledge calls for specialization, but public understanding also calls for an initial perspective that is broad enough to include all the main forces that have contributed to the making of modern China.

Thus my purpose in writing this book has been to introduce students and laymen to the many dimensions of Chinese politics and history. Surely there is a place for an introduction to China that brings together the Confucian, Republican, and Communist periods, and examines them in the light of China's physical characteristics and vivid cultural forms. The need seems particularly great at this time. China is becoming increasingly involved with the international community, and we must seek to understand this distinctive one-quarter of mankind. For too long China has been an abstraction — a devil for some and a utopia for others.

My writing was greatly facilitated by Alison Huey, who collected data and criticized my drafts. I am deeply indebted to Edwin O. Reischauer for helping me immeasurably with the chapters on the Confucian order. William E. Griffith checked my analysis of Communist relations and ideology; Takashi Inoguchi and James L. Foster carefully reviewed my summary of domestic development during the Communist period. Molly Morell and Joanna Hill skillfully and cheerfully deciphered my illegible hand and typed the different drafts. The assistance I received from Mary W. Pye went beyond that of an editor, and therefore she is rightfully recognized as my collaborator.

Chinese Spelling in the Third Edition

On January 1, 1970, the Chinese government officially adopted a system of spelling Chinese characters called *pinyin*, and since then most Western publications have used that system for words associated with contemporary China, that is, the People's Republic. Prior to this change the most commonly used system was Wade-Giles, developed by two Englishmen. Because all historical works found in libraries use Wade-Giles, as do the people of Taiwan, while contemporary publications, especially newspapers, journals, and the United States government, use *pinyin*, the situation is confusing. There seems no alternative but to become familiar with both systems.

Since our purpose is to be as helpful as possible, the ideal would be to use for each Chinese word the style spelling that a student would most likely encounter in other contexts — which would mean *pinyin* for contemporary Communist names and words and Wade-Giles for the more historical ones. In practice, however, we found that no such neat division is possible because some older words are being frequently used now, while many Communist names that are embedded in history in Wade-Giles are now officially spelled in *pinyin*. Ultimately, we were driven to using throughout mainly *pinyin* with Wade-Giles romanizations given in parentheses where appropriate. We have, however, made some exceptions, in order to use whatever spelling individuals or institutions may have chosen for their own names. Although it may seem disrespectful to alter the spelling of Mao Tse-tung and Chou

En-lai, we have adhered to the current Chinese practice and used Mao Zedong and Zhou Enlai.

Each system has its problems for English speakers. Most troublesome in *pinyin* are the following: *c* is pronounced like the *ts* in *ts*ar; *q* is like the *ch* in *ch*eap; *x* is like the *sh* in *sh*eet; *zh* is like the *j* in *J*oe.

The Wade-Giles system is complicated by the use of apostrophes after certain consonants to indicate that they should be aspirated. Thus, *p* is pronounced as *b* in the English *be,* while *p'* is *p* as in *p*ig. Similarly *t* is sounded as *d,* while *t'* is *t* as in *t*ea. Other peculiarities in Wade-Giles is the use of *j* for a sound much like *r,* and the use of the ending *-ih* for the sound *-er.*

Contents

CHINA

An Introduction

People's Republic of China
ADMINISTRATIVE DIVISIONS
International boundary
International boundary (indefinite or in dispute)
Internal administrative boundary
National capital
Internal administrative capital
0 100 200 300 400 500
Statute Miles
HEILONGJIANG
HARBIN
CHANGCHUN
JILIN
SHENYANG (MUKDEN)
LIAONING
SEA OF JAPAN
BEIJING DISTRICT
PEKING (BEIJING)
TIANJIN
HEBEI
NEI MONGGOL
HOHHOT
TAIYUAN
SHANXI
YINCHUAN
NINGXIA
JINAN
SHANDONG
YELLOW SEA
XINJIANG
URÜMQI
GANSU
QINGHAI
XINING
LANZHOU
XIAN
SHAANXI
ZHENGZHOU
HENAN
JIANGSU
ANHUI
HEFEI
NANJING
SHANGHAI
SHANGHAI DISTRICT
XIZANG
LHASA
CHENGDU
SICHUAN
HUBEI
WUHAN
HANGZHOU
ZHEJIANG
EAST CHINA SEA
NANZHANG
JIANGXI
CHANGSHA
HUNAN
FUZHOU
FUJIAN
FORMOSA STRAIT
GUIZHOU
GUIYANG
KUNMING
YUNNAN
GUANGXI
NANNING
GUANGDONG
CANTON (GUANGZHOU)
GULF OF TONKIN
SOUTH CHINA SEA
BAY OF BENGAL

CHAPTER ONE

An Abundance of Questions

China continues to attract Americans. First came the clipper ship traders, then dedicated missionaries, and now new generations of students, teachers, business executives, and not least, the tourists and cultural exchange delegations. After two decades in which Americans were cut off from contact with China, the thaw in antagonism between the United States and China in the 1970s reawakened the American yearning to know more about China. Although gratified by the apparent start of an era of goodwill, Americans remain puzzled about developments in China. Has the growing stream of tourists been allowed to see the "real" China? What is genuine and what is propaganda? Old myths have been dispelled, but are they being replaced by new ones that will continue to insulate Americans from the world's most populous country? How much has really changed as a result of the Communist revolution, and to what degree is China still "Chinese"? The more China has opened its "bamboo curtain," the more we realize how little we know about China and what an abundance of questions we still have.

During the turmoil of the Cultural Revolution, journalists, scholars, and diplomats spoke of the isolation of China and of how a quarter of mankind had turned its back on the rest of the world and was absorbed with itself. Red Guard youths captured the Chinese foreign office, attacked foreign diplomats in Peking, and generally denounced all manifestations of foreign as well as traditional Chinese influences on contemporary Chinese life. Strange events were these, yet China has always been alone in a sense, and the rest of the world has always viewed it with mixed fascination and revulsion. The mysteries of Cathay, the Middle Kingdom, the warlords, the Nationalists, and Mao Zedong's revolutionary visions have each in their time attracted and repelled the imaginations of those whom the Chinese designate simply as "foreigners." Under Deng Xiaoping China has opened her door a crack to the outside world, but much remains hidden.

Chinese civilization is one of the great achievements of the human spirit. Although many of its ancient forms and traditions are gone, the people most touched by it — Chinese, Koreans, Japanese, and Vietnamese — continue to show remarkable vitality in comparison with most non-Western societies. The grandeur and pretensions of the Confucian Way have crumbled, and the Confucian family system is no more, but the basic cast of personality that made China great still exists. To the extent that the character of the Chinese has persisted, China's potential for greatness has been continuous.

The puzzle that has been China grows more perplexing with the decades. Yet China in all its various forms has much to teach the rest of the world. Traditional China may reveal more about social order and political stability than any other society. The Chinese imperial system was the most enduring major political system in world history. For more than two millennia, from the second century B.C. until 1911, the Chinese essentially adhered to one form of government and, with only modest modifications, one political philosophy. Why did this amazing system of public order persist for so long?

In contrast to the theme of stability that characterized traditional China, the story of modern China is that of revolution — profound, intense, violent, and protracted. Like most non-European countries, China has been caught up in the complex problems of modernization, but the challenge has been more massive for the Chinese. For more than one hundred years they have been experiencing profound social change, and for decades they have lived through violence — political upheavals, civil wars, and foreign conquests. Behind the political and military turmoil lie deep intellectual and moral issues: The Chinese have grappled with the perplexing questions of how they should relate their traditions to modern experiences.

Just as traditional China had one of the most stable and enduring social orders in history, so the Chinese revolution has been one of the most far-reaching and fundamental upheavals of all time. The stereotypes of the "changeless Orient" and the "revolutionary East" persist precisely because China continues to surprise us with continuity when we expect change and change when we expect inertia.

In every age the story of China has been filled with perplexing contradictions. Traditional China extolled harmony and, more than most systems, emphasized morality and ethical precepts as the bases of legitimacy and authority. Yet every dynasty was founded by military force, and up to this very moment armies have been key factors at every critical turn of events.

Chinese political philosophy was elitist, sanctioning the rule of autocratic philosopher-kings, yet it praised the common man and the simple virtues. Among all the state ideologies of the ancient world Confucianism was unique because it was precociously secular, making no assertions of divine revelation or mystical origin. The greatest figure in the Chinese tradition, Confucius, was a mere mortal. But reason and morality, the ultimate foundations of Chinese imperial authority, were sanctified in the Mandate of Heaven, which suggested an element of divine influence in governmental affairs. Thus the Chinese confusedly mixed the secular and sacred in still another contradiction.

In a strange fashion, elements in the Chinese tradition seem to have given the Chinese unique advantages for establishing a modern state and developing a modern economy. The Chinese originated rule by a bureaucracy based on merit and were the first to recruit men for places of authority using competitive examinations. At a remarkably early date the Chinese eliminated formal feudalism and the concept of hereditary and landed aristocracy. The spirit of achievement and the virtues of hard work, frugality, and persistence were all central features of the Chinese social ethic. Yet in modern times nation-building has been peculiarly difficult for the Chinese, and despite their singular economic achievements in other societies the Chinese have failed in their own country to create a modern economic system and to achieve significant economic development. Capitalism has not emerged in China, and socialist institutions have yet to prove that they are the answer to China's needs. What are the reasons for these economic difficulties in the face of the manifest sophistication of Chinese civilization?

Furthermore, there is the puzzling contradiction that even though the Chinese achieved many remarkable technological advances at a very early date — the list goes well beyond such obvious items as the invention of paper, printing, gunpowder, and the compass — they failed to develop science. In spite of a tradition venerating the scholar and the role of reason, the Chinese did not significantly advance the art of reasoning, the study of logic, or the development of the physical sciences. Again we are led to wonder about the extraordinary strengths and limitations of the traditional Chinese intellectual achievements.

These challenging questions that compare traditional China with other great civilizations can be matched by equally intriguing questions about modern China, and particularly the Chinese version of communism. Why was Chinese nationalism so slow to produce effective government? Why did democracy fail in the Chinese setting? Why has Chinese communism presented so many faces to the world? The Chinese "model" has ranged from disciplined, well-mannered guerrillas, to an orderly planning and bureaucratic system, to radical and romantic revolutionary strife, and now to "pragmatic" economics.

Thus to know China is to learn about at least three political systems: the traditional, consisting of the remarkably coherent and integrated structures, institutions, and ideologies of the imperial era; the republican, or early modern, which found China reacting to the Western challenge and searching for a new destiny in nationalism; and Communist China, in which the theories and practices, the dogmas and disciplines, of Marxism-Leninism-Stalinism and Maoism are being applied to the modernization and development of the world's largest society.

The task of learning about any one of these Chinas would be demanding enough, but we need to know about all three, for there has been great continuity in Chinese life, and the contemporary generation of Chinese is still reacting to its cultural legacies. Mao Zedong, a worldwide symbol of radical revolutionary thought, was unmistakably a product of the intellectual confusion and striving of early twentieth-century China and thus took much from the earlier traditions and legends of China. Although Mao brought dramatic changes to his country, China today still reflects its prerevolutionary legacies. If, therefore, we are to understand the dynamics of China we must know both its Confucian and Communist forms.

In looking at traditional China, we shall be most interested in the distinctive harmony between Confucian thought and Confucian institutions. Confucianism was an ideology of the rulers and of officialdom, but it articulated values that were profoundly meaningful for even the humblest peasants. Confucianism influenced not just the institutions of government but also the traditions of the Chinese family system.

For a remarkably long time the formal institutions of the society meshed with and mutually reinforced nearly all social and private institutions. This was part of the source of Chinese stability. The dividing line between government and society was blurred. The result was a system of government that was both humanistic and autocratic. The authoritarian imperial system discouraged private efforts to make demands on the government: Popular sentiments had no channels for expression, and all forms of individualistic interests, whether economic, social, or regional, were considered improper. Accommodation between government and individuals occurred, but in ways that suggested impropriety and corruption.

The authoritarian spirit of Confucianism lacked the ideological firmness that went with the doctrines of absolutism in the West, and the Chinese did not have the pressure of competition that accompanied the fragmentation of Europe, with its clashes between nobles and nobles, between kings and kings, and finally between nation-states. Thus the Chinese state never became as rigid or as mobilized as the European states. According to the Chinese, the greatness of the civilization, and not the reasons of state, shapes history. If we are to understand the heritage that has formed modern China, we must look beyond institutions and ideology in order to capture the spirit of the artistic and philosophical traditions of ancient China.

The story of China's reaction to the West helps to highlight the essential differences between the two civilizations. The clashes illuminate the degree to which the Chinese tradition was based on human considerations, the search for the expression of virtue, and practical moderation and compromise, while Western culture was committed to the principles of law, competition, and individual self-interest. The story of this great meeting of civilizations has yet to be told from a perspective that does not seek to make moral points about the rights and wrongs of one or the other. In the meantime, however, it is important to see the story as an illustration of the Chinese efforts to find new foundations for their society and government. The breakdown of the imperial system caused profound economic and social changes, the rise of new classes, and the impoverishment of old ones. Above all it created a self-consciousness that produced shock waves of intellectual dissatisfaction and cultural humiliation.

After the revolution that brought down the imperial system, the Chinese began in earnest a search that is still going on. China avoided direct colonial domination but suffered the indignities of the treaty ports and foreign gunboats. It also suffered the humiliation of a period of ineffectual nationalist awakening. Finally — possibly most traumatic of all — China suffered through years of war with and occupation by the Japanese.

The Communist system that emerged from these travails seemed for a while to provide China with a new hope — the prospect for rapid development and an imminent return to world prominence. The turmoil of the Communists has made the future seem more clouded. They have, however, clarified the basic issues of Chinese modernization. The issues that tore apart the Chinese Communist party during the Great Leap Forward and the Cultural Revolution are more than just disagreements between Party factions; they touch the heart of China's modernization.

Does China need to find a new ideological and spiritual identity before it can truly find itself? Or do the Chinese need more the benefits of modern technology and science? The problem of how to modernize the world's largest and one of its poorest populations has challenged Communist authorities. Agriculture, industrial development, education, and national security have in their separate ways created uncertainties that have divided China's leaders. Such basic questions as whether China's hopes lie in greater ideological commitment or in greater professionalization have set one group of leaders against another. What struck the outside world as the bizarre and unexplainable behavior of the Cultural Revolution was in fact a natural culmination of fundamental differences about how

China could best resolve the problems of modernization. The issues were not, however, resolved. A decade later, the struggle over who should guide China after Mao's death continued to revolve around the same contending approaches.

In spite of these factional differences, China has made progress. Many elementary problems have been solved, and new issues have consequently emerged. How, for example, can the principle of self-reliance be maintained as the need for advanced technology grows? Will cultural exchanges dampen the revolutionary ardor of Chinese specialists and intellectuals? Will closer ties with capitalist powers, particularly the United States, produce confusion at home and among Third World revolutionaries?

We shall examine these subjects and problems in the hope of answering some questions and of raising new ones. In covering the full sweep of Chinese history, we shall seek matters that will provide insight into the mysteries of China, make its great culture more understandable, and set its current actions in a useful perspective.

China's remoteness and isolation and variety of political forms complicate the study of China. But even more troublesome is the extraordinary record of China's propensity to let down all who have sought to "understand" and champion it. The earliest Western defenders of Confucian and Daoist wisdom were not only ignored by the Chinese but abandoned by them when China turned away from the imperial tradition and sought to become a republic. Those who were quickest to see democratic potentialities in China were soon let down by events. Westerners emotionally attached to the idea of virtuous and decent China being violated by vicious Japan found that the Chinese leaders they had admired were not living up to their ideals. When the Communists came to power, their advocates suggested that they would be more pragmatic and less ideological than most Communists, but soon the advocates were shown to lack understanding of Mao's communism. When the Chinese seemed to move toward organizational efficiency, they attracted a new group claiming to understand them, who spoke unfavorably of the rest of the developing world on the grounds that Peking had a greater sense of economic priorities, technical competence, and no-nonsense discipline. These apologists of China were soon made to seem completely out of touch with the real China when the Maoist vision of revolutionary commitment replaced the Chinese "model" of development. Then radicals throughout the world began to wonder whether Mao's China had turned its back on them and the cause of revolution when Peking received President Richard Nixon and his national security advisor Henry Kissinger. The deaths of Mao Zedong and Zhou Enlai in 1976 prompted new speculation about the course China would take, as Deng Xiaoping sought to reach the goals of the "Four Modernizations" pragmatically.

The problem, of course, has always been that friends as well as critics have persisted in making China an abstraction and treating it as a symbol of good or evil. Subjective images have blurred objectivity. Before turning to the social and political puzzles of China, therefore, we need to be introduced to China as a physical entity.

PEOPLE'S REPUBLIC OF CHINA

Area

Total area — 3,691,500 square miles (slightly larger than U.S.)
Length (north-south) — 1,860 miles
Width (east-west) – 2,000 miles (average)
Cultivated acres per person — .25
Arable land — 25%

Population, Density, and Distribution

Total (1982 census) — 1,008,175,288
Per square mile — 273
Urban — 20.6%
Rural — 79.4%
Literacy rate (1964) — 61.9%
(1982) — 76.5%
Total university graduates — 4.4 million
Average annual population growth rate
(1950–1966) — 2 to 2.5%
(1965–1976) — 1.8%
(1976–1981) — 1.4%

Economy (in U.S. dollars)

	1952	1957	1965	1975	1979	1981
Total GNP (in billions)						
U.S. government estimates	99	138	185	368	468	515
Chinese government figures	51.9	72.4	97	193	245	270.2
Per capita GNP						
U.S. government estimates	172.2	249	255	400.1	482	516.9
Chinese government figures	90.3	112	133.7	302.9	253	271.2
Per capita national income						
Chinese government figures	52	71	87	137	174	N.A.

Foreign Trade (in millions of U.S. dollars)

YEAR	TURNOVER	IMPORTS	EXPORTS	BALANCE: SURPLUS (+) OR DEFICIT (—)
1952	1,890	1,015	875	−140
1965	3,880	1,845	2,035	+190
1975	14,575	7,395	7,180	−215
1980	38,040	19,940	18,100	−1,850
1982	38,600	17,000	21,600	+4,600

Currency

1 *yuan* = U.S. $1.96–$2.20 (1974–1982)

Grain Imports and Exports (in thousands of tons)

YEAR	IMPORT	EXPORT	BALANCE
1952	15	314	+299
1956	89	1,074	+985
1961	5,601	598	−5,003
1966	6,395	1,648	−4,747
1975	3,500	2,147	−1,354
1981	13,600	919	−12,681

Urban Households: Size and Income (1980)

Number of persons per household — 4.30
Number of persons employed per household — 2.35
Monthly per capita earnings — 42.80 *yuan*

Films, Radio, and Television

	1957	1965	1975	1979
Feature films produced	40	52	27	65
Film projection units (in thousands)	10	20.4	69.7	122
Radio broadcasting stations	61	87	88	99
Television transmitting and relay stations				238

Military

Regular forces	4.23 million
Atomic bomb detonated	October 16, 1964
Hydrogen bomb detonated	June 17, 1967
Space satellite launched	August 24, 1970

Sources: Economic Research Center, State Council of the PRC, and State Statistical Bureau, *Almanac of China's Economy, 1981*. Editor-in-chief Hue Muqiao; United Nations Economic and Social Affairs Office, Department of Statistics, *Statistical Yearbook, 1981;* and Willy Kraus, *Economic Development and Social Change in the People's Republic of China* (New York and Heidelberg: Springer Verlag, 1982)

CHAPTER TWO

Meeting China

The physical characteristics of China defy generalization. South China lies in the subtropics and blends into the world of Southeast Asia; at the other extreme, northern Manchuria and western Xinjiang are on a line with Newfoundland. On the east and south China has more than 4,000 miles of coastline, marked by excellent harbors, yet the country has always turned its back to the sea and contented itself with being a continental society. In looking inward, however, China has tended to ignore or treat with disdain the desolate mountainous reaches of its western interior, though the extent of that region makes China the world's third largest country in area, following Canada and the Soviet Union.

China has a population of more than a billion, making it nearly twice as large as India, the next most populous country. But this tremendous population does not seem to take advantage of China's physical size. The people are overwhelmingly concentrated in the eastern third of the land. This is because only about a quarter of China's territory is arable. About 245 million acres are in cultivation — an average of less than a quarter-acre per person — and these farmlands are concentrated along the eastern and northern coasts, on the Manchurian and the north China plains, along the main rivers, and on the Sichuan plateau.

More than 6,000 years ago Chinese civilization emerged in the Yellow (Huang He) River valley and spread across the north China plains. This region, with its vividly defined seasons and rich, good earth, has been the heart of the Mandarin-speaking region of China. The winters of north China, which begin in late November with the freezing of lakes and ponds, are dry and cold and sharply intensified by persistent and penetrating winds from across the Gobi Desert and out of Mongolia. By mid-February, signs of spring appear. Northern Chinese, like all people, talk much about the weather, but possibly to more purpose. They believe that every winter is made up of two "large colds" and three "small colds" — that is, two major and three minor cold spells — and therefore every change in temperature calls for judgments and classifications to determine what lies ahead. Men gather to compare impressions and test their judgments about what has been real and what mere illusion in the passing of the winter.

Spring in north China brings the harvesting of winter wheat and an early sowing of the *gaoliang* (capricorn), millet, and barley crops, which farmers hope will be helped by light spring rains. Summers are intensely hot, fueled by air that has moved across a whole continent. The rains arrive in July and August, but they are not as dramatic in their beginnings nor as continuous as the Indian monsoons. Sudden and intense storms, particularly in the mountains on the edges of the plains, cause flash floods but provide water for irrigation. About half of the cultivated land in China depends on irrigation. Every mountain stream and river is tapped to feed the fields. Electrically powered pumps exist, but frequently when water must be lifted the method remains the old one of manually working a bucket attached to a balanced pole that is weighted with a rock at the other end. In the past, the desperate shortage of water was often a principal cause of feuds within and between villages. Farmers clashed over the "stealing" of a few minutes of the flow of irrigation streams. Throughout the growing season the quiet night of the Chinese countryside would often be broken by shouts of violence and pain and the ring of picks and shovels smashing together, as one group of peasants attacked another caught in the act of trying to change the direction of a sluice surreptitiously. Long ago the requirements of irrigation taught the Chinese the need for cooperation and for a higher authority to adjudicate disputes and solicit fair shares in maintaining the dikes. The peasants also learned from the preciousness of water that one man's advantage was always another's loss, and that it was naïve to believe that everyone could benefit from change.

In central and south China water is less of a problem. There the brown flat plains of north China give way to a lush green and far more mountainous countryside. China is physically divided by the Yangtze River (or as it is now called, the Changjiang), which in west China moves through spectacular gorges and then races into the rich rice lands of central China, feeding numerous lakes before reaching the sea near Shanghai. In May and June the lower Yangtze has continuous rains called *mai-yü*, or plum rains, and the fog, clouds, and mists along its entire course are the source of the great Chinese landscape painting tradition. Along the lower reaches, river traffic includes sizable steamboats, but on the upper river the boats and barges have to be towed by men straining in harnesses as they plod along the rocky path by the churning water's edge. The scene enforces the impression that man is small and insignificant in contrast to the majesty and clouded mystery of nature.

Until recently the Yangtze could be crossed only by boat. The principal north-south railroad journey was interrupted while the train cars were ferried across the river and reassembled on the other side, a procedure requiring from two to three hours. A source of great pride to Communist China is a railroad bridge over the Yangtze at Nanjing, under which 10,000-ton ships can pass.

In south China the countryside is far more broken up by mountains. Although the land around Canton (Guangzhou) is level, other principal south China cities, such as Fuzhou and Xiamen, back right into mountains. The isolation of the population in China south of the Yangtze is reflected in the great variety of mutually unintelligible dialects spoken in the different communities.

Contrasts between north and south China exist in nearly every aspect of life. In the north, farms are large, and a farmer working with a donkey or mule can cultivate as much as twelve acres of wheat, millet, or *gaoliang;* in the south, working with a water buffalo and planting rice by hand, a farmer can cultivate three acres at most. In north China herdsmen tend flocks of sheep and goats on the hilly slopes of the loess valleys and on the mountainsides surrounding the plains. In south China livestock is limited to work animals and such scavengers as pigs, fowl, and dogs. Today the communes in north China have sought to increase production by improved water conservation, reforestation, and expanded acreage; in the south the communes are smaller but the warmer weather makes it possible to have as many as three crops a year.

Beyond the agrarian regions of north and south China lie the mountainous plateaus of Tibet (now known as Xizang) and the deserts and mountain ranges of northwest China, where in the past nomads roamed. Today the scenery of Tibet is much as it has always been, in spite of the destruction of the Lama theocracy and the construction of military roads. The Kunlun Mountains separate the Tibetan plateau from the deserts of northwest China, which in recent years have received several million migrants from east China. But the deserts still have vast empty areas marked by isolated settlements, at water spots along the recently extended railroad from Lanzhou through to the Soviet Union and Alma Ata.

The physical features of China have created great social differences. People near the mouths of the Yellow and Yangtze rivers live in some of the most crowded rural areas in the world; those who live beyond the atomic test site near Lake Lop Nor in Xinjiang are in one of the most sparsely settled regions in the world. These differences have probably increased over the centuries and continue to do so in spite of major efforts by the Peking government in recent years. Before Buddhism came to dominate Tibetan society and cause more than a quarter of its males to practice celibacy, Tibet supported a larger and more militant population, which spread out and conquered much of the rest of northwest China and Mongolia. From Roman times to the last Chinese dynasty, the desert regions in the northwest were the site of extensive trade caravans and restless, raiding nomadic peoples. The sharp upsurge of population in east China has occurred mostly in the last two hundred years.

China's population growth — a baby is born in China every two seconds — has forced an ever larger number of people to work on its limited arable land. While 80 percent of China's total population is rural, Japan has twice as much cultivated land per person, and India three-and-one-half times as much. Moreover, the expanding need for village housing has taken up nearly 20 percent of the better arable land and caused marginal lands, particularly forest and grasslands, to be brought under cultivation. In the last two decades Sichuan and Yunnan provinces lost 30 to 40 percent of their forests, respectively. The result has been a serious problem of soil erosion and a loss of irrigation water. Only farming skills and the increased use of chemical fertilizers have kept China's food production from dropping behind population growth.

The diversity of China is accentuated by the fact that although 80 percent of the people live in rural settings, Chinese civilization was built out of a great urban tradition. Thirteen of the fifty largest cities in the world are in China. Because most of these cities emerged not in response to industrial development but as administrative and trading centers, they generally reflect an orderly scheme and attention to comfort and beauty. The bustle of life in Chinese towns is largely centered on the marketplace and consumer interests. Matters of taste and choice, of novelty and quality, are important to the Chinese, and it is striking today that Communist China, with a poorer economy, surpasses the Soviet Union in the production of goods that can compete in international consumer markets.

Peking was once unquestionably one of the greatest cities of the world. It blended majestic orderliness and comfortable neighborhoods. Its broad avenues and open squares, the massive paved courtyards and golden roofs of the palaces in the Forbidden City, all succeed in humbling the individual. But these were juxtaposed with the intimacies of parks and narrow, wall-lined, sharply turning residential streets called *hutongs*. Old Peking had a low architectural profile, with only Coal Hill and the walls of the Forbidden City and the Tartar City breaking the skyline.

During the republican years many of the old imperial buildings of the capital were converted into museums and public parks, but when the peasant armies of the Communists captured power their leaders readily converted the Forbidden City into their own habitat. In much the same way that the Russian revolutionaries took to the Kremlin, the Chinese Communist leaders have turned the elegance of the imperial scene to their advantage. They have even cleared a massive square for their huge political parades.

Under the Communists the city still takes pride in being an elite center of government and education and a place for civil servants and scholars, but now, much like Moscow, it is also a showpiece for heavy industry and manufacturing. Urban sprawl has pushed out in all directions, and blocks of Soviet-style housing dominate the skyline in many sections. Peking, however, still maintains a sense of superiority, and its people are the best dressed in the country, with the exception of those in more cosmopolitan Shanghai. The Peking accent is the model for the national language, and the common and even unschooled people of Peking often sound more cultivated than the educated people from other places. (Chinese accents reflect geography more than class or social distinctions.)

The high points of a visit to Peking are usually trips to such ancient sites as the Great Wall, the Ming Tombs, the Temple of Heaven, the Forbidden City, and the Summer Palace.

Canton (Guangzhou) is in many ways the opposite of Peking. It is a massive, formless city, abounding in streets that teem with constantly moving people. In recent years it has been the scene of annual trade fairs at which China displays its products to buyers from abroad. Historically Canton was China's gateway to the sea, and it retains a tradition of fishing, but it is not located on the sea. It is situated about eighty miles up the Pearl River. Along the waterfront are old buildings once associated with foreign trade. The 3,025,000 people of Canton are thought of by many Chinese as industrious traders and merchants, and as hot-blooded revolutionaries always ready to challenge central authority.[1]

Before the Communist regime, Shanghai, the largest city, was a strange blend of East and West, cosmopolitan and provincial; exciting and vibrant to some, depressing and degenerate to others. From one perspective its International Settlement was a ghetto where Europeans and Americans huddled together, isolated from the main currents of China as a whole. From another perspective it was a place where haughty foreigners showed their scorn for the Chinese. In contrast to the International Settlement, which was dominated by the British but accommodated the pretensions of several nationalities, the French Concession in Shanghai reflected a Gallic spirit of shabby dignity and of going it alone.

After the arrival of the Communists, Shanghai continued to display extraordinary economic and industrial vitality. Communist propagandists had long portrayed Shanghai as an example of foreign exploitation of China, but on coming to power they discovered that what had been created in Shanghai was substantial enough to be permanently "exploited" for the benefit of the rest of China. Indeed, even after 2.5 million skilled workers had been sent out

[1] For the full story of Canton in modern times see Ezra Vogel, *Canton under Communism: Programs and Politics in a Provincial Capital, 1949–1968* (Cambridge, Mass.: Harvard University Press, 1969).

from Shanghai to help industrial development elsewhere, Shanghai's industries still remained supreme and continued to provide nearly half of all the revenues of the national government.

Paradoxically, in the 1960s Shanghai was the power base of the radical faction that advocated rural values, opposed technology, and sought equality to the point of insisting that every province should become self-sufficient. It was from Shanghai that Mao Zedong launched the Cultural Revolution. In the years since Mao's death the people of Shanghai have proved that they surreptitiously preserved their cosmopolitanism, and the city has come alive as the artistic and intellectual center of China.

Since the opening of China, and especially after the death of Mao Zedong, tourists from abroad have visited a group of historic and scenic cities in growing numbers. Xian (Sian) is the oldest, the first great imperial city of China, the capital of eleven dynasties, and once the largest city in the world. It was laid out in orderly rectangular blocks of streets, which became the model not only for Peking but even for Kyoto, Japan. Another popular tourist's stop is Hangzhou, also an ancient city, which was visited and admired by Marco Polo. Hangzhou is built around picturesque manmade lakes, dotted with islands and walkways so close to water level that they evoke in the visitor the sensation of walking on water. Possibly the most spectacular tourist city is Guilin (Kwelin) in South China, whose scenic outlooks provide photographers the blend of mountains, clouds, and water that has been standard in 1,000 years of Chinese brush painting.

In contrast to such attractive cities, China has a large number of relentlessly growing, nondescript, drab industrial centers. These include such cities as Tianjin (Tientsin), Taiyuan, Shenyang, Anshan, Dalien (Dairen), Chengdu, and the Wuhan complex. While each may have an area of distinctiveness, they are on the whole, massive company towns made up of factories, railroad yards, workers' living quarters, and support facilities — all contributing to the sooty gray sprawl. True, Hankou and its companion cities of Wuchang and Hanyang, which make up the Wuhan complex, have the spectacle of the Yangtze River to relieve the drab, industrial tone. In Tianjin, the old British Concession, surrounded by the dilapidated buildings of the former French and Japanese concessions, gave to the heart of an otherwise undistinguished industrial complex a nest of European town houses and some winding residential roads. These roads originated at what were a country club and racetrack but now a military barracks, and terminated at a neat, orderly Victorian park, adjoined by a town hall and clock tower built of imported stone. At the edge of the British Concession once stood the gray, soot-covered barracks of the Fifteenth Infantry Regiment of the United States Army, the "Can Do Regiment," posted in China during the Boxer troubles of 1900 only a few weeks after coping with the Philippine insurrection. Many of the older buildings of Tianjin were damaged or destroyed in the July 1976 earthquake that leveled the city of Tangshan, killed about 665,000 people, and damaged more than 30,000 houses in Peking.

Shenyang and Anshan, while largely industrial in character, offer innumerable examples of what might be called Japanese colonial architecture. The large, boxlike buildings, plain in form and decorated with disproportionately small towers, are much like those found in Taipei.

Harbin is much more distinctive architecturally, because more than a quarter of the city was at one time inhabited by a half-million Russian refugees, and many of its public buildings were once churches and synagogues with onion spires and arched domes. Its streets are wide and empty, its buildings now run down. In the principal square stands a huge monument to the few Russian soldiers killed in the last-moment Soviet involvement in the campaign against Japan in World War II.

The principal Chinese cities blend, in different amounts, Chinese culture and western impact. Although the "barbarian" has always been scorned by the Chinese, the foreigner, most especially the westerner, did leave a mark on China more indelibly than might be supposed in an essentially isolated culture.

The provincial cities of China that were less influenced by foreigners are usually low-built, with little design or plan. They do sometimes possess a historic center, formerly contained within high city walls. The heart of such a city was generally the area around the railway station and the central market. The Chinese practice was to congregate similar shops and businesses, devoting entire streets (Silk Street, Jade Street) to a single activity.

Historically, the distinctive features of provincial cities and large district towns were the high city walls, each broken only by massive gates closed each evening and guarded from above by towers in which a company of men could be stationed. The walls of small towns were generally straight and brick-faced, indented at the top with ramparts; such walls averaged from forty to sixty feet in height and were about twenty feet wide at the top. In the large towns the walls were higher, some of them reaching to nearly one hundred feet, with solid, well-placed battlements so the troops could cover all possible angles of fire. The tops of these walls were as wide as modern two-lane roads, and their rectangular lines gave an orderly pattern to the streets of the towns.

Now, except where shops open onto them, most streets are lined by the walls of private residences, government offices, and other establishments. Many streets in provincial and district towns are still unpaved. The Communist government has systematically leveled many of the ancient city walls, including Peking's, and has often used the bricks to pave the streets.

Throughout China, rural life centers on villages, not isolated farmhouses. Farmers must travel to their fields, starting the day early and usually ending it in long chats with neighbors. The men often bring their chopsticks and bowls of noodles out to the roadside, where they have their evening meal, squatting together in groups.

Chinese communes are remarkably similar in appearance in all regions of the country. In south China, however, the houses may be closer together, and more bamboo and straw is used in their construction. In north China most village walls are higher, and made of adobe brick. In parts of Liaoning, Hebei, and Shandong, houses are built with baked brick. Everywhere in China, village life traditionally centered on places of public or collective activity, such as a common well, an ancient shade tree, or even a small grove. There was also a tablet or shrine dedicated to the local gods or to the ancestors of the dominant clans. If the village was large enough or thought to be auspiciously situated, it might have a temple, usually without priests or monks but possibly tended by an aging caretaker. Periodically the temple served as a marketplace, and it would be the scene of annual festival celebrations, such as the Autumn Festival on the fifteenth day of the eighth lunar month, or the Dragon Boat Festival on the fifth day of the fifth month. From time to time, if things were not going well for the village or for people who lived there, villagers would refurbish their generally dilapidated clay idols, which had originally been painted in vivid colors, and which occupied secluded positions of honor in the temple.

After the arrival of Communism, temples were neglected and became devoted to secular concerns. They frequently became the storehouse for the collective's grain, the administrative center of a commune, or the location of a visiting clinic. Shrines and tablets were replaced by bulletin boards, which first appeared in villages during the Kuomintang (Guomindang) days and now are ubiquitous. Converting temples from religious to civic centers conveys little sense of sacrilege; in Chinese culture the separation of the sacred and secular was never sharp, and the conduct of worshipers usually disguised any sentiments of reverence. Significantly, after Deng Xiaoping consolidated power and sought to signal a more tolerant rule, many temples, including the Lama Temple in Peking, were restored.

The most visible transformation of the countryside since the Communist regime began has been the extensive reforestation. Roads are now lined with more trees than ever before, and groves cover hillsides, helping to hold the soil and adding moisture to the air. Within the settlements or communes are new buildings housing the variety of light industries that the national policy of self-reliance has encouraged.

In northwest China, through parts of Shanxi, Shaanxi, and Gansu where the loess plains have been eroded by rivers to produce cliff-lined valleys, are villages of caves. The most famous of these is Yan'an, which was Mao Zedong's headquarters from the end of the Long March until the end of the Japanese war. In this region cave villages are quite the equal of adobe ones in livability and status. The caves are usually arranged in a neat line on the side of a cliff, well above the high-water line of floods. Most dwellings consist of a single cave dug into the rockless, brownish-yellow soil, with an arched ceiling from twelve to fifteen feet high, a width of fifteen feet, and a depth of from twenty to thirty feet. The front of the cave is filled in with an adobe brick wall, the doorframe, and possibly a window or two. At night a wooden door is pulled shut; during the day the doorway is covered by a quilted mat in the coldest weather and by a bamboo curtain in summer.

The chambers of the caves tend to be of uniform size, and the dwellings differ only in the number of parallel chambers linked together. The largest units might have additional rooms whose doorways connect them to the main chamber, which has the only exit. The secondary rooms, generally bedrooms and storage rooms, often do not have windows, because the front facing the cliff is either entirely filled in with adobe brick or is the original wall of the cliff, in which case the room was dug out through the door to the main cave. If the caves are close to the top of the cliff, a chimney is drilled through to the surface above, which has to be roofed to prevent seepage. When the caves are at mid-cliff level, the stove pipe comes out through the front wall. Ventilation is generally poor, but the caves are snug in winter and cool in summer. In adobe and brick houses in northern China there are also few windows, and when windows do exist they usually cannot be opened and more often than not are covered with sheets of glued paper rather than glass.

Village life is geared to the rhythms of agriculture, but Chinese villages have not always been quiet pastoral places. In the past the shifting in the fortunes of families created tensions. Clashes and rivalries between clans were often intense, and because primogeniture did not prevail, hostilities could arise over the division of family holdings. In north China more often than in the south, landlords and tenants lived together as neighbors. The children of rich and poor peasants had the same schooling, but in the past, and probably still today, those who were inclined to command and those who were destined to obey found their respective roles at an early age.

Compared with other underdeveloped countries, China has a sound agricultural technology. Chinese farmers have long appreciated the differences in the quality of seeds and the advantages of using fertilizer. In the south the pattern of planting is relatively static, but northern farmers rotate their crops and respond quickly to changes in market and weather conditions. It is of historical significance that Chinese farmers have been able to keep pace with population growth. They have long understood that they can benefit by growing more than what is needed for self-sufficiency and by producing for larger markets that might be far away.

Indeed, rural China was never made up of only isolated, autonomous villages. Its communities usually clustered around marketing centers which were in turn parts of larger regional marketing systems. The centers moved rice from south to north along the Grand Canal and, after the introduction of the railroads, tied together not only regional grain markets but also the distribution of fresh fruits and vegetables.

Although today it might seem that the Chinese have an inadequate and antiquated system of transportation, in fact they have always, within the limits of their technology, invested enough in transportation to have a fairly complete national network. In modern times the system was built around roads for animal-drawn carts and the railroads. Less attention has been given to roads for motorized vehicles.

One of the extraordinary documents in Chinese history was the decree issued by the "first unifier," Emperor Qin Shi Huangdi, in 211 B.C., that the axles of all carts should be the same length. Uniform axle length made ruts in roads throughout the empire the same width, allowing military transport to reach any area without difficulty. In the plains of north China, over the centuries, the carts cut away the soil, causing erosion. Because many roads have sunk, heavily loaded carts pulled by as many as four teams of mules along such roads can be lost from the sight of a farmer plowing adjacent fields. The peculiarities of such sunken roadways have had some interesting consequences. They have made ambushing and banditry relatively easy. They pose problems for the passing of carts going in opposite directions and have given rise to the Chinese rule of the road that the lighter loaded cart must give way to the heavier — a principle the Chinese carried over to the motorized era, so that pedestrians must give way to bicycles, bicycles to cars, and cars to trucks. The bigger the vehicle, the more haughty the driver.

China lacks paved roads for automobiles and trucks; consequently such vehicles are mainly confined to cities or to a few well-established intercity routes. In the 1950s the Chinese claimed only 160,000 miles of usable highways, most of which were made of dirt or gravel; by the end of the 1960s there were about 225,000 miles of "all-weather" roads. By 1976 China had expanded its road network to 340,000 miles, though more than half were still dirt roads. Until the Japanese conquest of north China, the road between Peking and Tianjin was unpaved. Because of flooding, motorized roads in the north are usually raised, almost dikelike structures. Even today a common means of road freight transport is still big carts pulled by either animals or men, and at times by both.

There were inland waterways, the most impressive of which was the Grand Canal that linked the rice region of the lower Yangtze to Peking, but China had only 46,000 miles of navigable waterways when the Communists came to power in 1949. By 1958 the system had doubled, and by 1966 it totaled nearly 100,000 miles. It was planned in the 1950s to connect the basins of the Amur, Yellow, Yangtze, and Xi rivers by canals. Except for improving the southern half of the Grand Canal, however, little has been done because the Communists have focused on improving the railroads.

The railroads did not, however, come to China as a coherent system. On the contrary, and quite unlike Qin Shi Huangdi's unified rut system, different sections of China's railroads were capitalized by different sources, and thus used different equipment, including different gauges of track. The railroad from Shijiazhuang to Taiyuan, for example, was built by French capital. Its *wagonlits,* or sleeping cars, had French signs and pictures of the Seine and the French Alps, and its narrow, one-meter gauge gave it a miniature appearance. From Shijiazhuang to Peking the railroad used British equipment and a wide gauge. The Chinese Communists have continued to build railroads with different gauges, and while they do build large main lines, they still construct local lines with narrow gauges. A relatively uniform way of life is associated with the railroads. Railroad stations are usually central to Chinese cities. People who work on a railroad have real status, and no one with any connection to the railroad is too lowly to wear a uniform.

From the outset, Chinese railroads followed the European pattern of providing different classes of passenger service. Most lines had three classes. First class consisted of compartments with seats convertible to berths; second class offered less luxurious compartments; and third class generally had wooden seats and no privacy. The Communists have maintained these class differences, but refer to them, respectively, as "soft sleeper," "hard sleeper," and "hard seat."

Foreigners first pressured the Chinese for rights to build railroads in the 1860s, when the Taiping Rebellion was being crushed and when developments in America after the Civil War and in Latin America set off worldwide interest in the promise of railroads. From the beginning the Chinese reacted with caution: Li Hongzhang, at the time governor of Jiangsu, rejected a joint British and American request in 1863 to build a railway from Shanghai to Suzhou, saying that "railways would only be beneficial to China when undertaken by Chinese themselves and conducted under their management."[2] Chinese officials, without a tradition of eminent domain, immediately sensed the possibly insurmountable problem of building roads through fields dotted with ancestral graves. Nearly 3 percent of China's arable land was given over to the mounds of graves, for the Chinese did not have separate graveyards. They buried their dead in their own fields and then built large mounds of earth over the graves. The mounds were ten to fifteen feet high depending upon the importance of the person. Family fields were always marked with grave mounds.

The first railway in China was constructed in 1876 by subterfuge. British authorities claimed that a tramway was being constructed at the edge of the International Settlement in Shanghai, but then a locomotive was brought in. For a little over a month, six times a day, the train, loaded with passengers, covered the five-mile trip. Then a pedestrian was killed, under conditions that to the British mind suggested "either extreme dense stupidity or a malicious intention to commit suicide and thereby create a prejudice against railways"[3] — a not untypical example of how the Western mind thought the Eastern mind operated. Probably the unfortunate coolie was merely trying to use the locomotive, as countless later Shanghaiese have used motor cars, to run over the evil spirit he believed was bearing down from behind, and he simply played it too close. In any case, public wrath forced the line to be closed down; Chinese authorities bought the track and the rolling stock and shipped them off to Formosa, where they were never reassembled.

[2] Hosea Ballou Morse, *The International Relations of the Chinese Empire*, vol. 3 (London: Longmans, Green, 1918), p. 74.
[3] Ibid., p. 76.

The first successful railroad was a Chinese venture inspired by Tong King-sing, head of the China Merchants Steam Navigation Company, who wanted to get the coal from the Kailan mines in Tangshan, Hebei, to the seacoast and his ships. An Englishman, C. W. Kinder, was hired to construct the line, and he first laid the tracks and used mules to pull the carts while he went about building a locomotive out of odd parts and scrap iron. In 1881, on the hundredth anniversary of the birth of George Stephenson (the founder of the railroad), Kinder's steam engine went into operation and was christened "Rocket of China."

A few years earlier another English engineer had tried to convince the imperial Chinese authorities that they should engage in railway building only on the basis of a coherent general plan. He submitted such a plan: Hankou was the hub, with trunk lines going east to Shanghai, south to Canton, north to Peking, and west to Sichuan, Yunnan, and Burma, with spur lines connecting Shanghai and Ningbo; Fuzhou and the interior; and Peking, Tianjin, and Nanjing. Eventually much of the plan was completed, but initially it had been rejected. It provoked a split within Chinese officialdom. Some used military arguments to support an expansion of Kinder's efforts in order to link up Tianjin and Peking with the Great Wall and Manchuria; others rejected such arguments, saying that railroads that could carry troops north toward Korea could be used by an enemy to go in the opposite direction, toward the capital of the empire. The latter faction pressed for an interior system radiating from Hankou, which was far from the capital.

The imperial court saw merit in both arguments and allowed both projects to proceed. Li Hongzhang had been transferred by then to the north and strongly supported Kinder's design. When the line reached into Manchuria he used his appointment as ambassador-extraordinary to the coronation of Tsar Alexander III to work out a secret agreement bringing Russian capital into the south Manchuria program and to allow Russian construction of the Chinese Eastern rail line across northern Manchuria to Vladivostok. So began the complex schemes whereby European capital, working through special banks and under agreements with the imperial government, competed to build railroads. Money carried influence, though not always decisively. The Russian ambassador sought unsuccessfully to have Kinder removed, "not because he is an Englishman, but because he is not a Russian."[4]

The central China program, and in particular the Peking-Hankou railway, began as a completely Chinese effort in both capital and materials, but eventually foreign capital was sought, first from America and eventually from Belgium. In time, capital and engineers from Britain, France, Germany, and America produced other lines, but control and management of all lines in China proper remained always with the Chinese.

By the first decade of the twentieth century the spread of railroads was beginning to alter Chinese society and politics significantly. The traditional system of transportation, involving networks of canals and riverways, could be maintained by local and provincial authorities with limited centralized direction. Railroad revenues, though collected locally, had to be passed on to the central authorities in order to service the foreign loans that had provided the initial investment. Imperial authorities were thus compelled to penetrate more deeply than ever before into the domain of provincial authorities. In fact, a controversy over this issue of railroad revenues was the catalyst for the 1911 Revolution, which overthrew the Manchu (Qing) dynasty and brought the Republic.

When the Communists came to power in 1949 China had 13,700 miles of war-damaged railroads; by 1972 there were 8,000 additional miles of main and branch lines. Except for Tibet, every province and region was connected with the national network.

From this review of the physical features of China and its problems with communications it is apparent that China is not geographically homogeneous and it is not easy for people in the different parts to know each other. Diversity abounds, the pulls of regionalism are real, and national institutions, aside from government, hardly exist. Yet China is a cultural entity. The diversities of language and dialect that separate northerners from southerners and southerners from each other are as great as the differences in European tongues; yet the Chinese have held together. Behind the physical realities of China lies a deeper reality, that of Chinese culture, an extraordinary tradition that continues to provide a sense of national unity for China's massive population.

[4] Ibid., p. 77.

The physical differences of China have precluded the development of a homogeneous lifestyle. The wheat-growing peoples of the arid north and the rice-growing peoples of the semitropical south live differently. The key to their sense of common identity has been the existence of a superior culture, a great tradition, which has been spread throughout the land largely through the requirements of government and has provided a thin bond of cohesion for otherwise parochial peoples. At one time the bond consisted of the mandarinate and all the literary, artistic, and artisan traditions that went with the Confucian order. Now it is Communism and the rule of the Party.

The history of China is the story of how all the diversities of a continental society have been kept in check while also challenging the authority of the unifying forces, Confucianism and communism. The drama has become intensified as the problems of modernization have increased the strains and posed perplexing questions about how China should take its rightful place in the modern world. With this introduction to the physical reality of China, we are ready to consider the Confucian tradition.

THE CHINESE LANGUAGE

Mandarin Chinese (*putunghua*) is spoken by more people than any other language in the world. There is greater variety of dialect or "accent" among Mandarin speakers than among English speakers. In addition, China has a number of non-Mandarin dialects, such as Cantonese, Hakka, Fuzhou, and Shanghai, which differ from each other as much as Italian, French, and Spanish do. All Chinese dialects employ the same written characters, so that Chinese who cannot speak to each other can still communicate with no difficulty in writing.

Mandarin is essentially monosyllabic; every character is one syllable. Because certain compounds or pairs of characters do frequently stand for a single word, however, the language is not strictly monosyllabic. All words end in a vowel or an *n* or *ng*. All Chinese words have one immutable form; there are no declensions of nouns or conjugations of verbs. In Chinese grammar no distinctions are made between object and subject, for example, and there are no tenses. Time must be indicated by a specific qualifier and not by inflectional endings; e.g., "I come today," "I come yesterday," or "I come [in] ten minutes."

Chinese abounds with homonyms. In the spoken language distinctions between words are indicated by tones or musical accents. Mandarin has four tones. The first is even; the second is a quickly rising tone similar to English "who?"; the third is a broken rising note or a longer note that dips before rising; and the fourth is a falling tone, much like the last word in an ordinary English sentence. It is necessary to distinguish words with entirely different meanings merely by their tone; there is *chū* (pig), *chú* (*bamboo*), *chǔ* (*master*), and *chù* (to dwell). The same sound with the same tone can also mean different things. For example, the sound *yi* in the fourth tone has more than ninety characters, all representing different words. Context, sentence structure, and the coupling of words are used to reduce the confusion.

Chinese script was originally ideographic, or picture writing, and not phonographic, or according to sound. In the evolution of characters the step beyond the picturing of concrete nouns, such as "man," "sun," and "mouth," involved combining elements of concrete pictures to express abstract concepts. For example, the pictograph for "pig" was placed under that for "roof" to give the character for "house," "home," "family." The character for "good," "right," and "excellent" combined the characters for woman and child. The next step was to use pictographs of concrete nouns to represent abstract words of similar sound. For example, "to come" (pronounced *lai*), being abstract, was hard to depict. However, the word for "barley" was also pronounced *lai*, so the scribes simply used the pictograph for "barley" whenever they needed to write "to come," confident that anyone who read "king barley" would understand it to mean "king comes."

The development of phonetics meant that characters could be formed with part giving a sense of the sound and part the meaning. For example, the word for "mouth," which is simply written as a small box, is pronounced like the word for "to beat"; because "beating" is done with the hand, the character for "hand" was combined with that for "mouth" to form the character "to beat." The Chinese language has more than 40,000 characters, but most Chinese books use only 6,000 or 7,000, and knowing 2,000 or 3,000 is enough for general purposes. Hoping to make literacy easier to acquire, the Chinese Communists have sought to simplify the characters.

The strokes used in writing Chinese characters are precise and follow a set order. The art of writing, calligraphy, was a greatly appreciated feature of traditional Chinese culture. There are two basic styles of calligraphy: clear and bold, the equivalent of printed letters in English; and fluid and less legible, the equivalent of cursive writing. In classical brush writing these two categories were further subdivided into eight established styles.

CHAPTER THREE

The Confucian Tradition

For more than 2,000 years, without interruption, the evolving Chinese civilization was shaped by a distinctive political system and based on a humanistic ideology. Beginning in the sixth century B.C. and extending into the twentieth century, the Chinese functioned within a social and institutional framework that was the most enduring and stable in history. In the world of traditional societies, Chinese civilization ranks at the forefront in enlightenment and sophistication, in artistic achievement and ethical sensitivity, and above all in the imaginative development of the arts of government and the harmonious conduct of social life.

The stability and success of the traditional Chinese order stemmed from the preeminent place the Chinese gave to a remarkable ideology — Confucianism. Confucianism was remarkable because it was secular and was considered valid and appropriate for the problems of everyone — emperor, bureaucrat, landlord, and ordinary subject. It spoke to authority and for the common concerns of all who must look after their children. Other societies have in their time been bound together by the authoritative hold of religious beliefs. Indeed the grip of custom throughout most of the traditional world was stiffened by an awe of divine authority that was never far removed from temporal authority. China is unique because its social order was based on a secular ideology. Although the emperor was called upon to perform critical rituals of a religious character and his rule was identified with the Will of Heaven, the government set humane and decent standards and acted according to ethical principles based on learning rather than on divine revelation.

It is hard to say why the Chinese were inclined to give up the advantages for ruling inherent in the principle that the ruler's will, whether just or unjust, is coequal with divine authority. For unexplainable reasons the Chinese, as early as the first millennium before Christ, during the Zhou (Chou) dynasty, developed an awareness of government and began to ask what the ideal form of the state should be. Early in history thinkers articulated a sense of social malaise and proposed tactical and strategic ways for altering conditions, making the Chinese unique among ancient peoples.

At an early stage in their history, the Chinese also abandoned the traditions of an aristocracy based on birth and invented the great principle that those who manage government should do so because of merit and individual attainment in competitive examinations. In developing, by the second century B.C., the technique of bureaucratic rule by men of superior education, the Chinese created a form of centralized government that was not to be adopted by the West until the nineteenth century.

According to the Confucian ideal, government is at the heart of civilization. For the Chinese the most exalted task for mankind was devising proper and just government. They were concerned not only with the problems of rulers; their ideal also involved a sense of cultural and political unity for all members of their society. The result was an early and powerfully enduring sense of cultural identity and a profound sense of the unity and greatness of the Chinese people.

The Chinese people's sense of greatness was historically justified, not merely because of their cultural and material superiority over all their neighbors in Asia, but also because they were constantly reminded by their dealings with non-Chinese that they were unique in holding to the principle that government was basically a matter of ethics. While others believed in gods or sought the advantages of crude power, the Chinese thought of government as a moral force and suggested that princes should rule by example through the force of their superior moral conduct.

The Confucian tradition also linked government to scholarship. The Chinese early developed a profound faith in education and held that human nature could be perfected. Running through Chinese civilization has been the ideal that all individuals ought to perfect themselves, find virtue in performing their allotted roles, and contribute to the general good. Whenever the Chinese have sensed that all is not right with the collective state of affairs, they have believed that their troubles might be overcome if all people would try to improve their conduct, work harder at achieving cultural ideals, and conduct themselves more properly in their relations with others. This tradition outlasted the Confucian era and was constantly appealed to by both Chiang Kai-shek and Mao Zedong in seeking to motivate modern Chinese.

Although the Confucian ideals favored an elitist view that stressed the responsibilities of rulers, Chinese civilization also gave its members a belief that virtue and merit would be rewarded and that hard work and striving for achievement would provide the proper approach to life. Thus the Confucian emphasis on stability and order was tempered by an insistence that, ideally, those who held superior positions should have worked to obtain their advantages and should subsequently display more merit and more virtue than those beneath them.

The Confucian ideal was eminently appropriate for an agrarian society but was detrimental to the development of commerce and industry. Eventually the Confucian tradition of distrust for all that might unsettle the agricultural order worked against the Chinese in their confrontation with the modern industrial and technologically oriented West. This final failure of the Confucian system should not, however, obscure the remarkable greatness of China's polity in comparison with other traditional systems.

THE BEGINNINGS OF CHINESE CIVILIZATION

Chinese civilization originated in the Yellow River valley, first spread through north and east China, and only gradually extended into the southern regions. Substantiated Chinese history begins about 1500 B.C. with the Shang dynasty. The history of the earlier Xia (Hsia) dynasty is based more on legend than on fact. Archaeologists have been able to reconstruct much of the Shang culture through excavations and the analysis of "oracle bones," which had been used for divination. Questions scratched on bones were in an early version of the Chinese script. The bones were heated and the cracks that formed were "read" to give answers to the questions. Shang society was agricultural; it had a dominant ruler or emperor

CHRONOLOGICAL CHART

Principal Dynasties		Western Developments	
c. 2000 B.C.	XIA (HSIA)		
		CRETE	c. 3000–1400 B.C.
c. 1500	SHANG		
1122	ZHOU (CHOU) Feudal states Confucius Daoist (Taoist) school Legalist school Warring states		
		GREECE REACHED ITS GREATEST HEIGHT	c. 500–300
211	QIN (CH'IN)		
206	HAN Centralized rule End of feudalism Establishment of Confucianism		
		ROME AT ITS GREATEST PERIOD	100s
A.D. 222	SIX DYNASTY PERIOD		
		FALL OF ROME	A.D. 476
589	SUI		
618	TANG (T'ANG) Bureaucracy Examination system		
		CHARLEMAGNE	800
907	FIVE DYNASTIES PERIOD		
960	SONG (SUNG)		
1127	SOUTHERN SONG Neo-Confucianism	CRUSADES	1096–1291
1279	YUAN Conquests of Genghis Khan and Kubla Khan		
		RENAISSANCE	1300
1368	MING Model Chinese period		
		REFORMATION	1517
		FOUNDING OF AMERICAN COLONIES	1607–1670
1644	QING (CH'ING)	THIRTY YEARS WAR	1618–1648
1911	REPUBLIC		
1949	COMMUNISTS		

and a class of feudal nobles. The most striking feature of Shang culture was the creation of magnificent bronzes. Shang craftsmen developed techniques of bronze casting that exceeded any developed in Europe until the time of the Renaissance.

The Shang dynasty fell in 1122 B.C. to a conquering Zhou ruler who emerged in the northwest and established a dynasty that lasted until 211 B.C. The Zhou conquest did not bring about a sharp break in social organization. The feudal aristocracy continued, and the Zhou emperor could not effectively control his vassal lords, whose domains eventually became semiautonomous kingdoms and city-states.

In reaction to the decline of the Zhou dynasty and the rise of aggressive competition among the kingdoms, the Chinese experienced a great awakening about the need to question what constitutes proper government. The philosophical awakening in the later years of the Zhou dynasty, during the era of the "contending states," was marked by such self-awareness that the Chinese spoke about having "one hundred contending schools" — the phenomenon Mao Zedong referred to when he used the metaphor about allowing "one hundred flowers" to grow and contend. The Chinese mood was one of deep disquiet and concern that there should be such confusion and uncertainty about the political order. The Chinese reliance upon ideology came in response to what seemed to be basic disorder. The authority of the Zhou emperor had declined, and at the same time numerous city-states and petty kingdoms had emerged with separate rulers.

Western historians might view the period as unexceptional because it seems to be characterized by princes seeking security through diplomacy and alliances and generally participating in a competitive multistate system. The Chinese, however, thought there was something improper in such an unruly scheme of things, and wise men and prophets emerged to express their deep feelings of dissatisfaction and to suggest different routes to a better set of arrangements. The intellectual and ideological differences were great and the arguments were subtle. In the end, however, three principal views emerged about how Chinese, or rather Zhou, society could escape its difficulties: the Confucian, the Daoist, and the Legalist schools.

According to the Confucian school, which ultimately dominated China, society was in disarray because standards had deteriorated and people were not living up to their highest ideals. All would be improved if each person would work more conscientiously to fulfill his role in society. The ideal state of affairs that had once existed could be restored by using moral persuasion to make everyone be on his best behavior. Confucianists reasoned that if each individual were perfect in his behavior, society as a whole would likewise be perfect.

The Daoists (Taoists) called for almost the exact opposite course of action. They rejected the Confucian view that society was in trouble because standards had declined, and suggested instead that the basic trouble lay in the concept of standards. The fundamental problem was that society had become too artificial. They thought the Confucianists were introducing artificiality into life and were working against the Daoist ideal of harmony with nature. According to the Daoists, people should ignore the ethics and etiquette that the Confucianists preached and seek only to come to terms with nature, to become one with the natural forces of the universe. The Daoists contended that it was quite easy to deal with the Confucian problem of how to reduce evil and increase virtue. Simply lower standards for defining virtue, and immediately there would be an increase in virtue and a decline in sin. Because the Daoists thought all was relative, they insisted that the Confucianists were increasing the amount of evil in the world by attempting to raise standards for defining virtue.

The Legalist school responded that the others were champions of nonsense and that the only way to deal with a disintegrating and confused social order was to rely upon the powers of law. The Legalists argued that the problems of the day could be readily swept away if the ruler would establish clear and unambiguous laws and strictly enforce them. When people saw that violation of the laws would be dealt with severely, they would quickly and quite naturally change their behavior, thus ensuring a tranquil and orderly society. The laws could be quite arbitrary; indeed, there was a certain advantage in making laws arbitrary, for the people would constantly be reminded that power ultimately rested with the state and not with their personal notions of what was just and reasonable.

In the confusion at the end of the Zhou dynasty, the Legalists triumphed. In the longer flow of Chinese history the Confucianists became the champions of orthodoxy. The Daoists persisted, however, and contributed a vital ingredient to Chinese popular thought and an escape valve for officials and bureaucrats who needed some balance to the heavy and unsubtle moralism of Confucianism.

THE SHORT VICTORY OF THE LEGALISTS

The *Fa Jia,* or Legalist school, made its great but brief contribution to Chinese institutional development when Li Si (Li Ssu) became prime minister in the state of Qin (Ch'in) and set about putting into practice the theories of Han Feizi (Han Fei-tzu), the leading Legalist thinker. Li Si convinced his ruler, Qin Shi Huangdi, that he would be able to reunite China and establish a centralized dynasty if he would commit all his powers to a rule of law based not upon moral law or justice but on state fiat. The combination of Qin Shi Huangdi's military prowess and his reliance upon the uncompromising legalism of Li Si was successful, and China was united in 211 B.C. under its first centralizing emperor, who initiated the practices that were to evolve into bureaucratic rule.

In establishing his capital at Xianyang on the Wei River near present-day Xian in Shaanxi province, the "Great Unifier" Qin Shi Huangdi gave to his rule a sense of physical grandeur that was continued by all succeeding emperors. His palaces were not as densely concentrated or grand in size as those of later dynasties, but they did extend over twenty-five miles, and all the connecting roads and paths were covered to protect travelers from rain. Qin Shi Huangdi, especially as he got older, was obsessed with a fear of assassination and the idea of death. He never slept on consecutive nights in the same chamber or with the same woman. He insisted that the most influential people in the empire maintain residences at the capital so that they could be kept under surveillance while participating in a ceaseless round of parties and extravagant social life.

To his great credit, Qin Shi Huangdi established numerous lasting features of Chinese civilization. He is credited with standardizing weights and measures. He introduced uniform currency, contributed to the building of the Great Wall, established a set of written characters, and standardized the length of axles on carts.

A major accomplishment of the Qin regime was the destruction of the feudal aristocracy of ancient China. From the Legalist philosophy, Qin Shi Huangdi derived the idea that he should abandon the practice of rewarding loyal lieutenants with holdings of land that they and their families might hold in perpetuity. Li Si impressed upon him the dangers of such a policy, which would create within the empire self-contained power centers, each with its own resource base. Li Si suggested that loyal officers be given territories to govern, not to own, and that they should continue in office only so long as their behavior was consistent with the emperor's wishes and the rule of law.

Feudalism, as a system of hereditary local rulers governing independent estates and giving loyalty to the emperor, was abolished in China because of military rationale and legalistic demands — two elements of the Chinese tradition that Confucianists always thought to be of secondary importance. Elsewhere in the world the forces that eliminated feudalism — the emergent commercial class and the strength of kings — dominated the next phase of their societies' history. Not so in China, for the factors that eradicated feudalism were soon replaced by the new institutions of bureaucratic government.

The Legalists did not survive the death of Qin Shi Huangdi. In no small part this was because Li Si had been excessively vigorous in pressing Han Feizi's doctrine that all, including emperor and ministers, should be equally obedient to the law. He had, it turned out, offended the emperor's son, so when the latter succeeded his father, he quickly put Li Si to death. The dynasty could not long survive this double loss, and it was succeeded by a brief period of conflict during which the previously deposed feudal lords sought to reassert themselves. The idea of a unified empire had been effectively established in the Chinese mind, however, and the issue during the interregnum after the fall of Qin was who would be the man to establish the next dynasty.

Eventually the struggle became one between the colorful, romantic Xiang Yu (Hsiang Yü), who represented a revival of feudal traditions, and the cautious, doughty Liu Bang (Liu Pang), who had a peasant background and had mobilized a massive army of commoners. Although Xiang Yu and his dashing knights won battle after battle, they failed in the campaign and could not consolidate political power. Liu Bang, in establishing the Han dynasty, had to turn to others for advice and assistance, and he soon discovered the usefulness of those who had sustained the scholarly and ethical traditions of Confucius, Mencius, and Xun Zi (Hsün Tzu). The stage was thus set for the emergence, under an emperor of peasant origins, of a government of gentlemen and scholars who were quick to develop both a bureaucratic tradition and the concept of an orthodox ideology.

China became a powerful empire during the Han dynasty, which lasted from 206 B.C. to A.D. 222. The institutions of Chinese imperial rule evolved, and China expanded its territory, particularly to the north and west, and engaged in extensive foreign trade through central Asia. During this period Confucianism became the state ideology, and the traditions of Chinese scholarship that were the basis for the remarkable examination system for recruiting officials were established.

CONFUCIANISM: THE ETHIC OF MORALISTIC GENTLEMEN

Although eventually Confucianism became the essence of Chinese civilization, it was almost obliterated before it had a chance to shape Chinese institutions. Once he had conquered the Zhou dynasty, Qin Shi Huangdi sought with all his autocratic vigor to destroy the emerging Confucian tradition. He went so far as to declare that all the scholars' books should be burned. Yet clearly the words and sentiments of Confucius spoke to the majority of thinking Chinese. Indeed, the unsystematic but pithy statements of a relatively obscure and modestly successful scholar-official of Lu, a small insignificant Chinese state, became one of the most influential doctrines of human history.

Strangely, little is known about the man Confucius, who lived, according to tradition, from 551 to 479 B.C. What is known is wrapped in myth, for later generations sought to give him a divine dimension. It is generally believed that he was brought up by a domineering mother who wanted him to rise above the modest achievements of his deceased father, a low-ranking official. Another interpretation, however, is advanced by Fei Hsiao-t'ung: "Confucius' origins were quite doubtful. He was said to be the child of an illegitimate union. His mother would not tell him where his father's tomb was, and only when his mother died did he learn from someone else where his father was buried so that he

---

THE ANTI-CONFUCIUS AND PRO-LEGALIST CAMPAIGN

In 1974 Peking authorities initiated a nationwide anti-Confucius campaign, claiming Confucius was a "revisionist" who schemed to restore a "slave society" at a time when Chinese society was entering the Marxist stage of "feudalism." The germ of the campaign came from an article in which a leading ideologue sought to divide Chinese history into the conventional Marxist stages of society's progression from primitive communism to slave society, feudalism, capitalism, socialism, and eventually to communism. (Marxists have always had some problems in relating their schema to Chinese history; the institutionalized aristocracy associated with feudalism was destroyed during the early Han Dynasty; thereafter China did not experience real capitalistic development, and forms of slavery and indentured servitude lasted into the twentieth century.) At first the campaign seemed to be directed against Zhou Enlai, because it linked mandarin manners, the welcoming of foreign ways, and the abatement of conflict to Confucius and hence to "revisionism," which in that context meant desiring to restore "capitalism," as the Soviet Union allegedly had done. Zhou Enlai, even though mortally ill with cancer, adroitly deflected the attack by coupling the criticisms of Confucius with denunciations of Lin Biao, the disgraced and deceased heir apparent. The anti-Confucius/anti-Lin Biao campaign soon began to extol the merits of the Legalists and revived Mao Zedong's earlier attempt to identify himself with Qin Shi Huangdi. Since historically the Legalists had been defeated and Confucianism had endured, it would seem that Mao was associating himself with a lost cause, but presumably the major ideological point was the continuing need to oppose incipient Confucian sentiments and "revisionist" tendencies.

---

could bury his mother also in that spot."[1] Both versions provide an interesting psychological background for speculating about the man who made ancestor worship and filial piety the keystones of Chinese civilization.

In addition to stressing the vital importance of the family to society, Confucius concentrated on the art of government. Yet his personal record of governmental performance was unimpressive. After he left the service of the ruler of Lu, he wandered about from state to state seeking employment as an advisor to local rulers. In his travels he attracted a following of disciples who transcribed what are believed to be his sayings. Possibly the fate of Confucianism was determined by Mencius, a later disciple also from the state of Lu, who lived from 373 to 288 B.C. and devoted his life to spreading the thoughts of his master. He too wandered from state to state, preaching good government, seeking to advise rulers, and helping to establish the legitimacy of Confucian doctrines. After Mencius came Xun Zi (Hsün Tzu), who also taught that education was the basis of good government. But, unlike Mencius, who believed man to be inherently good and only in need of education to bring out latent virtues, Xun Zi believed man to be inherently bad and in need of education to tame his immoral and violent qualities.

Early Confucianism was a humanistic and pragmatic moral system. It dealt with worldly problems and assumed that its powers of persuasion rested entirely upon its self-evident reasonableness. Over the centuries, and especially after the appearance of Buddhism during the Tang (T'ang) dynasty (A.D. 618–907), when the Chinese learned more about sophisticated metaphysical systems, Confucianism became more than just an ethical system, especially during the Southern Song dynasty (1127–1279), when neo-Confucianism emerged.

Both early Confucianism and neo-Confucianism were less impressive as formal philosophical systems than as guides for elite behavior. Confucianism was a powerful force in shaping attitudes and giving a common orientation to generations of leaders, but it

[1] Fei Hsiao-t'ung, *China's Gentry* (Chicago: University of Chicago Press, 1953), p. 38. Copyright 1953 by The University of Chicago. Reprinted by permission.

was not a vigorous or elegantly logical system of thought. In a sense, the starting point of Confucianism was the requirement for proper philosophical definitions before discussion and action could begin. The Confucianists argued that trouble in human affairs began whenever there was confusion over the definition of roles. Thus the first step toward good government and the realization of a harmonious society was for each person to know his role and perform it well, according to the strictest interpretation of that role. Confucianism identified five key role relationships — between ruler and subject, neighbor and neighbor, father and son, husband and wife, and brother and brother. If everyone involved in any of these roles adhered to the highest standards for that role, the country as a whole would achieve a condition of collective perfection.

The stress on the achievement of perfection in role relationships, rather than the search for individual salvation or self-realization, gave to Confucianism and to Chinese culture its distinctive emphasis on human and social relationships, at some expense to the individual and his autonomy. Confucianism taught that people should be sensitive to what others thought of their behavior, that they should seek always to act with an eye to how others might respond, and above all that they should never be shameless but instead constantly anxious to do the right thing.

Confucianism treated man as a social being whose identity is determined by where he stands in relation to others in the web of social relations. Each individual had his unique place in the total scheme, and each individual's behavior differed according to his station and according to the station of the particular person with whom he was dealing. An elder brother had responsibilities different from those of a younger brother, and one's manner toward an individual changed according to whether the other person was older or younger, a stranger or a member of one's community.

The importance of correct behavior was related to the need for education and sincerity. Confucianists assumed that people were naturally eager to behave properly and would spontaneously seek guidance in how to find the Way, the correct path of the upright man. By the same token, they assumed that people would inevitably act in the wrong way if they were not properly trained. Whether one took the view that men were inherently good or basically evil, the absolute importance of education was stressed. The corollary was that educated men were inherently superior to the uneducated, and therefore that rulers and governors should be educated.

The key to correct behavior was sincerity, but the Confucian concept of sincerity had nothing to do with spontaneity or open good-heartedness. Confucianists believed that what kept people behaving properly was their inner sense of sincerity. The test of whether one was sincere was one's willingness to pay the price of practicing good manners. The sincere man obeyed completely all the requirements of proper etiquette. Bad or crude behavior suggested a lack of sincerity.

Partly as a reaction to the Legalist views and partly as a logical extension of their own views, the Confucianists argued that officials should be allowed considerable freedom and that as long as they displayed sincerity their small faults could be condoned. Toleration and understanding of anyone who was sincere led to an easy acceptance of corruption in government. By assuming that officials desired to act correctly and by refusing to be arbitrary or harsh about their behavior, the Confucian tradition arrived at the practice of describing in abstract terms the qualities of the perfect official while tolerating in practice considerable personal corruption.

Confucianism thus raised an issue still present in Maoism, whether the actual performance or the inner spirit of officials is more important to perfect government. Neither Confucianist nor Maoist has believed that objective measures of behavior should be the sole basis for evaluating the worth of officials, and both have stressed the importance of the inner state of mind and spirit. In both ideologies the criterion for the sincerity of the inner person has been correct behavior rather than effectiveness or efficiency. Neither the Confucianists nor the Maoists have preferred efficiency in attaining goals to perfection of the inner man.

Correct behavior was closely associated with five Confucian virtues — goodness or benevolent compassion, *ren* (*jen*); righteousness, *yi* (*i*); propriety, *li*; wisdom, *zhi* (*chih*); and faithfulness, *xin* (*hsin*). Confucian scholarship was an endless process of discussing all the possible meanings and connotations of these and other words, such as virtue, *de* (*te*); filial piety, *xiao* (*hsiao*); princely or superior man, *junzi* (*chün-tzu*); and, of course, sincerity, *cheng* (*ch'eng*). Over the centuries the meanings of these terms have changed. For example, in earliest times *ren* was identified with the notion of free man, in contrast with *min* or subject, but later *ren* became associated with gentlemen and thus with benevolence and goodness. In modern times, particularly with the establishment of the Republic, *min* became the word for citizen — a reflection of the positive concepts of nationalism and people's democracy.

Much of early Confucianism dealt with what were presumed to be the official problems of government. In the main, these were questions of the proper behavior of rulers, the correct rituals or manners for all situations, and the correct moral perspective for officials. The Confucian assumption was that if rulers and officials behave in a model way, all who are exposed to them will act with equal propriety. Personal behavior was considered decisive in public events.

The belief that emperors and fathers could rule by example gave to the Chinese the view that virtue and any public manifestation of virtue result in power. Contrary to the Western view of the conflict between morality and power, the Confucian idea was that goodness produces power. To show concern about moral issues suggested that one had power. Rule by example also encouraged the view that superior people were obliged to strive for virtue (*de*) and could expect deference from all who recognized this virtue.

Neo-Confucianism incorporated mystical concepts from early pre-Confucian texts and religious formulations from Daoism and Buddhism. The increasing complexity of Confucianism called for more authoritative interpretations, resulting in the rigid orthodoxy that came to dominate Chinese thought from Song times down to the Western impact. Neo-Confucian orthodoxy led to the identification of sacred texts, and the Four Books and the Five Classics became the basis of all education and of the examination system. This stultification of knowledge produced the classical Chinese concept of the "eight-legged essay" that was required in many examination answers. It was thought that all subjects were best dealt with as eight points; every idea introduced called for a balancing opposite idea; and sentences should alternate between being four and six characters long.

THE MATURE TRADITION AND HIGH SCHOLARSHIP

After the fall of the Han dynasty in A.D. 222, China experienced a prolonged interregnum, lasting more than three and a half centuries. A series of local dynasties rose and fell in north and south China, central government disappeared, and nomadic bands from central Asia (called "barbarians" by the Chinese) penetrated the agricultural domains of the north. The lack of central authority left the country open to outside influences, the most prominent of which was Buddhism, rapidly introduced from India. Chinese monks traveled overland to the subcontinent to bring back sacred texts, and some of the local "emperors" accepted Buddhism as their dynastic religion.

The reunification of China followed the pattern of a short-lived dynasty being succeeded by a great one, as the Qin was followed by the Han. In A.D. 589 the Sui dynasty was established, but in 618 it fell and was replaced by the Tang, which lasted until 907. The Sui emperor established an examination system and sought administratively to extend central control to the local level by dividing the provinces into districts or *zhou* and counties or *xian*, divisions that persisted into modern times.

The Tang period was a high point of Chinese culture. Reunification and peace brought a flourishing of commerce and a growth of urban culture. The Tang was the last dynasty to have its capital in the Wei valley in the northwest. In the realm of government the Tang was notable for giving China a codified legal system and the most formal ordering of the bureaucracy. When Japan and Korea sought to adopt Chinese institutions, their model was the Tang system. By the end of the Tang period Chinese traditions and institutions were firmly formed, and would change little until the end of the imperial system in 1911. During the period came the development of a form of lyric poetry called *shi* (*shih*), which stressed a mood of tranquility and remembrance of pleasures, in contrast to *fu*, the didactic poetry of the Han period. Tang military conquests carried Chinese civilization toward the southwest.

The high point of the Tang was the reign of Xuan Zong (712–756), during which the court in Changan (present-day Xian in

Shaanxi) became the center of scholarship, art, music, and high cultural style. At the same time, however, court intrigues became intense; even the emperor was involved in scandals, especially when he took his son's wife Yang Guifei, the most famous courtesan in Chinese history, as his favorite. Intrigues led to revolts. The military commanders on the frontiers had become semiautonomous; they had established alliances with the Turkish frontier people whom they were supposedly opposing.

The half century after the fall of the Tang, called the Five Dynasties period by the Chinese, saw a series of petty states struggling for power. During the Song (Sung) period (960–1279) there were additional innovations in philosophy and the arts, and neo-Confucianism, with its metaphysical dimensions, developed. Printing became widespread, and great numbers of historical writings and encyclopedic compilations were produced. In the arts the dynasty was most notable for excellence in landscape painting and the production of porcelains—especially celadon and figured white porcelains — and the rough brown *dianmu* (*tien-mu*) ware.

By the end of the Song dynasty the Confucian tradition was so firmly entrenched in Chinese life that even when alien rulers from central Asia and Manchuria conquered China, they could bring little change to Chinese society, and in fact had to accommodate themselves to Confucian institutions and ideals to rule the Chinese. Evidence of the remarkable strength of the Confucian system is shown by the fact that during the 632 years from the fall of the Song to the fall of the Qing (Ch'ing) dynasty in 1911, the Chinese controlled their own empire for only 276 years; yet because the alien dynasties had to employ Chinese scholar-officials, there was little basic change in the Confucian bureaucracy.

The vitality of the scholar-official class in China stemmed from the cultural ideals they embodied from generation to generation. Their commitment was to a moral view of power, to a personal search for artistic sensitivity, and to intellectual excellence in a highly disciplined form of scholarship.

In some respects, Confucian scholarship resembled medieval European scholasticism, except that the Chinese worked with a far larger body of literature. In addition to the Four Books and the Five Classics, which might be compared to the New Testament, and eight other classics, which in a less accurate analogy could be thought of as the Old Testament, the traditional Chinese library contained several other groupings of books. A feeling for the mass of Chinese literature can be gained from noting that one of these categories consisted of the *lei shu*, or encyclopedias, which reached huge proportions and consisted mainly of selections from other books rather than original articles. The *Yonglo Dadian* (*Yung Lo Ta Tien*), which was not strictly an encyclopedia, was compiled in the Ming dynasty (1368–1644) and ran to nearly 12,000 volumes; because of the cost only three sets were produced. During the Qing dynasty (1644–1911), under Emperor Qianlong, scholars compiled the *Si Ku Quan Shu* (*Ssu K'u Ch'üan Shu*), which sought to reproduce or excerpt all books of the time and was followed by an annotated bibliography that included more titles than had been published in the entire Western world up to that date (about the time of the American Revolution).

During the Song Dynasty the neo-Confucianists sought to "canonize" certain texts as works that had a particularly close relationship with the Master. The Four Books, which consisted of *The Analects* (*Sayings of Confucius*), or *Lun Yu* (*Lun Yü*); *Great Learning, Da Xue* (*Ta Hsüeh*); *Doctrine of the Mean, Zhong Yong* (*Chung Yung*); and *Mencius,* did have a somewhat close association with the spirit of early Confucianism. The Five Classics reached back earlier into history and brought to Confucianism an element of mysticism. The five were *Book of Changes,* or *I Ching* (*Yi Jing*); *Book of History, Shu Jing* (*Shu Ching*); *Book of Poetry, Shi Jing* (*Shih Ching*); *Book of Rites, Li Ji* (*Li Chi*), of which the *Da Xue* (*Ta Hsüeh*) and the *Zhong Yong* (*Chung Yung*) of the Four Books were parts; and *Spring and Autumn Annals, Chun Qiu* (*Ch'un Ch'iu*).

The *Analects* is presumably the sayings of Confucius, transcribed as he discussed problems of good governance with his disciples. Much of it, however, includes statements about the Master's views as well as his sayings. The style of *Mencius* is much the same, using the device of disciples, or straight men, asking questions or making incorrect statements to set the stage for Mencius' wise responses.

Great Learning and *Doctrine of the Mean* were two parts of the *Book of Rites* that Confucius had supposedly identified as being the most significant. The first is a rather brief text filled with Chinese aphorisms and sequential reasoning. For example:

> What a man dislikes in a superior, let him not display in the treatment of his inferiors; what he dislikes in inferiors, let him not display in the service of his superiors.
>
> When the ruler, as a father, a son and a brother, is a model, then people imitate him.
>
> Let the producers be many and the consumers few. Let there be activity in the production and economy in the expenditure. Then the wealth will always be sufficient.

Great Learning also contains a classic example of Confucian logic:

> The ancients who wished to illustrate illustrious virtue throughout the kingdom, first ordered well their own states. Wishing to order well their states, they first regulated their families. Wishing to regulate their families, they first cultivated their persons. Wishing to cultivate their persons, they first rectified their hearts. Wishing to rectify their hearts, they first sought to be sincere in their thoughts. Wishing to be sincere in their thoughts, they first extended to the utmost their knowledge. Such extension of knowledge lay in the investigation of things.
>
> Things being investigated, knowledge became complete. Their knowledge being complete, their thoughts were sincere. Their thoughts being sincere, their hearts were then rectified. Their hearts being rectified, their persons were cultivated. Their persons being cultivated, their families were regulated. Their families being regulated, their states were rightly governed, the whole kingdom was made tranquil and happy.

The *Doctrine of the Mean* stresses the great Confucian and traditional Chinese value of harmony. The book was attributed to the grandson of Confucius and could be seen as an effort to reconcile Mencius' concept of the inherent goodness of men with Xun Zi's skepticism. For example:

> When we have intelligence resulting from sincerity, this condition is to be ascribed to nature; when we have sincerity resulting from intelligence, this condition is to be ascribed to instruction. But given the sincerity and there shall be the intelligence; given the intelligence and there shall be the sincerity.

Much of the rest of the *Book of Rites* is given over to instructions about ceremonial behavior, including, for example, how one should hold the bow and finger the arrow while engaged in the gentlemanly art of shooting. The *Book of History* was supposedly edited by Confucius and therefore was profoundly important. It is in fact an odd collection of speeches, oaths, rituals, and observations of how rituals were more precisely performed in earlier ages. *Spring and Autumn Annals,* which was also attributed to Confucius, deals with affairs in the state of Lu from 722 to 481 B.C. and makes observations about how rites and rituals were performed, the conduct of officials and sacrifices they performed, and their manners in various relationships. It lists numerous historical events, ranging from diplomatic meetings to such natural phenomena as eclipses and the birth of two-headed lambs. Confucian scholars did not have an easy time figuring out what to make of such a collection, and since they had to assume that Confucius would never have wasted his time with trivial and irrelevant matters, they produced the *Commentary* (*Tso Chuan*), which sought to interpret the deeper meanings of *Spring and Autumn Annals* but goes off in enough directions of its own that it seems to have been written independently of any interest in *Spring and Autumn Annals,* and it certainly can be read without reference to it.

The *Book of Poetry* also caused great trouble for the later moralistic Confucian scholars, who felt that because the Master had read and commented on it, it must have meaning deeper than its obvious rustic simplicity. In a sense it occupies a place comparable to the Song of Solomon in the Bible. The poems are early folk verses that were sung by the people before the days of Confucian moralizing, and generally they describe boys and girls frolicking and playing erotically in the spring and at harvest time.

The *Book of Changes,* a mystical text dealing with divination and the forces of destiny, was an early work, elevated to classical status in later periods. Its key feature is the *bagua,* a formation of eight trigrams, that since earliest history has been used by Chinese fortune-tellers. Another classic was *Er Ya,* an early dictionary, which seeks to explain the obscurities of the *Book of Changes* and the *Book of Rites* but, like the *Commentary,* seems only to muddy the waters.

In identifying the literature that shaped the Confucian mind, mention should be made of the *Book of Filial Piety*, or *Xiao Jing* (*Hsiao Ching*), on which countless generations of Chinese children have been raised. This book taught them that others with parents far worse than their own had displayed exemplary behavior toward their awful parents.

Another dimension of the Chinese scholarly tradition was the writing of history, which produced the *Standard Histories*, or *Zheng Shi* (*Cheng Shih*). These cover twenty-six dynasties. The first history, *Historical Records, Shi Ji* (*Shih Chi*), deals with the pre-Han and early Han periods, and the last covers the Qing and was completed in Taipei in 1961. The tradition was established by a father and son combination of Sima Tan and Sima Qian, who wrote the *Shi Ji* during the early Han dynasty. The son in particular, who took over after his father's death, set the style of straightforward, unambiguous, terse statements with a minimum of moralizing.

The pattern of the *Standard Histories* was clear-cut. Each history was written by the court historians of the succeeding dynasty; each describes the dynasty beginning in glory and ending in disgrace as its successor rightfully takes over the Mandate of Heaven. The *Standard Histories* have four parts: annals, tables, treatises, and biographies. The annals follow very much the style and content of the *Spring and Autumn Annals*. The chronology was often incomplete, and considerable attention was given to natural events. The tables are a compilation of genealogies (which unfortunately record only the eldest son and are therefore of no help in providing demographic statistics) and lists of who held what office at what time. The treatises are essays on a wide range of subjects. They include significant imperial documents (the Chinese called such official papers "memorials") and impressive imperial decrees, as well as dissertations on foreign travels, calendars, rituals, music, administration, punishments, and other topics relating to state affairs. The subjects are generally interesting, but often the essays turn out to be lists of names and identifications of little substantive value.

The final sections of the *Standard Histories*, the biographies, are generally the most useful for modern scholars. They tell about the lives not only of great public officials of the dynasty but also of various virtuous and exceptional individuals, such as an exceedingly dutiful son, a virtuous widow, and even a butcher exceptionally skilled in cutting thin slices of meat. Although the biographies provide almost no sense of individual human development and portray most subjects as rather stiff and stuffy paragons, they do reveal career patterns and social practices and thus give some feeling for the times.

Confucian scholarship produced a rich and demanding intellectual tradition. Men had to spend years exploring its different reaches, and it was not supported by anything resembling a formal educational system or such religious institutions as monasteries. The individual, with the help of a tutor, had to work his way through the classics, memorizing long passages and striving to interpret obscure meanings. Since the language of the classics was not the same as the spoken tongue, this endeavor was much like engaging in scholarship in a foreign language.

Study of the classics provided a shared experience for that thin layer of men who held Chinese civilization together. Regardless of where they came from in the empire or their native accent or dialect, they could all speak to each other in the official's language, which was also the scholar's language. They used the same metaphors and aphorisms and could use the same allusions in making their points to each other. They were in much the same situation as the products of traditional British public schools and of Oxford and Cambridge, who received their classical education as a background before entering government service.

The limits of the Confucian world view, its smugness, its self-centeredness, its noninquisitive approach to all that lay outside its immediate concerns, became dramatically self-evident once it confronted the dynamic spirit of modern science and technology. Yet in comparison with other belief systems of the ancient world, Confucianism was most sophisticated and enlightened. In making morality a central feature of government, it not only tempered the autocratic propensities common to ancient governments and gave to Chinese rule a humanistic dimension, but also mobilized the great social powers of reasoned morality for service to the political system. Many systems of government have tapped the human sentiments of parochialism, nationalism, and religious convictions to strengthen the basis of the ruler's authority; Confucianism was outstanding because it insisted that government could be based on ethics and man's instinctive desire to avoid shameful behavior.

DAOISM (TAOISM) AND BUDDHISM: THE UNCERTAIN RELIGIOUS TRADITIONS

In all formal respects the Confucian scholarly tradition concentrated on the ethics of government, the moral behavior of citizens, and a pragmatic, conservative view of the importance of the secular social order. Yet as neo-Confucianism demonstrated, the scholar-official could not entirely divorce himself from otherworldly, mystical, and metaphysical considerations. Thus, although the Chinese talked of different schools of belief the divisions were not particularly sharp. Early Confucian scholars casually indulged in Daoist speculations and later ones took an interest in Buddhist metaphysics. Over time distinctions between the traditions became increasingly blurred, and in many respects all three became vulgarized.

Early Daoism did present some of the most sophisticated blending of philosophy and metaphysics in Chinese history. The Daoist concern with how man could go beyond the confines of reason and achieve identification with the central forces behind nature went far beyond the Confucian search for meaning in man's existence. Much in early Daoism, however, bordered on the merely clever. For example, Zhuang Zi (Chuang Tze) awakens from a dream that he is a butterfly and then finds that there is no way to answer the question of whether he was really a butterfly dreaming that he was Zhuang Zi or Zhuang Zi who had dreamed that he was a butterfly. (Zhuang Zi failed to find the solution Kant did for this problem: Because in the waking world, unlike the dream world, things hang together in a coherent manner, in waking life we can make sense of dreams, but not the other way around.)

The great contribution of Daoism to the Chinese political tradition was its stress on the value of "nonaction" and the argument that much can be accomplished by it — a belief that became a justification for a laissez faire view of the role of government. Essentially the Daoist position was that most actions are counterproductive because things will occur in their own time; much of the tension and confusion in life come from people's pressing for specific objectives when the time for them is not ripe. When conditions are appropriate, the desired outcome will occur automatically.

A contemporary Daoist argument might be that although individuals assume they have complete freedom to decide the time of their marriage, aggregate marriage statistics clearly show a uniform time when marriages have occurred and seem to deny the significance of personal choices.

After the introduction of Buddhism to China, Daoism became more a religion and less a philosophical system. Daoist monasteries spread, and in time a pantheon of Daoist gods came to be recognized and depicted in paintings and statues. The highest Daoist god was usually called Yü Huang, or the Jade Emperor. Beneath him came an array of holy men, or *sheng ren* (*sheng jen*); ideal men, *zhen ren* (*chen jen*); and, possibly most popular of all, the Eight Immortals, *Ba Xian* (*Pa Hsien*). The Daoists also had a spiritual leader, known in English as the Daoist pope, who was presumed to be the lineal descendant of an early Han believer in Lao Zi and who codified Lao Zi's writings and helped to establish *The Way and Its Power, Dao De Jing* (*Tao Te Ching*) as the classic of Daoism. The current pope is a young man who lives on Taiwan. He succeeded his uncle, who fled with the Nationalist remnants from the mainland when it fell to the Communists.

Both Daoism and Buddhism were more popular with the common people than Confucianism, and in many respects their sacred texts became the basis of learning for those who could not aspire to a Confucian education. For those who had no hope of making the civil service, it was still possible to find security by joining a monastery. Some of the tensions between Buddhism and Daoism on the one hand and the Confucian mandarinate on the other stemmed not just from conflicting doctrines but possibly even more from class tensions and an awareness that as the monasteries grew they could become centers of power and wealth.

The political and cultural influences of the Daoist and Buddhist monasteries were, however, always limited by the fact that clerical life and celibacy never had great appeal to the Chinese. Consequently, Daoist monks usually were only part-time religious practitioners and often were married, had their own secular occupations, and performed their priestly roles for supplementary income on such special occasions as weddings, funerals, and the opening of new enterprises, and to help people who had personal needs, ranging from rainfall to a change in luck and the restoration of health.

China never produced any great religious spokesmen — an indication of the basically secular spirit of higher Chinese culture. Historians have not recognized any great spiritual leaders; priests were not a part of the established elite; and the Chinese spirit was never profoundly influenced by the inspirational example of any man of God. But this does not mean that religion had no place in the lives of Chinese, particularly the common people.

Although Daoism, Buddhism, and ancestor worship in Confucianism were the principal formal religions of traditional China, the vast majority of the Chinese also responded to the pervasive, local forms of animism. Cults of gods, spirits, and ghosts were never organized to the point of becoming institutionalized, but they did provide most Chinese with a feeling for the supernatural. Shrines, temples, and tablets dotted the Chinese countryside. At frequent intervals along Chinese roadways, particularly beside mountain paths, there were piles of stones tossed one on top of the other by travelers concerned with their own fortunes and the moods of the local spirits. A traveler approaching a pile would pick up a slate or stone and toss it on the pile. If it stayed in place the trip would continue in peace, but if it slid off there would be trouble.

Hardly any event of significance could take place without an attempt to placate the appropriate spirits. In particular, the construction of a sizable building called for calculating the mood of *feng shui* (wind and water) — the supernatural forces and spirits of a location, which had to be reckoned with before a building meant for human occupancy could be safe and unhaunted. Within each household, in addition to tablets or paintings placed in reverence to the ancestors, there were usually tokens of respect for the kitchen god at New Year's time and to other spirits at the appropriate festival periods.

The conventional Western interpretation of Chinese civilization has tended to suggest a sharp division between the secular philosophical tradition of the Confucian elite and the religious superstitions of the uneducated common people. Modern Chinese scholars have contributed to this view by insisting that the Chinese were basically rational and unreligious. In particular they have pointed to several quotations of Confucius to support their claim that the tradition he initiated was essentially agnostic:

> Since we do not know all about life, how can we speculate about the afterlife?
>
> While we are not able to serve men, how can we serve the spirits?

And of course there was a long Chinese tradition of poking fun at or raising commonsensical objections to the antics of ghosts or *gui*. For example, Sima Guang dismissed the concept of Hell: "When the body has decayed, the spirit fades away. Even if there be such cruel tortures in Hell as chiseling, burning, pounding, and grinding, whereon are these to be inflicted?"[2]

The distinguished Chinese sociologist C. K. Yang, has, however, shown how limited this agnostic current was and how much it has been exaggerated by Western and modern Chinese scholars who were themselves agnostics. In fact the Chinese were neither devoid of spiritual interests nor particularly embarrassed about their supernatural concerns. Chinese social conventions meant that they did not generally talk about their beliefs any more than they would discuss their sex lives. A careful review of all aspects of Chinese life reveals that concern about the supernatural and correct ritual behavior was ubiquitous, but not glorified.

Probably more significant than the extent of agnosticism in traditional China is the lack of severe tensions between the sacred and secular domains and between the various religions. The ease with which Chinese accepted Daoism, Confucianism, Buddhism, and animism has been frequently mentioned, and the Chinese practice of hedging bets about eternity by inviting priests of all religions to participate at funerals is equally well known. In the isolated and self-contained conditions of traditional China the culture probably was able to accept certain contradictions and feelings of dissonance. Secular philosophical views and religious and supernatural beliefs could be as easily held by the same man as, say, the modern social scientist holds his different economic, psychological, and sociological theories without demanding total coherence.

[2] C. K. Yang, *Religion in Chinese Society* (Berkeley: University of California Press, 1961), p. 247.

STABILITY AND THE DYNASTIC CYCLE

Western characterizations of Confucian society have often stressed such negative features as its emphasis on the past, its opposition to innovation, and its failure to develop science and industry. It is true that the Confucian order valued continuity more than novelty and placed great importance on filial piety, ancestor worship, and maintenance of a division between the cultured and ethically concerned elite and the humble and hard-working masses. The Chinese were concerned more with social relationships than with exploring the physical world; their imaginations turned more to poetry and painting than to science and inventions. Yet the Confucian order succeeded in establishing the most stable and enduring culture in human history. It set forth the remarkable ideal that government should help the individual to realize his full moral potential. The Confucian concept that government should be involved in seeking the perfectibility of man has persisted into recent times with Chiang Kai-shek's New Life Movement and, even more dramatically, with Mao Zedong's massive attempts to inspire the Chinese with his version of the puritan ethic.

The Confucian stress on continuity and orthodoxy did not snuff out all attempts at innovation in China. For example, during the Song dynasty, Wang Anshi, a prime minister, sought to bring about fundamental structural changes in the Chinese polity and economy. His proposed reforms were ambitious and remarkably farsighted. He proposed a state budget that would control expenditures, a system of state purchases of grain designed to maintain an "ever normal granary," a system of loans to peasants, a form of graduated taxation and land reform, a limited system of military draft and militia organization, and a change in the emphasis of the examination system from the classics to current problems. The proposals were far too radical for the mandarins in his government, but they are evidence that Chinese officials were capable of innovative thinking. Although dramatic changes did not take place, the Confucian order was far from static. There were vigorous political struggles in the bureaucracy and significant incremental changes in practices.

There was also a rhythmic cycle in Chinese history, reflected in the rise and fall of dynasties. Chinese historians traditionally attributed the success or failure of the dynasties to the moral character of the emperors and the behavior of their officials. The first emperors of each dynasty were seen as vigorous, conscientious, and virtuous; their officials were diligent; the land prospered. The last emperors of the dynasty were venal, lazy, and not interested in ruling, and their officials were corrupt and without virtue.

The moral theory of the dynastic cycle was encouraged by the concept of the Mandate of Heaven, by which emperors could legitimately rule so long as their conduct was consistent with the Will of Heaven. When heaven was displeased with the quality of rule or the character of the ruler, the mandate to rule could be revoked and revolt was then legitimate. Evidence in support of this theory was readily provided by classical historians who were commissioned to write about the preceding dynasty. They were inclined to be generous in their praise of the founders of the former dynasty because that was long ago and they needed to establish a contrast with the later emperors. They had to picture the last emperor as an evil force, justifying his removal and setting the stage to legitimize the new dynasty, in which they always wrote.

Modern historians have rejected the view that Chinese history was governed by "good" and "bad" emperors. Yet the need to account for the differences between the early stages of a dynasty and its eventual decline still exists. This historical problem has produced the theory of the dynastic cycle, for which evidence is most convincing for the most recent dynasty but somewhat weak for several of the earlier ones because of the absence of adequate data.

The theory of the dynastic cycle begins with the period of disorder between dynasties and notes that when military force succeeded in establishing a new ruling house most of the people were anxious for peace and order, and thus each dynasty began with a "honeymoon" period characterized by great vitality. The disorder before the establishment of the dynasty had sufficiently reduced the population so that with peace the ratio of people to land was relatively favorable and the land could be fairly evenly divided among the rural people. Peace, however, brought change. The population grew and the officials began to accumulate wealth. This produced an increase in the numbers of landless peasants and absentee landlords. It also reduced the size of the tax base, for officials skillfully avoided taxing their growing holdings. This meant that the tax burden became heaviest on the poorest peasants, who eventually had to sell out. Concentrations of holdings grew, as did the peasants' frustrations. Under these conditions natural disasters would have particularly disturbing effects because so many people lived a marginal existence. The scene was set for rebellions, which generally began at the fringes of the poorest areas. The need to suppress the rebellions resulted in tax increases in the loyal areas, and these would cause the rebellion to spread. The emperor would then have to squeeze his shrinking domains harder and harder. (During the last years of the Ming dynasty the government needed more than four times its normal amount of resources to fight rebellions and foreign conquerors. The Qing dynasty never recovered financially from the strain of putting down the Taiping Rebellion.)

Finally the dynasty would be overthrown, and a period of strife and civil disorder would reduce the population and equalize holdings. The estates of the corrupt former officials would be redivided, and the stage would be set for another dynasty to emerge and for the cycle to repeat itself. But such changes in response to social and economic forces had little effect on the ideals of the culture. To appreciate the dynamics of the Confucian tradition, it is necessary to examine in detail the specific institutional arrangements that gave order to Chinese political and social life.

CHAPTER FOUR

Imperial Institutions and Practices

Chinese behavior did not always achieve Confucian ideals. In their personal lives emperors were not the paragons they were supposed to be. Officials could be crass and self-seeking, lacking ethical sensitivity. But in examining the institutions of traditional China, one must keep in mind that although they did not always meet the ideals of Confucianism, those ideals did inspire both rulers and subjects.

Important to remember also is the fact that much of the stability and endurance of Chinese civilization came from the extraordinary compatibility and integration of public and private institutions. The subtle meshing of philosophical ideals, family practices, controls on social advancement, formal arrangements of government, and career patterns that sustained public institutions was the basis of Chinese greatness. Indeed, when the separate parts of Chinese civilization are examined independently, out of context, weaknesses and flaws are all too apparent. Chinese emperors often seemed much too arrogant and remote to provide leadership for such a vast society. Chinese mandarin officials were often far too dedicated to acquiring irrelevant knowledge to effectively manage the great enterprises of the empire. Chinese fathers were generally so repressive and demanding that one might have expected them to produce deep alienation and rebellion in their sons. Yet the system worked with little tension and great stability. The contradiction between the parts and the whole makes it difficult to describe the traditional Chinese order, for attention to the separate institutions tends to exaggerate the problems.

The emperor and his court were at the apex of a hierarchical establishment composed of a civil bureaucracy of scholar-officials who were balanced by military authorities and their troops. The three basic elements of the government were thus the emperor and his court, the bureaucracy of mandarin scholars, and the military. The emperor was supreme in his capital, and the viceroys and governors-general were comparably powerful at the regional and provincial levels; in the local district the dominant official was the magistrate. This structure based its claims of legitimacy on Confucian ideals.

In theory the great masses of the people were controlled by and benefited from the system of distant government by their betters, but in practice they were kept in line primarily by the extremely demanding, immediately accessible institutions of family, clan, and community. Parental power and imperial power were based on the same doctrines and upheld by the virtues of obedience and loyalty to authority. As the rulers and opinion-makers of China, the scholars and philosopher-kings who adhered to Confucius ceaselessly stressed the need for harmony in all aspects of life, the legitimacy of classes, and a priority of occupations that rewarded compliance and penalized antisocial behavior.

THE EMPEROR AND HIS COURT

Although the institution of a supreme emperor began only with unification in 211 B.C., when the state of Qin conquered its neighbors and set the stage for the Han dynasty, the Chinese traditionally were never able to think of themselves as being without an emperor. Thus, in seeking to imagine the origins of their civilization, they have assumed that at the start there must have been great emperors, and they have always measured time by the reigns of emperors and their dynasties. For the Chinese, neither gods nor mystical beings, but the images of emperors, dominated legends of how life and culture began and history unfolded.

Emperor Pan Gu was believed to have separated heaven from earth. Of the nine Human Sovereigns (*Ren Huang*) who ruled for 45,600 years, Yu Chao taught people how to build houses, Sui Ren showed the Chinese how to start fires, Fu Xi invented the technique of fishing with nets, and Nu Guan introduced the regulations for marriages. Another mythical emperor, Shen Nong, taught the people agriculture. Musical instruments, ox carts, the development of silk, and other useful inventions were attributed to Huangdi, the Yellow Emperor. The succeeding Five Sovereigns (*Wu Di*) were identified with the five elements of traditional Chinese science (earth, metal, water, fire, and air). Finally, there were three great legendary Model Emperors (*San Huang*): Yao, who passed over his incompetent son to pick Shun as his successor; Shun, who subdued the barbarians and divided the empire into provinces; and Yu, who drained the world of water after the great floods and founded the Xia (Hsia) dynasty.

The mythical emperors, and particularly the Model Emperors, or Three August Ones, were depicted as doing things for the common people or acting as highly moral and virtuous rulers, thereby setting an example for all subsequent emperors.

The institutions of the emperor and his court were to a remarkable degree shaped by the first emperor of a unified China, Qin Shi Huangdi of the Qin dynasty. He established the tradition of the autocratic supreme ruler who relied not upon autonomous lords and nobles but upon technically competent officials to carry out the tasks of government.

After Qin Shi Huangdi the Chinese evolved doctrines that placed the emperor in a unique and interesting relationship to sacred powers. The Chinese emperors never had close ties with centralized religious authorities whereby ruler and priest reinforced each other. In Chinese theory the emperor, representing the benevolence of heaven, ruled according to the Mandate of Heaven. This doctrine legitimized the right of rebellion. If the emperor's conduct violated celestial norms, the anger of heaven might be expressed in natural disasters. People might regard floods or droughts as signs that heaven was withdrawing its mandate to the current ruler. In practice the doctrine was useful for justifying the overthrow of a dynasty and for legitimizing a new one without requiring any structural or organizational changes. It tempered the behavior of emperors and made them sensitive to the importance of correctly adhering to ceremonies. No doubt it also reminded them that they were mortal and might be destroyed if they failed to use their power correctly and effectively.

The throne was surrounded with ritual, and the emperor had

to perform many religious tasks even though Confucianism was a secular ideology. Every spring, for example, at precisely the right moment the emperor would go to the Temple of Agriculture and plow the first furrow of the year. From Ming times, when the capital was moved from Nanjing to Peking, until the fall of the Qing dynasty in 1911, every emperor, after a day's abstinence from food and women, faithfully performed ritual sacrifices at the blue-tiled Temple of Heaven and the yellow-tiled Altar to Earth, which were a few miles south of the outer wall of Peking.

It is not easy to evaluate the significance of individual emperors in Chinese history. The Western mind, with little more to go on than the age of absolutism and the grandeur of Louis XIV, has never known anything to compare with the powers of the Chinese emperor. The fact that the imperial court was concerned with ceremonial duties, acted as the arbiter of manners, and contributed to the arts — much as the European courts did — should not obscure its tremendous political and economic power. Indeed, it is exceedingly hard for us to grasp the breathtaking scale of the imperial enterprise.

The Forbidden City in Peking, now the seat of the Communist government, was once the private inner domain of emperors. Immediately outside its two miles of walls and moats were a series of parks built around large lakes, and an artificial mountain with pavilions and rest spots where the emperor and his favorites could enjoy themselves. Next in importance was the Tartar City, where those who had duties within the court or who were related to the emperor resided. Outside Peking and toward the Western Hills was the Summer Palace, with its marble boat and its outdoor theaters.

The imperial establishment involved far more than grand buildings. The number of retainers and personal household attendants surrounding the emperor placed him clearly above all others and in a sense removed him from easy contact with his government and his officials. The emperor's household was headed by his consort and usually four or five other recognized wives, as well as concubines and maidservants. All the imperial offspring were formally recognized as the children of the consort, who held the title of empress. The number of palace women was always impressive. By the end of the Ming dynasty there were over 9,000 concubines in the Forbidden City, and during the Qing there were over 12,000. By accepting as completely reasonable the idea that the emperor needed and could use so many women to satisfy his personal and sexual needs, the Chinese demonstrated their belief in the natural superiority and hence legitimacy of their emperor.

The development of a class of nobles was deterred by the refusal of Chinese emperors to dilute their power by allowing marriages to elevate the in-law families. Most of the consorts and palace women did not come from powerful families but were usually daughters of lesser, even humble, families. The emperor did not need alliances by marriage to enhance his power; rather he had to counter the danger that consort families would exploit their imperial connections. He did this by having such numbers of women that no one of them could claim special advantages.

Within the Forbidden City there were also eunuchs, whose duties, like those of the palace women, were entirely directed to the person of the emperor. In theory the eunuchs had no role in the management of government or the making of public policy,

---

TITLES OF EMPERORS

Emperors generally had several designations, a practice that led to many complications. A Chinese taboo forbade the mention of the personal name of a reigning monarch. Scrupulous scholars would in fact never put on paper any of the characters used in the emperor's name as long as he was alive. During other dynasties scholars might use such characters, but they would interrupt the column of their writing and place the character at the top of the next line, one space above all the other characters on the page. When the emperor died, he received a temple name, or posthumous title, such as "Grand Progenitor" or "Martial Ancestor." During his lifetime an emperor would assume a reign name, or reign title, called *nian hao,* which was used to reckon dates. A reign name was generally of an auspicious nature so that people could speak, for example, of the seventh year of "Eternal Contentment." Starting with the Ming, emperors were known by their *nian hao* and not by their temple names; in the early dynastic histories temple names were generally used.

---

but the fact that they had access to the emperor and controlled his appointments — even to the extent of holding off ministers and preventing them from seeing the sovereign — meant that in practice they had great power. The theory for surrounding the emperor with castrated men was that this would not only ensure that all children of the palace women were his, but would also surround the emperor with men who, not having families of their own, would be relatively uninterested in amassing fortunes. Nevertheless, during periods of dynastic decline the chief eunuchs freely used their powers for self-enrichment.

When the capital was moved to Peking during the Ming dynasty, the emperor had about 10,000 eunuchs. By the end of the dynasty there were 70,000 eunuchs in Peking, and during the Qing the number exceeded 100,000. Surprisingly little is known about who the eunuchs were. As far back as the Tang dynasty it was illegal for an adult to be castrated, but fathers could have it done to their sons. Presumably this meant that family lines were not threatened, for only fathers with several sons would sanction the castration of one. Most eunuchs came from very humble backgrounds and were usually illiterate. For no obvious reason, a few districts in Henan seem to have produced a disproportionate number of them.

In addition to the palace women and eunuchs, the emperor's inner court was composed of expositors-in-waiting and readers-in-waiting, who drafted imperial proclamations and helped the emperor peruse the memorials sent to him. The one formal and disciplined institution in the inner court was the Hanlin Academy, whose members maintained the Confucian ideology and assisted the emperor in making sure that the imperial examinations singled out the best scholars to serve in the state bureaucracy.

There is some debate over how tyrannical the emperors were with their public officials. Writers as different as Fei Hsiao-t'ung and Karl Wittfogel, for example, claim that even the highest bureaucratic officials were essentially helpless before their tyrant and that all policies came from the emperor, who could crush his subordinates. Others, including Wolfram Eberhard, believe that officials and emperors worked together to maintain the interests of the landed gentry. There were frequent struggles between emperors and bureaucrats to control state resources, and certainly the bureaucrats could protect their interests, if in no other way than by being excessively incompetent. Indeed, Fei Hsiao-t'ung argues that the tyranny of the emperors drove the civil service to develop the fine art of inefficiency as a means of self-protection. Much of the time, however, emperors were absorbed with their own concerns, and their officials were left free to conduct public affairs in their own manner.

On occasion emperors would be arbitrary and humiliating in their treatment of senior officials whom they seemed to feel they had to intimidate in order to control. Charles Hucker describes how frequently the Ming emperors brutally treated their officials — arbitrarily imprisoning and torturing them or executing them for very little reason: "On one occasion, 107 officials of the central government were even sentenced to kneel outside the palace gate for five successive days. What was most humiliating of all was that officials could be seized in open-court assembly, stripped naked, and flogged with bamboo poles, sometimes to death."[1] Officials were thus in much the same position as courtesans, trying to please every whim of the emperor and avoid his wrath; and rulers, in spite of Confucian rhetoric about how compassionate they should be, in practice were frequently autocratic and arbitrary.

The autocratic behavior of emperors did not, however, produce an administrative or executive style of ruling. At times the clashes between emperor and scholar-bureaucrats were over policy issues, but just as frequently they were of a more personal nature. As a consequence the basic style of emperors was a blend of ruling and reigning, of projecting personal influence on decision-making at one moment and of withdrawing into supreme isolation the next. Emperors could display their ultimate powers by making their officials work frantically or by ignoring them and forcing them to wait upon the imperial pleasure. Sometimes they would leave everything to an official, and at the next moment they would have every detail of his life and work checked by other subordinates. The intensity with which emperors at times attended to the affairs of state is documented by Hucker's statement that during the Ming dynasty, "In one ten-day period late in Taizu's reign,

[1] Charles O. Hucker, *The Traditional Chinese State in Ming Times, 1368–1644* (Tucson: University of Arizona Press, 1961), p. 98.

1,660 memorials dealing with 3,391 separate matters are reported to have been presented for imperial decision." [2]

In the contemporary world, Mao Zedong, Deng Xiaoping, and Chiang Kai-shek, though acting far more civilly than the dynastic emperors, all tended to blend ruling and reigning, to intervene in the details of governing at one moment and then to pull back into aloof isolation for prolonged periods. Mao, much like an emperor, depended on his bureaucracy, yet he felt compelled to clash with it and to distrust its most professional members. To be sure, the tradition of castigating bureaucratic behavior is as old as the bureaucratic tradition itself. But in China, unlike the West, it was a tradition that came from above, from the court itself, and not from below.

THE CIVIL SERVICE

The concept of a professional civil service, based on competitive entrance examinations, regularized evaluations, and systematic promotions, was possibly China's greatest contribution to the modern world. While European states were still relying on ancestry, aristocracy, and patronage, the Chinese had refined several times their competitive and merit-based civil service. When the American and the British governments felt the time had arrived to professionalize their services, they looked into Chinese practices.

In developing a professional civil service, the Chinese as early as the Han dynasty hit upon the remarkable idea that officials should be regularly transferred from place to place and never serve in their own home districts. The object was to reduce cronyism and opportunities for corruption and to free officials from the awkwardness of dealing with the problems of friends and neighbors. Impersonal posting did, however, have some practical disadvantages. Officials did not build up long-range interests in the welfare or economic development of particular regions.

The Chinese civil service was based on a body of shared knowledge and ethics — Confucianism — which gave its members a common approach to problems and to life. Members of the civil

[2] Ibid., p. 48.

service had all proved themselves in national competitive examinations, which tested their scholarship and the depth of their knowledge of the Confucian tradition. Since the Chinese social structure was essentially monolithic and government service was the principal avenue of advancement, competition was intense and men would study for years and keep coming back for reexamination in the hope of gaining admission to the service. The rewards were so great for those who passed that families, clans, and whole villages were willing to invest in years of education and tutoring for bright young candidates.

The starting point in the examination system was certification, which occurred every three years, when examiners from the capital went out into the provinces to identify the people who had done the proper studying and were of good character and certified them as *Xiu Cai* (*Hsiu Ts'ai*), having the bachelor's degree. Certification qualified the candidate to take additional examinations and was good for three years, after which it could be revoked if there was no evidence of further intellectual progress and continuing moral virtue. Full provincial examinations took place every three years and involved three days of continuous writing. Only one percent of those who went through this ordeal received passing grades. They were designated *Ju ren* (*Chü-jen*), or Licentiate (M.A. level), and were qualified for lower positions in government service, but unless they continued their scholarly progress and passed higher examinations they could not hope to reach the top grades and hold the highest posts.

The ultimate imperial examinations were held every three years at the capital. The candidates were locked into small, isolated cubicles with slits under the door though which food was passed. The cubicle had a single window and contained a desk at which the candidate stood while writing and a brick bed where he slept during the seven days of the examinations. Each candidate was given a number, which he put on his examination papers so that the graders would have no hint about his identity. Those who passed became *Jinshi* (*Chin-shih*), or Doctor, and were admitted to the higher service and could hope to reach the topmost positions in the government and become ministers and grand counselors. During the 276 years of the Ming period only 24,874 men became *Jinshi*.

Failure in the examinations could be shattering and resulted in many suicides. Disappointed candidates often became rebels, the most famous of whom was Hong Xiuquan, who became the leader of the Taiping Rebellion, the most disastrous conflict anywhere in the nineteenth century — it took 20 million lives. Most men who failed merely went back to study more for the next round of examinations. Their education, of course, had not taught them to be rebellious, and its content was essentially useless except for a career in government: Confucian knowledge made no concession to practicality except in the realm of governing.

A much-debated issue about Chinese history is the extent to which the examination system was vigorously applied and whether it brought a significant flow of new blood into Chinese ruling circles. Certainly during many periods, especially near the end of a dynasty such as the Qing, corrupt practices developed and men were allowed to buy office. The quest for office in such cases was not inspired solely by a search for greater wealth; it often signified a craving of the newly rich to gain the stamp of culture, for government service had been the mark of the cultivated gentleman throughout Chinese history. The system was also compromised from time to time by the open designation of categories of special candidates. For example, during the Qing dynasty Manchus and Chinese did not take the same examinations, and in several of the earlier dynasties the heirs of the founding family could take separate, and presumably easier, examinations.

These exceptions aside, the system was, on the whole, highly competitive, and it certainly succeeded in impressing upon most people the idea that they were being ruled by their intellectual and cultural superiors. It is hard to answer the question of whether the examination system facilitated or impeded elite mobility and recruitment. There are no comparative criteria for determining the norm for the "circulation of elites" in a genuinely open society. Bright fathers sometimes do have bright sons, and in a society in which there was only one channel for advancement a high proportion of exceptional sons would have had to enter their father's professions and compete to enter the ranks of officialdom. Moreover, in traditional China the sons of mandarins obviously had cultural and psychological advantages because they were brought up in a home environment in which education and the achievement of official status were stressed. Children of nonmandarin families, on the other hand, had little exposure to the classical literary traditions. It is therefore not surprising that during the Ming and Qing dynasties sons of elite families outnumbered sons of nonelite families in holding official office.

However, few families had more than two generations in office.[3] E. A. Kracke has found that during the Song dynasty, of those who passed the examinations in 1148 and in 1256, 56 percent and 58 percent respectively were "new men" in the sense that there had been no officials on their parental side for three generations.[4] On the whole, it would seem that there was more mobility throughout most of Chinese history than in even eighteenth- and nineteenth-century England.[5]

The examination process instilled a cast of mind blending the amateur ideal of the gentleman-scholar and a feeling of superiority over all others. The Confucian tradition developed no sense of professionalism or specialization. It encouraged people to think about their lifestyles. For the best men this meant reflecting on the humanistic values desirable in government; for the rest it meant thinking about careers in the bureaucracy.

The civil service was divided into nine grades, each of which was divided into two parts, making a total of eighteen steps. It is not clear why the Chinese bureaucrats (and subsequent European bureaucrats) found it natural and reasonable to divide authority and careers into eighteen stages. The pattern seemed to fit the life cycle rather well. The individual's final promotion usually came shortly before his vigor declined. Retirement was not institutionalized. Men stopped working either when they had the inclination or when their superiors no longer had an appropriate post for them. A unique feature of the Chinese career pattern was the break of about three years for mourning after the death of one's father. According to Arthur Waley:

[3] Ping-ti Ho, *The Ladder of Success in Imperial China: Aspects of Social Mobility, 1368–1911* (New York: Columbia University Press, 1962).

[4] E. A. Kracke, Jr., *Civil Service in Early Sung China, 960–1067* (Cambridge, Mass.: Harvard University Press, 1953).

[5] Rupert Wilkinson, *Gentlemanly Power* (London: Oxford University Press, 1964), ch. 12.

> This was a sort of "sabbatical," occurring as a rule towards the middle of a man's official career. It gave him a period for study and reflection, for writing at last the book that he had planned . . . , for repairing a life ravaged by official banqueting, a constitution exhausted by the joint claims of concubinage and matrimony.[6]

The Chinese imperial bureaucracy averaged 10,000 officials. The trend during each dynasty was Parkinsonian. There were only 4,900 officials at the beginning of the Ming dynasty, but there were 15,000 at the end: These were only senior mandarins. In addition, however, vast numbers of government employees supported these officials and were in some degree participants in official decision making. John Fairbank has estimated that there were as many as 100,000 such men.[7] This is not a large number, for these men were managing a country of 100 million people — a population that became nearly 400 million by the end of the imperial era.

Thus as large as the imperial court was and as extensive as the bureaucracy became, when it came to control at the local level, there were few officials. During the Ming dynasty the magistrate at the *xien* or county level had, on the average, 50,000 people to rule, and by the Qing period the magistrate at the *zhou* or district level was responsible for an average population of nearly 250,000.

It was possible to have so few officials as contacts between government and people because Chinese society had built in powerful forces for self-regulation. The traditions of the family and clan and other associations and occupational groupings made government intervention to maintain routine order rare. Most disputes were settled informally and by appeal to middlemen and village elders, and as little recourse as possible was made to courts of law.

In spite of the early role of the Legalists and the impressive body of administrative codes developed by the Tang, the imperial tradition did not identify government with law. The Chinese did little about civil law, stressing instead the virtues of accommodation, mediation, and compromise. The Confucian emphasis upon

[6] Quoted in John K. Fairbank, *The United States and China* (Cambridge, Mass.: Harvard University Press, 1948), p. 103.

[7] Ibid., p. 104.

ethics and reason precluded the adversary approach of Western law, and above all the Chinese rejected the idea that the law should protect the individual. For the citizen law meant punishment—the degrees ranged from prescribed numbers of strokes with heavy or light bamboo to death by strangulation, and incarceration was rare. For officials law meant administrative practices and punishments that ranged from demotion to exile.

The Chinese generally accepted a theory of collective rather than individual responsibility. When a crime occurred, it was not necessary to ensure that the perpetrator of the evil act was apprehended and punished; the government had only to identify the community or the family to which the criminal belonged and then hold the group responsible. Fathers were not inclined to accept punishment for their sons' deeds and hence vigorously sought to make sure that their children did not misbehave. Since one brother could be punished for the act of another, there was a tendency for all to be their brothers' keepers. Patricide in a town would bring lasting shame to all: in the short run higher taxes and, far worse, the perpetual stigma of having one corner of the city's walls rounded rather than at the normal ninety-degree angle. Any traveler approaching such a city could instantly recognize its moral shame, even though the ignominious event might have happened generations earlier.

Although informal social pressures were powerful forces easing the tasks of government, there was also a somewhat more formalized system of community and family controls called *baojia*. Although the numbers varied according to population and the natural size of the community, the *bao*, or community, usually consisted of 110 households. The heads of the ten most prosperous or established families were the community chiefs, and under an annually rotating leadership they would deal with the county (*xian*) magistrate and the tax collector and haggle over how to reduce and divide their collective tax burdens. They decided whose sons would be sent off to military service or to answer the imperial decree for corvée labor.

The remaining hundred families were divided into ten *jia*, or units of ten households. In theory the head of each *jia* was also selected on an annual rotating basis, but the position tended to rotate only among the few family heads who were deemed competent. At the *jia* level pressures could be extreme and painfully conflicting because the leaders had to live closely with their neighbors and enforce some of the most biting regulations of government. For example, the tax collector at the county level usually did not care to decide on his own the individual tax bills of each family but would present the *bao* or the *jia* with its collective quota and allow the people close at hand to deal with problems of equity.

THE SWEET AND SOUR CHARACTER OF GOVERNMENT

By now it should be clear that there was ambivalence about government and authority in imperial China. On the one hand, government was manifestly society's principal industry and elite activity. The higher the level one reached, the greater were one's rewards. Regardless of what one wanted in life — money, prestige, art, social refinement, action, leisure — the best career to follow was in government. On the other hand, the emperor could brutally mistreat those who were most successful, and the routine of service meant assignment to communities where one had no ties, did not know the spoken language, and would be seen by the local people as an agent of suppression.

The same ambivalence about power existed for those outside of government. There were advantages in being recognized as a negotiator with government, for one could look after one's personal interests while representing the community. Yet there was also the awful pain of having to serve as the government's agent in bringing bad news to one's neighbors.

These features of the hierarchy of authority in China produced schizophrenic behavior among those who were in any way involved with government. They had to learn how to display complete and abject servility toward all who were above them and to be harsh and repressive toward those beneath them. The highest officials in the land had to show degrading self-abasement before the emperor, and quite naturally they were gloriously haughty in their dealings with lesser figures. And so it went down the hierarchy. Local magistrates at the bottom had few face-to-face contacts with their superiors, and most of their time was given to showing their superiority over ordinary citizens. These attitudes, carried over into modern China, have contributed to what has been called the "bicycle complex" — that is, bending the knees to those above and kicking those below.

The sweet and sour character of government service was also to be found in the lack of material reward and the need to live constantly in the shadow of illegality. The official pay scale provided negligible salaries. Fairbank has estimated that a governor-general responsible for two provinces, often with populations exceeding the populations of modern France or Germany, was paid the equivalent of $300 a year plus an expense account, or "anti-extortion allowance," of $41,000.[8] Nevertheless he was expected to maintain a household and staff of several thousand people and to conduct himself in a style appropriate to the imperial representative. The result was a system of government by corruption, in which those who had dealings with officials tended to pay for services with "gifts." Just as the formal flow of tax moneys was extracted out of the people at the bottom of the hierarchy and passed up each step of the bureaucratic ladder to the imperial court, with vague amounts taken off at each level to maintain government operations, there was a private flow of resources, with subordinates seeing that superiors were taken care of. Fairbank tells of one Manchu official who, on falling from favor, was revealed to have had an estate of 425,000 acres, $30 million worth of gold, silver, and precious stones, and shares in ninety banks and pawnshops.[9] The fact that all officials had to breach the line of corruption, whether they amassed such large fortunes or not, meant that any official who displeased the emperor could be readily charged with misconduct in office and severely punished.

The basic logic of the system was that officials at every level of the hierarchy wanted tranquility and peace beneath them while they extracted enough from below to keep those above satisfied. Model magistrates were those who could keep their people from publicly complaining or disturbing the peace while they were passing to those above them gratifying amounts of revenue. Their third concern was to satisfy their own entourages and their own private

[8] Ibid., p. 105.
[9] Ibid., p. 104.

needs. The strains could be considerable, but that was the essence of government.

Fei Hsiao-t'ung has mentioned the Chinese tradition of poetry in which officials, in spite of their lofty estate and the grandeur of their offices, bemoaned their conditions, as for example Tao Yuan-ming:

> Why should I be an official?
> I bend my back
> For only three piculs of rice.
> Why should I not go back to till the land.[10]

Although the material benefits of office sufficiently outweighed the hardships so that people strove to get into the bureaucracy, the sour qualities of service were sometimes strong enough to inhibit their efficiency in carrying out their duties. Fei Hsiao-t'ung probably overstates the degree to which officials consciously or effectively fought back by doing a poor job and thereby frustrating the will of the emperor, but his words are helpful:

> Inefficiency and parasitism, on the one hand, remoteness of imperial control and a do-nothing policy by the emperor, on the other — this has always been the ideal. Yet this ideal of government, of a "good emperor" as one who presided but did not rule, has rarely been attained. As far as the officials were concerned, the next best thing, then, could only be to protect themselves, to keep a back door open for their relatives, and to be able to use their position as a shield against the emperor's whims. To protect not only themselves but their relatives and their whole clan from the unchecked power of the monarch, and to do this not by constitutional or by legal means but by personal influence — this is what they sought. Not by challenging the emperor's authority but by coming close to him, by serving him and from this service gaining an advantage in being enabled to shift the burden of the emperor's demands onto the backs of those lower down, did the propertied class attempt to neutralize the emperor's power over them and to avoid the attack of the tiger.[11]

The officials did not specialize in function or commit themselves to particular policy goals. Instead, officials followed a life-

[10] Fei Hsiao-t'ung, *China's Gentry* (Chicago: University of Chicago Press, 1953), p. 29. Copyright 1953 by The University of Chicago. Reprinted by permission.

[11] Ibid., pp. 26–27. Reprinted by permission.

time of moving from post to post, accumulating contacts and friendships, trying not to make enemies, and picking up subordinates who would be willing to throw in their lot with them. As an official's seniority increased, he accumulated a larger and larger following of staff assistants who accompanied him from one post to the next. Eventually, if he faltered, his staff might split up and his principal lieutenants would become figures in their own right and would in their turn begin to accumulate followers.

THE STRUCTURE OF OFFICIALDOM

For members of the bureaucracy tensions existed at two extremes: at the top in their relations with the emperor and at the bottom in dealings with the citizens. It is remarkable that within the bureaucracy, except for certain superior-inferior relationships, there were almost no institutionalized points of conflict. The reason that differences of interest among the ministries or boards did not often come into the open was the lack of professionalism and specialization. The bureaucrats were all generalists, trained only in the Confucian tradition, and they did not have strong loyalties for particular offices. For example, what might be assumed to be a natural clash between the interests of the Board of War and the Board of Revenue or between the Board of Public Works and the Board of War would never develop. If an official became excessively skillful and aggressive in obtaining funds for the Board of War, the ministers would transfer him in a year or so to the Board of Revenue or to the Board of Public Works so that he could argue the case against the Board of War. The combination of the amateur's ideal and constant movement among ministries kept officials from becoming personally specialized even though the government itself was organized by functional divisions.

Organizationally the imperial government had three layers. At the top were the highest officials who were closest to the emperor and concerned with general policies. The nature of their offices changed from time to time in response to relations with the emperor. Next came the operational offices, which, amazingly, changed little after they had been fully institutionalized into six boards or ministries early in the Tang dynasty. The third level consisted of the hierarchy outside of the capital, at the provincial and local levels.

When the Chinese bureaucracy first took shape, during the Qin and Han dynasties, the emperor was surrounded immediately outside his inner court by his three consultants (*sangong*): the chancellor (*chengxiang*), who was closest to being a chief administrator; the imperial secretary (*yushidafu*), who promulgated decrees and thus had legislative functions; and the grand commandant (*taimei*), who commanded the military. By the early Ming dynasty these top officials had formed the Grand Secretariat (*neigo*). Emperor Taizu (T'ai-tsu) discovered that they were becoming so powerful that they were usurping some of the imperial prerogatives. In 1380 he abolished the Grand Secretariat and suggested that bureaucrats of the capital might improve their claim to merit if they got out into the countryside.

Under the Qing rulers the most powerful group was the Grand Council (*juejiju*), of which half were Manchus and half Chinese, who acted as a cabinet or advisory council to the emperor. This body of the most august men in the empire was expected to conduct its business early each morning, starting before sunrise — a tradition that made it easy for those below to observe when standards were slipping and decline was setting in — which may help to account for emperors' petulance toward their ministers, for meeting with them so early in the morning after the active imperial nights could not have been easy.

As important as the officials around the emperor were, the hierarchy of Chinese officialdom did not point to any particular office as the commonly acknowledged goal of all careerists. Not all mandarins aspired to become members of the Grand Council or the Grand Secretariat. On the contrary, for most officials the preferred position was that of viceroy; one could rule with great autonomy as "little emperor" over sizable domains.

The Six Boards (*liubu*) were the principal ministries of the government and administered basic policies. The Board of Civil Appointments (*libu*) handled the personnel of the civil service, controlled appointments and promotions, and evaluated the performance of all officials. The Board of Rites (*libu*, but a different Chinese character) was responsible for ceremonies, sacrifices, and relations with foreigners, the rationale for the last responsibility being that visitors would not know proper etiquette and would appreciate guidance from specialists. This board had extensive and important duties; the Ming administrative code devoted 75 of its 228 chapters to its responsibilities.[12] The Board of War (*pingbu*) controlled the military, which, in spite of the Confucian scorn of soldiers, was never an insignificant force. For example, early in the Ming dynasty there were 15,000 officers and 1,100,000 men, and by the end of the dynasty there were 100,000 officers and 4 million troops.[13] Throughout their history the Chinese have maintained a remarkably high proportion of the population under arms, even when not engaged in conquest or defense against invaders.

The Board of Finance or Revenue (*hubu*) supervised the collection of taxes, set general quotas on what was expected from each province, managed census-taking, handled the financial accounts of the entire government, and managed such state enterprises as the granaries. The amateur spirit of the entire bureaucracy ensured that businesslike methods were not closely followed even in this apparently technical ministry, and the style was one of getting along as well as possible. The land tax in the Qing dynasty, for example — which lasted until 1911 — used assessments made in 1713 as the baseline for all subsequent haggling. The amount of revenue collected depended largely on the urgency of the emperor's concerns and the avariciousness of the particular officials involved. The Board of Public Works (*gungbu*) had some duties that came close to those of the finance board, such as the management of some state manufacturing, but specifically it was responsible for water control and irrigation schemes, canals and transportation systems, the construction of public buildings, and the mobilization of manpower for state services.

The Board of Punishment (*xingbu*) administered justice by codifying the laws, managing courts, and capturing and punishing criminals. Magistrates had considerable discrimination in decreeing punishments, but the most serious sentences were supposed to be reviewed by higher officials in the ministry. The review process helped to ensure standardized policies throughout the empire.

Outside of the capital the highest officials were viceroys or

[12] Hucker, p. 68.
[13] Ibid., p. 17.

governors-general (*zongdu, zhijun, or zhitai*), who as "little emperors" presided over two provinces. At the provincial capital were two governors, the provincial judge, the salt comptroller, and the grain intendant. Provinces were subdivided into circuits (*fu*), districts (*zhou*), and finally counties (*xian*).

Officials changed positions every two or three years among all these offices. Their ranks were proclaimed to all by the size of their entourage, by the number of banners they flew, by the color of the buttons on their skullcaps, and by the square insignia they wore in the middle of the front and back of their state robes.

THE CENSORATE

Possibly the most novel feature of the Chinese institutional arrangement was the Censorate (*du cha yuan*), which served as special watchdog over the entire civil service and performed as a blend of inspector-general and secret police. The institution was formed because of the suspiciousness of Qin Shi Huangdi, but its development eventually reflected the personal styles of many emperors. In general its task was to keep a sharp eye on the performance of all officials and to criticize any deviation from established norms. It reported to the emperor any misconduct of any of his officials. It could also, however, criticize the emperor himself, which some Censorates did. In return for that action they gained in the long run immortal recognition for their courage and honesty, but in the short run they generally lost their jobs, if not their heads. The Censorate might have brought a remarkable corrective influence to the Chinese system, restraining emperors and punishing evil officials. In practice, however, members of the Censorate were relatively lowly officials who were outside the flow of policies and revenues and their influence was usually marginal. Officials might worry about a censor's finding them adhering to the wrong forms, making a mistake in a document, or violating official etiquette, but generally they did not expect the censors to take up more fundamental matters. Consequently the Censorate was generally staffed with low- and middle-grade officials of little personal influence who were always vulnerable to the emperor's wrath.

THE SCHOLAR, THE GENTRY, AND THE MERCHANT

The boundary between state and society in imperial China was quite imprecise. The government dominated the society, and much of its authority was used to enforce behavior and punish offenses that in the West would be private matters. Exemplary moral conduct was also a matter of state concern. Authority thus could be humane and highly paternalistic.

The citizen had no claim on government, however, and there was not the slightest inkling of an idea that government should respond to the competitive forces among the people. The emperor's rule was supposed to bring tranquility and universal contentment, and officials were expected to support justice and decency, for all government rested on ethical considerations.

Because citizens had no legitimate mechanism for organizing and openly pressuring the government, influential people outside government sought to have their interests protected by officials. The lack of any formal machinery for registering the demands of special interests meant that such demands took on a subversive character, and the officials who responded to the realities of competing interests had to act in ways that were essentially corrupt. In the gray area beyond governmental jurisdiction existed a wide range of organizations that lacked respectability and were not honored in the formal histories, but did give protection to collective and special interests.

The most extensive and best organized of these groups were secret societies, the most famous of which included the White Lotus, the Elder Brother, the Triads, the Yellow Turbans, the White Lily, and the White Cloud. Each had its elaborate rituals and its areas of special concentration. The members looked after each other and took care of each other's funerals and bereaved widows and children. Most of these secret societies cut across class lines; their membership included not only representatives of the rural gentry but also ordinary peasants and even a few thugs who could be called on for the physical protection of the collective interests.

Most analysts of Chinese social classes observe that in a predominantly rural society there are always distinctions between landlords and rich peasants on the one hand and tenant workers and lowly peasants on the other. In China, however, those who were better off were not really an aristocracy. Early Western observers of China were struck by the lack of a formal aristocracy based on landholdings, and many of the contemporary interpretations of the collapse of the imperial system identified its weakness as precisely its lack of a hereditary class committed to aristocratic values.

More recent studies of Chinese society have focused on the existence of a gentry class that may not have had much sense of style or collective identity (in comparison to such classes in the rest of the world) but was a force for stability and even repression. Whether the gentry identified its interests with those of the government or whether it was victimized by the officials, it is clear that most of the scholar-officials came from this class. The gentry's values were Confucian, and they did tend to see the good life in much the same terms as the scholar-officials. In general, the gentry had pathetically small landholdings, and only those who got into government could hope to amass fortunes significant by any standards.

In contrast to the rather tense closeness of gentry and officials, there was a relatively unambiguous feeling of contempt and animosity among gentry and scholars toward merchants. As has so often been the case in agricultural societies there was distrust of those who dominated the marketplace and sought wealth without regard to sentiment or tradition. The Chinese had a great history of trading, and from the early Han dynasty they traveled extensively across central Asia. Yet those who ruled the empire never accorded status or recognition to the merchants. Instead, social and political pressures encouraged successful merchants to abandon money-making and enter government, even if they had to buy office. If they were not so enticed into the ranks of officialdom, it was still likely that their sons would be given a Confucian education and instilled with antimercantile views.

Social values were a prime reason for the failure of capitalism to develop in China. Government policies further impeded economic development by controlling much of the foreign trade on the pretense that it was really an exchange of tribute and gifts between the emperor and foreigners. The government also controlled certain critical commodities and industries, such as salt and iron in the early period and liquor and tea at later dates. In a sense the Chinese always had a "mixed economy" in which the "public sector" restrained the "private sector."

CHAPTER FIVE

The Sweep of Change

The collapse of the stubbornly durable structure of traditional China and the effort to erect in its place a modern Chinese nation-state is the central theme of the history of modern China. A system that had lasted for over 2,000 years and had experienced several periods of alien conquest, each time absorbing its foreign rulers, was unable to withstand a century of Western contact.

So long as the outside world reached China by land, its traditional society and economy were well protected. For many centuries the Chinese had coped with the probes and the raids of nomads, though at times the "'hordes" beyond the Great Wall were well enough organized to conquer the agricultural Chinese. But power relationships in central Asia generally favored the Chinese, and they had few reasons not to cling to their belief that those beyond their cultural reach were mere barbarians.

The challenges of the nomads to the agrarian Chinese had strengthened Chinese civilization. In reacting to the need to defend themselves, the Chinese developed their centralized empire and also their sense of cultural identity. The impact of the West, however, was of a completely different order, for it represented a political and military threat based on modern science and technology. As long as China was threatened only by familiar forces, Chinese civilization was secure. The collapse came when China was confronted with enemies who had the advantages of science and modern forms of military, economic, and political organization.

When Western civilization first reached China, it was not a major threat; only in the modern age of science and industry did it become a profound problem for the Chinese. Once British ships with advanced forms of firepower began to appear off the China coast early in the nineteenth century, the balance of power between China and outside "barbarians" began to change, and the Chinese became aware that they were facing a challenge unknown in their previous history.

Throughout the eighteenth and nineteenth centuries the West became steadily more effective in producing military power. The modernization of Europe generated a capacity for organizing large economic enterprises that could pressure the Chinese to adhere to Western terms for conducting trade. Although divided into nation-states competing for special advantages, Europe confronted the non-European world with the demand that European norms govern all interstate relations.

The West challenged China at many levels. In addition to presenting a military challenge, its impact created a historic confrontation between a traditional, agrarian society and a modernizing, urban-industrial one. For the first time China was confronted with enemies who were not isolated but were in close communication with each other. The traditional Chinese diplomatic technique of playing one barbarian off against the other by the careful management of favors backfired; granting a favor to one European power resulted in all demanding similar concessions.

The fundamental balance between China and the rest of the world began to change, and Chinese domestic society began to experience the profound effects that inevitably accompany the decline of a traditional order and the creation of a modern, technological society. The old order was threatened, but there was no clear indication of what the new should be. The self-assurance of the emperor was broken, and members of the civil service found their skills and cast of mind irrelevant to the new problems of the day. By the end of the nineteenth century, human relations throughout China were to undergo wave after wave of upheaval as new forms of urbanization pulled people in from the countryside and as rural life reacted to the broadening of the monetized economy. Members of such once-despised classes as soldiers and merchants were to find new opportunities, while such previously secure classes as scholars and gentry were to have their most basic values and their self-esteem threatened. The Chinese family was to experience great stresses and fundamental changes.

CHINESE VULNERABILITIES

It would be wrong to give the impression that the sweep and the rate of change in Chinese society resulted only from the military effectiveness of the Western nations. Certainly China, like all the rest of the world, in time would have had to accommodate and absorb the essential features of the modern world based on the scientific and technological revolution. However, at the moment of Western impact China was experiencing a phase of domestic decay and was therefore peculiarly vulnerable to outside influences.

By the middle of the nineteenth century the imperial system was displaying many characteristics typical of dynastic decline. Even if there had been no Western impact the Qing dynasty might have been nearing its end. Such speculation aside, the policies and practices of the imperial court and the mandarinate were exceptionally ineffectual at the very time that the system was experiencing its greatest challenge from outside forces.

China was also experiencing some historically unique developments that made the country peculiarly vulnerable to basic social change. There was an abnormally sharp rise in Chinese population in the eighteenth century, before the impact of the West began. China's population doubled between 1740 and 1790 and continued to grow by another third in the next fifty years, fundamentally changing the historic man–land ratio and in doing so possibly weakening the fabric of Chinese society.

The basic patterns of Chinese social and economic life had evolved when the population numbered well below 100 million, and indeed most of the time the population was closer to 60 million people. Although minor technological changes and the introduction of new crops (potatoes, sweet potatoes, peanuts) provided some support for a growing population, the inescapable fact is that China's resources expanded barely as fast as its population, and thus Chinese society was under considerable stress on the eve of its exposure to the challenge of the West.

The growth of population had brought about an expansion of urban centers long before there was any industrialization. Chinese cities emerged as administrative rather than as trading centers, and most of the people who lived in them were artisans and persons engaged in service functions. An increase in population without a concomitant increase in investment in productive enterprises tended to debase the old handicraft trades and make service activity servile and degrading. Even before industrialization, Chinese urban culture was based on a surplus of labor and reflected a spirit of abject poverty. When China began to industrialize early in the twentieth century, there was an overriding tendency to exploit the cheap labor, and there was less compulsion than in Europe and especially in the United States to substitute machinery for manpower.

At the beginning of the period of intense contact with the West, the Chinese government, though too weak to deal effectively with foreign pressure, was strong enough to play its classic role of obstructing China's merchant and commercial classes. Those active in the Chinese economy could not react on their own terms to the challenge and stimulus of Western traders. Arbitrary taxation prevented the natural development of a more integrated national economy and trade within China was impeded by a variety of internal levies and tariffs called *likin.*

In later years even a weak government was able to delay the growth of a modern intellectual class because it still served as the major employer of the intelligentsia. A weak government could also allow traditional standards of scholarship to decline and tolerate the practice of buying degrees and admission to the bureaucracy. Those who were in government service at the end of the Qing dynasty were second-rate by traditional Chinese and Western standards of scholarship. For the first time in Chinese history the stage was set for the development of an intellectual class that was divorced from government and that would increasingly reflect the frustration of imaginative but powerless and inadequately employed intellectuals.

AN ABUNDANCE OF THEORIES AND A SHORTAGE OF FACTS

Chinese intellectuals and officials were not alone in being puzzled about the broad sweep of change that came to China after the impact of the modern West. All thoughtful observers of the Chinese scene have felt it necessary to seek interpretations of the fundamental causes and the basic character of the prolonged "Chinese revolution" that eventually brought the downfall of the old order and massive turmoil when attempts were made to establish the new. As might be expected, interpretations of the causes of such a major historical occurrence have been numerous, reflecting individual points of view and preferences in theories of history. Until recently most students of China accepted such theories as partial explanations of what happened. They believed that the Western impact challenged the traditional Confucian order in all spheres: The immediate diplomatic and military confrontation of the mid-nineteenth century merged with fundamental economic and sociological changes, which in turn contributed to intellectual and cultural confusion and tension.

Recent scholarship, however, has shown that the process of modernization was not so coherent, and has raised doubts about the two most sophisticated theories. According to the first, the breakdown of the Confucian order resulted from the undermining of the agricultural economy and the rise of rural discontent. According to the second, the breakdown of the Confucian order stemmed from the collapse of the Chinese family system as a consequence of urbanization.

Doubts about the validity of these economic and sociological interpretations have led to the view that modernization in China has been unique because of the central importance of intellectual conflict. Although military and political considerations dominated China's initial reaction to the challenge by the West, the issue soon became a choice between clinging to the past or replacing traditional Chinese values, views, and practices with the ideas and values of a modern scientific and technologically oriented society.

Because the economic and sociological interpretations have been so popular, it is appropriate for us to examine them and comment on the evidence in their support.

THE BANKRUPTCY OF CHINESE AGRICULTURE

Since both the society and the economy of China were agricultural, it would seem logical to assume that developments in the countryside were basic to the breakup of the traditional order. A conventional interpretation of the economic history of China traces the collapse of the Confucian order to changes in tenant-landlord relationships. According to this view, which ignores the doubling of the population that occurred before the Western impact, the processes set in motion by the Western impact began with a rise in population, which increased the supply of cheap labor. At the same time those who made money in the cities as a result of new developments tended to cling to old practices and invest in land. This meant that land prices were driven steadily upward. Consequently there was a disturbing increase in the number of both landless peasants and absentee landlords. The gentry, who had once been a stabilizing factor in the countryside regardless of whether they acted as allies of a domineering government or as opponents of the bureaucracy, were compelled to become more distant and exploitative. The lot of the peasants became desperate, and rebellion increasingly seemed their only hope. In time, class lines were more sharply drawn, and eventually the entire social and political order was toppled by the frustrations and demands of the landless and poor peasants.

This theory is challenged by facts suggesting that the processes of change were much more complex. Undoubtedly the rich took advantage of the poor when they could. The facts that are available, however, do not suggest any dramatic increase in tenancy and landlessness, and there is no solid evidence that the size of the largest holdings increased markedly from the 1850s to the 1950s.

Dwight A. Perkins has shown that China's agricultural production grew at a rate consistent with the growth in population. This growth was achieved largely because the opening of new areas and the expansion of irrigation increased the amount of arable land. During the eighteenth and nineteenth centuries publicly and collectively owned lands were steadily transferred to private ownership. Lands once owned by the imperial family, the government, the army, the temples, and clans were transferred to individuals. At the beginning of the Qing dynasty the entire area of Manchuria was reserved for the Manchus, and in theory Chinese were not allowed to own land "beyond the Wall." But even before the end of the dynasty there was a flow of migrations, particularly from rural Shandong and Hebei, which greatly increased after the revolution of 1911.

The expansion of acreage and the reduction of lands reserved for tenancy meant that during the nineteenth century there was a rise in the proportion of small, independent holdings and a decline in the percentage of peasants who rented rather than owned their fields. These facts do not support the view that the changes that might have followed the Western impact on the Chinese economy produced a significant increase in tenancy and landlessness among China's peasant populations.

There is no evidence that after the Western impact there was an expansion in the size of landholdings. The Chinese never practiced primogeniture, and with the passing of each generation individual holdings were invariably broken up among all the heirs. Indeed, because of the Chinese custom of leaving equal shares to all sons, the tendency was to fragment holdings in order to ensure that each got the same amount of good as well as poor land. Wealthy people tended to have large families, and the usual Chinese pattern was that increases in the number of heirs ran ahead of increased accumulation of land. As a result, holdings were broken up almost as fast as they were accumulated, as in each generation sons split up what their fathers had put together.

Consequently Chinese "estates" were rather trivial by the standards of most agrarian societies. A 1935 government survey of eleven provinces revealed that there were only 1,545 "big landlords," and these averaged less than 350 acres per family. In 1937 the largest holding in Hebei province, which contains Peking and Tianjin, was only 165 acres. In south China the "estates" were even smaller, and holdings of four and five acres were enough to permit one to have tenants and to become a member of the "gentry."

Although there is little evidence to suggest either that the landlords were becoming more numerous or that they possessed larger holdings, some facts suggest that the peasant owner was having more trouble avoiding bankruptcy. By early in the twentieth century rural indebtedness had become endemic. The difficulty stemmed in part from the tenacity with which the Chinese peasant clung to traditions and customs more appropriate to an earlier period of less intense population pressures. He persisted in living well beyond his means in his observances of weddings and funerals and other festive occasions, and years of indebtedness generally followed such major events. Possibly in earlier ages it had been easier to maintain old customs because they were supported

LAND TENANCY

Statistics on land use and tenancy over time and for the various parts of China do not exist. At best we have isolated figures for different locations at different times. The problem of understanding tenancy is further complicated by the great variety of land rights and forms of ownership. In some areas sharecropping was practiced. In others peasants had permanent rights to the land they worked. They could will the rights to their sons, but they could not sell their rights, and the landlord could not evict them. In other areas the general practice was for a high proportion of tenants also to be owners of part of the land they worked. In many areas the relation between landlord and tenant was that of a clan organization to one of its members.

Size of holdings differed greatly according to population density, crops raised, and general economic conditions. These factors in turn influenced the tenancy picture.

A study by Dr. R.T. Ts'ui of the University of Nanjing College of Agriculture showed the following historical pattern for central China:[1]

Percentage of Total Number of Farmers

	1912	1934	1937
Tenants	28%	29%	30%
Part-owners	23	25	30
Owners	49	46	46

The China Handbook, the semiofficial statistical abstract, in its last report before the Communists came to power, stated that in 1947 about a third of the farmers were tenants, a quarter were part-owners, and from 40 to 45 percent were full owners.[2]

Dr. John Lossing Buck found that in a sample of 16,796 farms taken in the mid-1930s, only 17 percent were tenants, and "only 28.7 percent of the total Chinese farm area was rented (12.7 percent in the wheat region and 40.3 percent in the rice region)." [3] Compared

[1] Gerald F. Winfield, *China: The Land and the People* (New York: William Sloane, 1948), p. 279. Reprinted by permission of William Morrow & Co., Inc.

[2] The Chinese Ministry of Information, *The China Handbook* (Shanghai: Commercial Press, 1947), p. 172.

[3] Quoted in Winfield, p. 280. Reprinted by permission.

to American, European, and South Asian patterns of tenancy, the Chinese situation was not in any sense extreme, according to these studies.

Other studies, particularly those by the Communists, suggest that there was greater inequality in distribution. One non-Communist study suggested that from 10 to 15 percent of the farm population owned from 55 to 63 percent of the land.[4]

Equality certainly did not exist, for even though China lacked the large-scale estate holdings common to many other agricultural societies, there were always differences in wealth among village families. What is less clear is how stable the inequality was. Chinese folk culture includes a strong notion of the constant rise and fall of family fortunes. In the United States, "shirt-sleeves to shirt-sleeves in three generations" and "rags to riches" stress upward social mobility; similar Chinese concepts have emphasized the idea that when one family rises another must go down, and the notion of social decline and decay is more vivid in China. Inequalities did not imply security for some. The search for equality did appear in the Chinese practice of dividing inheritances equally, both with respect to size and quality; thus the tendency toward fragmentation of plots was traditionally a more serious obstacle to productivity than excessive concentration.

[4] T. H. Shen, *Agricultural Resources of China* (Ithaca, N.Y.: Cornell University Press, 1951), p. 96.

by a larger collective, either the extended family or the clan. The trend toward individualized agriculture meant that many peasants who owned their own land were not able to maintain such elaborate traditions.

More importantly, peasants were increasingly driven to indebtedness because the expansion of the monetized economy and closer trade links with the cities meant that they had more fixed and inflexible obligations and fewer possibilities for relying on handicrafts for additional income. Peasants traditionally could pay their taxes or rents in kind, as a proportion of their crops. In bad years they would pay less, and they could even bargain for special considerations that might further lighten their load. The Chinese pattern was that government, landlord, and peasant all suffered losses during bad harvest years, and the peasants, being closest to the situation, could often look after their own interests so as not to suffer proportionally more. By the end of the nineteenth and the beginning of the twentieth century, peasants had more standardized taxes and rents because the government needed a predictable income, mostly because it had to borrow more and had to meet the schedules of debt payments. This was also true of the landlords, who not only had to pay their taxes in cash but also had more fixed obligations. They had once been able to educate their children by supporting a tutor-teacher in the household, for example, but now they had to pay tuition at schools and universities. The process of moving toward more impersonal and generalized practices tended to hurt the peasants most because they were confronted with increasingly rigid obligations while nature remained unpredictable.

The indebtedness of Chinese peasants was rarely related to investments to increase production; the weight of their debts tended to erode only their positions as landowners. Yet the fact that concentration of landholdings and the ratio between owner-operated and rented lands did not appreciably change, and certainly not at a rate proportionate to the rising level of indebtedness, suggests that those who owned their lands were somehow able to survive economically in spite of their indebtedness. No doubt the main explanation is that these people usually maintained some personal contacts, including family connections, so that indebtedness brought help from friends and relations. This might mean that relatives who had moved to the city were sending back some of their earnings. For these farmers, then, the generally unfavorable terms of trade between countryside and city were balanced by private remittances.

Tenant farmers had the greatest problems with indebtedness. To borrow the money they often needed to survive from one harvest to the next they would usually turn to their landlords. The result was that even when rents remained constant, the proportion of the crop that went to the landowner could be increasing. Since tenants usually did not have family connections as economically beneficial as those of the landowners, they could only mortgage their future earnings.

These patterns suggest that the only way indebtedness could

rise without an increase in the amount of rented land was with a significant turnover of tenants — as those who collapsed under their burden of debt were replaced by new tenants who would soon be likewise indebted. Though plausible, this theory is contradicted by evidence from village surveys, which show that until the Japanese occupation Chinese villages were extremely stable. Landowners tended to rent only to long-established tenants and rarely to strangers. Neither north or south China showed any significant tendency toward the creation of an impersonal market of tenants. If a peasant wanted to rent land, he could hope to do so only if he were known and trusted by the landowner. Indeed, the trend toward more absentee landlords — which developed as landowners moved to larger towns to take part in new economic activities or as people from the distant cities invested in land — increased the need for reliable tenants. The farmer who worked part of his land and rented out part was more likely to rent to a stranger than would an absentee landlord who could not keep his eye on the tenant.

Thus although indebtedness probably increased, and life certainly was not easy for Chinese peasants who worked their own land, the basic structure of the rural economy was not severely shaken, and the proportion of landless farmers to peasant owners probably did not greatly change during the decades in which the traditional Confucian order was decaying.

The thesis that political changes stemmed from a sharp rise in rural economic discontent is also put into doubt by the pattern of rebellions. The great peasant rebellions that shook imperial China took place in the nineteenth century. They occurred, however, either before the Western impact could have produced extensive economic changes — as was the case with the Taiping Rebellion, from 1851 to 1864 — or in the areas least affected by the Western impact — as was the case with the Muslim rebellions in Yunnan province from 1855 to 1873 and in Xinjiang from 1877 to 1878. In the twentieth century, when the effects of rural bankruptcy should have been increasingly intense, there were no significant peasant rebellions until the emergence of the Communists, who did not rely solely on rural economic discontent but appealed to Chinese nationalism during a period of Japanese war and occupation. In short, it is not possible to establish a clear connection between peasant rebellions and the cumulative consequences of rural bankruptcy.

Another historic indicator of the condition of the Chinese countryside has been the frequency of famines. From 108 B.C. to 1911, 1,828 famines of significant proportions were recorded. In 1921 there was a major famine in north China. But, interestingly, in the next decades there were no famines of such proportions. Although not a particularly reliable measuring rod, the reports of travelers in the Chinese countryside do give the impression that after the turn of the twentieth century the most extreme forms of human suffering seemed to be declining with each decade. Female infanticide was widespread in the first two decades of the twentieth century, but it was rarely noted by the 1930s. Daughters were sold into various forms of bondage in the first decades, but this practice had largely disappeared by the 1940s. The quality of textiles and of clothing improved during the very period when, in theory, conditions were deteriorating.

We are thus left with a complicated story filled with contradictions. The most plausible theory, that of steady rural pauperization, is not fully supported by the facts. No measure unambiguously shows the landlords getting richer and the peasants getting poorer as China was exposed more and more to the international commercial world. On the contrary, the more objective the data and the more precise the study, the greater is the doubt about the validity of what in general terms seems to make sense. From a distant perspective that sees only the collapse of the traditional order and the emergence of Communist China, the theme of increasing exploitation of peasants by landlords seems so reasonable as hardly to require accurate data for its validation. Yet in village studies made before World War II little evidence was uncovered to support such a pattern of change in economic relationships. Scholars currently examining the voluminous economic and social surveys conducted by the South Manchurian Railroad are discovering that although the work was done by Japanese social scientists personally inclined toward Marxism, the results were almost identical to those of some Kuomintang-supported studies done in Shandong and Hebei, and both groups of studies show that not until the mid-1930s did tenancy and size of landholdings begin to change. The proportion of the population that was landless showed almost no increase until the eve of full-scale war with Japan, and by then other political and social factors were at work.

The best available evidence thus demands further speculations, for no direct correlation between economic factors and the collapse of the Chinese social and political order can be established. There must have been something more to the story, something that tempered the economic trends and intensified the degree of political and social change. In looking for such intervening considerations, it would seem reasonable for sociologists to begin with the institution that traditionally was the most decisive in giving shape to Chinese society — the family.

Perhaps the Chinese family moderated and accommodated the stresses in Chinese life, for a long time preventing them from becoming too explosive but eventually itself collapsing, thus opening the way to the final disintegration of the old Confucian order and the advent of Communism.

FORM AND SUBSTANCE OF THE CHINESE FAMILY

The conventional account of the transformation of the Chinese family is even more entrenched than the conventional account of the breakdown of Chinese agriculture. Available facts about the family, however, seem to contradict this interpretation more emphatically than the facts bring into doubt the theory that agricultural bankruptcy was the prime cause of the disintegration of the Confucian system.

The standard view, held by Chinese and foreigners alike, is that historically the Chinese family consisted of three, four, or even five generations living together as a social and economic unit. The Confucian ideal of filial piety presumably required that children look after their parents in such an unbroken line that the extended family, in which a son brought his wife to live with his father and grandfather, was a cultural ideal violated only by extreme economic necessity.

In a society dominated by extended patrilineal families, an individual had unquestioning obligations to look after his relatives and to share with them whatever good fortune might befall him. The strength of the extended family presumably gave stability to the entire society. The conventional wisdom about Chinese society has generally held that only with modernization did the traditional family structure begin to break down and be replaced by the stem or the nuclear family consisting of parents and children or just husband and wife.

This theory, like the one attributing agricultural collapse to increasing repression by landlords of peasants, is not easily supported by the data. Wherever it is possible to find solid evidence of how the Chinese actually lived, the facts uniformly suggest that they rarely achieved their cultural ideal of the extended family. The Chinese family, even during the Qing dynasty, often consisted of no more than parents and children. As soon as sons could support themselves, they were expected to go out and seek their own fortunes. Moreover, there is little evidence that the pattern of family institutions changed much in the last 150 years. In villages, elder sons usually stayed close to family enterprises and younger sons drifted away, but the pattern was little different from that in Europe. The fact that the Chinese did not practice primogeniture meant that there was possibly less difference in the treatment between eldest and youngest sons than in Europe.

The ideology of the Chinese family was indeed severe. There were no conceivable grounds for challenging the institution. Children were expected to be unquestioningly dutiful regardless of parental behavior. Divorce was exceedingly rare and could never be initiated by the wife. The husband had seven possible grounds: if the wife was disobedient, was excessively talkative, was caught stealing, had a reputation for loose morals, displayed jealousy, had a contagious disease, or was childless. Like the structure of the extended family, however, the ideology of marriage was more firmly embedded in the culture than was the achievement of the ideal.

Modernization did not bring quick changes to the structure of the family or to the practices of marriage and divorce, but it did make the Chinese aware that they were not meeting their cultural ideals. These strains made clear the gaps between their ideology and their practices. Economic stress from the increasing monetization of the economy and from the increasing population competing for a limited amount of land did cause the Chinese to turn to their families for help. Faced with immediate problems and responding to their own sense of isolation and insecurity, the Chinese rationalized that earlier generations escaped the problems they were having. They idealized the security of the past by suggesting that the extended family had once been very widespread, although it never really had been.

Notable changes in marriage practices suggested that great changes were taking place in the Chinese family. During the 1920s and 1930s increasing numbers of Chinese refused to accept marriages arranged by their parents, but chose to select their own mates instead. Such independence was a bold act, limited in the 1920s largely to the urban and educated segments of society. By the time of the Japanese war, however, personal choice in marriage was also more common at other levels of society. As significant as this development was for creating a sense of autonomy among modernized Chinese, it did not greatly affect the prevalence of extended families.

Established facts about Chinese social life indicate that the composition of families did not change very much in modern times. Attitudes, sentiments, and cultural ideals were changing far more than the actual family structure. The breakdown of the Chinese family was thus more a change in attitude than in behavior. There were about as many extended families in modern as in traditional times, but the number of people who felt threatened because they lacked the protection of an extended family rose significantly.

The key to the collapse of the traditional social order was neither economic dislocation nor a perceptible change in family patterns. Rather, the old order collapsed because there were fundamental changes in political attitudes and emotional commitment. Statistics about landholdings and family practices show that physical upheavals lagged behind changes in beliefs and feelings. During the nineteenth century and early in the twentieth century, life in China did not actually undergo major disruptions, but there was widespread belief that conditions were in fact different. In particular, Chinese intellectuals were frustrated because they believed conditions had severely deteriorated, far more than the facts now available would suggest. Others were disturbed because they wanted changes to be more rapid.

THE TRADITIONAL CHINESE HOUSE

The architecture of the traditional upper-class house in China was designed to accommodate the extended family. Old, large houses in Chinese cities had a series of courtyards, each of which could hold one or more family units. A high wall and a large gate separated the compound from the street. Immediately inside and usually to the left was a gate house, or a room or two, where the gate-keeper lived. The rest of the first courtyard was usually given over to the servants and to stables and storerooms. The courtyard was roughly square in shape, and in its center there was likely to be a well and maybe a tree. The passage between the first and second courtyards was usually in line with the front gate; behind it was likely to be a large screen or wall so that when the doors were opened one did not have a direct view inward. The Chinese believed that evil spirits could move only in straight lines, and thus the screen protected the living quarters from them and gave privacy and a break between living units. The second courtyard repeated the first, but on a grander scale. On both sides of the entrance were two or three rooms, usually accessible only through the center room. The roof extended over the front to create a covered walkway or narrow veranda on three sides of the courtyard. This courtyard might serve as quarters for the staff and personal servants. Then, depending on the size of the total establishment, the next, and in some cases the fourth, courtyard, housed the living quarters for the junior members of the family.

Depending on the wealth and station of the family, each son and his family occupied either one side of a courtyard or a whole courtyard. Certain courtyards might also be the quarters for the master's concubines. The innermost courtyard belonged to the master. Domiciled here were the first wife and often the second and third wives, who lived in rooms along the sides. The eldest son's courtyard was located immediately before the master's and, depending on whether the father had a second wife or concubines, the second and third sons and their wives might occupy the rooms on the two sides. Questions of precedent were important. Hurt feelings could result from decisions about whether the younger son or the unmarried daughters should rank above favored concubines, the issue being less the status of the concubines and more the physical convenience of the master, who might prefer not to stumble through too many courtyards on a dark night.

Traditional Chinese House and Courtyards

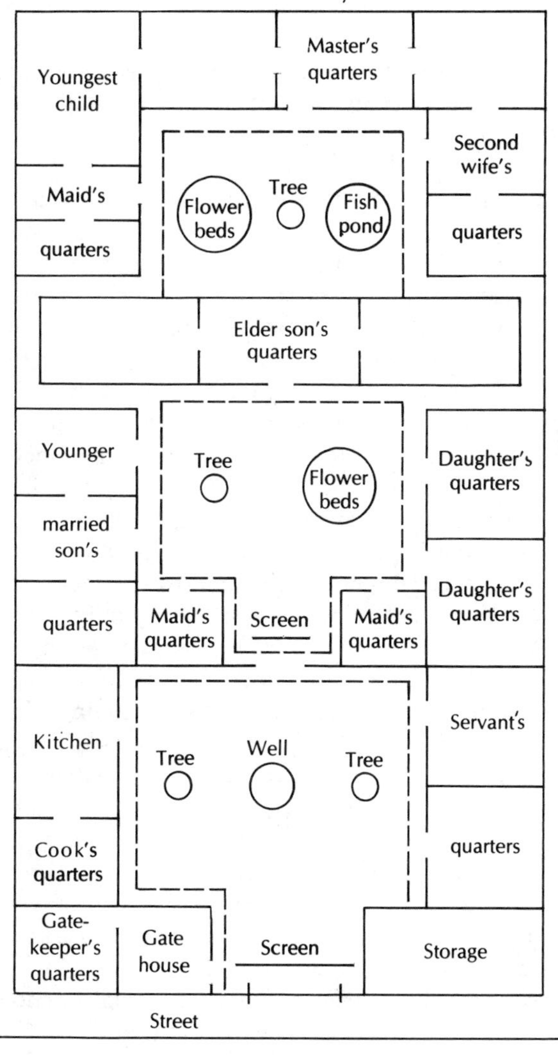

THE DECLINE OF IDEOLOGY

An analysis of the intellectual and economic history of the period reveals that major shifts in the importance of Confucianism and in the acceptance of foreign ideas had already occurred before there were significant changes in the economy and in established social institutions.

During the first decades after the Opium War (1839–1842) the Chinese were experiencing profound self-doubts and wondering whether they should incorporate Western technical knowledge to protect what remained of the Confucian system of values. Mary C. Wright, a most careful historian of modern China, identified the Tongzhi (T'ung-chih) Restoration, the remarkable effort of the throne to modernize China on Confucian terms after the Taiping Rebellion, as "the last stand of Chinese conservatism," by which she suggested that thereafter there was no effective formal defense of the Confucian order. Certainly by the end of the nineteenth century the "traditionalists," as so ably described by Joseph Levenson, were self-consciously defensive and haunted by doubts, and were thus no longer true Confucianists.

China's intellectual vulnerability to Western ideas can be seen from the fact that the ideological basis of the bureaucratic system — the classical examinations for the civil service — was completely eliminated by 1905, long before there had been significant structural changes in the economy. In the 1860s leading officials were arguing that the traditional amateur and belletristic ideals would have to be supplanted by more professional and technical skills. In the next two decades there evolved a debate on issues about knowledge that are still plaguing the Chinese Communists. Within the leading circles of the mandarinate there was general agreement that it was possible to distinguish between basic values, of which the Confucian tradition presented the supreme examples, and technology, in which the West was more advanced.

Chinese intellectuals tried to make a sharp distinction between fundamental values, including their Confucian ideals, and utilitarian and practical knowledge. The scholar-officials debated about "controlling the barbarians through their own superior technology," and many advocated that Chinese students learn Western science and use foreign technical knowledge to defend Confucian civilization.

The debate itself, however, began to spread doubt about the superiority of Confucian knowledge. By the 1890s the most vigorous reformers in the government were pressing for the all-out adoption of foreign knowledge in order to protect Chinese culture. In the summer of 1898 these reformers had one hundred days of complete control during which they sought to open the way for a constitutional monarchy supported by modernized governmental and educational systems. The reformers went too far, and a group of conservatives began to challenge the validity of the distinction between cultural values and utilitarian knowledge. They advanced the extraordinarily sophisticated view that Western technology could not be separated from the underlying values of Western Judeo-Christian civilization, and similarly, that Confucian values depended on the integrity of all aspects of Chinese civilization. Their concern was that if Western science and technology were accepted as the basis of the new education, Chinese students would soon come to doubt Confucian values and turn to foreign values. Even though some of the conservatives recognized the superiority of Western technology, they felt that it would be better for Chinese civilization to go down to defeat honorably clinging to the Confucian world view than to insist that the old could be defended by incorporating select elements of the new.

The conservative argument, which was defensive and lacked the easy self-assurance of the traditional Confucian view, sowed doubts among the reformers, causing some to become pessimistic about any hope for China and others to become even more radical, to the point of rejecting the need to defend Chinese "civilization" and favoring the idea of preserving the Chinese "nation."

The clash between values and knowledge became a central ingredient in the development of Chinese nationalism. It has in a strange fashion survived to this day, appearing now as the "red and expert" problem, in which "redness" is political correctness and values and "expertness" is technical knowledge and skills. That Chinese nationalism was shaped by questions about values and knowledge reflects the degree to which the Chinese experienced the most fundamental intellectual changes in a much shorter time than any other society. It has been argued that the mental climate of China changed more during the first half of the twentieth century than that of the West changed between the thirteenth and twentieth centuries.

The clashes of values did not occur in a calm, intellectual atmosphere; often they were at the vortex of considerable violence. For example, the reformers led by Kang Yuwei (K'ang Yu-wei), who gained the support of the young Emperor Guangxu (Kuang Hsü) for the hundred days of reform in 1898, realized they might have to counter the reactionary forces by assassinating Ronglu (Jung-lu), the close adviser of the Empress Dowager Cixi (Tz'u Hsi). The chosen agent for the act, Yuan Shikai (Yüan Shih-k'ai), who later became the first president of the Republic of China, informed the Empress Dowager of the plot, and she quite ruthlessly had the young emperor seized and placed under house arrest in the palace, while she executed several of the reformers. Kang Yuwei fled the country. In the following years the incompetence of reactionary leaders and the fiasco of the Boxer Rebellion encouraged more and more Chinese to think of the need for change, and reformers became revolutionaries as national self-consciousness stimulated resentment against Manchu rule.

The extent to which intellectual life was breaking out of the Confucian mold can be seen in the spectacular rise in the number of students studying in modern, westernized schools as soon as the examination system was changed. In 1905, when it was decreed that the Confucian classics were no longer the basis for the examinations, only slightly more than 100,000 students were in modern schools. By 1907 the number had increased more than tenfold, and there were more than 1 million students in nearly 38,000 schools. At the time of the 1911 Revolution there were more than 1.5 million students and 52,650 schools, and by 1916 the number had risen to nearly 4.3 million students in 129,739 schools. By 1923 more than 6.6 million students were learning modern sciences and mathematics instead of the Confucian classics. During this period, numerous universities were founded by both foreigners and Chinese; some floundered and failed while others became noteworthy centers of knowledge. By 1931 thirty-four universities and sixteen technical institutions of higher learning had been established in China.

In addition, large numbers of Chinese students began studying abroad, starting with Yung Wing, who had graduated from Yale in 1847. At the time of the 1911 Revolution there were 800 Chinese students in America, 400 in Europe, and from 10,000 to 15,000 in Japan. By 1930, almost 2,000 students left the country each year for university work in America and Europe. The speed with which the Chinese turned to modern education reflected not only their rejection of Confucianism and their continuing faith in education but also the remarkable efforts of foreign missionaries to establish schools and universities along the east coast and in the interior. The first major schools and universities were supported by missionaries. Many of the people trained to teach at these schools were encouraged to spend some years abroad. By the 1930s twenty-one Protestant societies and twelve American universities were supporting a dozen or so Chinese universities and colleges ranging from Yenching, near Peking, to Lingnan, near Canton.

In 1919 the intellectual ferment in China became highly politicized with the May Fourth Movement, which was occasioned by the announcement of the decision of the Allies at the Paris Peace Conference to give Japan rights in Shandong province which had once belonged to Germany. Since China had declared war on Germany as a consequence of American persuasion, there was a strong feeling that China had been unjustly treated by Woodrow Wilson. More than 3,000 college students demonstrated in Peking; the home of one cabinet member was burned; and two other ministers had to escape over their back walls. In the days that followed, students poured down to Shandong in commandeered trains. The government sought to restore order, but by mid-May the students had called for a general strike, and there was widespread sympathy on the part of merchants who were anxious to boycott Japanese products and workers who were inflamed by the spark of nationalism.

John Dewey happened to be in China at the time and inspired the intellectuals with his views of the pragmatic and utilitarian focus appropriate to modern education. Cai Yuanpei (Ts'ai Yuan-p'ei), the chancellor of Peking National University, and Dr. Hu Shih, a former student of Dewey's and China's leading philosopher, gave constructive intellectual leadership to the students' movement. Student unions were established in the major cities, and a variety of new journals, such as *Young China, The Construction,* and *Young World,* made their appearances and, along with such established journals as *The New Youth, The New Tide, Weekly Review, The Modern Critic,* gave the Chinese intellectual scene a heavy dose of utopian idealism that stressed the purity of youth and nationalist sentiments.

THE MYSTERIES OF CHINA'S POPULATION

The history of Chinese demography offers several mysteries. First it is startling that the first census taken in A.D. 2, when the population was still concentrated in the Yellow River valley, reported 59.5 million people, which compares with the estimated 54 million in the entire Roman Empire at about the same year. But in the next 1,500 years there was apparently very little change, as the Malthusian balance must have been at work:

A.D. 2	59.5 million	1651	60 million
742–755	51	1741	143.4
900	53	1775	264.5
1200	45	1793	313
1292	53.6	1849	413
1393	60.5		

These figures probably underestimate the actual population by at least 20 percent; as the census was the basis for establishing tax quotas, both households and districts benefited by understating their sizes. Official estimates often fluctuated greatly from year to year: The figure for 1774 was only 221 million, and for 1775, 264.5 million. The deepest mystery of China's population is that it more than doubled between 1741 and 1793, before the Western impact, industrialization, or any changes in public health standards. The explanation seems to lie in a combination of minor technological innovations in agriculture and the introduction of new crops.

The mystery of China's population continues today. Between 1849 and 1949 the assumption was that the population was growing slowly and at the most totaled only some 450 million. The first Communist census, however, taken in 1953, revealed a figure of 580 million. The second published census, in 1982, reported that China had passed the 1 billion mark by 8,125,288, and therefore constituted a quarter of mankind.

With the May Fourth Movement the Chinese intellectuals deserted the faltering regime of the warlords and set the stage for the founding of both the Kuomintang and the Communist Party as mass movements heavily influenced by students in search of allies in the rest of society. These developments carry us well ahead of our story. These trends, however, demonstrate the degree to which intellectual currents came to dominate the fate of China as the old imperial structure crumbled.

The Western impact also challenged the Qing dynasty politically by questioning its legitimacy and setting in motion the currents of nationalism, which were at first strongly anti-Confucianist and promodern but in time became increasingly antiforeign in spite of (or because of) their dependence on foreign knowledge. The political dimensions of the Western encroachment on China suggest that the dynamic element in China's modernization was primarily the problem of attitudes and intellectual perspectives and less one of material or economic changes. For this reason, Joseph Levenson, Benjamin Schwartz, and other intellectual historians unquestionably discovered what was both critical and distinctive in China's modernization when they focused on the clash of ideas.

CHAPTER SIX

Confronting the West

A paradox of China's external relations is that in spite of prolonged periods of alien rule, the Chinese throughout most of their history felt secure, to the point of complacent smugness. Far richer and stronger than their nearest neighbors and exposed only to "barbarians" who might conquer but who could never rule without employing Chinese ideas and personnel, the Chinese understandably developed a deep sense of cultural superiority. Others might be rude and militarily vicious, but the Chinese had no reason to doubt in spite of some unfortunate experiences, that they were culturally the center of the world, the Middle Kingdom, as they called themselves.[1] Although during the last 1,000 years of the imperial order all or part of China was ruled by alien conquerors, the Chinese persisted in feeling supremely self-assured.

The first contacts of the Chinese with the West were not threatening and indeed reinforced the Chinese view of themselves as the center of civilization. As early as Roman times the balance of trade with Europe heavily favored China. The Chinese were able to export tea, silk, chinaware, paper, and art objects, while the Romans could supply only such exotic objects as "ostriches' eggs and jugglers; dwarfs and musicians; horses that sweat blood; parrots; peacocks and apes; incense, perfumes, and aphrodisiacs; ivory, rhinoceros horn, and tortoiseshell; and even pretty girls for concu-

[1] The Chinese word for their country is *Zhongguo*, which means central or middle country. The Western word *China* may have come from a faulty transliteration of *Zhongguo*, or more likely it may have been derived from the Qin (Chin) dynasty.

bines."[2] And, above all, they sent gold and silver bullion. Indeed, the drainage of gold to China during the Roman Republic was so great that a decree was passed that Romans should no longer wear silk togas. (Thereafter they could only wear silk surreptitiously under their outer garments, which may have been the origin of silk lingerie.)

The arrival of Christianity in China created little disturbance. The Nestorian Christians who wandered into China from Europe by way of Central Asia during the Tang dynasty were hardly noticed by the Chinese. The emperor Tai Zong (T'ai Tsung) apparently welcomed some Christians to his capital at Changan as early as 635 and had parts of their sacred book translated for the enlightenment of his people. Some 600 years later William of Rubruck made his way across central Asia to the Mongol capital and sought to convert Mangu, the grandson of Genghis Khan. Mangu welcomed him warmly and gathered a great audience for him to preach to. After the performance Mangu commended the good friar for his high fervor and his manifest sincerity but told him if he were to succeed in his divine mission he would have to drop such implausible doctrines as the virgin birth and the resurrection.

By the Ming dynasty (1368–1644) more Westerners, particularly Portuguese, were reaching the Celestial Empire. In the middle of the sixteenth century the Portuguese established a colony at Macao, where they have remained to this day. The Spaniards and the Dutch soon settled on the seacost, and the Russians began to make an appearance in the north. The most remarkable achievement during this period was the patient and highly successful mission of the Jesuit Matthew Ricci, who arrived in Macao in 1582 and set about carefully analyzing Chinese society and Confucianism. After twenty years of study he came to the conclusion that Confucianism was not a religion, that one could be both a Christian and a Confucianist, and that it should be possible for Jesuits to compete in the examination system and become mandarin officials and so gain the emperor's attention. The strategy was to convert the emperor so that he in turn might decree that all Chinese should embrace Christianity. Eventually the dedicated and tolerant Ricci

[2] George B. Sansom, *The Western World and Japan: A Study of the Interaction of European and Asiatic Cultures* (New York: Knopf, 1950), p. 18.

made his way to Peking and the Imperial Court. He became a tutor to the heir to the throne, helped develop Chinese astronomy, and wrung from the emperor permission to establish a church near the palace. Before he died in 1610 he had converted two members of the Hanlin Academy — the height of the Confucian elite — and an imperial prince to his faith. The Jesuits demonstrated their commitment to the Chinese court when they served as the chief negotiators for the Chinese in arranging the Treaty of Nerchinsk with the Russians in 1689. This first modern treaty involving the Chinese was drafted in Latin, and because of Jesuit determination it was truly a treaty of equals, without the humiliating features that became a part of subsequent Chinese treaties with the European sea powers.

The Jesuits' commitment to the Ming court was also demonstrated when they helped design and direct the artillery in the last battles against the conquering Manchus. When the Manchus established the Qing dynasty, the missionaries returned and were usually received with tolerance. Once again the Jesuits found themselves in particular favor in the imperial court. By early in the eighteenth century they were joined by Dominican and Franciscan friars from the Philippines, who, true to the spirit of their mendicant orders, were horrified at the elite style of the Jesuits. The new arrivals denounced the Jesuits for treating with the rulers rather than serving the common people and for tolerating Confucianism, which, they insisted, was indeed a religion and thus incompatible with Christianity. The Emperor Kangxi (K'ang Hsi), was amused by the debate and found in favor of the Jesuits, but in the meantime Pope Clement XI had become involved in the "rites controversy," and his legates arrived in China to adjudicate the matter. On the basis of their reports the Pope found in favor of the mendicant orders and against the Jesuits. The Chinese emperor promptly decided that his right to be the sole authority over what took place in his empire had been challenged, so in 1732 he decreed that all missionaries should leave China.

This was the first sign that relations between China and the West would not always be untroubled. The missionaries gradually withdrew. Meanwhile the West was developing more effective sailing vessels, culminating in the development of clipper ships in the mid-nineteenth century. Once again trade became the main form of contact between China and the West.

Although the clipper ships could make the trip far faster than overland caravans, the balance of trade still favored the Chinese. New England traders from Salem and Boston were soon deeply involved, carrying tea, silk, chinaware, and other Chinese products abroad, while desperately trying to find enough American goods to send to China in return. Yankee ingenuity came up with the shipment to Canton of ice from Massachusetts ponds, roots of trees that New Englanders hoped would be thought of as ginseng (a favored medicine of the Chinese), and furs from Oregon and the Northwest. The balance, however, was so much in favor of China that the Americans had to make substantial shipments of bullion. Indeed, during the first years of the American republic the export of specie was so alarming that one of the first congressional investigatory committees looked into the problem and reported that "the whole amount of our current coin is probably not more than double that which has been exported in a single year to India, including China in the general term." Subsequently the United States Treasury minted a special coin to be used only in the China trade. In time the Americans obtained silver from their trade with Mexico and shipped it to China, and in this way the Mexican dollar became the principal unit of currency along the China coast.

Shortly after the turn of the century an item was found that dramatically altered the terms of trade: opium. Very early in the nineteenth century the British East India Company encouraged the production of opium, especially in Bengal and Madras in India. By the 1830s the flow of opium into China had reached major proportions, and China was now beginning to experience an outflow of bullion, for all its exports were not enough to pay for the amounts of opium that were being imported. Long before the trade began to affect the economy, the Qing government declared the opium trade illegal. This, however, did not stop the flow, because the Western merchants had without delay established working relations with Chinese officials, paying them handsome prices to allow the trade to continue.

At that time the West had no sympathy for China's problems. Western traders took the attitude that opium smoking was beneath contempt, that even the lowliest animal would not engage in it, but the principle of free trade was absolute and all the Chinese had to do was to stop being addicts. They were contemptuous of the Chinese officials they had bribed to keep the trade open, precisely because they were corruptible. The Western view at that time was similar to the attitude of those who today supply the American hard drug market and rationalize that any society that cannot effectively prohibit such awful practices should not expect others to do their policing for them.

The rise in the opium trade coincided significantly with a Western, particularly British, movement toward free trade. The case for not interfering with the opium trade rested on the theory of free trade, which logically required that the British government abolish the charters it had once given to certain companies that had legal monopolies on all trade in a specified area. The greatest of the charter companies was the British East India Company. The principle of free trade finally triumphed in 1833 when the British East India Company was abolished and free competition was allowed to reign.

Before then the "John Company," as the British East India Company was called, had regulated the China trade and assumed full responsibilities for working out the conditions of trade and the adjudication of all controversies associated with it. The Western traders generally accepted the special role of the British East India Company and allowed it to conduct all informal relations with the Chinese officials so that trade could flow. Matters of status and pride were easily handled because company officials did not have official rank and as private citizens their concern was only with keeping trade moving. Ending the special status of the company created a need for a new basis for regulating relations between the traders and the Chinese government. For the Westerners, at least, the only logical alternative was the customary legal sovereign-to-sovereign relationship common to the European state system. The fact that the West was engaged in illegal, immoral, but highly profitable trade greatly complicated the problem of arriving at any mutually acceptable basis of official intercourse with the Chinese.

As soon as the British government sought to establish diplomatic relations with China it became apparent that the Chinese and English saw the world completely differently. The English assumed that the Chinese would be anxious to behave according to European standards of international law, or that at least they would want to learn what those standards were. The Chinese on their part were convinced that Britain was merely another barbarian country that should welcome the opportunity to partake of Confucian culture.

The problem of establishing workable diplomatic relations was made nearly insurmountable by the Western notion that official acts and private commercial contacts were completely separate matters and the Chinese attitude that, as far as the Middle Kingdom was concerned, trade and tribute were the same. According to the Chinese view, all trade with China was a political act: Barbarian countries showed their reverence for the Son of Heaven, the emperor, by sending him "tribute," while he in turn showed his magnanimity by giving gifts in return. Foreign trade for the Chinese was really just a way in which others showed respect for the emperor and were rewarded with his bounty. This was why the Imperial Court believed that all dealings with foreigners should be left either to local officials, who did not have to abide by protocol, or to officials of the Board of Rites who would teach the foreign barbarians the correct rituals so they could avoid embarrassment.

By the 1830s an absolutely irreconcilable situation had developed. Each side was convinced of its unquestionable righteousness. The Chinese were prepared to insist that the opium trade be stopped, and in 1839 the emperor appointed a vigorous and incorruptible mandarin, Lin Zexu (Lin Tse-hsü), to Canton to see that this was done. The British were equally insistent that the Chinese give up their pretensions of being the center of the world and accept standard conventions of diplomacy. The British were also frustrated by Chinese insistence that trade could be conducted legally only at the port of Canton and with the few recognized Chinese merchants of the Canton guilds, or *cohongs*.

As early as 1793 the British had sent a mission under Lord Macartney to try to establish official relations with the Imperial Court. That mission, like those that followed, ran into the irreconcilable but essentially ludicrous controversy of the *kowtow*. The Chinese insisted that the ambassador would have to prostrate himself three times before the emperor, touching his forehead to the floor with each prostration. The responses of Emperor Qianlong

(Chien Lung) to Macartney's requests for a straightforward audience give the flavor of the times (and may help to explain why King George III suffered fits of madness):

> You, O King, live beyond the confines of many seas; nevertheless, impelled by your humble desire to partake of the benefits of our civilisation, you have dispatched a mission respectfully bearing your memorial. Your Envoy has crossed the seas and paid his respects at my Court on the anniversary of my birthday. To show your devotion, you have also sent offerings of your country's produce.
>
> I have perused your memorial; the earnest terms in which it is couched reveal a respectful humility on your part, which is highly praiseworthy. In consideration of the fact that your Ambassador and his deputy have come a long way with your memorial and tribute, I have shown them high favour and have allowed them to be introduced into my presence. To manifest my indulgence, I have entertained them at a banquet and made them numerous gifts. . . .
>
> Swaying the wide world, I have but one aim in view, namely, to maintain a perfect governance and to fulfil the duties of the State: strange and costly objects do not interest me. If I have commanded that the tribute offerings sent by you, O King, are to be accepted, this was solely in consideration for the spirit which prompted you to dispatch them from afar. Our dynasty's majestic virtue has penetrated into every country under Heaven, and Kings of all nations have offered their costly tribute by land and sea. As your Ambassador can see for himself, we possess all things. I set no value on objects strange or ingenious, and have no use for your country's manufactures. This then is my answer to your request to appoint a representative at my court, a request contrary to our dynastic usage, which would only result in inconvenience to yourself. I have expounded my wishes in detail and have commanded your tribute Envoys to leave in peace on their homeward journey. It behooves you, O King, to respect my sentiments and to display even greater devotion and loyalty in future, so that, by perpetual submission to our Throne, you may secure peace and prosperity for your country hereafter.[3]

[3] Harley Farnsworth MacNair, *The Real Conflict between China and Japan: An Analysis of Opposing Ideologies* (Chicago: The University of Chicago Press, 1938), pp. 26–27. Copyright 1938 by The University of Chicago. Reprinted by permission.

Lord Macartney recognized the failure of his mission, but before he left Peking he received another memorial, which said in part:

> You, O King, from afar have yearned after the blessings of our civilisation, and in your eagerness to come into touch with our converting influence have sent an Embassy across the sea bearing a memorial. I have already taken note of your respectful spirit of submission, have treated your mission with extreme favour and loaded it with gifts, besides issuing a mandate to you, O King, and honouring you with the bestowal of valuable presents. Thus has my indulgence been manifested. . . . But your Ambassador has now put forward new requests which completely fail to recognize the Throne's principle to "treat strangers from afar with indulgence," and to exercise a pacifying control over barbarian tribes, the world over. Moreover, our dynasty, swaying the myriad races of the globe, extends the same benevolence towards all. Your England is not the only nation trading at Canton. If other nations, following your bad example, wrongfully importune my ear with further impossible requests, how will it be possible for me to treat them with easy indulgence? Nevertheless, I do not forget the lonely remoteness of your island, cut off from the world by intervening wastes of sea, nor do I overlook your excusable ignorance of the usages of Our Celestial Empire. I have consequently commanded my Ministers to enlighten your Ambassador on the subject and have ordered the departure of the mission. . . . My capital is the hub and centre about which all quarters of the globe revolve. Its ordinances are most august and its laws are strict in the extreme. The subjects of our dependencies have never been allowed to open places of business in Peking.[4]

The British tried again in 1816 by sending Lord Jeffrey Amherst to Peking. The issue of the *kowtow* again appeared, and the new Jia Qing (Chia Ch'ing) emperor delivered an equally haughty mandate,

> My dynasty attaches no value to products from abroad; your nation's cunningly wrought and strange wares do not appeal to me in the least, nor do they interest me.
>
> For the future, O King, if you will keep your subjects in order and strengthen your national defences, I shall hold you in high esteem, notwithstanding your remoteness.[5]

[4] Ibid., pp. 28–30. Reprinted by permission.
[5] Ibid., pp. 43–44. Reprinted by permission.

Once issues of honor, prestige, and relative political importance were compounded with the moral and legal issues of the opium trade, the accommodations that had brought East and West together in Canton began to wear thin. These earlier adjustments had been easier when the British East India Company dominated commerce and assumed the role of informal representative of the traders. Given the Chinese philosophy of collective responsibility, relations were most tranquil when there was a representative who could be held accountable for the behavior of all traders. As more countries entered the trade and the East India Company lost its monopoly, the problem of regulation increased.

The differences between the Western view of individual accountability and the Chinese view of group responsibility are well illustrated by the Terranova case. In 1821 the *Emily*, out of Baltimore, was at anchor off Canton and surrounded by sampans on which hawkers were selling vegetables and trinkets. Someone threw some garbage overboard and somehow a boat woman toppled into the water and drowned. The Chinese authorities insisted that someone, anyone, be handed over for punishment so that all could see that justice was being upheld. The American captain insisted that the drowning must have been an accident and that in any case the authorities would have to establish proof of criminal guilt before justice could be done. The Chinese threatened to stop the *Emily* and all other American vessels from trading. They arrested the Chinese merchants who were the trading partners of the Americans and who owed them large sums of money. The American captain then felt he had to yield to necessity, and so he handed over to the Chinese an illiterate Italian seaman who a few days later was executed by strangulation.

During the early nineteenth century Chinese policy was mostly directed toward controlling foreigners in the classic imperial way — by trying to isolate and herd together members of each alien group. The "barbarians" were then ordered to govern themselves according to their own rules in their own circles but to observe Chinese usages in all relations with Chinese. This tradition was extremely important, for it set the pattern for the emerging treaty port system.

In Canton the foreign traders (also called "factors") were restricted to their "factories," which were long narrow buildings of two or three stories and served as both warehouses and living quarters for the merchants. The compounds were owned by the Chinese businessmen with whom the factory traded. The Westerners were constantly frustrated by Chinese refusal to allow commerce with anybody, but the Chinese authorities felt that they could only maintain control over the foreigners by holding the Chinese merchants accountable for the foreigners' behavior. The frustration of the traders was intensified because they were confined to their factories and could not move about within the city, to say nothing of visiting the countryside. The Chinese believed peace would be best maintained if the "barbarians" were kept in their ghettos.

Lin Zexu, a determined and honest official, was working to abolish the opium trade. At the same time the British were seeking once more to force the Chinese to establish diplomatic relations with England. They were particularly annoyed that the representative of their king was being treated as a lowly figure by mere provincial authorities in Canton instead of being received by the central authorities in Peking. Tension quickly mounted when Lin set about confiscating all the opium in Canton, and events soon led to the Opium War, which, in a desultory fashion and with almost no casualties, lasted from November 1839 to August 1842. (When the British frigate *Amethyst*, withdrawing down the Yangtze River in 1949, ran a gauntlet of Communist guns, it sustained more casualties than the British suffered in the Opium War.)

Peking's ability to deal with the British was profoundly hampered by almost complete ignorance of Europeans. The situation was not helped by the flow of memorials from high officials to the emperor. (Often they were as irrelevant as some of the proposals that officials in Washington get from American university professors.) One official, for example, proposed to the Son of Heaven that in order to defeat the British the emperor should assemble a group of men who could stay under water for two or three hours, and send them to pull the plugs out of the bottoms of the British boats. Another official observed that because the British were like locusts large locust traps should be set on the beaches to snare them if they came ashore. Still another mandarin remarked that since the British "barbarians" were peculiarly stiff-legged, all that had to be done was to topple them over and they would not be able to get up again.

The war produced the Treaty of Nanjing, the first of the "unequal treaties" that Chinese nationalists over the next hundred years saw as a principal source of China's humiliation. According to the terms of the treaty, the island of Hong Kong was ceded to England, and the five cities of Canton, Xiamen, Fuzhou, Ningbo, and Shanghai became treaty ports in which British traders resided and conducted business in "concessions" where their own authorities would govern them. The *cohongs* were abolished and the British received permission to trade with any Chinese merchant. British and Chinese officials would deal with each other on a footing of equality. A schedule of tariffs was established, and China agreed to pay an indemnity of 21 million *taels* to cover the cost of the opium that Lin Zexu had destroyed, the debts of the *cohong* merchants, and the cost of the war to Britain.

On the heels of the British successes, other Western powers pressed China for comparable treaties. Caleb Cushing, dispatched by President Tyler to negotiate an American arrangement, obtained the Treaty of Wanghai in July 1844. It specifically formulated the rights of extraterritoriality (Americans would be governed by American laws in China) and established the principle of the most-favored nation, which meant in practice that the United States would receive whatever benefits were given to the European powers, especially the British. In the same year the French obtained a comparable treaty that also contained clauses protecting missionaries. The Belgians signed a treaty in 1845, Sweden and Norway in 1847, and Russia in 1851.

The treaty system that followed from the initial unequal treaties was only gradually and painfully established. The principle of diplomatic representation and of equality in official relations was not easily accepted by the Chinese, who persisted in believing that the "barbarians" were still best handled by the Ministry of Rites, which would teach them civility and proper awe for the Emperor's Way. In 1856 an incident involving a small Hong Kong registered craft, the lorcha *Arrow*, triggered off a second war. British and French troops occupied Tianjin and approached Peking, capturing the Summer Palace. The subsequent Treaty of Tianjin created ten more treaty ports, established the right of foreigners to have embassies in Peking, opened the interior to travel, provided additional protection for missionaries, arranged new tariffs, and ceded to Britain Kowloon, the tip of the mainland across from Hong Kong island.

By force of arms the Western powers also compelled the Chinese to establish a foreign office and send diplomatic missions abroad. One of the early missions was headed by Anson Burlingame, who had just retired as American minister to Peking but enthusiastically took up the Chinese cause. Washington and London negotiated treaties that provided for the territorial integrity of China and for unrestricted immigration of Chinese laborers into the United States.

In 1861, under constant prodding from the Western ambassadors, the Chinese established the *Tsungli Yamen*, or foreign office, for the management of foreign affairs. Since the new office lacked traditional status and had to deal with unpleasant matters, it was initially staffed by officers who seemed to the foreigners to be peculiarly incompetent. There was suspicion that the Chinese had designed a clever stratagem for dealing with foreign officials — forcing them to conduct their business with the most dim-witted officials in all the empire. Many Western officials were nearly driven out of their minds. The tactics ranged from a persistent tendency of officials to "forget" all that had been agreed to at previous meetings, to the practice of confusing and mixing up the policy demands and interests of the various foreign powers. The diplomatic corps took upon itself the task of trying to educate the Chinese in Western diplomacy, a reversal of the earlier efforts of the Ministry of Rites. The effort was marked by the frustrating ways in which the Chinese repeatedly failed to understand what was involved in "playing the game." For example, the diplomatic corps was completely undone when the emperor ordered some Chinese diplomats executed because a treaty they had negotiated with Russia displeased him: How could one press for advantage in negotiating with the Chinese if they refused to recognize the principle of diplomatic immunity — not just for foreign diplomats but for their own?

CULTURAL CONFLICTS: MISUNDERSTANDINGS AND FRUSTRATION

Detailed analysis of the early nineteenth-century meeting of East and West along the China coast reveals a host of misunderstandings stemming from cultural differences. Each side proceeded to treat the other according to its own perceptions of what was called for, and consequently the behavior of each often provoked the other to even more unintelligible acts.

The Chinese frustrations were compounded by the discovery in case after case that traditional techniques that had once worked masterfully in controlling the "barbarians" of central Asia backfired when applied to the Western "barbarians." For example, the cardinal aim of Chinese foreign relations had always been to play off one barbarian against another. In the past the Chinese had been extremely successful in giving and denying favors to nomad groups to pacify them or encourage them to fight another group. The attempt to use the distant barbarians to control the nearer ones completely collapsed when the Western countries uniformly demanded the most-favored-nation principle in all their treaties. All at once the Chinese discovered that by giving a favor to one country in the hope of winning its goodwill or pacifying it, they were in fact giving the same favor to all the treaty powers.

Similarly, when applied to Westerners, the traditional Chinese practice of insisting that alien communities rule themselves according to their own customs — which provided the original rationale for the treaty port system — produced not isolated cells of "foreign bodies" but virulent centers that spread "cultural contagion" throughout the Chinese community. Instead of the treaty ports becoming isolated settlements within which the foreigner was contained, they became the dynamic centers of much of China's economic life and a source of humiliation to all Chinese leaders.

By the last decade of the nineteenth century it appeared that China, like Africa, might be carved up by imperial powers. Parts of the country became spheres of influence of different powers. Russia dominated Manchuria, especially after 1896, when it obtained the rights to build the Chinese Eastern Railroad across the province;

in 1898 Russia obtained a twenty-five-year lease for a base in Dalien and Port Arthur. Great Britain sought to counter the Russian advance in Manchuria by demanding a lease to Weihaiwei, a seaport in Shandong across the Yellow Sea from the tip of the Liaodong peninsula of Manchuria, "for as long a period as Port Arthur shall remain in the possession of Russia." The principal British sphere of influence, however, was Shanghai and the Yangtze River valley. Germany, after the murder of two German Catholic missionaries in 1898, obtained a ninety-nine-year lease on the tip of Shandong. In the same year France got a ninety-nine-year lease on the Bay of Guanzhou in southwest Guangdong, just above the French colony and protectorates in Indochina.

The constant foreign demands for concessions involved more than just treaty port arrangements. It has been estimated that between 1842 and 1911 China on 110 occasions had to make indemnity payments to foreign governments. The problem of providing cash for such payments was severe; between 1895 and 1900 China had to pay Japan 200 million *taels* of silver, although the government's receipts totaled only about 90 million *taels* in 1900. The problem of government revenues resulted in odd arrangements whereby the Chinese Maritime Customs Service was organized and staffed by foreigners. China lost control of its own tariffs, but the service did come to provide the government with one of its most reliable sources of income.

In 1900 the Boxer Rebellion, an atavistic, antiforeign movement that had the tacit support of the Manchu court, provided an occasion for much more severe demands by the European powers, and for a brief period it appeared likely that China would at last be partitioned. Britain, however, was in no mood to assume additional imperial responsibilities because the demands of India were heavy and the Boer War was just commencing in South Africa. The British did not wish to see China divided among other powers, and they were confident of their ability to compete for trade and influence on equal terms.

Immediately before the Boxer uprising, Britain had cooperated in supporting the American declaration of the Open Door policy, under which all countries would recognize the principle that no sphere of influence could interfere with the vested interests of any other state, thus eliminating the commercial advantage in claiming such a sphere. In 1899 John Hay, the American secretary of state, had sent notes to all interested countries proposing the "open door," and because no country was prepared to answer publicly in the negative, hypocrisy triumphed and compelled all to act more honorably than they might otherwise have done, saving China from almost certain dismemberment.

China's problems were not limited to the unruly demands of Westerners. Just as threatening to the Confucian order was the behavior of China's immediate neighbors, Japan, Korea, Vietnam, Burma, and even Thailand. At one time they had recognized the Middle Kingdom by extending tribute but, sensing China's weakness, they had become as intimidating as the Westerners. China had been the suzerain of its neighbors; China was considered the "elder brother" and the vassal country was the "younger brother" who had to show proper Confucian deference to the elder. The tribute system called for periodic missions, usually every three years, to the Peking court. Members of these missions would perform the proper rituals to show their submissiveness to the Celestial Empire and present to the emperor their gifts. The effect of this practice was to provide the basis for significant foreign trade while not giving power or status to private merchants whom Confucian officials distrusted. It made the Chinese feel superior to all their neighbors and allowed these neighbors to marvel at how vulnerable to flattery the Chinese were.

In theory, in return for tribute the emperor would protect the vassal country and take care of its foreign affairs, while allowing it freedom to manage its internal affairs. In the Chinese mind the relationship was precisely that of the elder and younger brother, but this relationship was not acknowledged in Western international law and could not be easily explained in non-Confucian terms.

According to the Western mind China either must be held accountable for all the actions of those over whom it claimed suzerainty or forfeit the right to such claims. The French soon concluded that the Chinese were not able to be responsible for what the Vietnamese did. Similarly the Russians challenged Chinese rights in central Asia, in the area of Ili, and proved to their own satisfaction that the Chinese claims of suzerainty were pretentious.

Most shocking was the behavior of the Japanese, who had

been influenced by the Confucian ethic but, ever since their exposure to the West, had developed an ability to demonstrate the faults of the Chinese according to both the Confucian and the Western world view. They vigorously challenged China's claim of suzerainty over Korea and sought to "open" the Hermit Kingdom to contacts with other countries. China was compelled to back up its claims of suzerainty by trying to manage Korea's relations with Japan, but the outcome was a disastrous war in 1894 and 1895, which resulted in a humiliating defeat for China, and ended in the Treaty of Shimonoseki by which China not only had to give up claims of suzerainty over Korea but was also forced to cede to Japan Formosa, the Pescadores islands, and the Liaodong peninsula in Manchuria.

The fact that Japan felt no awe of the Celestial Kingdom and could handily defeat the Chinese was possibly the most demoralizing blow of all to China. It opened the way for a flood of Chinese students who were eager to learn more about how Japan had adopted modern technology. By the end of the nineteenth century no country in Asia still thought of China as the Middle Kingdom, deserving of awe and capable of bounteous protection. Furthermore, increasing numbers of Chinese were questioning traditional Confucian values and were eager to replace them with assertions of Chinese nationalism.

With the twentieth century came a significant drop in the importance of the China trade with all Western powers. The industrialization of Europe and America made the China market less attractive, for more lucrative possibilities were to be found nearer home. By World War I the dominant impulse of Western contact with China had become the missionary endeavor, and the underlying spirit of the relationship became less one of trying to outwit the Chinese and more one of seeking to help them.

Several generations of Americans were brought up with the belief that China needed the help of missionaries, but few had any idea of the reality of that endeavor. Whereas in the middle of the nineteenth century the focus of Western activities in China was the treaty port and the "factories" of the traders, by the early twentieth century it was the mission compound with its Westernized schools and hospitals.

Scattered throughout China and often far removed from the

treaty ports of the businessmen were the compounds of American and European missions. Most contained Western-style houses made of brick, with Chinese gray-tiled roofs. The dominant buildings were the school complexes — primary, elementary, and high school, with boarding facilities — perhaps a hospital (often of major proportions), and always a church. The relationship of Chinese and foreigners in these compounds was exceedingly complex, possibly as complex as any intercultural situation and certainly one that has never been effectively studied. Within the compounds were Chinese who desperately sought to identify with all that was alien to China, from religious belief to secular knowledge; others who hoped to gain something of value while not yielding their identity; and many who simply sought material benefits from contacts with the foreigners.

Whether it came from the early trader and the activities in the treaty ports or from the missionaries and their schools, colleges, and hospitals, the incessant message for the Chinese was that others had found a more exciting and significant way of life and that the old Chinese virtues were inferior. Young Chinese who attended the new schools dreamed of a new China that would be rich and powerful, fully capable of competing with the West on Western, not Chinese, terms.

The Western impact brought deep humiliation and physical suffering to the Chinese people. More than this, however, it made the Chinese dissatisfied with their traditional ways and anxious to prove themselves in modern terms. The stage was set for a profound cultural and political revolution.

CHAPTER SEVEN

Rebellion, Revolution, and Warlordism

The goal of Confucian China was harmony and tranquility; the theme of modern China has been revolution and war, both civil and international. The politics of traditional China was based on matters of ethics, the pretensions of philosophers, and the accommodating spirit of scholar-officials. Nevertheless, violence occurred, torture was used, and rebels were harshly dealt with. Indeed, every dynasty arose out of successful military operations, and they all relied on huge armies, although the source of legitimacy in ancient China was not military power.

In modern China, once the mystique of Confucianism had dissolved, the search for a new basis of legitimacy began. Instead of harmony, sincerity, and virtue, the modern spirit called for more activist values. Rebellion against what lingered of the old authority blended with aggressive assertions that China had lost its way by being too passive for too long.

In old China people revered their elders, and believed that the best things came late in life; in the twentieth century the mood was one of youthful exuberance and naïve innocence. Behind the Chinese spirit of rebellion and revolution was a quest for purity and a higher morality, for the decadent old order was judged weak and contemptible.

In the last years of the Qing dynasty the traditions of the ageless imperial system came under siege as the West, seeking its own objectives in China, began to thrust new visions into a once closed society. Inexorable trends that had been present for a long time were picking up force and eroding the Confucian order, and historic domestic processes of rebellion and disintegration were gathering strength.

The Confucian system was no match for this dual challenge. The fact that the old order was toppled by two separate and divergent forces profoundly shaped subsequent Chinese history. The force of rebellion was almost entirely peasant based and reflected the demands and the lifestyles of the countryside. The rebellions, such as the White Lotus Society (1796–1804), the Taiping (1851–1874), the Nien (1853–1868), and the Boxer (1900), at times took on ideological or pseudo-religious trappings, but they were all partly supported by banditry, which had always been practiced by Chinese peasants when they found life otherwise insupportable.

The force of revolution in modern China, in contrast to rebellion, was associated almost entirely with the urban culture, and particularly with the educated classes who were the most responsive to foreign ideas and the most sensitive to the need for fundamental changes in society. The goals of rebellion were the reduction of suppression, fewer taxes, and more freedom to live according to tradition; the goals of revolution were the elimination of China's humiliations and the achievement of greater national power and wealth. Chinese rebellions did not seek to make basic changes, but they did have the ideal of greater freedom and autonomy for all individuals. Revolutions, on the other hand, idealized the need for greater discipline, self-sacrifice, and the denial of individualistic desires.

The spread of rebellions during the declining years of the Qing dynasty stimulated an increase in the imperial military forces and transformed civilian authorities into the mobilizers, and even commanders, of armies. The necessity to put down rebellions brought about a structural change in Chinese government, elevating the military over traditional civilian authorities. It is probably accurate to say that since the time of the Taiping Rebellion, armies and those who command them have been the decisive factors in Chinese politics.

Paradoxically, then, the forces of rebellion, which were largely of the rural folk, tended to encourage the growth of autocratic army rule in China. Although international wars and domestic conflicts also contributed to the growing influence of the military in Chinese society, a basic reason for the persistent escalation of the importance of the Chinese military has, to this day, been the presumed need to react against the spirit of rebellion.

The revolutionary forces in modern China, responding to the Western impact, were able to undermine the intellectual foundations of the old regime but did not provoke as physical a counterreaction as did the rebellions. Instead, the thrust of revolution remained the frustrated and ineffectual search for a new order. Eventually, however, the spirit of revolution, first with the Nationalists and then with the Communists, allied itself with military power. To the extent that the revolutionary quest became allied to military power, as it did during the first republican years and then with the Nationalists in the late 1920s and early 1930s, it became a force opposed to the spirit of rebellion in China. Only during brief periods have the thrusts of revolution, rebellion, and military power merged into a common force, at which times modern China seemed to be finding an appropriate new identity.

Possibly an oversimplification but perhaps a useful approximation is the notion that modern Chinese history has been marked by a dynamic tension among rural rebellion, urban-intellectual revolution, and pragmatic military power. Over the years there has rarely been a stabilization among these forces. When pressed to the extreme the spirit of rebellion has usually stimulated atavism and traditional prejudices completely inconsistent with the modernistic ideals of revolution. The forces of revolution in their purest form have not only been ambivalent toward the older tradition of rebellion but have distrusted military authority as well. The Nationalist revolutionaries never took an interest in the peasants, and Mao Zedong, after using the peasants to gain power, sought his revolutionary goals by turning his back on their desires for autonomy. Whenever those in command of armies have been supreme they have tended to distrust the proponents of both rebellion and revolution.

Chinese nationalism has erratically fluctuated from glorification of the vitality of the ordinary peasantry, to reverence for the idealism of the intellectual revolutionaries, to blind worship of martial practices. With this overview of Chinese modernization in mind, we can more closely examine each of these forces.

THE FORCES OF REBELLION

Repeatedly in Chinese history, and most frequently near the end of a dynasty, peasants and dissatisfied members of the gentry have banded together and asserted their independence from imperial control. When the government could no longer collect taxes in a local area, a secret society, with its own quasi-religious ideology, would assert itself as an alternative goverment. The consequence was rebellion, which eventually brought to the scene government armies and pacification programs that were generally a blend of coercion and seductive appeals to rebel elements.

The White Lotus Rebellion, which lasted from 1796 to 1804, was typical of such movements. Based on a blend of Buddhism and an appeal to the most economically depressed peasants for a life of action, the movement began in the mountainous areas of the northwest. The hill peoples raided the homes and lands of the richer plains people and banded together to resist the demands of the imperial tax collectors. The lawlessness that the movement produced encouraged more and more people to seek the security of membership in the secret society that had initiated the disturbances. Efforts of the government to suppress the rebellion only increased peasant insecurity and support for the White Lotus.

The process by which the rebellion was eventually eliminated by the government was a classic example of brutal repression. Imperial forces called into Sichuan, Shaanxi, and Shanxi to suppress the rebels had to live off the land. Thus the peasants, who wanted only to live in peace, had to provide food for both the government armies and the rebels. In time the government broke the White Lotus Society by confining the villagers within walled areas and separating them from all contacts with the rebels. In the late 1930s there were still remnants of some of these walled enclosures, built of adobe or loess and still maintained by villages as a refuge for peasants and their possessions when bandit bands approached their defenseless settlements.

The far more extensive and violent Taiping Rebellion was inspired partly by foreign ideas, particularly Christian ones. Some scholars argue that it was really the beginning of the Chinese revolution, because the Taipings accused the Manchu rulers of being both foreign and Confucian and sought to satisfy the diffuse rebellious demands of the economically distressed peasants. The leader was a strange and remarkable man, Hong Xiuquan (Hung Hsiu-ch'üan), who originally studied to become a Confucian scholar-official. Three times, however, he failed to pass the provincial examinations. On the last occasion he fell ill, became delirious, heard voices telling him to save mankind, and saw visions of a figure who he later became convinced was Jesus Christ. At about this time Hong picked up a Protestant religious tract, and subsequently he came to know and briefly live in the home of an American fundamentalist missionary, Reverend Issachar J. Roberts, who filled his mind with Christian doctrine and practices. Hong for the moment was following the custom of the frustrated examination candidate, teaching school, but he became a local nuisance when his new Christian doctrines inspired him to rove about smashing idols in the temples. He was finally run out of town and took to the hills to organize his *Taiping Tianguo* (*T'ai-p'ing T'ien-kuo*), or Heavenly Kingdom of Great Peace. Hong had earlier baptized himself and was convinced that in one of his fits he had ascended to heaven, met with God and Jesus, and learned that he was Christ's younger brother, assigned to bring Christian morality to the world.

In very short order, Hong Xiuquan surrounded himself with a band of followers who began in the usual manner of secret society rebels but were soon convinced that they were divinely appointed, many of them identifying themselves with the various Apostles. Hong continued to have visions, each of which produced doctrines for the movement, and in time his lieutenants found that they too were having visions that they felt should also contribute to the ideology. The issue of what was divine inspiration and what was spurious opportunism eventually split the leadership.

Hong created an enthusiastic and remarkably puritanical movement. All property was to be held in common, no one was to be selfish, material corruption was a great sin, the sexes were to be equal, and people were supposed to devote all their attention to simple homilies. All in all it was remarkably similar to the utilitarianism and antisexual puritanism of Mao Zedong. Men and women were to treat each other as brothers and sisters, and the women were placed in separate battalions and even engaged in combat.

Through some strange reasoning, which is still not clear, Hong and his most saintly associates were able to argue that although everyone else should abstain, they were entitled to harems.

This unlikely movement caught the imagination of hundreds of thousands of peasants and swept up from south China to take over the Yangtze valley. One army column reached the outskirts of Shanghai and another nearly reached Tianjin. Taipings ravaged the countryside, isolating and starving out cities, so disrupting life that disease and pestilence took their toll. The conventional estimate is that the Taiping Rebellion took 20 million lives, but some careful judgments place the figure closer to 40 million.

This rebellion, with its Western ideas, was finally beaten back by a combination of traditional methods and foreign assistance. Western elements initially looked with some sympathy upon the Taipings and their enthusiasm for spreading their version of Christianity mixed with ethics of honesty and righteousness, but in time they became increasingly doubtful. Also, as the Manchu court committed itself to more and more treaties with the Western powers, the latter had an increasing interest in the preservation of the Qing dynasty. An extraordinary adventurer from Salem, Massachusetts, Frederick T. Ward, organized an army to fight the Taipings when they began to threaten Shanghai. He died during the campaign but his troops, called the Ever Victorious Army, continued under the command of a series of Americans and Europeans until the Englishman Charles George Gordon took over and led them to their final victories. This was the famous "Chinese" Gordon, who later met his end in the siege of Khartoum.

More significant than Western actions in suppressing the Taipings were the huge armies organized by some of the most outstanding Chinese officials of the time. Confronted with rebellion, civilians Zeng Guofan (Tsêng Kuo-fan) and his associate Li Hongzhang (Li Hung-chang), who later became China's ablest statesman, mobilized provincial forces and led them against the Taipings. Raising an army in such a way called for a tightening of taxation and the cooperation of the imperial court in diverting resources from the rest of the empire to the authorities in central China. After victory, however, this method of fighting rebellion proved to be disastrous, for it contained no answer to the problem of how to demobilize armies — a dilemma that has continually plagued modern China. To simply disband the forces would be to instantaneously create widespread banditry.

The armies raised by Zeng Guofan, Zuo Zongtang (Tso Tsung-t'ang), and Li Hongzhang were later used to put down the Nien Rebellion and the Muslim rebellions of the 1870s and early 1880s. They became the nucleus for what were to be "model armies" after China's defeat by Japan in 1895. Later, these modernized forces were made into the Beiyang army, which became the core of the warlord armies that dominated China during the Republican period. Later still the Nationalists had to raise an army to crush the warlords, and eventually the Communists depended on their own armies to rise to power. Thus, from the time of the suppression of the Taipings, Chinese politics has been shaped by military power and the fact that large numbers of men have consistently been under arms.

In suppressing the Taipings the practice of raising armies on a personal rather than national basis complicated the role of the military in the modernization of China. In Zeng Guofan's army each unit took the name of its commanding officer, increasing the tendency of troops to see themselves as private forces. The subsequent effort to modernize the imperial armies did not eliminate the importance of personal ties; it only raised the personal armies to a higher level and set the stage for warlord politics.

Although the ideology of the Taipings was touched to a degree by foreign influences, the rebellion was basically an indigenous movement that expressed popular discontent and identified the Manchu government as foreign. In contrast, the Boxer Rebellion was an atavistic movement, with no taint of foreign concepts, that was manipulated by the government and directed against foreigners and, more importantly, against Chinese who had been influenced or converted by them.

The Boxer movement reflected in part the conservative reactions of some officials who opposed the efforts at moderate reforms in 1898. It exploited famine conditions and popular local reactions to the disruptions that accompanied the introduction of railroads. There were enough problems in China at the time to tap xenophobic sentiments and stir up passions against foreigners. The Boxers emerged out of the local militia in Shandong and Shanxi. (These poorly armed forces practiced Chinese "boxing," a form of karate; hence their name.) Initially, the movement enjoyed official sanction, but in time its violent anti-Christian attacks went beyond government control. The high point of the rebellion was the siege of the foreign legations in Peking, which eventually had to be relieved by an international contingent of troops consisting mainly of British, American, Japanese, and Russian soldiers, with representations from the German, French, Italian, and Austrian armies.

To the extent that foreign military units remained stationed in Peking from the time of the expedition until World War II, it can be said that the Boxer Rebellion followed the Chinese pattern in which rebellions evoked rural populist or atavistic sentiments but resulted in an increased role of military force in Chinese politics.

THE THEME OF REVOLUTION

Revolution began with attempts to overthrow the Manchu dynasty and has persisted in Chinese politics to this day. The most active forces opposing the imperial system were the "overseas" Chinese and returned students who had learned of political alternatives elsewhere and deeply felt the national humiliation that came from the weaknesses of the Manchus.

The most important figure in this early revolutionary tradition was Sun Yat-sen, who was born near Canton, educated first at a British mission school in Hawaii, then trained as a doctor in British Hong Kong, and later practiced medicine in Portuguese Macao. Sun's limited experiences in China were generally unhappy. He returned from Hawaii a vigorous Christian and made himself unpopular by smashing idols in his ancestral village. Later he wrote memoranda to Li Hongzhang about reforming the country and became a bore to all who were trying to make Confucianism viable in the modern era. Sun Yat-sen became increasingly revolutionary and secretive, founded the *T'ung-meng-hui* (United League), an organization of Chinese students studying abroad, especially in Japan, and anti-Manchu intellectuals in China.

In the fall of 1911, while Sun was abroad trying to raise funds and sympathy for the revolutionary cause, and when the clash of interests between central and provincial authorities over the control of railroads was reaching crisis proportions, a bomb accidentally went off in the house of some *T'ung-meng-hui* members and attracted the attention of the police, who searched the premises and found a list of the full membership.

The crisis called for immediate action. The officers in the imperial army who had been secretly in sympathy with Sun's cause, now had to act in support of the revolution and they forced their superior, Li Yuanhong (Li Yüan-hung), to declare himself to be with the revolutionaries. The imperial court at Peking responded by calling upon Yuan Shikai (Yüan Shih-k'ai), the general who had informed the Empress Dowager of the ambitions of the reformers in 1898 and who was at the moment out of favor. Yuan's response was to ask coldheartedly what each side was prepared to offer him, and when the revolutionaries offered to make him president of their new republican regime, he abandoned the Manchus, thereby undermining the dynasty.

Sun Yat-sen welcomed these developments, accepted Yuan as the new president, and turned his attention to the economic development of China, a subject about which he was both passionate and ignorant. Yuan quickly disposed of the Manchus and professed a belief in republicanism, but he also proceeded to consolidate his own power and began to visualize himself as the founder of a new dynasty. Before this could come about he died in 1916, leaving military commanders with supreme power in all the provinces.

The next two major political groups that sought to reunite China, the Nationalists and the Communists, spoke of "completing the revolution." In contrast to the indigenous quality of the rebellions, the concepts of revolution were cosmopolitan, elitist, and above all concerned with giving China strength and unity rather than individual freedom.

The theme of modern Chinese politics has been revolution, but revolution directed by those in command of state power. On their assumption of power, both the Nationalists and the Communists proclaimed that the revolution should overthrow existing authorities and replace them with a more effective system. The aim of revolution in modern China is not to topple authority but to establish power.

In making power a central feature of the revolutionary mystique, the Chinese in the Republican era pursued their revolutionary quests with a heavy reliance on military force. The tendency to use military means to seek revolutionary ends became clear when, after the death of Yuan Shikai, warlords dominated Chinese politics.

WARLORDISM AND THE PHANTOM REPUBLIC

From 1916 to 1927 China was fragmented and ruled by warlords with separate provincial bases. For the Chinese this was a period of unrelieved humiliation because all the warlords seemed to be shortsighted, selfish, and unconcerned about the national interest. The experience of the period convinced the intellectuals that China's salvation lay not in competing power centers but rather in the establishment of a monolithic, single-party, hierarchy of power.

A case can be made that competition among the warlords opened China to greater ideological and intellectual diversity than it had ever known. It also exposed the country to the challenges of a more pluralistic and competitive form of politics. Although the warlords misappropriated resources and failed to provide a sense of national cohesion, the period was intellectually exciting, and the currents of change set in motion by the May Fourth Movement continued to be strong in the universities and among the intellectuals in the larger cities and the foreign concessions. Numerous foreign intellectuals, including John Dewey and Bertrand Russell, made prolonged visits. Dr. Hu Shih pressed on with the drive to give spoken Chinese respectability and to break the grip of classical Chinese as the only language of literature. This was also a period of popular reforms that included the efforts of "Jimmy" Yen to counter adult illiteracy and the programs of some of the warlords themselves to establish "model" provinces and towns. Change seemed to be sweeping the country, and China won much sympathy in the West, for it seemed to be a society pulling itself up by its own bootstraps. Although the figure of speech at the time was of China's "awakening" (not "developing"), the country was in a sense the first of the newly emerging nations that have been of such interest in world politics since the end of World War II. Socially and intellectually China seemed to be on the move.

Politically, however, the Chinese were deeply dissatisfied with their version of "competitive politics." Seeing power in the hands of the warlords convinced the intellectuals that national salvation lay in some form of one-party or one-man rule. Diversity seemed to offer only divisiveness and the end of the utopian dream of a democratic republic.

After the death of Yuan Shikai the government in Peking steadily lost its ability to rule; the office of the presidency was filled by a succession of weak military men without effective control of the resources of even a single province. The Parliament, established immediately after the 1911 Revolution and composed of civilian notables and supporters of the *T'ung-meng-hui*, lacked authority and did not even effectively participate in the selection of cabinets. After the fall of the imperial system the civilian bureaucracy throughout the country lost its dominant power because without the legitimizing force of the Confucian order it was of little utility to the new rulers.

The military commanders in the provinces, however, had responsibility for their armies, and their troops had to be supplied, paid, and generally maintained. It might be all right for civilian governors not to pay their bureaucrats, but when soldiers are not paid from the central treasury, they have, with their weapons, the means of getting what they want. The provincial military commanders (*duchuns*) first sought merely to extract from their territory what they needed to keep their armies intact. Soon they were the actual rulers of those territories, for they had the only organizations capable of mobilizing resources and providing order. The problem of maintaining their organizations led them in time to seek alliances with other warlords and to expand their power bases, all in the search for greater security. The politics of warlordism became a complicated balance of power among leaders whose influence depended on their ability to support their armies.

Control of Peking was a prize because it offered the prospect of obtaining foreign loans and the revenues of the customs services. Alliances were formed in order to gain such control, and on some occasions individual warlords sought either by coup or by conquest to take the capital.

The balance of power among the warlords and their struggles to control the formal institutions of government produced two fairly well recognized factions. The first was the Anfu group led by

Duan Qirui (Tuan Ch'i-jui) and supported by such warlords as Xu Shuzeng (Hsu Shu-tseng), his immediate lieutenant; Ni Sichun of Anhui; Yang Shande of Zhejiang, Li Hoji of Fujian; and Lu Yunxiang, the commander of the Shanghai Special Area. The Anfu group focused on controlling Parliament and the office of the presidency, and thus sought to become champions of republican legitimacy. It had, however, a questionable reputation, particularly among the intellectuals, who suspected it of being subservient to Japanese interests. It was badly discredited at the outset of the May Fourth Movement because it had been in charge of the Peking government at the time of the Shandong decision at the Paris Peace Conference and thus became the object of attack by the newly aroused student nationalists.

The Zhili faction was the second clustering of warlords. It was first under the leadership of Feng Guozhang and then of Cai Kun, a senior commander in the Beiyang army. Its most powerful warlord was Wu Peifu of Honan.

A third major factor in the warlord system was Zhang Zuolin, of Manchuria, who had the largest and most secure power base of all. Other principal warlords included Feng Yuxiang, the so-called Christian general, who was at times loosely associated with the Zhili faction but generally operated quite independently (executing two coups d'etat and developing a private source of Soviet assistance), and Yen Xishan, the "model governor" of Shanxi, who avoided alliances and concentrated on maintaining his autonomy.

In the early 1920s there were two major but inconclusive military clashes between the Zhili faction and Zhang Zuolin's Manchurian forces. The balance of power among the warlords prevented anyone from gaining complete superiority, and there was a state of relative equilibrium. The balance operated in such a fashion that even when all the warlords were threatened in 1927 by the Northern Expedition of the Kuomintang they could not band together in a common effort.

Some of the warlords were avaricious and shortsighted, with little sense of public responsibility, but others were exceptional leaders. Wu Peifu, who dominated central China, had great organizing ability and worked effectively with a wide range of people. Zhang Zuolin in Manchuria came from a lowly peasant family and began his career as a bandit before becoming a soldier. Although scarcely educated, he proved to be a skillful negotiator who sensed the international play of forces in his domain and resourcefully balanced relations between Japan and Russia.

Possibly the most colorful warlord was Feng Yuxiang (Feng Yü-hsiang), who lacked a definite power base and had to live by his wits. The other warlords distrusted Feng for his unorthodox actions: Twice he executed coups d'etat in Peking. He was said to have converted his troops to Christianity (some say by marching them under fire hoses to baptize them) so they would lead moral lives and abstain from wine, women, and cigarettes and thus require less pay than the troops of other warlords. He was willing to violate the warlords' code and seek help from the Communists. As a consequence of an invitation from Soviet agent Michael Borodin, Feng visited Moscow and received military support from the Soviets, but at the critical juncture, when he was expected to show his gratitude, he failed to support the Chinese Communists and sided with Chiang Kai-shek. He never became an influential figure with the Nationalists, and on the eve of the Communist takeover of the mainland in 1949, while on a trip to the United States to "study water conservation," Feng declared his support of the Communists. He then took a Russian freighter from New York to return to China by way of Russia, but when the ship was two days out of Odessa the Russians announced that Feng had burned to death when a movie projector caught fire. No one else was hurt. There certainly was no clear future in the Communist scheme for the old warlord, especially since all his old subordinates had already given their allegiance to the new regime.

Other warlords, like Yen Xishan (Yen Hsi-shan), ended up with the Nationalists on Taiwan. For a brief period they had been the main actors on the China scene, but even as they carried out their personal struggles the forces that were to be more enduring in Chinese politics were becoming effectively organized. In the early years of the warlord period the followers of Sun Yat-sen, who by then had organized themselves first into the *T'ung-meng-hui* and then the Kuomintang, hoped they could influence national politics by working through the Parliament in Peking. It was soon apparent, however, that such a democratic and representational institution could have little influence in a situation in which real power lay with those who physically commanded armies. In spite of the important role Sun Yat-sen had played in mobilizing anti-Manchu sentiments, he had been nearly helpless from the time the Republic was established. In 1917, Sun accepted the support of the warlord of Canton and became the leader of a regime that was in competition with the Peking government.

In the years that followed Sun again became active in seeking international support for his version of a Chinese nationalist and democratic movement. The Western powers, however, continued to recognize the Peking government, despite its ineffectualness. Although Sun's arguments were often sympathetically listened to by foreign officials, no government felt inclined to intervene in Chinese affairs by withdrawing its recognition of the Peking government and extending it to Sun's southern-based government. So, for nearly a decade, from 1917 to 1927, there were two governments in China seeking international recognition, just as there have been the two regimes since 1949 claiming to be the legitimate government of China.

The shameful reality of warlord politics convinced Chinese intellectuals and modernizers that the country needed another revolution, which, to be successful, would have to be based on military power. Thus modern Chinese history, which began with the growth of military influences designed to suppress rebellions, culminated in the emergence of ideologically oriented revolutionaries who were compelled to turn to military power to achieve their goals. The success of the Kuomintang revolutionaries in becoming a national regime depended on the strength of their arms; similarly the Chinese Communists' road to power was by way of military victories.

CHAPTER EIGHT

Kuomintang Rule and Japanese Occupation

For a brief time during the decade from 1927 to 1937 it appeared that China might be reunited. The prospect of centralized rule under the Kuomintang was seen by most Chinese political observers as an advance over the warlord period, but in actual fact provincial leaders continued to have considerable autonomy. Chiang Kai-shek, however, began to emerge as a national symbol, welcomed, at least at first, by the modernists and feared by the idealistic elements.

The period of Nationalist rule was characterized by an attempt to forge a popular ideology out of Sun Yat-sen's writings, create a new structure of national authority, and inspire new loyalties. It was a time when China briefly seemed on the road to greater progress and economic development. The Great Depression and the struggle with Japan, which began in 1931 and became a full-scale war in 1937, compelled the fragile regime to deal with far more problems than it was capable of managing. The war did stimulate a great outburst of patriotic support, but the strains of the war years and the increasingly authoritarian character of Chiang's rule gradually weakened his claims of legitimacy.

Although the Nationalist period was a short one, it was significant because it revealed the problems inherent in China's effort to modernize and set the stage for the eventual victory of the Communists. Much that has since happened in China had its roots in those years.

THE RISE OF THE KUOMINTANG

In June, 1922, Sun Yat-sen was at a low point in his political career. Frustrated by his inability to attract either Western or Japanese help and out of sorts with his Canton warlord host, he withdrew to Shanghai and there contacted the Comintern, seeking Soviet help. Adolf Joffe was responsive, and early in 1923 the Sun-Joffe Agreement was announced. The Soviets declared that although China was not advanced enough for a Communist revolution, they were prepared to aid the Chinese nationalist revolution. At the time there was considerable disagreement about whether Joffe was dissembling by asserting that the Soviets were not seeking Communist domination of Sun Yat-sen's revolutionaries. Technically, his statement that China was not ready for Communism was entirely consistent with basic Marxist-Leninist doctrine, which maintains that a bourgeois-democratic revolution must precede socialist revolution and that a country is only "ready" for Communism after a socialist period. The agreement had profound consequences for the subsequent history of China.

The Comintern dispatched Michael Borodin, a former Chicago schoolteacher, to Canton to direct the reorganization of the Kuomintang. The Soviets invited Chiang Kai-shek to come to Russia for three months before he became the head of Whampoa Military Academy in Canton. Most important of all, the Comintern decision forced the fledgling Chinese Communist party to agree that its members as individuals would work within the framework of the Kuomintang, thus bringing together most of the principal actors who have shaped the subsequent history of the country.

As a consequence of Borodin's work the Kuomintang and the Chinese Communists have nearly identical organizational structures. Borodin sought to make the Kuomintang into a disciplined, purposeful organization, capable of both conducting revolutionary warfare and controlling whatever government it might establish. In addition to building a strong party, the Russian advisors began to plan a military force that would be politically disciplined under officers trained at the new Whampoa Academy (where Zhou Enlai was the chief political commissar under Chiang Kai-shek).

Although in retrospect it appears that the Russians moved

rapidly, Sun Yat-sen was impatient and, needing medical attention, visited Peking in 1925, hoping while there to negotiate a reunification of the country. Borodin, accompanying him incognito, had a secret meeting with Feng Yuxiang and sought his support. In what must have been one of the most unlikely debates in history, the Bolshevik agent belittled the reformist spirit of the Christian general, while Feng shrewdly defended humanitarian values against the violence of revolution. Feng was unconvinced at the time but later did accept Borodin's invitation to visit Russia and seek Soviet military assistance.

While in Peking Sun Yat-sen died, leaving an uncertain power situation in Canton. The Communists were under orders to cooperate with the Kuomintang and hence would not claim leadership. Also on the left were some less disciplined but aggressive individuals, the most notable of whom was Wang Jingwei, who felt he had a personal bond with Sun Yat-sen. In the middle, less ideological and most pragmatic, was Chiang Kai-shek, whose strength came from the Whampoa Academy and the military forces being trained to conquer the north and its warlords. To the right of Chiang were several individual leaders, generally older and still sympathetic to elements of the great mandarin tradition. The most notable of these was Hu Hanmin, a very close, old friend of Sun Yat-sen. Soon after Sun's death Hu and his associates sought to reunite the country through a conference convened in a major temple in the hills beyond the Summer Palace to the west of Peking. Thereafter they were referred to as the Western Hills clique.

In this confused situation it was Chiang Kai-shek who made the decisive moves and thus became the principal figure in Chinese politics. Acting with authority, he assumed command and declared that the goals of Sun would be realized. He thereupon unleashed his cadets and elements of his army for a series of raids on the leftist elements in the Kuomintang. Some of those chased out of Canton in 1926 scattered to Southeast Asia and, becoming more radicalized, founded the Communist movements in Singapore and Malaya, thereby bringing a Chinese tone to the Communist movements in the region.

In spite of Chiang's sharp attacks on the left, the Communists, particularly Stalin in Moscow, continued to declare that the Kuomintang was the hope of China and to praise Chiang's leadership. In the next year, 1927, the stage was set at last for the military reunification of China, and Chiang led the Northern Expedition out of Canton. One army under his own command moved to the northeast, approached central China at Nanjing, and enveloped Shanghai. The other army, which included Communists and the remaining leftwing elements of the Kuomintang, moved more directly north to central China and occupied Wuhan. Arriving in that major industrial center, they declared that the "capital" had been moved from Canton to Wuhan. Chiang Kai-shek's forces were just then approaching Nanzhing. Shocked by the Wuhan declaration, Chiang tested his own authority by calling a meeting of the Central Executive Committee of which he was nominally chairman, but no one from Wuhan came to Nanzhing.

The events that followed were critical for the subsequent development of China. To some degree they are still obscure because all the participants have given different versions of what happened. It is known that Chiang reacted to this rebuff by moving his forces toward Shanghai. Probably, although it is hard to prove, he established contact with the Shanghai business community, promising them a combination of order and stability on the one hand and a nationalist, anti–treaty port program on the other.

At this juncture one of the most controversial and confused incidents in modern Chinese history took place. With Chiang's troops on the outskirts of Shanghai, the workers and trade unionists in the city staged a remarkable insurrection, taking power from the police and the militia of the local warlord. With power in their hands they were prepared to welcome Chiang Kai-shek's armies, but when his troops finally entered the city they turned on the workers and soon destroyed that revolutionary power. The drama of these events has been movingly depicted in André Malraux's great novel *Man's Fate.*

Since the unions were Communist-controlled, it was generally assumed that Chiang was retaliating against the Communist-inspired act of setting up the Wuhan government. Chiang's position was that the trade unions had been supplied by the Soviet Union with arms shipped down the coast from Vladivostok and that they were supposed to give these arms to him so that his forces could complete the Northern Expedition to Peking. He charged that the unions had refused to carry out the plan because they wanted to conceal their arms and deliver them only to the Wuhan commander.

In Moscow at this time the Communists were being torn apart by the clash between Stalin and Trotsky that followed the death of Lenin. The Trotskyites would later claim that Stalin had ordered the Shanghai unions to hide their arms precisely because he wanted Chiang to react by destroying the unions and their leaders. In any case, Chiang acted decisively in crushing the unions and after capturing their arms, he confronted the Wuhan group with the charge that they were antirevolutionary.

Meanwhile, in Wuhan there was considerable confusion over what should be done. The Wuhan group included dedicated and disciplined Communists led by Michael Borodin; some more romantic and ideological Communists such as M. N. Roy (the Indian representative of the Comintern who had his own channels to Moscow); the radical, undisciplined, non-Communist left wing of the Kuomintang; and the completely unideological military officers who were simply seeking to carry out their professional task, conquering the rest of the country.

The massive power struggle in Moscow between Stalin and Trotsky was reflected in the clash of forces in Wuhan to determine the course of the Chinese revolution. Trotsky was pushing the view that as the armies moved north from Canton they should carry out a social revolution by breaking up significant landholdings and establishing soviets of peasants and workers. Stalin insisted that the Communists should work within the Kuomintang, wait until the entire country had been conquered, and then by a coup d'etat take over the country and commit it to the socialist world.

In this situation, Stalin was in the awkward position of calling for patience while at the same time trying to prove that he was a champion of revolution. He sent Borodin instructions that were impossible to carry out: Stalin ordered that the Communists continue to accept Chiang and the Kuomintang as leaders but at the same time train Red Army units within the Kuomintang that could surface at any time and take over.

Borodin recognized that the instructions were irreconcilable and asked Moscow for clarification. M. N. Roy learned of the orders and felt that Borodin was dragging his feet. At this point Borodin showed the Moscow instructions to Eugene Ch'en, a leftist

Kuomintang propagandist from the West Indies, who immediately recognized Moscow's cynical game of supporting the Kuomintang with the expectation of gaining domination over the country for itself and the Chinese Communists. When Ch'en publicized the instructions from Moscow, he shattered the Wuhan government. The idealistic left wing of the Kuomintang felt helpless; it was caught between an angry Chiang Kai-shek, who was clearly moving to the right, and an opportunistic Communist party. Historically this was the end of any non-Communist leftist group in the evolution of Chinese politics.

In his moment of triumph, Chiang was prepared to make a pragmatic arrangement with any force that might help in the reunification of China. The Communists were driven to desperation. In the fall of 1927 they attempted a series of military operations, known as the Autumn Harvest uprisings, but they were easily crushed; in Canton they sought to establish a commune, which also failed within a few days. In the meantime Chiang struck an agreement with the powerful warlord Feng Yuxiang (Feng Yü-hsiang). The Communists had earlier approached Feng with the proposition that in return for all the help the Soviets had given him he should declare himself against Chiang and in favor of the Communists, for otherwise the Communists would certainly collapse. Chiang's approach to Feng was more assertive and positive: If Feng did not support the Nanjing government, he would be opposing a force that would inevitably be triumphant. Feng, never one to support a losing cause, declared himself for Chiang and the Nanjing government and was promptly rewarded by being named minister of war in the new regime.

THE NATIONALIST SYSTEM OF RULE

From 1927 to 1937 Chiang Kai-shek and the Kuomintang achieved the high point of their rule of China. At no time, however, were they in full and unqualified command. Domestically, they had to contend with remnants of the Communist forces and a series of challenges from warlords who were not prepared to sacrifice their autonomy to Nanjing. Indeed, in nearly every year the Nanjing government had some local revolt or international incident that dramatized the weaknesses of the regime. For example, in the spring of 1929, Li Zongren (Li Tsung-jen), the general in Guangxi, revolted against the national regime and later that year Dang Shengchi (Tang Sheng-chih), also in the south, followed suit. In 1931 Feng Yuxiang joined with Yen Xishan in a revolt, and in the same year the military in Canton challenged Nanjing's authority. In 1933 the Nineteenth Route Army in Fujian revolted, and in 1936 the generals in Guangdong and Guangxi again sought to assert their independence. In each case the issue was whether central authority was to replace traditional localized warlord autonomy.

The Japanese occupied Manchuria in 1931, further extended their influence over Jehol province in 1933 and over Hebei and Chahar provinces in 1935, and then on July 7, 1937, initiated the war that lasted until 1945. Thus the Nationalist regime had little peace either at home or abroad during the ten years of its most effective rule. Nanjing's authority never really reached into Manchuria and was limited in northeastern China. Elsewhere Chiang had direct clashes with the Guangxi generals in 1929, and with Feng Yuxiang and his ally Yen Xishan the governor of Shanxi.

Chiang Kai-shek's method of ruling was to balance contrasting elements and seek alliances between all manner of groups. The Kuomintang itself was never a coherent or monolithic party; it contained an array of cliques and notable personalities. Two brothers, Chen Guofu and Chen Lifu, headed what was known as the C. C. Clique, which pushed a rightist ideology and organized the so-called Blue Shirts, a secret group of Kuomintang activists who employed bullying methods to maintain discipline. At the other extreme were the few remaining Kuomintang leftists, who looked to Wang Jingwei for inspiration. Chiang's power was augmented by his ties with the Soong family through his marriage to Soong Meiling in 1927. The oldest Soong sister was married to Sun Yat-sen, and the second to H. H. Kung, one of the wealthiest bankers in China. Their brother, T. V. Soong, was the minister of finance in the Nanjing government.

Members of the Kuomintang elite generally came from the urban, educated, and somewhat more cosmopolitan elements of Chinese society. They were not, however, modernized intellectuals with extensive foreign training, as have been the leaders of many of the newly independent states that experienced colonial rule. In the main, members of the Kuomintang political class had their roots in Chinese culture and society. Many of them wanted China to become a strong power, but they were ambivalent about social change, for they still valued much in Chinese tradition.

Kuomintang rule rested on the new civil and military bureaucratic structures established by the Nanjing regime. The new bureaucracy was quite different from the imperial one: It was not composed of gentlemen-scholars, nor were its members as much the modern technocrats as some of them thought they were; they were functionaries committed to a semimilitary ethos. Wearing blue uniforms cut like "Sun Yat-sen tunics," these officials tried to blur individual distinctions and inspire the idea that they were part of an efficient governmental machine. Their technical and administrative abilities, however, were not up to coping with the problems confronting a narrowly based government that had some ideological appeal but no substantial organizational strength.

In the early years, the Nanjing regime received most of its support from the merchant and industrial classes in the Yangtze valley. These were in the main newly emerging middle classes that lacked a tradition of respectability and seemed to be primarily interested in making money. The industrialists were concerned with China's economic development, and they were forward-looking and technologically progressive in their outlook. They could accept the idea of change. Many were self-made men: H. H. Kung came from a modest Shanxi banking family, and the father of the Soong sisters came from even more modest circumstances.

After the Japanese occupied the industrial centers of east China, these men steadily lost influence within the Kuomintang. Indeed, after the government was driven to Chongqing, the problem of collecting revenues to maintain the war effort forced the Kuomintang to become increasingly dependent on the rural gentry, the elite of interior China. Thus during the war years the Kuomintang became allied with conservative and reactionary elements in China.

Kuomintang rule was based on agreement about China's need for ideological and moral revitalization, but above all, the party emphasized its commitment to the doctrines of Sun Yat-sen, known as the *San Min Chu I*, or Three People's Principle. Coming out of a series of lectures Sun once gave, they reflect his uneven reading of Western authors. The first and most emphasized principle was nationalism. Sun emphasized the extent to which China had been victimized by imperialism and unequal treaties, and he diagnosed national weakness as the source of most of China's ills.

The second principle was democracy. Sun's interpretation of democracy blended with his concern about China's national power. He had argued that China had had an "excessive degree of liberty" and that "people's sovereignty" called for greater unity and authority. The Chinese people were like "loose sand," in need of more vigorous leadership. Sun rejected the concept of equality and stressed the need for wise leaders, advocating a version of democracy quite different from that generally known elsewhere. Sun did, however, add to his doctrine the idea that the people had four rights — rather modern ones — suffrage, recall, initiative, and referendum. These eventually would be implemented, but in the meantime Sun insisted that China needed "political tutelage."

One feature of Sun's theory of democracy that affected the structure of the Nanjing government was his view that government in China should be divided into five powers (*yuans*) — the executive, the legislative, the judicial, the civil examination system, and the Censorate. The last two were seen as distinctive contributions of traditional China to the organization of government. The Confucian examination system and the independent Censorate, which checked on the performance of officials, were thus added to the traditional European and American three-way division of power.

The Kuomintang established the Nanjing government on the basis of the five powers, and accepted completely the concept of "political tutelage." As for the four rights of the people, it spoke of the desirability of ultimately realizing them.

The third of Sun Yat-sen's three principles was people's livelihood, which was a vague form of socialism. Although Sun praised Karl Marx, he was probably influenced more by an obscure American dentist, Dr. Maurice William, and by Henry George, the advocate of a single tax system. Sun's livelihood principle did include the ideal that land should belong to the tiller and that people should not make profits from real property. Although he offered little substantive guidance about how the goal of people's livelihood was to be achieved, he did suggest that the government buy back all the land in the country. Under his scheme the landlords would declare the value of their holdings, and the government would then have the option of buying the land (if the price was low enough) or taxing it (if the value was set too high).

The *San Min Chu I* accurately reflects the distinctive blending of Western ideas and traditional Chinese virtues that characterized Kuomintang rule on the mainland of China. Strange mixes of foreign ideas were brought together and sanctified into a revered body of poltical doctrine. The outward forms suggested a commitment to change and modernization; the words evoked concepts of popular involvement and a belief in the sovereignty of the people. The substance of the doctrine, however, was ambiguous and could justify much that was antidemocratic.

Above all the *San Min Chu I* revealed the confused state of Chinese thinking as the country sought revolutionary change. It acknowledged a need to look abroad for ideas and techniques for modernizing the society, but it suggested that the Chinese were not happy in having to do so. The new mood did not encourage a systematic, hard, and critical examination of foreign ways, nor was it explicit about which traditional Chinese values should be maintained.

In short, the doctrines of the Chinese Nationalists went far in teaching the Chinese people that they had to take a broader view of their place in the world. But though they called for a mixture of foreign and Chinese ideas and practices, the doctrines did not capture what was best in each. The *San Min Chu I* tapped much that was second-rate. Sun Yat-sen was not to blame for this, for he had thought of his remarks only as the substance of lectures that he hoped would stimulate a youthful audience. It was the later Nationalist government that elevated his words into a sacred ideology for the Chinese people. The doctrines and the "Last Will and Testament" of Sun Yat-sen were made into articles of faith and became the basis for national loyalty training in all Chinese schools. In every school on every Monday morning during the Nationalist period students ceremoniously recited Sun's will and fervently bowed to his portrait.

Ideology aside, the Kuomintang committed itself to a system of government far stronger and more centralized than it was able to establish. In practice, the Nanjing regime was relatively ineffectual and not able to penetrate very deeply into Chinese society or bring about the new order and structure to which it aspired. In its rhetoric, however, the Kuomintang consistently stressed autocratic and elitist themes.

Despite the rising threat from Japan and the instabilities that came from the lingering warlord forces, China did experience some significant advances between 1927 and 1937. The impending international crisis with Japan sharpened the nationalistic sentiments of students and intellectuals. The national unity achieved by the Kuomintang set the stage for an upsurge in economic activity, even under the conditions of the Great Depression.

Against this accomplishment must be set the fact that the Kuomintang, wherever it had control, became increasingly authoritarian and antidemocratic. State power often became arbitrary power. Although there were many dedicated and hard-working lower- and middle-level officials in the government, charges of corruption against higher officials became a major problem, especially during the upheavals of the Japanese war period. Nor were the specialists and technicians within the various departments of government generally effective in using their skills. All government organizations were under party domination, and most party officials had little appreciation of technical matters.

THE WAR WITH JAPAN AND A DIVIDED NATION

By 1936 Chiang, in spite of many shortcomings, was making significant progress in increasing national unity. Most of the remaining warlords had been neutralized and were giving support to the Nanjing government. Chiang had carried out a series of "extermination" campaigns against Communist guerrilla base areas, compelling the Red Army under Mao Zedong and Zhu De to leave Guangxi and make the Long March to the northwest and Shaanxi province, where they were surrounded by the Manchurian forces of Zhang Xueliang (Chang Hsüeh-liang), the son of Zhang Zuolin. The Manchurian forces had been driven from their home provinces by the Japanese and were being used to "suppress the Communist bandits." The Communists were quite successful, however, in demoralizing the Manchurian armies by declaring that, instead of fighting the Japanese invaders of their home provinces, they were fighting against the only Chinese force that had "declared war" on Japan.

In December, 1936, Chiang flew up to Xian in Shaanxi province to press upon Zhang Xueliang the urgency of completing the "annihilation" of the Communists before confronting the Japanese. Upon arrival he was ignominously kidnapped by Zhang, who had been influenced by the Communists' argument that the Chinese were shamefully fighting other Chinese at a time when Japan threatened. The mutinous act shocked the nation and for a few days it appeared that China was about to lose whatever sense of national leadership it had. At this juncture, according to some reports, the Soviet Union intervened: Stalin sent a telegram to the Chinese Communists declaring that unless they arranged for the release of Chiang he would publicly disavow them as Communists and declare them to be mere "bandits." In any case Zhou Enlai did enter the scene and negotiated for Chiang's release.

Finally an agreement was worked out between the Communists and the Kuomintang. Chiang declared that he would firmly lead the national resistance against any further Japanese demands, and the Communists committed their forces to operating under the national command and promised to cease their partisan revolutionary propaganda. Chiang was released on Christmas Eve, 1936, and the Chinese nation seemed again to be moving toward genuine national unity.

Half a year later, on July 7, 1937, at Marco Polo Bridge near Peking, the Japanese attacked Chinese units, an incident that opened the all-out war that was to drive the Kuomintang government out of Nanjing, first to Hankou and then to Chongqing. The Japanese forces soon occupied all the principal cities of east China and controlled the railroad system. In the early months of the war there was a great outpouring of national sentiment, and thousands of people trekked to west China to escape the Japanese. Factories were dismantled and the machinery moved piece by piece to the west; entire schools and colleges picked up all that was movable and headed west, by foot if necessary and by bus and train where possible. Those trains that did move were packed, and refugees clung to the outsides. The country seemed united and committed to a heroic purpose. This idealism gradually gave way to greater and greater cynicism during the war years as the Chongqing government displayed both its ineffectualness and its autocratic proclivities.

Although the brutalities of the Japanese and their exploitation and suppression of the Chinese created widespread hostility and strengthened the national awakening of China, the Japanese demand for an East Asian co-prosperity sphere and their successful establishment of puppet states did win some converts and spread confusion and self-doubt among the Chinese. The Japanese propaganda approach was in fact rather skillfully tailored to exploit local and regional sentiments.

In Manchuria, for example, they appealed to the old Manchu loyalties and restored the last Manchu emperor, Henry Pu Yi, to the throne of the state they called Manchukuo. In Inner Mongolia and Jehol they appealed to Buddhist sentiments and held out the vision of a theocracy functioning under Japanese supervision. In north China they appealed to the pride of the greatest of the imperial cities and made Peking once again the national capital; they brought out the old five-bar flag that had been China's national emblem during the republican, pre-Kuomintang period and installed in visible but powerless offices men who had been notable in that era. All this set in motion the confusing battle of names between "Peip'ing" and "Pei-ching." When Chiang Kai-shek made Nanjing the capital, he changed the name of Peking from Pei-ching (northern capital) to Peip'ing (northern peace). Most Pekingese, however, continued to cling to their old name and resented their loss of capital status. As soon as the Japanese gave them back their cherished name, however, they displayed their nationalist ardor by uniformly calling their city Peip'ing. This continued to be the practice until the Communists came to power in 1949 and declared the name to be Pei-ching once again, or, in the *pinyin* spelling, Beijing. Thereafter the battle of names became one between Communists and Nationalists, with the United States State Department adhering strictly to Peip'ing until President Nixon announced in 1971 that he planned to visit Peking.

In central China the Japanese made Nanjing a capital. They shamelessly adopted the Kuomintang flag and the *San Min Chu I* ideology, placed Wang Jingwei in a position of nominal leadership and surrounded him with men, both Chinese and Japanese, who had known Sun Yat-sen well during his years of exile in Japan.

The fact that both Chongqing and the puppet Nanjing regimes could profess to be the legitimate heirs to Sun Yat-sen and hold sacred the same set of symbols tended to undermine all that the Kuomintang seemed to represent.

While the Japanese were systematically seeking to turn the Chinese against each other in the occupied regions, the Chinese in the west were also becoming more sharply divided. For a brief period at the beginning of the war the Communists and the Nationalists achieved a degree of cooperation and coordination, but it did not last long. The Nationalist armies were short of arms and equipment, so Chongqing was not inclined to supply the Communist armies as specified in the Xian (Sian) Agreement that followed the Chiang kidnapping incident. The Communists, however, were soon operating in north China behind the Japanese lines, and running an effective government in the countryside surrounding the Japanese-occupied cities. It was no longer feasible for them to take all their orders from Chiang's headquarters, as required by the agreement.

Whatever cooperation existed before December 7, 1941, evaporated after the attack on Pearl Harbor, for all politically conscious Chinese knew from that moment that Japan would certainly be defeated by the United States regardless of what the Chinese did. Thus, while Americans were concerned with how and when the war might be won and expected everyone to be equally dedicated, the Chinese were beginning to worry about what was to be the balance of domestic forces in the country once the Japanese were beaten.

Before World War II ended, the stage in China was set for a civil war. The Communists steadily expanded their guerrilla base territories, built larger armies, and extended their capabilities for civil rule. The Party also engaged in a major self-disciplining campaign, the *zhengfeng* (*cheng-feng*), to raise its ideological level and improve its revolutionary spirit.

The Nationalists were equally concerned with maintaining and strengthening their domestic political position. Although the Nationalist armies carried on the main war against the Japanese, they seemed increasingly less concerned with pushing back the foreign conquerors and more with husbanding their resources for the postwar period. The strain of prolonged war and the realization that victory depended little on what the Chinese did and almost entirely on the Americans created a pervasively cynical and depressed mood in Chongqing. Authority tended to respond with increased repression and dependence on military rather than political or ideological power.

The final defeat of Japan left China deeply divided — between Nationalists and Communists, and between those who had collaborated or lived accommodatingly with the Japanese in east China and those who had gone to the west. Immediately following the surrender of Japan to the Allies, the United States helped move Nationalist armies from west China to the major coastal cities, and soon the Nationalists were in almost exactly the same situation that the Japanese had occupied — in command of the cities and the railroad lines while the Communists held the countryside.

During the next four years the country gradually slipped toward civil war. The Communists grew steadily in strength and benefited from the confusion while the Nationalists just as steadily lost morale and the capacity to rule. The divisions between city and countryside, the inability to unite the country into a single economy, and the tremendous costs of maintaining huge armies contributed to an acute inflation that hurt, above all, the civil servants and the urban middle classes, the very groups whose support was most essential for the Nationalists. Inflation was probably the most immediate cause of the fall of the Kuomintang on the mainland. It not only wiped out the middle class but also encouraged ever more flagrant corruption among higher officials.

During this period the United States sought to achieve a truce and establish some form of national integration in China. Shortly after the Japanese surrender, President Truman sent General George C. Marshall to China to bring together the Nationalists and the Communists. Negotiations aiming at some form of coalition government broke down because of mutual distrust. The effort to freeze the military situation also failed, largely because both armies were drawn into Manchuria to fill the void created by the withdrawal of Russian forces, who had defeated the Japanese troops there during the last week of World War II. The intense fighting in Manchuria gradually spread to north China, and by

1948 the country was embroiled in a major civil war. Peking was surrounded and finally fell to the Communists in 1949, and by autumn the Communists had crossed the Yangtze.

Finally Chiang K'ai-shek was driven to the island of Taiwan, where the remnants of the Kuomintang armies and party members gradually were able to reorganize themselves and established a more efficient regime than they had on the mainland. The Nationalist government and the Kuomintang party remain the principal foe of the Communists and an alternative government to Peking's, aspiring always to return to the mainland but in practice concentrating on ruling their island country, achieving impressive economic development but limited civil liberties.

CHAPTER NINE

The Rise of the Communists

The People's Republic of China was established on October 1, 1949, but for the previous twenty years the Communist party had controlled territory in various parts of China and thus brought with it unique experience in governing. Before the Party captured national power it had had more practice in ruling than in being a revolutionary party without governmental responsibilities. The Chinese Communist party made tactical judgments from the outset; it never experienced a period comparable to that of the early Russian Marxists, when ideological disputations were all-absorbing.

The speed with which the Communist party became a major force in Chinese politics was amazing. Before the Russian Revolution of 1917 there was almost no awareness of Marxism in China, even within intellectual circles. In 1921 the First Congress of the Chinese Communist party was held, and by 1927 the Party seemed to be on the brink of capturing national power. Thereafter, for more than twenty years the Chinese Communists were a military force, beyond the ability of the Nanjing government to eliminate. They controlled territories, ruled over citizens, collected taxes, and even issued their own postage stamps and currency.

The spectacular spread of Communism reflected both the craving of intellectuals for ideas that might revive China and the Communists' ability to act when they felt they had found their answer. After the Paris decision to give Japan the former German rights in Shandong, the upsurge of Chinese nationalism (the May Fourth Movement) was most intense among the students and faculty of Peking National University. Its sprawling, unimposing campus of gray brick buildings located to one side of the Forbidden

City was an intellectually vital scene where students returning from Japan, America, and Europe, sought to share their new knowledge with younger compatriots who were equally anxious to find answers for China's impotence. Peking National University (or Beida as it was conventionally shortened in Chinese) became the preeminent intellectual center of China. It was also a center of Chinese nationalism largely because of the qualities of Chancellor Cai Yuanpei (Ts'ai Yuan-p'ei), who encouraged independent and unorthodox thinking among his faculty and political activism among his students.

Cai, a highly competent philosopher, was interested in synthesizing Chinese and Western intellectual traditions. As a young man he had been one of the last of the Hanlin scholars, but after China's ignominious defeat by Japan in 1894 and 1895, Cai gave up his concentration on Confucian learning and vigorously sought out Western knowledge. Before the 1911 Revolution he visited Japan and spent four years studying at Leipzig. After a brief return to China during the presidency of Yüan Shih-k'ai, he returned in disillusionment to France, where he helped organize the Société Franco-Chinois Education, which sponsored a work–study program that brought to France more than 2,000 Chinese, including Zhou Enlai and Deng Xiaoping, leading figures of Chinese Communism. Indeed, participants in this program became in time an important channel of recruitment to the fledgling Chinese Communist party.

When Cai Yuanpei became chancellor of Beida in 1916, he recruited a talented faculty that included Hu Shih, who, as a disciple of John Dewey, pressed for pragmatic approaches to Chinese ills, and also Li Dazhao (Li Ta-chao) and Chen Duxiu (Ch'en Tu-hsiu), two leading figures both in introducing Marxism into China and in founding the Chinese Communist party.

Li Dazhao was educated in Japan. As a student at Waseda University in Tokyo he had become a politically active publicist who was soon recognized as a passionate champion of Chinese nationalism. In 1918 Cai invited him to become chief librarian at Beida, and two years later he became professor of history, economics, and political science (in those days discipline differences were not great). He and Hu Shih and other leading intellectuals devoted considerable energy to literary and cultural movements, focusing around *The New Youth* magazine, which was founded by

Chen Duxiu, dean of social sciences at Beida. In the fall of 1918 Li Dazhao hired a young man from provincial Hunan who had just graduated from the Changsha Normal School, Mao Zedong, to serve as an assistant librarian. Mao was strongly influenced by Li's enthusiasm for a better China, and he sought contacts with both Hu Shih and Chen Duxiu.

In the spring of 1919, when the May Fourth Movement swept the campus and brought all classes to a halt, Cai, Li, Chen, and Hu Shih all adopted strong positions in support of a student strike and in opposition to the Peking government that financed their university. Cai's threatened resignation helped gain the release of imprisoned students and faculty, including Chen Duxiu, who, however, had to resign and withdraw to the security of the International Settlement in Shanghai as a condition of his release.

During the rest of the academic year and into the following fall the confusion continued. When funds were cut off, Cai Yuanpei and Hu Shih sought to turn the momentum of the strike in more constructive directions. They proposed that students and staff return to their home districts to spread the message of the May Fourth Movement and help illiterates learn to read. Hu Shih's proposal to replace classes with a politicized work-study program sent Mao Zedong back to Hunan to study rural conditions.

In the following year the radicalizing of the university continued with the introduction of Marxist-Leninist study groups under the leadership of Li Dazhao. Early in 1920 Li was approached by Gregory Voitinsky, an agent of the Comintern, to see what help the Chinese intellectuals might need if they were to become serious Communists. Li suggested that Voitinsky contact Chen Duxiu in Shanghai and provided a letter of introduction. Chen at that time was busily contacting former students and colleagues and welcomed any help that would facilitate his organizational work.

Within a year's time cells had been established in Shanghai, Peking, Changsha, and other cities by former associates of the Beida leaders, and the first group of Russian-language students, including Liu Shaoqi, had been sent to Moscow. In January 1921, Chen Duxiu left Shanghai for Canton to become head of the education department of Guangdong province and to establish Communist cells in the area controlled by the southern government.

Voitinsky was joined by a Dutch Comintern agent, Sneevliet,

who operated under the name of Maring and who had brought Marxism to Indonesia before World War I. The time seemed right to link the separate cells into an organized party. In the previous spring the Chinese work-study group in France had formed the Communist Youth Corps, which included Zhou Enlai, Li Lisan, and others destined to become important figures in the Party. When Maring arrived in Shanghai, he sent out the call for an organizational meeting that would establish the Chinese Communist party.

THE FIRST CONGRESS OF THE CHINESE COMMUNIST PARTY, JULY 1921

There has been some confusion over who was present at the creation of the Chinese Communist Party, but it is generally recognized that there were twelve Chinese, Maring, and either Voitinsky or an agent named Nikorusky. Chen Duxiu was not able to be there because of his new duties in Canton, and Li Dazhao was busy in Peking so he sent Zhang Guotao to represent the Peking group. Mao Zedong and He Shuheng came from Hunan. Some of those present at the initial meeting later turned against the Communists or dropped out of politics. For example, Zhou Fohai became the personal secretary to Chiang Kai-shek and a leading propagandist for the Kuomintang and later went over to the Japanese; Li Da drifted away from disciplined Communism to become a university professor and intellectual Marxist. Chen Gongbo also left the Communist Party after a few years and became closely associated with the left wing of the Kuomintang and finally helped Wang Jingwei to establish the Japanese puppet regime in Nanjing. Liu Renjing became a Trotskyite in the 1930s and only came back to the Party he helped establish after the Communist victory of 1949. Deng Biwu spent much of the rest of his career as a liaison man between the Communists and the Kuomintang and was the only Communist representative on the Chinese delegation at the founding conference of the United Nations at San Francisco. Chen Tanqiu spent several years in Moscow and was finally executed by the warlord of Xinjiang after serving as the Communist liaison officer in that province. In the 1927 disorders Li Hanjun also met a violent death. The last two, Wang Jinmei and Deng Enming, had relatively undistinguished careers in spite of participating in the founding of the Party.

The meetings took place on Perbalu Street in the French Concession in a private girls' school whose custodian allowed the delegates to use the rooms vacated for the summer holiday. On the evening before the last session the delegates were crowded into Li Hanjun's apartment when a mysterious man wandered in, claiming he was looking for someone. As soon as he left, the meeting adjourned and a few minutes later police raided the apartment but found nothing incriminating. In search of a safe place to finish their business, the delegates retired to Neibu Lake, outside Shanghai, where, posing as a group of vacationing sightseers, they rented a boat, provided themselves with a picnic lunch, and finished their deliberations in isolation on the lake though still in public view.

The group had not found it easy to arrive at any ideological agreement, for the various delegates had divergent interpretations of history and of the current state of the world. They did, however, decide that Chen Duxiu should be chosen secretary-general of the Party, and by this decision the fledgling organization avoided intellectual disputes and focused on action. Chen was an extremely articulate intellectual as well as a straightforward believer in the need for change and the importance of science. He was ready to be pragmatic and to do what had to be done to make the Chinese Communist Party into a significant political force.

Chen immediately left Canton and returned to Shanghai to take command of the Party. Maring worked closely with him, and during the next year they both concentrated on helping Zhang Guotao establish the secretariat of the Chinese Labor Union and carry out railway and seamen's strikes, which were relatively ineffectual.

THE SECOND PARTY CONGRESS, MAY 1922

When Chen took office as secretary-general, the Party had possibly fifty members. By the following May, when the Second Party Congress was held on West Lake, in Hangzhou, it had nearly one hundred. The growth in numbers was not impressive, but significant political changes had occurred in China and the stage was set for a momentous decision by the Party. The Kuomintang was becoming a significant force in Canton and had successfully carried out a seamen's strike in Hong Kong. Zhang Guotao had attended the Conference of the Toilers of the East in Moscow early in the year and learned of Soviet interest in creating a broad nationalistic force in China that could drive out the warlords. The currents of revolution seemed to be running high in Asia.

When the Second Congress met, Maring shocked the delegates with the proposal that the Party seek to cooperate with the Kuomintang. Most of the delegates were committed to the belief that the Party should not compromise its proletarian integrity by allying with the Kuomintang, which contained clearly bourgeois and even "semifeudal" elements. There have been conflicting statements about what transpired. Maring, many years later, told Harold Isaacs, leading chronicler of the period, that he had no trouble convincing the delegates of the wisdom of simply entering the Kuomintang and using its organization as a means of reaching a larger public and that the only uncertainty was whether the Kuomintang was in fact a potentially effective organization. Chen Duxiu, years later when he was in disgrace, insisted that Maring had forced the decision of the first united front upon the Party by asserting the authority of the Soviet Comintern.

The ultimate decision was clear: The members of the Chinese Communist party would enter the Kuomintang as individuals and, while maintaining their Communist Party discipline, would seek to shape the Kuomintang into a force that would unite the country and lead to a socialist revolution. This decision was unambiguously ratified in August 1922, at a special plenum of the Central Committee of the Chinese Communist Party called by Maring at Hangzhou.

THE THIRD PARTY CONGRESS, JUNE 1923

In the last weeks of 1922, at the Fourth World Congress of the Comintern, Karl Radek, the German socialist and close supporter of Lenin, publicly called for closer collaboration between the

Kuomintang and the Communists. This was followed immediately by Moscow's encouragement of the Sun-Joffe Agreement in which the Soviets pledged to help the Kuomintang while claiming that China was not ready for communism.

By June 1923, when the Third Congress of the Chinese Communist Party met in Canton, membership had grown to possibly 300 persons and Maring was still having trouble making the twenty delegates support the Comintern line of working within the Kuomintang. Chen Duxiu, who had just returned from the Comintern Congress, strongly defended the Kuomintang-Communist alliance. At this stage Zhang Guotao began to advocate a more independent line. The final manifesto of the congress supported the alliance but included some criticism of the Kuomintang and called for closer ties with the world proletariat. Chen Duxiu was again confirmed as secretary-general.

In September 1923, Michael Borodin arrived in Canton, replacing Maring as Comintern representative. By January 1924, he had reorganized the Kuomintang to the point of calling for its First National Congress. At the congress the Kuomintang admitted the Communists to membership, declared an alliance with the Soviet Union, and elected three leading Communists to the Central Executive Committee and six as alternate members, including Zhang Guotao and Qu Qiubai.

THE FOURTH PARTY CONGRESS, JANUARY 1925

During the next year the Kuomintang established the Whampoa Military Academy and commenced serious planning of a northern expedition from Canton that was to reunify the country. The Communist members within the Kuomintang were beginning to encounter resistance and suspicion. When the Fourth Party Congress of the Chinese Communist party met in Shanghai, the delegates, who now represented more than 1,000 members, eagerly pointed out that the Kuomintang was composed of several factions and that the Communist Party members should join the left wing of the Kuomintang to try to weaken the right and center factions. At the same time the congress called for some activities that would go beyond the Kuomintang. The congress urged the development of workers' unions and peasant associations in central and north China. The Central Committee also set up two regional offices extending beyond Kuomintang territories: one for north China headed by Zhang Guotao, and one for central China under Cai Heshen.

Opportunities for political action outside of the Kuomintang framework were becoming increasingly tempting. When Sun Yat-sen died in Peking on March 12, 1925, many Communists called for more independent action. In October, Chen Duxiu told an enlarged session of the Central Committee of the Chinese Communist Party in Peking that actions independent of the Kuomintang were to be welcomed. The Party was also having apparent success among laborers, which was particularly gratifying to the intellectuals who had little experience with the working classes. Li Lisan was organizing strikes in Shanghai, and the Comintern was enough impressed with the labor unions to supply them with arms so that they could cooperate in the northern expedition of the Canton forces.

The Communists were also quick to exploit a clash between the Shanghai police and students, which became known as the May Thirtieth Incident and they called a brief general strike. In the meantime, Mao Zedong was beginning to organize the peasants in the Hunan countryside. For the first time Party membership was growing at a pace that suggested that the Chinese Communist Party might become a mass party. In the two years between the Fourth Congress in 1925 and the Fifth in 1927 membership increased from a little more than 1,000 to more than 60,000.

These substantive advances by the revolutionary leaders strained relations with the Kuomintang and hence created tensions between the Chinese Communists and Moscow. Stalin and the Comintern still insisted that the character of the Chinese revolution demanded that the Chinese Party continue to work within the Kuomintang. The anomalous feature of the relationship was dramatized after Chiang Kai-shek staged his military coup against the Communists and the left wing of the Kuomintang in Canton on March 20, 1926. Even after the Soviet advisors were placed under house arrest, with leading revolutionaries having to flee the country, Moscow blindly continued to insist that Chiang was a hero of the working classes whom all Communists should continue to support.

Chen Duxiu and the other Communist leaders were beginning to learn the true meaning of revolutionary discipline. Borodin continued to display the required loyalty to the Kuomintang and was soon again helping with plans for the Northern Expedition. In July 1926, the armies began to move out from Canton. In the meantime in the Soviet Union, the struggle between Stalin and Trotsky was centering increasingly on interpretations of the Chinese revolution. Trotsky impatiently argued that as the Canton forces moved toward the Yangtze they should set up soviets along the way, initiate land reform, and carry out a social revolution. Stalin persisted in his view that although the Chinese Communist Party should encourage peasant rebellion, it would have to contain "peasant excesses" and continue to operate within the Kuomintang until the country had been united. Stalin felt that introducing a social revolution as an adjunct of military operations would be a disruption certain to bring about failure.

THE FIFTH PARTY CONGRESS, APRIL 1927

In November the left wing of the Kuomintang moved the "government" from Canton to Wuhan. The act challenged the leadership of Chiang Kai-shek, who was leading his troops toward Nanjing and Shanghai. In spite of the strains among the revolutionary forces in China, in Moscow at the Seventh Enlarged Plenum of the Executive Committee of the Comintern, Stalin's views about the need to support Chiang dominated, and criticism of the Kuomintang was declared counterrevolutionary.

Early in 1927 the Chinese Communists joined the left Kuomintang government in Wuhan. Meanwhile the Communist trade unions in Shanghai launched a series of remarkable attacks on the warlord garrisons in Shanghai, facilitating Chiang's ultimate conquest of the city. On April 12, however, Chiang turned his troops against the workers, stating that they had failed to hand over their arms to his command.

Only fifteen days later the Fifth Congress of the Chinese

Communist Party met at Hankou, one of the three cities that made up the Wuhan complex where the left Kuomintang government was located. The debates at the congress were confused, and there was even disagreement between Borodin and M. N. Roy, the watchdog of the Comintern. Borodin was pressing for new ties with Feng Yuxiang, which would carry the Party into the northwest, while Roy argued that if there was further trouble with the Kuomintang rightists, the Party should return to its base in the south and strengthen its revolutionary forces there. Also discussed was mobilizing the peasantry by advocating land confiscation. In the previous year Mao Zedong had actively worked to organize peasant associations in Hunan, and he was anxious for the Party to take a strong stand legitimizing the destruction of "local bullies and bad gentry."

The Fifth Congress acknowledged Chiang's attack upon the Shanghai workers but insisted that the Communists should continue to work with the Kuomintang leftists in Wuhan. Wang Jingwei, the leader of that government, attended sessions of the congress and heard M. N. Roy expound the theory that the Communists should continue to work within the Kuomintang to be in position to take it over at the appropriate moment of revolutionary success.

Mao's more extreme views about peasant confiscations did not win the day, and when the Central Committee established the first Politburo in the Party's history, he was not on it. The members were Chen Duxiu, Zhang Guotao, Zhou Enlai, Qu Qiubai, Li Lisan, Li Weihan, Su Zhaozheng, Tan Pingshan, and Cai Heshen.

While the congress was in session, Zhang Zuolin, the warlord in control of the north, sanctioned a raid on the Soviet embassy in Peking, seizing large quantities of documents revealing the extent of Soviet involvement in both the Chinese Communist Party and the Kuomintang. The raiding troops also captured several Communist leaders, including Li Dazhao, on the embassy grounds, and they were summarily executed. The stakes were clearly rising for the Chinese Communists. At this juncture, in June 1927, Borodin received his contradictory instructions from Stalin ordering both continued cooperation with the Kuomintang and the building of an anti-Kuomintang force from below. Roy showed the communication to others, and Wang Jingwei finally recognized what the Communists had in mind. Shocked, he expelled them from the Wuhan government and from the Kuomintang left. Soon after this, the Nanjing forces under Chiang Kai-shek turned toward Wuhan, spelling the end of the Kuomintang left wing.

On the night of August 1, 1927, commanders of forces that were part of the Kuomintang Northern Expedition carried out an uprising in Nanzhing. The revolt was quickly put down and the troops scattered, but the remnants became the nucleus of the Red Army, which eventually would conquer its Kuomintang foe. The commanding generals He Long and Ye Ting, were secretly Communists and they were supported by Zhu De and Lin Biao. In the confusion at the time, however, it seemed that total disaster had suddenly struck a party that only months before was calculating on taking over total power in the largest country in the world.

On August 7, 1927, the Central Committee of the Chinese Communist Party held an emergency conference, and Chen Duxiu was charged with right-wing "opportunistic deviations." He was removed as secretary-general and replaced by Qu Qiubai. The Comintern, and particularly Stalin, was unwilling to share responsibility for the disaster that their policies had brought upon the Chinese Communist Party, so Chen was made the scapegoat. Stalin's contradictory orders made it easy to say that Chen had not followed all instructions. The charge that he had been engaged in "right deviation" — that is, that he had been excessively cautious and unprepared to support the more revolutionary elements — was peculiarly unfair because Stalin's emphasis had been on conservative tactics and he had picked up Trotsky's theme of peasant insurrections only after defeating Trotsky.

Soon after the removal of Chen it was Qu Qiubai's turn to become the victim of Moscow's inability to understand the Chinese situation. Stalin now insisted that the time was ripe for armed uprisings, and even after the failure at Nanzhing he insisted on additional revolutionary acts. Consequently, during September and November Mao Zedong led the Autumn Harvest uprisings in Hunan, but when these failed Mao was blamed and dismissed from all important Party posts. By December the Party was still trying to carry out Moscow's wishes and launched a disastrous uprising in Canton, under the general direction of the German Comintern representative, Heinz Neumann. For several days revolutionaries did manage to hold ground in the southern city and they proclaimed the establishment of a commune, but quickly they were scattered by troops loyal to Chiang Kai-shek.

THE SIXTH PARTY CONGRESS, JULY 1928

After the failure in Canton, Moscow could no longer ignore the declining fortunes of the Chinese Communist Party, and at the Ninth Plenum of the Executive Committee of the Comintern, in February 1928, Stalin declared that the Chinese Party was guilty of "putschism" — improper use of military power — and a series of "left deviationist" errors, all stemming from insufficient planning. Whereas Chen Duxiu had been removed for "right opportunism," Qu Qiubai was under attack for "left deviation" and "putschism." Yet both had merely sought to carry out the Comintern's unrealistic instructions.

On July 9, 1928, at the Sixth Party Congress in Moscow, Qu Quibai was removed as secretary-general and replaced by Xiang Zhongfa, who held the office in an administrative capacity until he was arrested and executed by the Kuomintang in June 1931, although he never was the actual political leader of the Party. The role of the Party leader went from Qu Quibai to Li Lisan, whose formal title was head of the Party's propaganda bureau.

The Sixth Congress decreed that "the degree of consolidation of the reactionary regime in different regions is uneven; therefore the revolution, in a general new rising tide, may succeed first in one or more provinces." For some members of the Party, including Mao and Zhu De, this meant that an effort should be made to consolidate rural base areas for the Red Army. Even before the congress met, Mao and Zhu had joined forces to establish the Fourth Red Army. Li Lisan, however, discounted the possibility of revolution by military means and instead compelled the Party to emphasize labor organization and agitation. He was convinced that only the proletariat could lead a successful revolution, and in this belief he thought he was carrying out the highest principles of Marxism-Leninism. By the time that Li Lisan had become the dominant figure in the Chinese Communist Party, its membership was down to only

15,000, and he was devoting all his time to meeting with secret cells in Shanghai, Hankou, Tianjin, and other industrial centers.

After the Sixth Congress a significant split developed within the Party, between those who were in close contact with the secretariat in Shanghai and those who were in isolation in a mountainous retreat in Jiangxi. During 1929 one part of the Party was vigorously seeking to expand within the urban workers' environment, and the other faction was becoming increasingly militarized and allied with the peasantry in some of the most backward and isolated parts of China. By August 1930, at the Third Plenum of the Central Committee at Lushan, there was widespread criticism of the "Li Lisan line" because it expected too much of the labor movement and in November Li Lisan was disowned by the Comintern. In January 1931, the Fourth Plenum of the Central Committee met secretly in Shanghai and formally declared that the Chinese Communist Party was abandoning the Li Lisan line because it was, like the Qu Qiubai line, too "putschist" in stressing the revolutionary potential of the working classes. Li confessed his errors and agreed to retire to Moscow to study and improve his capacity for revolutionary analysis.

At this point Party leadership in the urban areas passed to a group of young Communists who had been trained in Moscow and were generally identified as the "returned students group." They included Chen Shaoyu, alias Wang Ming (who became secretary-general after Xiang Zhongfa was executed), Zhong Wentien, and Shen Zemin. Zhou Enlai, who was always with whatever faction seemed dominant at the moment, joined briefly with the Shanghai group.

THE JIANGXI SOVIETS

While the Party leadership, with its Comintern connections, continued to operate out of an unimportant office in Shanghai, the other element of the Party was busily building actual governmental power in the mountains of Jiangxi. After Mao Zedong and Zhu De were driven out of Hunan, they crossed to the east and sought safety in the mountainous isolation of Jiangxi where they established the Chinese Soviet Republic with Ruijin as the capital. Until

1932, the Politburo continued to operate out of Shanghai, but it commanded only a handful of people, while in Jiangxi a system of government and a military force were beginning to evolve. In the fall of 1932 Chen Shaoyu, Zhong Wentien, Liu Shaoqi, and the other members of the Central Committee left Shanghai and escaped to Ruijin.

Zhu De was the recognized military commander in Jiangxi, and all the resources available to the Communists went into building his army. Mao Zedong emerged as the political leader. The anomaly of the time was that the Comintern in Moscow continued to pretend that revolutionary currents were running high in China and that the only reason the Communists had not taken command of the country was the incompetence of the various Chinese Communist leaders. In fact the organization of the Chinese Party was exceedingly weak as a national institution, and whatever power existed lay with separate and isolated groups, whether in cells in the cities or in the separate soviets in Jiangxi. Even in the mountains there was no single command structure.

In addition to those headed by Zhu De and Mao Zedong, a group in Jiangxi was under the command of Zhang Guotao, who thought of himself as the senior Party representative. Thus Moscow assumed that the Chinese Communist Party had greater revolutionary potential than it had in fact, and furthermore Moscow was least aware of the developments that would in time give the Party its greatest advantages — the growth of the Red Army in Jiangxi.

The Jiangxi soviets were a blend of civilian and military rule. Party cadres served as both military commanders and political commissars, and by 1931 a clearly established tradition of political officers paralleled the military chain of command. The troops were subjected to daily propaganda sessions, and all sought to prove in the regular self-criticism sessions that they were unequivocally committed to the revolution. Peasants who lived on some of the poorest land in China willingly abandoned their farms and sought service and community in the new army that Zhu and Mao were building.

In the meantime Chiang Kai-shek was directing his armies against the remaining warlord forces and was attempting to meet the threat of Japan, which had invaded Manchuria in 1931. Chiang did, however, devote some of his troops to Jiangxi and began a series of five "extermination" campaigns, each of which was expected to annihilate the Communists. Thus, between his campaigns against Feng Yuxiang, the Guangxi generals, and the Japanese, Chiang moved against the Communists.

Finally in 1934 the pressures in Jiangxi became too great. With the *soviet* areas encircled, the decision was taken to abandon the Jiangxi base and seek security elsewhere. Thus began the Long March, which was to be the most significant experience in the early history of Chinese Communism. In the autumn of 1934 Moscow radioed Ruijin to advise the Chinese to seek safety as far away as Outer Mongolia if necessary. The Red Army, which broke out of the Kuomintang ring and started the Long March, totaled about 120,000 men. When the march ended in Yan'an in Shaanxi province 368 days later, only 10,000 men remained.

From the outset the Long March contained heroic, romantic, and tragic elements. When the troops set out, they left behind Qu Quibai, who was politically discredited and physically incapacitated by tuberculosis. He was captured by the Nationalist troops and dramatically executed. According to a story then current, Qu was carried on a stretcher from prison to the place of execution. He drank a glass of whiskey, asked for a brush and paper, and wrote this poem:

> The colorful splurge of the setting
> sun etches the mountains of Fukien.
> The rustle of the falling leaves and
> the sound of the running streams
> show that winter is near.
> These are eternal.
> Ten years I have passed in
> worldly undertakings, and now
> I am prepared to join heaven,
> But I leave with desires unfilled.[1]

Then "he met his death singing the 'Internationale' in Russian, a cigarette drooping languidly from his fingers."

The story may have been a bit romanticized by the Commu-

[1] Robert C. North, *Moscow and Chinese Communists*, 2nd ed. Copyright © 1953, 1963 by The Board of Trustees of the Leland Stanford Junior University. Reprinted with permission of the publishers, Stanford University Press.

nists because while Qu was a prisoner he wrote a remarkable introspective essay, quite un-Chinese, in which he suggested that it had been a historic misunderstanding for him to have been involved with Communism: "My basic nature, I believe, does not make for a Bolshevik fighter, or even a revolutionary novitiate. But because of pride, I did not have the courage, after joining the group, to recognize my own self and ask them to wash me out."[2]

THE ZUNYI CONFERENCE AND MAO'S RISE TO POWER

As the Long March columns moved out of Jiangxi and entered Guizhou, their leaders were consumed with debates about what had gone wrong. The political leaders close to the Red Army were convinced that the "returned students" led by Wang Ming had failed to understand the revolutionary potential of the countryside and of the Red areas. The fact that they had been faithfully following Moscow's orders was ignored. In time, however, each in turn sought to follow Moscow's instructions and they clashed, even disagreeing over which route to follow.

In later years the Communists would idealize the Long March, but much that happened during its course is still obscure. There was, for example, a conference at Zunyi, in Guizhou, at which, according to some accounts, Mao Zedong was recognized as the leader not only of the military operation but of the Chinese Communist party. Others have suggested that the leadership was more diffuse and collective. In any case, there was a major break between Mao Zedong and Zhang Guotao. Zhang had long been a major figure in the Party and had begun the Long March with more men under his command than Mao had, so when Mao asserted his leadership at Zunyi, Zhang refused to recognize the legitimacy of his decisions. By the time the two leaders reached Yan'an, however, it was clear that Mao had established his superiority in the eyes of such important figures as Zhu De, Zhou Enlai, Lin Biao, and Peng

[2] Chester C. Tan, *Chinese Political Thought in the Twentieth Century* (Garden City, N.Y.: Doubleday, 1971), p. 322.

Dehuai. Zhang at this juncture broke with the Party. Thus during the course of the Long March Mao Zedong became the great symbolic leader of the Chinese Communists.

YAN'AN AND THE SECOND UNITED FRONT

The decision to settle in Shaanxi was influenced in part by Stalin's increasing concern about the rise of Japanese power in the Far East. The Russian leader was anxious to have as strong and unified a China as possible to serve as a balance to Japan and provide security for the Soviet Union. On August 1, 1935, during the Long March, the Chinese Communist Party issued a "declaration of war" against Japan and called for all Chinese to unite in opposing the nation's principal foreign threats. The decision was made to seek a base area in northwest China from which the Party could continue to appeal for national unity in opposition to the Japanese.

An unexpected opportunity presented by the kidnapping of Chiang Kai-shek, in December 1936, gave the Communists the additional leverage necessary to extract from Nanjing the agreement for the Second United Front of the Chinese Communist Party and the Kuomintang. In Communist tactical jargon the First United Front (1922–1927) had been "a bloc within a bloc" and a "united front from below" — that is, it involved Communists working as individuals within the Kuomintang. According to class analysis this meant that the Communists worked directly with workers, peasants, petty bourgeoisie, and big bourgeoisie — that is, from "below" — to lead them into support of the Kuomintang. The result of such a united front should have been a bourgeois-democratic revolution, which would set the stage for a subsequent socialist revolution as the workers' and peasants' powers grew. The Second United Front was in Communist theory an alliance, and thus a "united front from above." It called for limited agreements between Communist leaders and those of other parties and for the various classes to pursue certain common but highly restricted goals. The distinction is significant. Neither form of united front was seen by the Communists as demanding a merging of interests or complete cooperation and they interpreted "united front from above" as binding the Party only to the formal conditions of the alliance. It could still build its own class base and subvert the power of enemy classes.

In short, with the First United Front the Communists had been seeking power and advancement in any way possible; with the Second United Front (1937–1945) the relationship was more an alliance between two mutually suspicious governments, each of which had its own territorial bases and constituencies.

During the war years Mao emerged not only as the symbolic leader of the Chinese Communist Party but also as an ideologue in the tradition of Marx and Lenin. Although Chinese Communism sprang from the activities of intellectuals and some of its earliest champions were among the liveliest minds in the nation, the early years saw few doctrinal disputes and nothing in the way of memorable ideological writing. The Party leaders were far too engrossed in mastering the intricacies of Comintern logic and tactics to treat Marxism as a subject of intellectual challenge. Men who had once been trained in philosophy and philology concentrated only on learning about "left" and "right" deviation, "adventurism," "putschism," and the other sins that beset the Bolshevik revolutionary.

In the relative security of Yan'an, Mao Zedong was able to devote more attention to larger questions about Communism in China. This was the time when Mao was most productive, and his essays ranged from military affairs(*On Protracted Warfare*) to political analysis and propaganda (*On New Democracy*), basic Marxist theory (*On Contradiction* and *On Practice*), and sermons and attacks (*Talks at the Yan'an Forum on Literature and Art* and *On Liberalism*). Mao was also busy meeting with foreign visitors and managing the public relations of the Yan'an regime.

Other leaders, especially Zhu De and Liu Shaoqi, assumed the principal responsibilities for military operations and civil administration. Even before the Japanese conquests had reached their greatest limits, the Chinese Communist Party had organized "border" governments that straddled provincial lines, enabling them to overlap jurisdictions and thus exploit the federal or provincial traditions of China. After the Second United Front was established, the Communist Party was supposed to end its propaganda and revolutionary efforts, but it continued to maintain the Shaanxi-Gansu-Ningxia Border Region government, and as early as December

1937, it also established the Shanxi-Hebei-Chahai Border Region government. These "governments" organized the peasants behind the Japanese lines and provided support for the guerrillas. The civilian populations were formed into various organizations that collected intelligence on Japanese troop movements, provided food and funds for the guerrillas, and produced uniforms, equipment, and even munitions. In the rural areas the Communists controlled, they introduced their own currency and stamps and collected taxes. When the Eighth Route Army moved about it had to live off the countryside, and when it obtained food and supplies it generally gave in exchange a form of IOU that would be honored once the war was over and the People's Republic was established. The Red Army thus left in its wake large numbers of people who felt that their interests lay with the establishment of a Communist government, for only then could they hope to be reimbursed.

During the war years the Chinese Communist Party grew not only in numbers but also in political sophistication and discipline. Early in 1942, after America had entered the war and the defeat of Japan seemed assured, Mao Zedong initiated the *zhengfeng* movement, which sought to instill in the Chinese Communists the Bolshevik traditions of party discipline. The target of his ideological attack was political liberalism and bourgeois democratic sentiments. The goal was to create a monolithic party, advanced in the use of political indoctrination, which regularly employed self-criticism and mutual criticism to eliminate deviationist tendencies.

By 1943 the Chinese Communist party controlled millions of people in north China, and through increasingly professional activists it was disseminating new attitudes and styles of behavior. The line between soldier and civilian was blurred, and everyone was expected to lead a frugal and austere life. Workers who labored long hours and asked for no extra pay were idealized as heroes. Army units were expected to provide their own support, as were schools and administrative organs of government. Soldiers, students, and officials divided their time between raising food, making handicrafts, and carrying out their primary functions.

During these years the Party gained extensive experience in both warfare and ruling a rural population. It introduced new guerrilla practices to China, and it upheld new ideals of civilian and military relationships, but much of its energy still had to be focused on reacting to the initiatives of others and coping with immediate circumstances. Mao and the other Communists had surprisingly little to say about the kind of China they were seeking to build. In his *New Democracy* Mao made it clear that, as a good Marxist, he did not expect that government by the Party could bring Communism to China because the country had not experienced the bourgeois-democratic revolution that must precede a socialist revolution. Yet he did say that because socialism existed in Russia the process might be speeded up in China. His discussion, however, dealt with historical generalities and not with programmatic considerations.

Although during the early years of the Communist movement in China Mao Zedong was identified with the most radical view on land reform, during the Yan'an period, when Mao was more clearly in authority, discussions of confiscation were strangely muted. In the base areas it was important to emphasize unity and avoid potentially divisive issues, so advocacy of extreme forms of social change was avoided. At the same time there was no mistaking the direction of Communist policies. Owners of large landholdings knew they had little to gain from the Communists, while the poor peasants saw the Communists as their natural ally.

The Communists' emphasis during the war years was thus less on social and economic issues and more on appeals to nationalism. Nationalism meant not only opposition to the Japanese conquerors; it also involved a historic process by which the rural and interior parts of China were being brought into the national political spotlight. The Communists were extremely successful in establishing contacts with villagers and making them feel that their actions could influence the fate of their country. The years of foreign, particularly Japanese, pressure on China had produced a general awareness of China's limitations, which the Nationalists' propaganda had further highlighted. The Communists at last offered the people something constructive to do: They could support the war against Japan by helping the guerrillas and becoming model, hard-working, unselfish citizens in the Communist-controlled areas.

By the time the war ended, the Communists had greatly strengthened their popular and their political positions. The Party was at last highly disciplined, well organized, and extensively distributed, with cells not only in the countryside but also in all the major east coast cities, where its underground had been active during the entire Japanese occupation. The Red Army had a dual structure of authority with political commissars paralleling the conventional military command chain. The Party's propaganda organization had many talents and provided the people with a steady stream of plays, dramas, speeches, newspapers, and radio programs stressing the themes of nationalism and the worth of the common man.

The Party, however, said little about what national policies would be under its rule. Many people assumed therefore that Communism would bring to China a system more democratic and less authoritarian than Kuomintang rule. Even within the Party there was little sense of what victory would bring. Probably few Chinese, either in or out of the Party, expected the extreme version of totalitarian government that emerged. The Communists had produced idealism and the mechanism of mass organization, but they had only the model of Stalin's Russia to tell them how to build socialism.

CHAPTER TEN

The Means of Ruling

In the summer of 1949, with the Kuomintang armies in demoralized retreat toward the island of Taiwan and Chiang Kai-shek in temporary retirement, Mao Zedong moved his government from the caves of Yan'an to the yellow-tiled Forbidden City in Peking. In June he had gathered the leading Party members and notables who were prepared to support the Communists in a Chinese People's Political Consultative Conference, and on July 1 he presented his concept of the Communist government-to-be — a "people's democratic dictatorship." Mao's mood and his words were confident, to the point of being aggressively self-assured, as he dismissed the rhetorical criticisms he made of himself:

> "You are leaning to one side." Exactly. . . . All Chinese without exception must lean either to the side of imperialism or to the side of socialism. Sitting on the fence will not do, nor is there a third road. . . .
>
> "You are too irritating." We are talking about how to deal with domestic and foreign reactionaries, the imperialists and their running dogs, not about how to deal with anyone else. . . . We must not show the slightest timidity before a wild beast. We must learn from Wu Song on the Jingyang Ridge. As Wu Song saw it, the tiger on Jingyang Ridge was a man-eater, whether irritated or not. Either kill the tiger or be eaten by him — one or the other. . . .
>
> "Victory is possible even without international help." This is a mistaken idea. In the epoch in which imperialism exists, it is impossible for a genuine people's revolution to win victory in any country without various forms of help from the international revolutionary

> forces, and even if victory were won, it could not be consolidated. . . . Internationally, we belong to the side of the anti-imperialist front headed by the Soviet Union, and so we can turn only to this side for genuine and friendly help, not to the side of the imperialist front.
>
> "You are dictatorial." My dear sirs, you are right, that is just what we are. All the experience the Chinese people have accumulated through several decades teaches us to enforce the people's democratic dictatorship, that is, to deprive the reactionaries of the right to speak and let the people alone have that right.
>
> "Who are the people?" At the present stage in China, they are the working class, the peasantry, the urban petty bourgeoisie, and the national bourgeoisie. These classes, led by the working class and the Communist Party, unite to form their own state and elect their own government; they enforce their dictatorship over the running dogs of imperialism — the landlord class and bureaucrat-bourgeoisie, as well as the representatives of those classes, the Kuomintang reactionaries and their accomplices — suppress them, allow them only to behave themselves and not to be unruly in word or deed.
>
> "Don't you want to abolish state power?" Yes, we do, but not right now; we cannot do it yet. Why? Because imperialism still exists, because domestic reaction still exists, because classes still exist in our country. Our present task is to strengthen the people's state apparatus — mainly the people's army, the people's police, and the people's courts. . . .
>
> "You are not benevolent." Quite so. . . .
>
> To sum up our experience and concentrate it into one point, it is: the people's democratic dictatorship under the leadership of the working class (through the Communist Party) and based upon the alliance of workers and peasants. This dictatorship must unite as one with the international revolutionary forces. This is our formula, our principal experience, our main program.[1]

On October 1, 1949, at three o'clock in the afternoon, Mao stood on the reviewing platform at Tiananmen (Gate of Heavenly Peace) Square, declared the establishment of the People's Republic of China, and hoisted the new flag. Government at that time — and for the most part ever since — involved three closely related

[1] Mao Tse-tung, "On the People's Democratic Dictatorship," *Selected Works of Mao Tse-tung* (Peking: Foreign Languages Press, 1967), vol. 4, pp. 415–22.

institutions: the Chinese Communist Party, the People's Liberation Army, and the state bureaucracy.

Since that day Communist rule has gone through several phases. Initially the chief task of government was to restore order and legitimize the new system. The search for order brought about an early reliance on the army for administering the country. The problem of legitimacy produced numerous populist policies, the recognition of minority political parties (that eventually had no independent powers), the creation of large mass organizations for mobilizing specific segments of the society, and above all, extensive propaganda campaigns to influence individual citizens.

The Korean War facilitated the restoration of order and the legitimation of the new regime. In the next phase the principal problem of government was to take up the tasks of socialist reconstruction and economic development. The government had to strengthen its administrative and technical capabilities, which resulted in the rapid growth of the civil bureaucracy. From about 1952 to 1958 the Communists made their most impressive achievements in bringing effective centralized government to China. The bureaucracy that emerged under Party control was the most efficient institution in Chinese history. The government reached down further into society than any previous administration, penetrating into villages and urban neighborhoods where officials in the past had tolerated a great deal of autonomy. Government reached out to encompass all phases of life. Never before in Chinese history, or for that matter in world history, had a government sought to rule so completely and involve itself in so much.

The third phase of Communist rule was the brief period from 1958 to 1960 when the leaders sought to achieve total mobilization of the Chinese population and go beyond the limits they believed the bureaucrats could reach in achieving economic and socialist development. This was the period of the Great Leap Forward and the communes. Whereas in the first years the government had used mass organizations to mobilize public support, beginning in 1958 cadres focused on activities in the places where people worked.

During the Great Leap Mao suggested that China was moving ahead of the Soviet Union in its advance toward the goal of complete Communism. By 1959 it was apparent that the policies were not working, and in the following three "dark years of hardship" there was such a breakdown, especially in agriculture, that famine and near famine occurred in many parts of the country. Governmental authority was solidly in the hands of state and party administrators, however, and from 1963 to 1966 China renewed its economic growth under pragmatic administrators.

But Chairman Mao was concerned that the Chinese were losing their revolutionary commitment. Thus was born the Cultural Revolution that raged from 1966 to 1969 and caused a complete breakdown of administration. The process of restoring order after the vicious factional clashes during the Cultural Revolution involved the introduction of "revolutionary committees" to manage nearly every institution in the country, from schools and factories to communes and provinces. In most cases the revolutionary committees were composed of representatives of three groups: the Army, the veteran cadres (who were usually former bureaucrats), and the workers and peasants (who were most often leftist cadres in the Party). Each committee had its "leading figure" or "responsible official" as chief administrator, but in most cases there was a delicate balance of power, with the representatives of the Army and the veteran cadres trying to introduce more orderly processes while adhering to radical rhetoric. The process of government became more complicated in 1971 and 1972 when Party committees were reestablished in nearly every institution.

After the death of Mao in 1976 and the emergence of Deng Xiaoping as China's paramount leader, the state bureaucracy was reestablished and strengthened. Yet because of factional problems and policy differences, Deng often found himself in conflict with the veteran cadres. As a consequence of this, he frequently called for older officials to retire to make way for younger and if possible more vigorous people. In the early 1980s Deng was still experimenting with organizational changes as he sought to find a means of ruling that might further China's modernization.

The formal structures of government that have emerged under Communist rule have generally been most obvious during periods of relatively systematic national development and have been weakened during such periods of revolutionary agitation as the Great Leap and the Cultural Revolution.

THE ARMY AS RULERS

The field armies that brought the Communists victory in the civil war provided the initial administrative capabilities for the Party. As the armies advanced and "liberated" rural areas and cities, they established military control commissions that maintained public order, arrested former Kuomintang officials, and provided political and ideological guidance for the population. These commissions in turn depended on the organization of the People's Liberation Army. Quite naturally, the military jurisdictions of the five field armies and of the central army command in the area of the capital became six administrative regions, which provided the critical dimension of government during the first five years of the regime.

Although in theory the People's Republic of China has had from its establishment a highly centralized government, in practice the great regional administrative councils became autonomous and in their separate ways sought to translate into practical administrative policies the general policy lines that emanated from the Party and the Politburo. In the early years of Communist rule the administrative regions were declared to be temporary subdivisions, to exist only until the government was fully centralized. By 1954, however, the leaders acknowledged that practicality favored decentralization. In June 1954 the administrative regions were abolished, and effective control was brought down to the level of the province. The number of provinces was reduced from thirty to twenty, the number of counties set at slightly more than 2,000, and the number of villages came to 214,000. In the years that followed, the Chinese Communists were compelled to follow the practice of all previous rulers of China: They had to treat the province as the key unit beneath the capital. Coequal with the provinces (*sheng*) were special cities (*tebie shi*), which included Peking and Shanghai.

In Communist China the provinces are divided into counties (*xien*), districts (*chu*), and communes (*xiang*). Before 1958 the village was the smallest administrative unit, but after the Great Leap it was replaced by the commune. On the average a commune has over 7,000 inhabitants, and a few Party activists manage it. A county is considerably larger, with an average population of over

250,000. From the earliest days of Communist rule, and more so in recent years, there has been a considerable clustering of technical specialists at the county level. Agricultural specialists, medical officers, visiting nurses, special police, and propaganda groups are county officials.

The Party had to look to the People's Liberation Army (PLA) for administrative capabilities, so, not surprisingly, most of the field army commanders became leaders in the new regime. Several were caught up in factional conflicts with Mao and the civilian leadership. Gao Gang, for example, in command of elements of the Fourth Field Army, took charge in 1948 of the Northeast People's Government, which soon became so autonomous that he was conducting his own relations with the Soviet Union. He was subsequently purged and is said to have committed suicide. General Lin Biao, who was Mao's designated heir apparent until he was caught in a purported plot to assassinate the Chairman, commanded the majority of the Fourth Field Army and administered the Central and South China Regional Committee. General Rao Shushi had the Third Field Army and was responsible for the East China Military and Political Committee until he was purged along with Gao Gang. Peng Dehuai, who was to be purged for challenging Mao's Great Leap policies, commanded the First Field Army and administered the northwest.

In spite of the problems Mao had with his generals, one of the most striking characteristics of Mao's rule was his frequent and extensive reliance on the PLA as a means of administering his revolutionary society. Before the Cultural Revolution the PLA was frequently called on to manage the civil government, and after the disorders of the Cultural Revolution Mao again turned to the army to help run the country. Not surprisingly, the effect was to create within the officer corps large numbers of cadres who developed a great interest in political affairs.

One of the most significant changes in China in the post-Mao era has been Deng Xiaoping's determined effort to get the army out of civil government and make it again a fighting force. Deng's efforts to depoliticize the PLA were not popular with the military, but by early in the 1980s he had nearly succeeded in removing the army from the domain of domestic administration.

THE STATE APPARATUS

In September 1949, the Party convened the Chinese People's Political Consultative Conference, which in turn legitimized the establishment of the National People's Congress. This body, which in theory was to be elected by county representatives, established the Central People's Governmental Council or, as it soon came to be called, the Government Council. The chairman of the council was Mao Zedong. It contained an executive body called the Government Administration Council, or State Council, which operated as a cabinet under the guidance of its premier, Zhou Enlai. The State Council is composed of a variety of ministries, generally grouped into three categories: political and legal, financial and economic, cultural and educational.

From the beginning, Communist rule was characterized by two practices: the incessant use of committees and liaison groups, and the integration of the government by giving many offices and posts to the same man. In theory the administrative regions were run by committees that included military officers (who were, of course, Party officials) and civilian officials. The ministries in Peking were staffed by specialists but were constantly being "coordinated" by various subcabinet committees. Coordination and integration were achieved by giving individuals high status in the Party hierarchy, definite commands in the army, and specific governmental responsibilities.

The practice of wearing several hats started with Mao Zedong, who was called "Chairman" because he was chairman of the Central Committee of the Party, chairman of the Governmental Council, and also chairman of the People's Revolutionary Military Council, which controlled the People's Liberation Army. Thus in theory Mao was in command of the three basic institutions of the new regime, the Party, the government, and the army.

In practice, however, during the first fifteen years of Communist rule the management of the government went to the premier, Zhou Enlai, and the management of the Party went to Liu Shaoqi, the vice-chairman of the Central Committee and of the Politburo. When the regime was established in 1949, considerable care was taken to separate the state apparatus from the Party organization. During the early years the principle was well established that the state organization was to be given over predominantly to technical specialists and not to political policymakers. Thus the State Council has never performed as a cabinet, and the heads of the various ministries are implementers of general policies and not figures of power.

The extent to which the state apparatus was made into a narrowly technical and administrative institution reflects a distinctive characteristic of the Chinese Communist style of rule: Policymaking and policy execution are clearly separated. In making this separation, the Communists emphasize the distinction between general policy, or the "line" (*fangzhen*), made by the Politburo, and administrative policy (*zhengce*), arising out of officials' efforts to implement the general line.

Because the state apparatus has been devoted entirely to the implementation of policy, the ministries lack a distinct character of their own. During the first five-year plan several separate ministries dealt with different parts of the economy. Since the Cultural Revolution the number of ministries has been reduced by nearly half. Government officials in state offices have tended to become increasingly specialized, in contrast to the gentlemen amateurs who filled the bureaucratic posts in the imperial system. Officials are expected to implement policies, although Communist rhetoric stresses the need for initiative and for everyone to be an activist. Over the years officials in the state bureaucracies have had to learn to uphold ideals of loyalty and obedience while creating the impression of being imaginative in figuring out how established policies can be carried out more efficiently. They have had to worry about the sin of bureaucratism (*guanliaochui*), the tendency to lose touch with the masses and become absorbed with questions of rank and status. Government officials must engage in constant study sessions to ensure that they do not develop wrong attitudes.

PARTY ORGANIZATION

The key to the processes of government and the behavior of officials is the role of the Party. Although descriptions of the mechanisms of rule have stressed the state organs, and although the army was the most conspicuous institution of government during the first years and again after the Cultural Revolution, the critical factors in the Communist system of government have been the Party and the individual cadre.

During the Yan'an period the Party had been exposed to a stern rectification campaign (*zhengfeng*), but as the Communists moved toward victory there was an upsurge in the number of candidates for Party membership and in the need for skilled and trusted people. In 1945 the Party had 1.2 million members; by 1948 the number had grown to 3 million; by 1950 it reached nearly 7 million, 12.7 million in 1956, and 17 million by 1961. During the confusion of the Cultural Revolution the Party organization was in disarray, but large numbers of radicals were recruited to membership. By 1978 there were over 30 million members, and at the time of the Twelfth Party Congress in 1982 there were nearly 40 million members.

Historically Party membership has required the candidate to demonstrate his loyalty and competence during a probationary period. In rural areas Party members are a distinct elite, numbering no more than 2 or 3 percent of the population. In urban areas, where there are more educated and technically skilled people, the number of members can be as high as one out of every seven or ten people. In the army, officers with the rank of company commander and higher are likely to be Party members.

The basic unit of the Party is the branch committee (*zhibu*), and in theory every Party member belongs to one. In most governmental organizations or large institutions (factories, research institutes, universities), a Party branch provides guidance to and surveillance of the actual hierarchy of officials. The Party chain of command constitutes an invisible inner framework for formal institutions. Each Party member must combine the duties of the office he holds with his higher obligation to his position within the Party. In this sense the Communist Party, even after the victory of 1949, remained a submerged organization, following semiclandestine practices.

The leadership of the Party theoretically resides in the Central Committee, but in fact it is in the hands of the Politburo, and more particularly, in its standing committee. According to the Party Constitution the Party Congress is supposed to meet every year. Its members, elected by the Party congresses of provinces and the special cities, have terms of five years. The Eighth Party Congress, however, held its first session in September 1956, and was not reconvened until May 1958; the Ninth Party Congress was not called until April 1969, in the wake of the Cultural Revolution; the Tenth Party Congress took place only in 1973, when Lin Biao supporters were purged; the Eleventh confirmed Chairman Hua in 1977; and the Twelfth removed him and certified Deng's victory in 1982.

Since Yan'an the Party congresses have generally been less significant than the meetings of the Central Committee and the various plenums at which policy lines have been announced. Strong policy conflicts have occasionally taken place in the Central Committee, which is not always a rubber stamp for the Politburo; but most of the time it is docile.

The Central Committee is composed of leading Party members, who manage not only the Party but also the army and the government. Although it rarely acts as a decision-making body, the Central Committee is the symbol of established authority, and its members derive considerable power and prestige from being identified with it. For these reasons the chairmanship of that body is the most prestigious office in Communist China, followed by the position of senior vice-chairman.

The Central Committee is a sounding board, a legitimizer of policies, and a device for indicating relative rank and status, but real power in the Party rests with the Politburo. In 1949 when the Chinese People's Republic was established, the Politburo had only eleven members. With the Party Constitution of 1956 the Politburo was expanded to seventeen full members and six alternates; at the time of the Cultural Revolution there were twenty-one full members. The Politburo actually runs the country and provides policy guidance for all institutions. Because it is too large to operate effectively, its standing committee of five members is the most powerful decision-making group.

Beneath the Politburo, and responsible for the actual administration of the Party, is the Central Secretariat. Until he was purged during the Cultural Revolution, Deng Xiaoping was the long-standing first secretary of the Party. The number of secretaries at any one time has varied from four to ten. The major task of the Central Secretariat is to communicate Politburo decisions and receive reports from all the offices of the Party. Yet in practice much of its power flows from its management of the personnel of the Party.

Separate from the Central Secretariat is the Party's Military Affairs Commission, which directs military policy, controls the People's Liberation Army, and supervises the work of the political commissars in the army structure. Although the commission theoretically deals with military and security policies, it actually has been an important political decision-making force, especially when the People's Liberation Army played a significant role in governing China in the early days of the regime and after the Cultural Revolution.

Early in the 1980s Deng Xiaoping became worried about the numbers of old men clinging to top posts in the Party. Without a system of retirement, and given the Chinese custom of venerating the aged, there was little prospect of promoting younger, and often better educated, cadres. Paradoxically, the purges that followed the arrest of the Gang of Four had the effect of raising the average age of the Central Committee. Those pushed out were generally in their fifties; they were replaced by older veteran cadres in their sixties and seventies. To carry out his new, pragmatic policies, Deng needed new blood. Thus at the Twelfth Party Congress in September 1982 he arranged for the establishment of a Central Advisory Commission, to be filled with the distinguished elders, who would now have appropriate positions with which they could preserve their perquisites (cars, housing, servants, and the like) and from which they could offer advice without being involved in daily matters.

Even though Deng himself assumed the Chairmanship of the Advisory Commission, many of the oldest Party members refused to join him and instead held on to their active positions. Deng himself held on to the office of Chairman of the Military Affairs Commission and to his membership on the Standing Committee of the Politburo. Thus the Chinese were not quite able to solve their gerontocracy problem.

BENDING INSTITUTIONS TO ACHIEVE POWER

Mao Zedong established the tradition of altering whatever institutional arrangements might be inconvenient to his ruling purposes. In the early years he elevated the importance of the army over that of the state bureaucracy. Then, as we shall see, he shattered the Party itself during the Cultural Revolution and ruled through the Red Guards and revolutionary committees. Mao so blurred the lines of bureaucratic authority that the Chinese came to speak of decisions being made by the "center" (*zhongyang*) without feeling it necessary to distinguish among the Politburo, its Standing Committee, the Central Committee, and any of the ministries at the capital.

Mao's successors have maintained the same tradition. Part of the explanation for Deng Xiaoping's success in outmaneuvering Hua Guofeng, for example, was his bypassing of the Standing Committee of the Politburo and making the State Council the dominant policymaking body. He was able to do this because the Standing Committee was divided, while he could command the State Council. At the same time, Deng signaled to everyone the unimportance of the formal hierarchy of the state and the Party by becoming China's strongman while holding only the amusingly unassuming title of vice-premier. Once his power was consolidated, he arranged for his protégés, Hu Yaobang and Zhao Ziyang, to become his technical superiors.

Another example of the way formal structures have been bent according to the wishes of powerful personalities was Deng's move, before and after the Twelfth Party Congress, to elevate the importance of the Party Secretariat over that of the still factionally divided Standing Committee of the Politburo. This development had ominous consequences for Party discipline: It meant that the policymaking center and the personnel management authority were merged, with obviously threatening consequences for the careers of cadres who might want to question any policy. (In American bureaucracies great care is usually taken to separate the personnel office from the true authority so as to protect officials from improper treatment by policy superiors.) Significantly, Stalin's totalitarianism emerged from the same tactic of making the Party Secretariat an inappropriate policymaking organ.

THE ACTIVIST CADRES

The secret of the strength of the Chinese Communist party is not its Leninist discipline or its hierarchy of unbending authority. It is the concept of the dedicated individual member, the Party cadre. Liu Shaoqi stated in his essay *On the Party*: "The cadres of the Party are the nucleus of the Party leadership and of the Chinese revolution. Everyone knows that cadres decide everything. . . . They are as Comrade Mao Zedong puts it, 'the treasures of the nation and pride of the whole Party.' "[2]

The most startling development that took place as the Kuomintang retreated in the civil war was the sudden surfacing of dedicated cadres in organization after organization. On university campuses, janitors and technicians, students and maintenance workers suddenly asserted themselves and revealed that they were long-standing Party members. In government offices, hospitals, and businesses, people who had previously appeared to be uninvolved stepped forward to become spokesmen for the new regime. In urban neighborhoods, in schools and factories, cadres emerged to guide their associates and colleagues in learning the new work styles demanded by the new rulers.

The ideal cadre (*ganbu*) is a Communist Party member who works with endless vigor and complete self-sacrifice for the goals of the revolution. As an activist he is a part of the elite, sensitive to the rationale of the correct Party line. At the same time he is completely in tune with the masses, aware of their interests and their problems. He is a paragon of Communist virtues, always striving to improve himself, constantly sensitive to his own failings, and completely obedient to the demands of the Party. Over the years the good cadre increasingly became one who was absolutely devoted to the Thoughts of Mao Zedong and an unquestioning worshiper of the demigod who led the Chinese Communist Party.

There are two kinds of cadre: Party and non-Party. Non-Party cadres are activist officials or military officers who lack official status in the Party but are leaders in their respective spheres. They are presumed to have a deep personal commitment to the Communist system. Under no condition would a cadre question policies or discount the goals of the revolution.

The outlook of a cadre is supposed to be that of a professional revolutionary inspired by ideals of voluntary dedication. He works

[2] Liu Shaoqi, *On the Party* (Peking: Foreign Languages Press, 1952), p. 101.

for promotion and is aware that he is part of a system that recognizes seniority and provides a career ladder. He works more for an honorarium than for a meaningful salary, however, and he is prepared at all times to sacrifice his own interests for those of the organization. He is in a sense the perfect "organization man" precisely because he denies that he is striving for material rewards and because he wants to work only for the collective good.

In the early years of the regime possibilities for advancement in the Party existed, but the hierarchy became more frozen and cadres had fewer opportunities to improve their positions. A symptom of the tendency toward rigidity is the practice of referring to cadres according to cohort groups. There are "old cadres" and "new cadres," "Long March cadres" and "Yan'an cadres." Promotions within the Party have been exceedingly slow because its expansion has brought in mainly young people. A major telescoping of generations has occurred within the Party hierarchy.

Partly because of decreasing promotion possibilities and partly because their pay is so low, cadres have been transferred quite freely from place to place to do any required task. The cadre is like a member of a modern army or large bureaucracy in which personnel is frequently assigned and reassigned.

The quality of the cadre's work is supposed to be related to the intensity and regularity of his study and his participation in indoctrination sessions and theoretical study (*lilun xuexi*). During drives and special campaigns the cadre may have to spend almost all his free time attending struggle meetings (*douzheng hui*) at which all engage in criticism (*piping*), self-criticism (*ziwo jiantao*), and mutual criticism (*hexiang piping*).

The ultimate discipline has been expulsion of the cadre for being an anti-Party and anti-progressive person. A less drastic threat has been criticism about one's inadequate work style. A unique Chinese form of discipline and retraining has been the practice of demanding manual labor of all cadres and of periodically "transferring downward" (*xiafang*) — that is, moving cadres to rural areas. Since 1950 nearly 40 million cadres and young people have been sent to isolated rural communities where they are expected to improve their outlook by learning from the peasants. This procedure has interjected into the most stagnant and tradition-bound rural villages of China millions of young and ambitious men and women who are anxious to prove themselves as leaders. Whether this has been effective in raising the ideological level of the Party may be questioned, but there is no doubt that it has indirectly served to reduce the gap between the backward villagers and the more politically conscious urban people.

The Chinese Communists have gone beyond the Russians in making class distinctions less a sociological phenomenon and more one of personal attitudes and convictions. A cadre can by his words and deeds prove himself to be a model proletarian revolutionary, and even people with no working-class experience can prove themselves ideologically. The Chinese, however, have certainly emphasized the values of manual labor more than any of the other Communist Parties. Factory managers are expected to spend one day a week working as common laborers; government officials are called upon to engage regularly in physical labor; and all cadres are believed to benefit from a regimen of some form of manual work. A. Doak Barnett has suggested the interesting hypothesis that the Chinese Communists' near-reverence for manual labor may be related to the work-study program in France that played such an important part in the early days of the Party. Certainly the intellectuals who founded the Party were very much in awe of workers, and all modernizing Chinese have tended to feel that a basic flaw in the ethic of the Confucian scholar-official was his contempt for working with his hands. Whatever the explanation, the fact is unmistakable that the Chinese Communists believe that physical labor is important for creating and maintaining correct political attitudes.

As the Chinese leadership has sought to direct the nation's energies toward economic development and modernization, one serious problem has been the educational deficiencies of the Party cadres. After the Twelfth Party Congress in 1982 it was revealed that less than 16 percent of the nearly 40 million Party members had had more than secondary schooling, and less than half had completed high school. Even more troubling was the fact that the least educated were conspicuously numerous among the younger age groups, many of whom had little formal schooling because of the Cultural Revolution.

Many of the veteran revolutionaries, reflecting sentiments that Mao Zedong once espoused, have remained suspicious of technically trained people, believing that in absorbing Western science and technology they must also have adopted bourgeois attitudes. Thus, even though the country is in desperate need of more modern skills, there are large numbers of Party cadres who distrust educated people and resist giving authority to people with specialized knowledge.

CONTROLLING THE INDIVIDUAL

The key to government's control over individual citizens is not a system of laws but rather a system of collective responsibilities, reinforced by the Chinese cultural emphasis on group identification. Under Confucianism the group was, as we have said, the family and the clan; under Communism it has become the unit or *danwei* and the street committee.

Every Chinese at his or her work place or school belongs to a small group called a *danwei*. Members of the *danwei* must share all their political thoughts in regular study sessions, and the *danwei* controls most aspects of their lives. Permission to marry or to divorce, to change jobs, to move to another town, or even to travel must be given by the *danwei*, and the *danwei* manages such critical matters as the ration cards and coupons needed to purchase such basic items as rice, wheat flour, cooking oil, cloth, and "industrial" coupons. (One industrial coupon is issued to each person every six months; ten are needed to buy a sewing machine, seven for a radio, five for a watch, five for men's leather shoes, and ten to fifteen for a bicycle, which also requires special permission from the *danwei*). Under the population control program, the *danwei* has authority to decide which couple may have a child next.

In the cities there are street committees that check on individuals, report any strangers in the neighborhood, and ensure that all regulations and government instructions are passed on to every resident.

Either the *danwei* or the street committee (and for Party members, the branch committee) maintains a secret dossier on every individual. The dossier not only includes all important biographical information but reports on political attitudes and opinions as well. Wherever an individual may be assigned, his or her dossier will be sent confidentially; one can never escape one's past. After the Cultural Revolution, people were told that all negative items in their dossiers from that period would be destroyed, but of course they could not know what had not been deleted.

If the fear of being labeled a "bad element" by the *danwei* is not enough to ensure control, the state has more coercive means. Relatively little is known about the Public Security Bureau, the Chinese secret police, and the labor camps and jails it manages. As a result of the rehabilitation of many people purged during the anti-Rightist campaign of 1957 and the Cultural Revolution, however, there are now many firsthand accounts of the Chinese *gulag,* with its numerous camps in Xinjiang in the northwest and Heilongjiang in the northeast. Many of China's leading writers have been incarcerated in Qin Cheng, the large jail operated by the Public Security Bureau in a suburb of Peking.

The Cultural Revolution was an exceptional period, and there may be some tendency among those who suffered to exaggerate, but it is still significant that during the trial of the Gang of Four in 1980 the government said that in one forty-day period the Public Security Bureau in Peking beat 1,700 people to death, "searched and ransacked" 33,600 homes, and drove 85,000 people out of the city.

MASS LINE AND DEMOCRATIC CENTRALISM

The stress on cadres' maintaining close contact with the common people, both workers and peasants, relates to the Chinese Communists' concept of the mass line, which in turn is based on the principle "from the masses, to the masses." Cadres are supposed to collect individual and general views of the masses — their complaints and their wishes — sum them up, relate them to policies, and finally take integrated ideas back to the masses and explain them so that the people will see their correctness and will accept them. The cadre is then expected to get people's reactions to the explained policies and to transmit those reactions upward so they can be reintegrated and expressed in modifications of policies, which are then once again explained to the people. The process is supposed to go on endlessly: Cadres tap public attitudes, report them, and seek to formulate policies in light of the public attitudes they have discovered.

The mass line means that policies are presented in ways that take some elements of public opinion into account. The mass line evolved while the Chinese Communist Party was a guerrilla movement and had to live close to the rural people. When the Party came to power, communication "from the masses, to the masses" became far more complicated. National policies had to be made from a national perspective, and increasingly the mass line became a means of instructing people about their responses to given policies. Paradoxically the concept of the mass line, which made a virtue of cadres' contacts with the population, provided the basis for the practice of "transferring downward," or *xiafang*.

The mass line is a generalized form of democratic centralism, to which all Communist Parties adhere in theory. Members of the lower branches of the Party are encouraged to discuss possible policies and pass along their views. When decisions are taken at higher levels, all subordinate levels must strictly obey. The Common Program, approved by the Chinese People's Political Consultative Conference on September 29, 1949, carried the concept of democratic centralism beyond the limits of the Party and the entire government. Article 15 stated:

> The organs of state power at all levels shall practice democratic centralism. In doing this the main principles shall be: the People's Congresses shall be responsible and accountable to the people; the People's Government Councils shall be responsible and accountable to the People's Congresses. Within the People's Congresses and within the People's Government Councils, the minority shall abide by the decisions of the majority; the appointment of the People's Governments of each level shall be ratified by the People's Government of the higher level; the People's Governments of the lower levels shall obey the People's Government of the higher levels and all local People's Government throughout the country shall obey the Central People's Government. . . .[3]

[3] *The Common Programme* (Peking: Foreign Languages Press, 1952), pp. 7–8.

THE PROCESS OF GOVERNMENT

In the first years of the Peking regime most contact between the people and the government came not through dealings with the Party, army, or state bureaucracy, but through a series of drives or campaigns in which mass organizations were established to mobilize various segments of the population. Such specialized organizations as the New Democratic Youth League, the All China Democratic Women's Federation, the All China Federation of Trade Unions, and the All China Federation of Industrial and Commercial Circles were established to link the new government with different groups. Cadres took the lead in organizing the mass organizations, which eventually became critical channels of communication between leaders and the Chinese people.

Early in the 1950s, much time and energy was expended in building the mass organizations, and it appeared as though the regime would seek to rule permanently through these institutions. There was a gradual trend away from the mass organizations, however. Then quite abruptly, after the Great Leap, greater reliance was placed on the basic structures of the Party, the army, and the state. Since the Cultural Revolution, mass organizations have nearly disappeared.

During the first years of the regime, most observers were extremely impressed with the ease of coordination among Party, army, and state. It was universally assumed that the coordination resulted from the fact that the top Communist leaders knew each other well and had worked together for a long time. Their personal relationships seemed to ensure that all the institutions of government worked smoothly.

Since the Cultural Revolution we have learned that more stresses and strains among the leaders existed than appeared on the surface. Policy differences emerged among the top rulers, and some of the erratic behavior of the regime can probably be attributed to such conflicts. Indeed, one of the persistent characteristics of the Communist system in China has been conflict over the relationship between ideological commitment and technical specialization — the "red and expert" problem, as the Chinese call it. This tension has contributed greatly to the retardation of institutional development in China. As procedures tend to become routinized, they are likely to be disrupted by the clash of ideological requirements and technical or pragmatic considerations.

The revolutionary legitimacy of the regime was only slowly routinized. In the early years the continued use of mass campaigns and special drives to accomplish objectives prevented the institutionalization of administrative routine. Later Mao's personal views about the need to maintain revolutionary order by opposing bureaucratic rule prevented standardized procedures.

FRUSTRATIONS WITH THE BUREAUCRACY

One of the most persistent themes in the political history of China has been the frustration of rulers over the unresponsiveness of their bureaucracies. One of the greatest achievements of imperial China was the development of a bureaucracy recruited by competitive examinations, but nearly all Chinese emperors came in time to distrust their ministries for failing to implement their wishes. Early in Mao Zedong's rule there were signs of the same frustrations and tensions.

Mao declared that his bureaucracies were less interested in carrying out policies than in the privileges of their offices. He felt that the cadres tended to lose touch with the people and their problems while they became excessively absorbed with their own rules and procedures. Many times Mao erratically changed policies in order to keep administrators on their toes.

Mao's frustrations with the bureaucracy exploded into the Cultural Revolution. Tens of thousands of officials were sent down to the countryside to work on state farms and communes or to do physical labor at May Seventh Schools. Government ceased to operate in many fields.

One of the main tasks that confronted Mao's successors was the reestablishment of effective administration. During the period from the end of the Cultural Revolution to the death of Mao (1969–1976), the first attempt to rebuild China's capabilities for administration involved establishing revolutionary committees at every level. Gradually and especially after Chairman Hua Guofeng lost out to Deng Xiaoping, these were transformed into chain-of-command systems of authority.

As China settled down after the turmoil of the Cultural Revolution, officials responded by seeking ever greater security for themselves. This led to two trends that were disturbing for Deng and his immediate colleagues. First, there was a marked increase in charges of corruption and of using the perquisites of authority for family benefit. Sons and daughters of bureaucrats and army officers were able to gain various forms of special treatment, including back-door entry into universities. Second, officials became extremely cautious in order to avoid the dangers of criticism. As a result, many citizens could get little satisfaction from cadres, who would put off their requests for help with such standard responses as "It's not convenient" (*bu fang-bien*) and "It's not clear to me" (*bu qing-chu*).

Almost as soon as Deng felt he was securely in command, he began to repeat the age-old complaint of China's rulers that officials were ineffective and that "veteran revolutionaries only end up as monsters and ghosts" when they hold office. Starting in 1979 and gaining great momentum in 1982, Deng sought to reduce the size of his bureaucracy and to bring younger people into positions of authority. In December 1981 he revealed that China had 1,000 officials of the rank of minister and deputy minister, and over 5,000 department and bureau chiefs. Since the time of the Cultural Revolution the central bureaucracy in Peking alone had grown to 600,000 people.

In carrying out Deng's order to reduce the size of the bureaucracy, Prime Minister Zhao Ziyang brought about in 1982 the most drastic administrative changes in the history of the People's Republic. In March he decreed that the ninety-eight ministries and commissions should be reduced to fifty-two; then in June there was a further call for reductions, to forty-one. This was achieved by merging several ministries, retiring the former ministers, deputy ministers, and their key staff members, and appointing as heads of the new combined ministries somewhat younger people. (Officials in their seventies were replaced by people in their mid-sixties.) In the first moves, twelve ministries and commissions were made into six, and their administrative staffs were cut from 49,000 to 32,000. Yet by the time the Twelfth Party Congress met in the fall of 1982 there appeared to be limits to how far Deng's desired reforms would go. The costs were becoming substantial. Retired officials were allowed to hold on to many of their perquisites of office and to draw their full salaries. The promotion of younger cadres did not always produce more qualified ones, especially when it meant advancing people whose education had been interrupted by the Great Leap or the Cultural Revolution. Finally, the problem of ideology could not be entirely dismissed, especially since ideology had been such a central feature of the first two decades of the People's Republic.

CHAPTER ELEVEN

Ideology: Marxism-Leninism and the Thoughts of Mao Zedong

As long as Mao Zedong lived, government in the People's Republic of China was distinctive not because of its institutional arrangements, but because of the use of ideology to justify policies and to control behavior. Concern for ideology and "correct thinking" pervaded social life. Wherever people lived or worked together, in their neighborhoods and their factories, farms, or offices, they were compelled to meet regularly for prolonged "struggle" sessions to ensure the universal acceptance of "correct thoughts."

Possibly the most dramatic change in Chinese society following the establishment of the People's Republic was the obligation imposed on everyone to go through "thought reform," or as it was called at the time, "brainwashing." Intellectuals in particular were required to confess their "erroneous" views and accept the validity of the new ideology. Actions and programs had to be explained and justified according to the principles of Marxism-Leninism–Mao Zedong Thought. In announcing Mao's death the Central Committee chose to emphasize the ideological correctness of his leadership and the contributions he had made to Marxism-Leninism, and, pledged that, "The radiance of Mao Zedong Thought will forever illuminate the road of advance of the Chinese people."

Yet within three years after Mao's death the Party was in a quandary over how to treat Mao's ideological legacy. Many of the urban cadres who had suffered during the Cultural Revolution believed that China's hope for modernization depended on putting aside the rhetoric of ideology and introducing material incentives and pragmatic policies. Many others, particularly the rural cadres, felt a deep need to preserve Mao's Thoughts and to respect his contributions to the revolution. It was finally decided at the Twelfth Party Congress, September 1982, that "whereas Mao made some mistakes," including in particular the Great Leap and the Cultural Revolution, "he was a great leader" and he made a "contribution to Marxism-Leninism and the Thoughts of Mao Zedong." Even before this, at the Third Plenum of the Eleventh Central Committee, in December 1978, when Deng began to consolidate his position over that of Mao's chosen heir, Hua Guofeng, the Party, in deference to the sentiments of the more ideologically inclined members, upheld the "four fundamental principles": the mass line; the dictatorship of the proletariat; the leadership of the Communist Party; and doctrines of Marxism-Leninism–Mao Zedong Thought.

The Chinese Communist Party has come a long way from its doctrinaire past, but it is still important to understand its ideological foundations, in order to understand its history and its current commitments.

THE MARXIST-LENINIST TRADITION

Marxism-Leninism remains the historic basis of Chinese ideology and many of the operational features of that tradition continue to endure or have only been modestly modified by Mao and now by the Chinese Party. Chinese Communist ideology is committed to belief in the "universal truths" of Marxism-Leninism and to dialectical materialism and historic materialism. Class struggle remains for them the prime force of history, and they have a continuing faith in a redemptive historic process. The Party ceaselessly stresses the identification of China's struggles with the forces of history, and its leaders seem to have no doubts that they are the chosen instruments of history.[1]

In the spirit of Leninism the Chinese revere the Party as the most powerful force in changing history. According to all three of

[1] Benjamin I. Schwartz, *Chinese Communism and the Rise of Mao* (Cambridge, Mass.: Harvard University Press, 1951), pp. 202–204.

their constitutions, "The Communist Party of China is the political party of the proletariat and vanguard of the proletariat." Everyone is to work for the Party, protect it against all enemies, and obey its every order. The basic rule of Party discipline holds that "the individual is subordinate to the majority, the lower level is subordinate to the higher level, and the entire Party is subordinate to the Central Committee."

As a Leninist elite party of the working class, the Chinese Party has the classic Marxist-Leninist ambivalence about the simultaneous need for secrecy in leadership decisions and popular participation in mass activities. The Chinese possibly have carried these imperatives of their ideology to ultimate extremes: Their governmental decision-making process is veiled in deeper secrecy than that of any country in the world, and they have gone further than any country in mobilizing their citizens for various forms of participation.

In the spirit of Marxism-Leninism the Chinese believe that there can be only one correct Party "line" and that the Party must be constantly vigilant against "left" and "right" deviation. Although the Chinese have never had the bloody purges associated with Stalin's rule, they do take pride in the number of "opponents" they have unmasked and removed from leadership positions.

The Chinese follow conventional Marxism-Leninism in stressing the need for the "unity of theory and practice." Theory or doctrine should guide practice, but practical experience must in turn bring modifications to doctrine. Doctrine should not become blindly rigid, yet at the same time experimentation without regard to theory can lead to all manner of errors.

As Communists, the Chinese have faith in economic planning and generally distrust the market processes. At the same time, they have idealized decentralized planning and accepted, as have all Communists, the need for private plots for peasants. Since 1981 they have also experimented with limited markets.

Finally, the Chinese adhere to the Marxist-Leninist principle of opposing individualism and encouraging collectivity. Individuals are expected to sacrifice themselves to the good of the state and to sublimate their private ambitions to an overriding desire to "serve the people."

THE DEVELOPMENT OF MAOISM

These standard characteristics of Marxism-Leninism have been embellished over the years by additional themes, most of them inspired by Mao Zedong. The drift of change has been toward Mao's increasingly popularized version of Marxism, a fanatical belief in the powers of the human will, and a form of puritanism expressed in slogans. The trend was accompanied by periods of intense concentration upon the *Quotations from Chairman Mao,* the "Little Red Book," and the elevation of the cult of Mao's personality.

In the first years after the Chinese Communist Party was formed, the problem of ideology was little more than learning the subtle nuances of Comintern debate and developing skill in relating the grand theoretical formulations and categories of Marxism-Leninism to Chinese circumstances. The intellectuals who first formed the Party strangely resisted the idea Lenin consistently espoused, that in "colonies and semicolonies" (China was an archetype of the latter) the historic class conflicts had been distorted by imperialism, and that therefore the fundamental "contradiction" was less the clash between proletariat and bourgeoisie than a uniting of classes in support of nationalism against imperialism. At first the Chinese comrades felt that they were being treated in a patronizing and less than revolutionary way when they were told, for example, that ideology dictated cooperation with the Kuomintang.

Throughout the 1920s the Communist leaders were constantly searching for proletariat-based power in order to become a truly revolutionary force in the traditional Marxist sense. But China had little in the way of an industial working class. During the time that Li Lisan led the Party a considerable effort was made to strengthen and radicalize the trade union movement, but even then power was most readily available in the countryside where the armies were. Lenin's and then Stalin's insistence on class alliance had produced the combined armies under Chiang Kai-shek and the Wuhan government and the Red Army.

In the meantime, Mao Zedong in his classic "Report on an

Investigation of the Peasant Movement in Hunan" said that considerable tensions existed in Chinese villages and that they could be exploited for revolutionary purposes. This discovery, plus the fact that armies in China, including the Communist army, depended almost entirely on peasants, raised the Communists' awareness of the importance of the peasantry. It also provoked considerable debate over whether Mao and the Chinese Communists had left the confines of orthodox Communism and had become peasant reformers. Lenin unmistakably had recognized the need to build upon the revolutionary potential of peasants while maintaining the "vanguard role of the party." [2]

Mao fully accepted the Leninist formulation that the "Party is the vanguard of the proletariat," and he gradually carried this to the point of defining "proletarian views" as "correct Party views." Mao thus contributed to the long-standing tendency of Marxism-Leninism to move away from a strict sociological view of classes; he regarded ideological or intellectual positions as bases of the historical dialectic. In short, just as Marx had turned Hegel upside down and made materialism more important than idealism, Mao turned Marx upside down and reasserted the supremacy of ideas. This feat of Mao was consistent with the historical propensity of the Chinese to attach prime importance to intellectual and ethical considerations.

During the Yan'an period Mao made his most substantial contributions to ideology. At that time he was concerned with theorizing about warfare and Party development. More than any other leading Communist, Mao sought to identify a category of war that could be called revolutionary and to explain the laws of such warfare. He wrote about guerrilla warfare and the importance of obtaining popular support, stressing the need for a close relationship between political and military considerations.

[2] Whether Mao was a heretic in identifying the revolutionary potential of the peasantry or an orthodox follower of Lenin has been vigorously debated by Karl A. Wittfogel, in "The Legend of 'Maoism,'" *China Quarterly* (1960), no. 1, pp. 72–86, and Benjamin I. Schwartz, in "The Legend of the 'Legend of Maoism,'" Ibid. (1960), no. 2, pp. 35–42. Schwartz is correct in saying that Mao was more in tune with peasants than any previous Marxist theoretician had been, but according to strict Communist "logic," Wittfogel correctly stated that peasants would be essential to the revolution in China and hence Mao merely conformed to Communist notions.

In the 1930s, while his armies were engaging in guerrilla warfare behind Japanese lines, Mao was busy writing about party-building and the need to get rid of incorrect attitudes. In books such as *Dialectical Materialism, On Contradiction,* and *On Practice* Mao made his most sophisticated efforts to continue the tradition of ideological and philosophical writings established by Lenin and Stalin.[3] His efforts were generally in the direction of supporting Communist orthodoxy, and indeed from 1938 to 1953 Mao's intellectual contributions were generally consistent with standard Russian Communist positions. He was concerned about the danger that the Chinese Communist Party would be influenced by liberal democratic tendencies that might dilute its professional revolutionary standards. Stuart Schram has uncovered the startling fact that in some of Mao's more theoretical writings of this period he rather freely plagiarized from the works of minor Russian theorists — no wonder the Russians were later to discount Mao as a theorist of Marxism.[4]

Mao specified that the task of ideology was to ensure that Party cadres maintained their revolutionary ideals even as the Party worked with popular nationalistic themes. He recognized that the Party would have to appeal to the masses, which included the bourgeoisie, the intellectuals, and petty bourgeoisie, and the peasantry, who wanted a more just existence though not necessarily a socialist society. He feared that the Party would lose its revolutionary identity as it sought to be all things to all groups.

Thus during the Yan'an period Mao developed a keen awareness that a gap existed between appearances and beliefs, and he worried that cadres' inner convictions would be eroded by pressures toward respectability inherent in propaganda. In a fundamental sense Mao's concern with Party rectification in the 1940s and his fear of revisionism, which became destructively obsessive in the

[3] Because of the gross difference in the sophistication of these three works by Mao, there has been some controversy over the order in which they were written, and even a suggestion that *Dialectical Materialism* must be forgery because it so clumsily explains elementary features of Marxism. See John Rue, "Is Mao Tse-tung's *Dialectical Materialism* a Forgery?" *Journal of Asian Studies* 26 (1967): pp. 464–468.

[4] See Stuart R. Schram, "Mao Tse-tung and the Theory of the Permanent Revolution," *China Quarterly* (April 1971), no. 46, p. 223.

late 1960s with the Cultural Revolution, reflected his basic anxiety about the vulnerability of the revolutionary spirit.

Mao was not the only person who linked ideology with party-building in the late 1940s. Liu Shaoqi, second in command at the time, was also active in pushing for a more disciplined and ideologically sophisticated Party. Liu's *How to Be a Good Communist* was a technical manual that made ideology the moral basis of a highly disciplined Party organization.

In recent years, as a consequence of the Cultural Revolution, it has been suggested frequently that as early as the 1940s Mao and Liu had different points of view. According to this argument, Liu was predisposed to champion order and Party discipline; Mao favored conflict and struggle. A careful review of the ideological contributions of the two men during the early period, however, does not suggest such consistency in the writings of either. *How to Be a Good Communist* contains sections extolling the virtues of contradiction and the need for ceaseless struggle, and it is not hard to find passages written by Mao Zedong in the 1940s and 1950s in which he praises order, patience, and discipline and in which he condemns sins of left deviation and petty bourgeois revolutionary romanticism.

After the Communist regime was established, the chief function of ideology went beyond Party building to guiding the reconstruction of Chinese society. During the first years, until the death of Stalin, when the emphasis of the Party was on emulating the Soviet Union, the Chinese developed a new ideological approach to revolution. They displayed an unquestioning faith in the possibilities of converting all people to Communism and, regardless of class background, everyone was treated as a potential convert to their viewpoint. The result was a vigorous application of persuasion and the development of the techniques of self-criticism and public confession. Ideology became a highly personal matter. Individuals had to reveal their erroneous views, denounce their past failings, and dedicate themselves to revolutionary ideals.

During this period ideological considerations focused also on the questions of loyalty to the regime and commitment to Chinese nationalism. The world was seen as divided between progressive (friendly) people and reactionary-imperialist (enemy) forces. All the subtleties and complexities of Marxism were made to stand for little more than a litmus test for distinguishing good and bad elements in international politics.

China's preoccupation with identifying and distinguishing the good and bad in the individual, in domestic society, and in international politics resulted in the late 1950s in Mao's acknowledgment that even in socialist countries there could be contradictions between true revolutionary feelings and inclinations toward bureaucratization, elitism, revisionism, and the restoration of capitalism. Both during the period of the Hundred Flowers and while Mao was defending the liberalizing tendencies in Poland under Gomulka, China's ideological assumption was that reason could win all intelligent people to the cause of revolution. From the Bandung Conference until after the Hungarian revolution, from 1955 to 1957, the tone of China's ideology was reasonable and moderate.

A more constant theme in Chinese Communism has been the importance of the human spirit in shaping history. The Chinese are unique among Communists in supporting the concept of voluntarism — that is, the idea that revolutionary success is possible if there is unity in commitment and desire. According to traditional Marxism, objective forces of history will inevitably produce the triumph of socialism, followed by the victory of Communism. Proletarian leaders were, of course, expected to push history along its inevitable course, but history itself was governed by objective factors and not by subjective sentiments. Mao stressed the importance of human willpower in directing the course of history. For him the dialectic of history was less the clash of class interests than the contradiction between the spirit of revolutionary progress and tendencies toward selfishness, capitalism, and status.

By the mid-1960s, when the clash between Peking and Moscow was being played out in a series of communications and responses, Mao made explicit his view that in socialist countries there was a permanent inclination toward revisionism and the revival of capitalism. Instead of the traditional Marxist view that progress toward Communism was inevitable and that attitudes basic to earlier periods could be "consigned to the dustbin of history," Mao, in a Confucian manner, upheld a cyclical view of history in which "feudal" and "capitalistic" attitudes can always reassert themselves regardless of how far a society may have objectively "progressed toward Communism." Mao transformed Communist ideology into a morality play between forces of good and evil in which there is a constant danger that evil will seduce even the most virtuous from the straight and narrow path of revolutionary dedication.

Mao gave to socialist morality a sense of omnipresent, if not original, sin. He suggested that man has a permanent potential for corruption because of selfishness. As long as individuals are ambitious they may be captivated by pride. Pride can lead to egotism, which is only one step from selfishness, which (as the source of corruption) is the principal cause of individual, family, and national decline. Despite his talk about the reconstruction of a new and more virtuous society, Mao was profoundly pessimistic about the course of history, suggesting that decline, like death, is certain — unless it can be resisted by superhuman efforts — because of the human potential for corruption stemming from human striving for attainment.

Mao's sense of the conflict of effort, the search for attainment, and vulnerability to selfish corruption is in a sense analogous to the traditional dilemma of the Puritans. They preached that man should be frugal, hard-working, and never slothful, and suggested that virtue would produce material success, but they had no answer for what would follow if their preachings worked. Would success not bring a decline in the striving for virtue? Mao's problem was not the consequence of material success but rather the consequence of revolutionary and political success. He recognized that the hard-working revolutionary of yesterday, having achieved power, was likely to become self-assertive and corrupt because success results in self-consciousness, which readily becomes egocentrism, which increases one's vulnerability to corruption.

By the late 1960s these contradictory tendencies dominated Chinese ideology. The Chinese belief in the importance of the ego reached its highest point in the extraordinary lengths to which they carried the cult of the personality of Mao. More than any Chinese emperor, Mao was revered, eulogized, and glorified. The central themes of Chinese ideological indoctrination became the praise of Mao and the acceptance of the presumably superhuman power of his words. Mao personally encouraged the most extravagant worship of his person and helped to give a semireligious character to his political appeal.

At the same time, however, Mao endlessly emphasized the

need for selflessness, for the depreciation of ego, and for sacrificing the personal for the collective. The Thoughts of Mao Zedong are simple, moralistic principles stressing the need for self-sacrifice and heroic self-destruction in favor of collective interests.

According to traditional Marxist precepts, Mao's Thoughts are more a reflection of petty bourgeois sentimentalities than proletarian attitudes. Although by the late 1960s Maoism was recognized throughout the world as more radical and emotionally revolutionary than conventional Marxism-Leninism, it also was considered more utopian, more voluntaristic, and hence more petty-bourgeois than orthodox Communism. From the classic perspective of Marxism-Leninism the fact that Mao was constantly concerned about the revival of capitalism and endlessly preached against the dangers of bourgeois attitudes is not enough to make his views correctly proletarian. His moralistic belief in willpower is traditionally identified with the petty bourgeoisie.

By the early 1970s, in the wake of the Cultural Revolution, it was clear that the Thoughts of Mao Zedong represented a corruption of both Marxist materialism and Leninist operational discipline. Ideology in China had become a form of personal morality instead of a view of the historical transformation of society. In spite of Mao's attacks on the corruption of Soviet society and the spread of revisionism in the "fatherland of socialism," the fact remains that his Thoughts are a deviation from conventional Marxism. Whereas under Lenin the demands of ideology were to advance the revolution and the building of a socialist society and economy, with Mao exemplary ideological conduct became almost an end in itself. The Maoists insist that they would prefer that China remain materially weak and backward rather than the Party lose its spiritual qualities.

The Thoughts of Mao Zedong represent not just a break with the traditional style of Marxism but also a change in Mao's intellectual style as he became the dominant, and indeed single, ideologue in the Chinese Communist Party. Although Mao's personal impact has shaped most aspects of Chinese Communism, he dominated ideology above all. During the Yan'an period when others were directing the guerrillas, Mao was busy studying and writing on ideological issues. In the 1950s when others were absorbed in the affairs of state-building, Mao, in his style of ruling and reigning, repeatedly drifted away from administrative concerns to devote himself to theoretical questions. In the 1960s he threw himself completely into polemics against the Soviet Union and proved that he had no equal in conducting a traditional Communist ideological debate. From the clumsy discussion in *Dialectical Materialism* of the late 1930s to the Ninth Commentary Letter of the late 1960s, Mao showed tremendous growth in the skills of Communist discourse. Yet his most distinctive writings, especially *Quotations from Mao Zedong* (known as the "Little Red Book"), reflect an earnest moralism that is not characteristic of most Communist writings.

THE FUNDAMENTALS OF MAOISM

In summarizing the principle themes of Mao Zedong's contributions to Chinese ideology it is necessary to appreciate above all that Mao was a man of ambivalences and hence at different times and in different circumstances emphasized contradictory themes. His successors are in much the same position as Lenin's successors in the Soviet Union have been — they can quote the Chairman to justify whatever changes in Party line they are likely to want. In Mao's later years he did stress utopian sentiments, but during his middle years it was generally assumed by Western scholars that Mao's contributions to Communist theory would be more in support of pragmatism. Benjamin I. Schwartz, in his classic study *Chinese Communism and the Rise of Mao,* published in 1951, analyzed Maoism in great detail but gave no hint that Mao's thinking ultimately would be in the direction of romanticizing the revolutionary spirit and discounting technological and pragmatic considerations.

Keeping in mind this inherent potential for ideological accommodation in Marxism-Leninism–Mao Zedong Thought, we can note that at the time of Mao's death the fundamentals of Maoism contained the following items.

Contradiction and Struggle. The major difference between Maoism and China's traditional ideology of Confucianism is that now the Chinese are told to welcome conflict and disorder, while in the past the highest values were harmony and social order. As Richard Solomon has insightfully noted, the most psychologically revolutionary aspects of Mao's Thoughts were his challenge to the conventional Chinese fear of *luan,* disorder and social confusion, and his celebration of the merits of confrontation and conflict.[5]

The essence of Marxism is the conflict inherent in the "dialectical process," but Mao went further and idealized conflict. As a Marxist he agreed that history proceeded out of conflict, but as a revolutionary leader fighting against the conformism of Chinese culture, Mao saw merit in struggle for its own sake.

Class Struggle and Class Attitude. Again Chinese doctrines begin with the classic Marxist view that class struggle is the most important fact of history, but Mao added a strangely subjective dimension to the concept of class attitudes. Mao Zedong expanded greatly upon Stalin's concept that even after "socialism" there would be class conflicts, and in particular he stressed the potential for "revisionism" — the revival of capitalism and bourgeois thought in a socialist country. Whereas the Russians customarily associated the danger of "antisocialist" sentiments with the existence of "imperialism" and hence contamination from abroad, the Chinese have stressed the likelihood of a spontaneous domestic revival of "revisionism" unless constant campaigns are waged against "class enemies."

Maoism is ambiguous about the essence of class. As we have seen, Mao tended to move away from sociological or empirical definitions of class and spoke largely about ideas or attitudes to which he gave class labels. "Proletarian" attitudes often became synonymous with "progressive" views. Yet at the same time the Chinese have made much of the actual class background of individuals. Indeed, class identification has frequently been treated as being of almost a genetic nature, in that sons and grandsons of former bourgeoisie are regarded as still being suspect, while descendants of "poor" and "middle" peasants are treated automatically with favor. This is not simply a matter of justice for the formerly disadvantaged, but is based on a strong presumption

[5] Richard Solomon, *Mao's Revolution and the Chinese Political Culture* (Berkeley: University of California Press, 1971).

that workers and peasants, and their children, have potential talents that should make them the superiors of others in all activities important for the country. Ideology dictates that people with poor peasant and worker backgrounds have the innate ability to understand political situations better than all others, and even people without the favored backgrounds are believed to benefit from contact with workers and peasants.

Human Spirit over Machines. A third distinctive feature of Maoism is the belief in the superiority of people over machines. Classical Marxism treated technology as a decisive factor shaping society and determining attitudes. Marx thought that the distinctive revolutionary quality of the proletariat came from the nature of the factory, which in turn was a product of industrial technology. His dream of Socialist and Communist utopia was premised upon constant advances in technology. Lenin and Stalin continued in that tradition and centered their economic planning on the growth of heavy industries and the building of more machines.

In Maoism machines and technology are depreciated and almost magical powers are attributed to human effort and willpower. Lack of technology can be compensated for by sheer determination and hard work. Maoists are convinced of the truth in the old adage, "Where there is a will, there is a way." Almost all activities take on the character of a moral crusade, and the preparation for any great enterprise requires instilling moral inspiration among the participants.

This feature of Maoism contains a large dose of making the best of necessity. China is a poor country with limited technology, but it does have a large population capable of hard work. The country's economy must be more labor-intensive than machine-intensive. As a result, in the past Maoist military doctrine dramatized the role of the guerrilla warrior, who, armed with primitive weapons but heroic courage, is the match of a soldier with more modern equipment.

The Maoist glorification of human motivations goes well beyond the dictates of necessity and strikes chords in harmony with certain traditional Chinese attitudes. The emphasis upon the primary role of "correct thoughts" and the right "spirit" seem to be modernized versions of the Confucian doctrines about the importance of "self-cultivation" and "correct behavior." As we have seen, in Confucian thinking the solution to all problems begins with the "rectification" of behavior and the need for people to subjectively commit themselves to proper values and attitudes. The particular values are, of course, different now, but the importance of human behavior and motivation remains the same.

Self-reliance. Consistent with the Maoist belief in the importance of human motivations is the value placed on self-reliance and the emphasis on the dangers of dependency. Mao Zedong consciously sought to break what he perceived to be the traditional Chinese cultural bonds of dependency, which he felt prevented China from taking initiatives and solving problems. Mao believed that the Chinese preferred to defer to their superiors, wait for orders, and seek the help of others.

Making self-reliance a virtue in Maoist ideology has affected policy in such areas as foreign trade and regional economic development. The Chinese seem to be wary of becoming dependent on foreign suppliers, especially since 1960 when the Soviets abruptly terminated all their foreign assistance to China. Internally the Chinese have encouraged each region, province, and commune to strive to be as self-reliant as possible. We shall note shortly some of the consequences of these trends toward autarky.

Distrust of Specialization. Maoism departs from traditional Marxism-Leninism in its intense distrust of technical specialization and its assumption that correct political attitudes can compensate for lack of specialized knowledge. Out of the slogan that "politics should take command" has come the view that the advice of engineers, economists, doctors, and other professionals should be discounted. In this respect the Chinese do not share the usual socialist reverence for "science." Chinese ideological discourse contains few appeals to "scientific socialism" and much praise for the insights and knowledge of untutored people.

On this theme Maoism goes against both traditional Chinese thought and the modernization experiences of the rest of the world. In traditional China, scholars were revered and those with more education and more esoteric knowledge were assumed to be the rightful elite, while people without formal education had little hope of getting ahead or of being respected by the community. Elsewhere in the world the entire movement of the Industrial Revolution has been to increase the importance of specialization and the division of labor.

Some Chinese leaders have opposed the anti-intellectualism in Maoism; hence the struggle over the question of "red and expert." They point out that if China is to become strong and modern it must have specialists who have more than just a political education. Mao Zedong himself, however, remained throughout his life deeply distrustful of intellectuals and ambivalent about the value of books and formal knowledge.

Rural over Urban. Mao Zedong's distrust of specialization also took the form of idealizing rural life and regarding cities as sources of moral and political corruption. Mao was, in this sense, more of a populist than Marx, who spoke of "rural idiocy," or Lenin or Stalin, who had little patience with the problems of agriculture in Russia.

In Maoist thinking a rural setting encourages the growth of proper revolutionary sentiments, while urban life favors the revival of capitalist attitudes. This is the exact opposite of the traditional Russian Communist view, which saw peasants as inclined to be antisocialist and interested only in their private affairs. Mao himself had come from the rural interior of China, and the Party developed deep rural roots through its struggles of the Long March and the war years.

This feature of Maoist ideology has unquestionably influenced Peking's policies by providing more support for agriculture than is the case in other socialist and developing countries. Although, as we shall see, the Chinese have not been able to achieve complete equality, they have minimized the usual disparity in income between urban workers and farmers. This trend was furthered by the policy of sending high school graduates from urban schools "down to the countryside" to "learn from the peasants" and to spread their own knowledge and skills to areas where the educational system is less developed. This policy of the "rustication of youth," which we shall return to in a later chapter, is possibly the most extreme manifestation of the Maoist idealization of rural values and distrust of the urban way of life.

The Collective over the Individual. A final important theme in Maoism is a deep distrust of individualism and an unquestioning belief that the interests of all individuals should yield to the interests of the group or collective. This spirit also pervaded traditional Confucianism in that the individual was expected to defer completely to the wishes of the family and clan. In Maoism, however, the collectivity has become the larger concept of the "state" and the "people" as a whole.

Today in the People's Republic the ultimate sin is that of selfishness, and China's heroes are people who have sacrificed themselves for the larger interests. Young people are taught that they should have no personal ambitions, only an overriding desire to "serve the people" and to do what the Party requires.

To find the sources of many of these striking dimensions of Maoism, we must look briefly into the personality of Mao Zedong and examine how he came to embody such distinctive values. By linking his thought to his life it is possible to see his contributions as a living force relevant to his times.

MAO'S PERSONALITY

Mao was born in 1893 on the day after Christmas in Shaoshan village, in an agriculturally rich part of Hunan province. The same region had produced two of the most outstanding mandarin officials of the Qing dynasty, Zeng Guofan and Zuo Zongtang, who had been masterful in suppressing the Taiping Rebellion. Hunan had long had a tradition of political activism, producing a disproportionate number of officials and rebels.

Mao's father was the dominant figure in his early life. Mao Rensheng, a tough-minded, ambitious, driven man from a poor family, had achieved some success in his community. Like his son, his great break in life came from his use of the army. As a consequence of a few years of service he was able to save and otherwise accumulate enough money to purchase a respectable farm. He owned fifteen *mou* (2.47 acres) of land when Mao was young — enough to make him a rich peasant according to Mao's later classifications. Working hard and displaying all the traditional peasant qualities of avarice and insensitivity to the problems of others,

Mao Rensheng accumulated land and established a small grain business by buying up his neighbors' rice crops as loans before the harvest. By storing and selling to the mills when the price was best, he worked to his advantage the two extremes of the annual marketing cycle.

Early in his life young Mao showed signs that, like his father, he had a larger horizon and a broader perspective than his schoolmates at the village school, which he attended until he was thirteen years old. He became a voracious reader of adventure and romantic stories. His mind was filled with the exploits of the heroes and clever bandits of the *Romance of the Three Kingdoms, Sanguo Yanyi* (*San-kuo Yen-yi*) and the *Water Margin, Shuihu zhuan* (*Shui-hu chuan*). He was fascinated by stratagems and deceptions and moved by the struggles of the poor and the dispossessed.

Mao Zedong was the eldest of four children. Apparently he had little feeling for his two brothers and sister. He never spoke of them except to tell how he mobilized them along with his mother and the hired hands to form a united front against his father. He told Edgar Snow, an American journalist, that in his struggles with his father he learned how to manipulate a united front. Mao's mother, an illiterate, superstitious peasant woman, was overwhelmed by her husband and awed by her eldest son. He thought of her as warm and generous, in contrast to his father, and felt he could dominate and manipulate her because of her fear of controversy.

The relationship of Mao and his father was seen by Mao as one of constant conflict, of a prolonged war that the son was able to win because of his greater stamina, his refusal to struggle according to his father's rules, and his willingness to risk all. Significantly, they clashed over two fundamental issues. The father constantly charged that the boy was lazy and lacked willpower and that he made too much of books, which, according to his father, were of no practical value. It is interesting that Mao will be known to history for his exaggerated faith in willpower and human energy and his determination to prove that books and particularly his "Little Red Book" could solve even the most mundane practical problems.

It is tempting to suggest that throughout his life Mao has been unconsciously striving to prove that his father was wrong, and if we carefully read Mao Zedong's own words this thought may not seem farfetched: "Against [my father's] charge that I was lazy, I used the rebuttal that older people should do more work than younger, that my father was over three times as old as myself, and therefore should do more work. *And I declared that when I was his age I would be much more energetic.*" [6] Mao said of books: "I succeeded in continuing my reading, devouring everything I could find except the Classics. This annoyed my father, who wanted me to master the Classics, especially after he was defeated in a lawsuit due to an apt Classical quotation used by his adversary in the Chinese court. . . . *My father considered such books a waste of time.*" [7]

The fact that Mao clashed with his father might not be too significant. But the fact that in a culture stressing filial piety Mao talked openly of his hatred for his father is indeed significant. Mao has admitted that he learned the tactical uses of hate and bluff when challenging his father's authority. He tells of a time when, embarrassed before others by his father's criticism of his laziness, he ran to a nearby pond and threatened to drown himself if his father did not humiliate himself by begging his son not to jump into the lake. (Mao later made much of his prowess as a swimmer.) In Chinese society for a son to threaten to destroy himself, particularly because of displeasure with his father, was an extremely unfilial act; and for a father to have to beg of his son not to act unfilially was the ultimate loss of face. Displaying hatred toward a person and expecting to damage him by threatening or actually harming oneself is a standard Chinese cultural practice.[8] In later years Mao frequently used the maneuver of threatening a foe, such as the United States and the Soviet Union, by daring the foe to attack him.

Since we have only Mao's version of his clashes with his father, it is impossible to judge whether the father was unusually unjust. Parents were customarily harsh and demanding of their

[6] Edgar Snow, *Red Star over China* (New York: Modern Library, 1938, 1944), p. 126; italics added.

[7] Ibid., pp. 127–28; italics added.

[8] Nathan Leites has rightly documented the prevalence of this Chinese practice in "On Violence in China," D-20517-PR (Santa Monica, Calif.: Rand, July 15, 1970).

sons. From Mao's account, his father's demands for physical labor do not seem excessive or out of line with cultural patterns. The pain Mao felt was no doubt excruciating, of the same order as that of a young American boy who is made to mow the lawn. We must wonder if Mao did not exaggerate the extent to which his father mistreated him, particularly when he claimed that his father treated him more harshly than he did his farm laborers: "On the 15th of every month he made a concession to his laborers and gave them eggs with their rice, but never meat. To me he gave neither eggs nor meat." [9] Indeed, in spite of Mao's statement that "I learned to hate him," we must wonder whether the relationship was not more complex, especially when Mao tells about how he and his mother were worried about their father's lack of piety and how "We made many attempts then and later to convert him, but without success." [10]

It is easy to find much in Mao's words to support the idea that rather than being damaged by a threatening father, Mao was self-assured and believed he was morally superior to him. Mao speaks of hating his father and of learning the art of rebellion in his relations with him. What can be inferred from his behavior is that he also learned that those with whom one has an adversary relationship may also be admired and even loved. By threatening to destroy himself by jumping into the lake, Mao learned that his father cared about him. Thus some question remains about how much Mao actually hated his father, just as some question remains about how deeply Mao hated such international foes as the United States.

What is of unquestionable significance is that when Mao was sixteen years old he defied his father and left home, an especially traumatic act in Chinese culture. To justify his behavior Mao stressed his desire for more education. He went to nearby Xiang Xiang and persuaded the teachers to admit him to the Dongshan Higher Primary School. A country boy, he felt ill at ease, and because he was several years older and many inches taller than his classmates, he thought they considered him a bit of an oaf.

Mao's relations with his peers were never easy. During his school years and as an ordinary member of the new Communist

[9] Snow, p. 125.
[10] Ibid., p. 128.

Party he did not develop close associations with his equals. He was a loner. Later in Jiangxi and Yan'an he and Zhu De shared authority, but in fact they were not personally close and usually operated in different areas of China. Mao always tended to set himself apart, and he seemed to feel most comfortable when being treated as a superior, slightly aloof from his colleagues.

As a child and as a young man Mao seemed to be extremely self-assured and yet highly sensitive to criticism and scorn. Not only did he feel that his classmates were laughing at him at primary school, but years later when he was working as an assistant librarian at Peking National University he said, "My office was so low that people *avoided me*. . . . They had no time to listen to an assistant librarian speaking a southern dialect."[11]

By the time Mao completed primary school he had been introduced to foreign cultures and was gradually becoming aware of the backwardness of China. When the time came to enter high school (middle school), he walked to Changsha, the capital of Hunan and a center of new and revolutionary ideas. Here he was confronted for the first time with Western knowledge and, dropping out of school, he spent every day for six months in the provincial library reading in translation works such as John Stuart Mill's *On Liberty,* Adam Smith's *Wealth of Nations,* Thomas Henry Huxley's *Evolution and Ethics,* and Charles Darwin's *Origin of Species.*

After returning to school, his high school education was briefly interrupted again by the Revolution of 1911. In a state of great excitement Mao cut off his queue and joined the army. A strange feature of his brief army experience — particularly in light of his distaste for physical labor under his father's direction and his subsequent demand when he was in authority that all who work with their minds should periodically be compelled to work with their hands — is that in recounting events at the time he said without shame or apology that carrying water was too much to expect of him because he was a student: "I also had to buy water. The soldiers had to carry water in from outside the city, but I, being a student, could not condescend to carrying, and bought it from the waterpedlars."[12]

[11] Ibid., p. 150; italics added.
[12] Ibid., p. 138.

In 1913 when Mao was twenty he entered the normal school in Changsha. During the next five years he participated energetically in a wide range of student politics and became secretary and then director of the Changsha Student Association. Mao also came under the influence of a modern and liberal teacher, Yang Changji, whose daughter he later married. In April 1917, Mao published his first article in the new journal *The New Youth,* founded by Chen Duxiu, the man who was to be the first leader of the Chinese Communist Party. The article was signed with the pseudonym "Twenty-eight-stroke Student" — the number of strokes in the three characters used in Mao Zedong's name; its title was "The Study of Physical Culture" (*Tiyuzhi yanjiu*).

This article, written in his pre-Marxist period, reveals fundamental features of Mao's thinking, features that became increasingly conspicuous as he became older and less inhibited in expressing his views.[13] In the article Mao seems to assume that national strength and military ability are synonymous: "Our nation is wanting in strength. The military spirit has not been encouraged. . . . The principal aim of physical education is military heroism." Mao reveals his pessimistic inclination to see national deterioration as inevitable if not countered by conscious human effort and willpower. He observes, "The physical condition of the population deteriorates daily."

Mao expresses his belief that subjective attitudes and willpower are decisive and the correction of the inner spirit is the starting point of all effective programs of action: "*If we wish to make physical education effective, we must influence people's subjective attitudes and stimulate them to become conscious of physical education.*" By merely substituting the word "revolution" for "physical education," one has a typical statement of the older Mao. One can find the seeds of Maoist voluntarism in the following passage:

> When one's decision is made in his heart, then all parts of the body obey its orders. Fortune and misfortune are our own seeking. "I wish to be virtuous and lo, virtue is at hand." [From the Confucian

[13] The excerpts from "The Study of Physical Culture" on pages 214–215 are taken from Stuart R. Schram, trans., *The Political Thought of Mao Tse-tung* (1969), pp. 152–60. Reprinted by permission of Praeger Publishers, New York, and The Pall Mall Press, London. Italics in original.

> *Analects.*] How much more this is true of physical education! If we do not have the will to act, then even though the exterior and the objective are perfect, they still cannot benefit us. *Hence, when we speak of physical education we should begin with individual initiative.*

We also find Mao as a young man writing, *"The will is the antecedent of a man's career."*

The central theme of young Mao's article is that self-cultivation should be a constant concern. If certain elementary steps are taken, all manner of grand outcomes are possible:

> Physical education not only strengthens the body but also enhances knowledge. There is a saying: Civilize the mind and make savage the body. This is an apt saying. In order to civilize the mind one must first make savage the body. [Why? No explanation is given or thought necessary.] If the body is made savage, then the civilized mind will follow. [The assertion is merely repeated in reverse order.] *Knowledge consists in knowing the things in the world, and in discerning their laws. In this matter we must rely on our body, because direct observation depends on the ears and eyes, and reflection depends on the brain. The ears and eyes, as well as the brain, may be considered parts of the body. When the body is perfect, then knowledge is also perfect.*

The style of logic here clearly links Mao to traditional Confucian reasoning and also oddly to Stalin's heavy-handed style.

A final basic theme of "The Study of Physical Culture" is the extolling of conflict, rage, and physical violence:

> Exercise should be savage and rude. To be able to leap on horseback and to shoot at the same time; to go from battle to battle; to shake the mountains by one's cries, and the colors of the sky by one's roars of anger; to have the strength to uproot mountains like Xiang Yu and the audacity to pierce the mark like Yu Ji — all this is savage and rude and has nothing to do with delicacy. In order to progress in exercise, one must be savage.

Over the years Mao adopted the language and abstract categories of Marxism-Leninism while continuing to preserve the sentiments expressed in his pre-Communist writings. Concern over Chinese national strength, faith in the power of the human will and subjective attitudes, belief in the importance of self-improvement and self-discipline, and an easy acceptance of the importance of violence and the value of being rude and aggressive have in varying amounts combined to form Mao's basic style.

By the late 1950s Mao's advocated policies, with the exception of his polemics with the Soviet Union, were less Marxist and more the views of a man educated in provincial China during the first decades of the twentieth century. The older Mao freely dipped into Chinese history for examples and often used earthy phrases and traditional Chinese modes of reasoning. Above all, he turned things around and made a virtue of either a necessity or a liability. For example, in a speech at the Supreme State Conference in January 1958, he said:

> Our country is both poor and blank: The poor own nothing, and the blank is like a sheet of white paper. It is good to be poor, good for making revolution; when it is blank, one can do anything with it, such as writing compositions or drawing designs; a sheet of white paper is good to write compositions on.
>
> We must have zeal so that the Western world will lag behind us. Aren't we prepared to rectify bourgeois ideology? No one knows how long it will take for the West to discard the bourgeois ideology. If John Foster Dulles should want to rectify his bourgeois style, he would have to ask us to be his teachers.[14]

A most revealing example of Mao's intellectual style was his speech at the Lushan Conference of July 23, 1959, when he was desperately trying to defend his policies of the communes and the Great Leap:

> You have spoken so much; permit me to talk some now, won't you? I have taken three sleeping pills. Still can't sleep. . . .
>
> There are three kinds of words; and the mouth has two functions. A man has only one mouth, which is used, first, to eat, and second, to discharge the obligation of speaking. With ears one must listen. He wants to talk, and what can you do about it? There are some who just don't want to listen to bad words. Good or bad, they are all words and we must listen to them. There are three kinds of

[14] Speech at the Supreme State Conference (January 28, 1958), translated in *Chinese Law and Government* 1, no. 4 (Winter 1968–1969): 10–14. Reprinted by permission of publisher, M. E. Sharpe, Inc., Armonk, NY 10504.

> words; one is correct, the second is basically correct or not too correct, and the third is basically incorrect or incorrect. Both ends are opposites; correct and incorrect are also opposites. . . .
>
> No matter what they say, it is muddled. This is also good; the more muddled they talk, the more one wanted to hear it. . . .
>
> One can't be rash; there must be a step-by-step process. In eating meat, one can only consume one piece at a time, but never hope to be a fatso at one stroke. X consumed one catty of meat daily, but did not even become fat in ten years. That Zhu De and I are fat is not due to a single day. . . .
>
> When I was young and in the prime of my life, I would also be irritated whenever I heard some bad remarks. My attitude was that if others do not provoke me I won't provoke them; if they provoke me, I will also provoke them; whoever provokes me first, I will provoke him later. I have not abandoned this principle even now. . . .[15]

The popularization of the Thoughts of Mao Zedong reached a high point with the publication of *Quotations from Chairman Mao Tse-tung* in 1964 at the beginning of the Cultural Revolution. Over half a billion copies of the "Little Red Book" were published. Indeed, the entire Chinese publishing industry was given over to the single task of publishing the country's most recognized author. This selection of quotations, which have been ceaselessly studied, memorized, and repeated by millions of Chinese, totals about 300 pages and includes some stark and aggressive statements:

> Every Communist must grasp the truth, "Political power grows out of the barrel of a gun."
>
> We should support whatever the enemy opposes and oppose whatever the enemy supports.
>
> A revolution is not a dinner party, or writing an essay, or painting a picture, or doing embroidery; it cannot be so refined, so leisurely and gentle, so temperate, kind, courteous, restrained and magnanimous. A revolution is an insurrection, an act of violence by which one class overthrows another.[16]

[15] From "Speech at the Lushan Conference," translated in *Chinese Law and Government* 1, no. 4 (Winter 1968–1969): 27–43. Reprinted by permission of publisher, M. E. Sharpe, Inc., Armonk, NY 10504.

[16] *Quotations from Chairman Mao Tse-tung* (Peking: Foreign Languages Press, 1966).

IDEOLOGICAL DECLINE AND THE RISE OF DISSENT

During the Cultural Revolution Mao's Thoughts were simplified into slogans which in the minds of the fanatical Red Guards had nearly magical force. For nearly three years Chinese were proclaiming that careful "study" of Mao's Thoughts could solve all manner of public and private problems.

Not surprisingly, after the frenzy abated in 1969 there was a gradual decline in ideological rhetoric in China. In 1973, three years before Mao Zedong died, there was the first sign of dissent against Marxism-Leninism. In that year there appeared in Canton a long "wall poster" written by three young men using the pseudonym Li Yizhe, which suggested that China needed the freedom of democracy.

It was not until two years after Mao died, however, that dissent came into the open, particularly in Peking, at the spot that came to be called "Democracy Wall." In November 1978, as he was preparing for the Third Plenum of the Eleventh Central Committee, Deng Xiaoping encouraged public criticism, which he assumed would be directed against the more ideological supporters of his opponent, Hua Guofeng. One of the most outspoken dissidents who accepted the opportunity was Wei Jingsheng, who called for a fifth modernization, namely democracy, to supplement Deng's Four Modernizations.

By early spring Deng had concluded that the criticisms would have to be curtailed, and in March 1979 Wei was arrested. After a one-day "trial" in November, he was sentenced to fifteen years in prison. By March 1980 Democracy Wall was closed and Deng had the guarantee of the freedom to write "large posters" or *dazebao* removed from the Constitution.

This brief thaw revealed that some young Chinese who had been brought up on Mao Zedong Thought craved greater freedom from the constraints of ideological conformity. But the ease with which the authorities were able to reinforce conformity demonstrated the regime's continuing powers of thought control.

The post-Mao era thus saw an end to ideological dramatics but not to political conformity. Under Deng the Party made several starts at reestablishing ideological institutions, but aside from preaching the slogan, "Seek truth from facts," it made no new definition of official ideology. For years orthodoxy had been based on proclaiming the Soviet Union "revisionist." Once Peking became as pragmatic and as willing to adopt Western technologies as the Russians were, it was no longer clear what defined the proper ideological standards. The need to experiment further to find the right mix of policies for facilitating China's modernization also meant that doctrinal issues had to be kept in abeyance.

In 1980 Western journalists stationed in China reported widespread cynicism, particularly among the youth. By legitimizing material incentives the regime had opened the door for individuals to try to accumulate foreign consumer goods, and there was less talk of "struggling" for utopian goals. What remained, however, was a commitment to conformity and to puritanical standards, which reflect Confucian traditions quite as much as they do Maoist values. For a brief period the leadership encouraged writers to describe the sufferings caused by the Cultural Revolution, in this way publicizing an implicit criticism of Mao Zedong's political thoughts. By the fall of 1981 Deng's associates had decided that such criticisms were going too far and bringing disgrace to the Chinese revolution. Writers and artists were told that they should "serve the people" and not damage national pride. Thus early in the 1980s the ideological vacuum created by the decline of respect for Maoism was filled by a combination of nationalism and Confucian authoritarianism, both of which called for conformity and consensus.

At the Twelfth Party Congress in September 1982, there was a call for a review of the work style of Party members, but no clear indication was given as to what should be the correct ideological standards. Deng Xiaoping's slogan, "Seek truth from facts," was not an adequate guide, especially because it was coupled with the ruling that Marxism-Leninism and Mao Zedong Thought were also the guiding principles of the Party.

In the continuing effort to reestablish a clear ideological basis for the government and the Party, the new leadership did make the interesting announcement that the Thoughts of Mao Zedong were not to be seen as the product of one man but rather represented the collective wisdom of the Chinese Communist Party, gathered over its entire history.

CHAPTER TWELVE

The First Years: Experimentation

During its struggle for power, the Chinese Communist Party devoted little attention to what its specific policies would be if it were ruling the country. The Party's propaganda concentrated on the deplorable conditions of Chinese weakness and backwardness and extolled the puritanical virtues practiced in the liberated areas. Programs and policies in these areas did not, however, provide guidelines for what would be done once the Party was responsible for managing the whole country. Even during the civil war the Communists emphasized tactics instead of describing ultimate objectives. In fact the stress in those days was so much on power considerations that the Party's propaganda dealt more with the question of coalition government than with what Communist rule by itself would mean.

When the Communist government was established, the first concern of the leaders was to create a sense of legitimacy and convince the Chinese people that they would be able to live on reasonable terms with their new rulers. In order to gain political acceptability, they focused attention on procedures, particularly on the claim that the regime was a united front incorporating non-Communist minority parties. Ultimate goals were left vague, and there was some question about whether the Chinese Communists were true Communists.

The Korean War, coming so soon after the establishment of the new regime, facilitated the growth of national unity and pushed the government toward forming policy programs. The leaders capitalized on the menace of the foreign foe and, using appeals to national security, attacked critics as traitors. The need to put the country on a war footing justified a rapid movement toward more centralized control of all aspects of life. The movement toward totalitarianism began with the requirements of war mobilization.

For the Communists, as for all modern Chinese leaders, the goals of policy have been to modernize the country, build up its economy, and reestablish China as a major world power. Because modernization and national power have been the common themes of all these Chinese leaders, the degree of their implementation provides a basis for measuring the relative successes and failures of the Communists' policies in various fields. The initial appeal of Communism for the Chinese intellectuals who formed the Party was that it offered a program to satisfy the universal Chinese desire for national power and wealth. Those who came into the Party after the civil war were eager to believe that Communism might bring China back to its rightful place as a major world power.

When the regime was finally established, the leaders came to realize that Communism did not offer as clear-cut answers to China's problems as had been presumed. A host of practical problems pressed in on them: What was to be done to restore the economy? How was industry to be regulated? What would be the relationship between the cities and the countryside now that they could be reintegrated into a single economy? In the face of such confusion, ideology provided valuable guidelines, for it made the Party discriminate between friends and foes, both domestic and international. In nearly all policies the Chinese sought to emulate Soviet practices, and they enthusiastically cast themselves in the role of "younger brother" following the ways of "elder brother."

Gradually, however, the Chinese began to search for their own path. It is still not clear that they have found it in many areas of life. The almost yearly vacillations and the ease with which they could move to the leftist, radical extremes of the Cultural Revolution and then swing toward a rightist course confirm the difficulties the Chinese have been having.

In addition to the guidance they received from their ideology, Peking's new rulers relied on their military organization to give them administrative direction. The army provided not only the structure for administration and for conveying orders but also a tradition for establishing priorities. The army's approach to such matters as public order, the mobilization of materials, logistics, and even production became the approach of the newly established regime.

From time to time it has been common to speak of a Chinese "model" for development applicable to the needs of newly emerging states of Asia and Africa. The "model," however, has not been a consistent one. Sometimes it has been highly revolutionary and ideological in its character; at other times it has been a "model" of orderly efficiency and businesslike economic growth. Sometimes Chinese policies have been pragmatic, down-to-earth, and based on science and technology; at other times they have been highly idealistic, rhetorically revolutionary, and founded on antiscientific faith in the human spirit.

Mao's personality contributed to both models, although certainly more to the radical one. Some of his colleagues contributed to the other. Before we examine the year-by-year shifts in policy emphasis more closely, therefore, it will be helpful to meet three important leaders who also shaped Chinese Communism: Zhou Enlai, a loyal leader who gave balance to Mao's policies until he died in 1976; Liu Shaoqi, who epitomized the disciplined, bureaucratic approach that, in its clash with Maoism, produced the Cultural Revolution in the mid-1960s; and Deng Xiaoping, who was at the center of affairs in the Party and, although purged in the 1960s and again in the 1970s, emerged as Mao's successor.

THE POISED SPOKESMAN: ZHOU ENLAI

Zhou Enlai was unquestionably the most cultured and sophisticated of all the Communist leaders. Whenever the Party sought to advance a genial and rational front, Zhou Enlai brought into play his quite considerable social and diplomatic talents. In the early years Zhou met with Western reporters and suggested that the Chinese Communists were pragmatic modernizers and not ideological fanatics. During World War II Zhou was stationed in the Kuomintang capital of Chongqing and carried out public relations activities for the Communists. After the Communists came to power Zhou played a leading role whenever Peking sought to beguile others. He emerged in the post–Cultural Revolution scene when

Peking was anxious to gain respectability and to suggest that nothing was out of order. With equal skill he carried out conversations with young American students and table tennis players, with correspondent James Reston and President Nixon's special assistant Henry Kissinger, and with Nixon himself. His personal skills, however, were never matched by actual power. His strength came almost entirely from his personality.

Zhou Enlai was born in 1898 in Huai'an, Jiangsu. His father, a member of the local gentry and owner of a small retail business, passed the initial provincial civil service examinations but never served in government. His mother was well educated for a Chinese woman of her generation. While Zhou was a small boy his father died, and during the subsequent years of his childhood he lived with various relatives in material comfort but with considerable loneliness. First he was sent to his grandfather in the ancestral home in Jiangsu, and then he went to Mukden to be with his uncle, a police official. After primary school he was sent to Tianjin to attend middle school. During these school years he became increasingly nationalistic and began to write essays about how to make China strong again. When he graduated in 1917, his uncle provided funds for him to go to Japan. He became a special student at Waseda University in Tokyo and then attended Kyoto University, where he first encountered Marxist economic theory.

Zhou became an active leader among the Chinese students in Japan. When news of the May Fourth Movement reached Kyoto he returned to Tianjin, enrolled at Nankai University, and was soon deeply involved in radical student politics. He traveled regularly to Peking to take part in the Marxist study group organized by Chen Duxiu and Li Dazhao. He attracted the attention of the Tianjin police and was arrested, but the university president persuaded the authorities to release him on the grounds that it was absurd to take seriously the radicalism of students from good families. Zhou next joined a group of students leaving for France on a work-study program. He never enrolled in any school in France but rather became a full-time professional political activist, working among the Chinese in Paris and Berlin and establishing the European headquarters of the Chinese Communist Party. Zhou was in Europe, mainly Paris, from 1920 until the summer of 1924, absorbed with the problems of unifying all the factions of left-wing Chinese student politics and propagandizing for the unification of China.

During these critical years in his intellectual development, Zhou did some writing of an uninspired nature, but mainly he was learning the art of bringing people together and conciliating different points of view while making sure that egos were not too seriously damaged. These were the skills Zhou would contribute to the leadership of the Chinese Communist Party. He developed a strong instinct for practical solutions and for making any position he advocated appear to be eminently reasonable. He learned never to argue from passion or by manipulating the passions of others. His style made it possible for him to work with many kinds of people. When he returned to China he became the deputy director of the political department of the Whampoa Military Academy, of which Chiang Kai-shek was commandant. Just before the Northern Expedition began, Zhou Enlai slipped into Shanghai and took the lead in organizing the trade unions that took over the city when Chiang's troops reached the outskirts. When Chiang sent his soldiers against the workers because they failed to relinquish their Soviet-supplied arms, Zhou was captured. Again he was able to so impress his captors with his reasonableness and decency that they released him. It has been surmised that the Communist hero Kyo Gisors in André Malraux's novel of the Shanghai events, *Man's Fate,* was modeled on Zhou Enlai.

During the next few months Zhou was consistently a halfstep behind events. He was never held responsible for anything that happened but benefited from always having been on the scene. He got to Wuhan just as the government there was collapsing. He went to Nanzhang just as the uprising there was being carried out. He was part of the Autumn Harvest uprisings but was not involved in the planning that led to failure. Stricken with malaria and shipped to Hong Kong for recovery, he avoided the issues of the split between the comrades in Shanghai and those in Jiangxi. He recovered in time to go to Moscow as a delegate to the Sixth Party Congress and thus became a member of the Politburo. He spent nearly two years in Moscow and became one of the most knowledgeable of the Chinese Communists on Comintern affairs. He also was in Shanghai working with the Returned Students there, but once again he left at the critical moment and went to Jiangxi to join Mao and Zhu De. He was a new arrival at the Ruijin conference of November 7, 1931, which elected Mao chairman of the Chinese

Soviet Republic. Zhou was likewise on the scene when the Long March took place, even though in previous years he had been closer to other factions of the Party. Mao benefited greatly by winning Zhou's support for his claim to leadership of the Party. Zhou had had more experience than any other Chinese in both European and international Communist affairs and was capable of legitimizing and giving professional respectability to Mao's claims.

When the Red Army reached Yan'an, Zhou Enlai became the chief negotiator with all non-Communist forces. It was he who dealt with the forces of Zhang Xueliang, particularly during the Xian (Sian) incident, when Chiang Kai-shek was kidnapped. Thus he set the stage for creating the united front to oppose Japan, but soon afterward reestablished his orthodox Communist credentials by spending half a year in Moscow. He returned to China in 1939 and went to Chongqing to be the principal Chinese Communist representative in dealings with the Nationalist government and Western officials and unofficial representatives.

Zhou Enlai's remarkable talent for reasonableness and lack of passion unquestionably helped to create the impression during World War II that the Chinese Communists were peasant reformers and not professional revolutionaries. After the defeat of Japan, Zhou continued to describe the Chinese Communist Party as moderate and democratic in contrast to the backward and venal Kuomintang. Those who observed Zhou during the period when General George Marshall was seeking to negotiate a coalition government judged him as either a devious influence or a sophisticated and reasonable man — and in either case a man who could not be a fanatical Communist. People generally discounted his radicalism, just as they had when he had been arrested in Tianjin and Shanghai.

After the Party came to power Zhou Enlai regularly sided with strength in Party councils, but publicly he was just as regularly seen as the voice of reason. When the Chinese Communists sought to create an international image of revolutionary zeal, Zhou was inconspicuous. When the image was one of wisdom and sound programs, Zhou dominated the scene. During the brief period in which China's policies conveyed the Bandung spirit of cooperation with Afro-Asian states, Zhou Enlai represented Peking. He carried Chinese diplomacy into Africa. Wherever he appeared it was almost unthinkable to identify him and China with foolish radicalism.

People have always found it hard to believe that anyone with his poise and genial sophistication could be a fanatical Communist.

In the Party's inner councils Zhou performed much the same role. He was consistently the conciliator and the unfailing champion of legitimate authority. As premier he was the spokesman for the administrative departments of the government. Indeed, he was the leading bureaucratic administrator of the regime. Yet when the Cultural Revolution turned against "bureaucratization," Zhou was somehow not selected as a leading target of the radicals, for just as constituted authority always found it hard to take Zhou's radicalism seriously, so radical dissidents refused to treat him as a serious enemy. Consequently, Zhou had remarkable survival capacity over the years. He added nothing to the ideological development of Communism but was a critical figure in providing a pragmatic basis for national policies.

THE PARTY TECHNICIAN: LIU SHAOQI

In contrast to Zhou Enlai, Liu Shaoqi, who was also a professional organizer and administrator, was always considered a challenge to Mao, in spite of the fact that he consistently sang Mao's praises more conspicuously than Zhou. While Mao Zedong was concentrating on ideological matters and becoming an object of veneration, and while Zhou Enlai was becoming a paragon of wise reason, Liu Shaoqi was learning how to be an impersonal revolutionary, dedicated to building the Party in the Bolshevik tradition. Because of his concern with Party matters, Liu became the administrator of Party policies. His power derived from his appointment of officials, and he became the supreme organization man of Chinese communism.

Liu Shaoqi was born in 1900 only a few miles from Mao Zedong's native village in Hunan. His father, like Mao's, was a hard-working and relatively successful owner of a small farm. Liu, the youngest of nine children, was his parents' favorite. He developed early a sense of group loyalty and understood the need for contributing to a collective cause without expecting public recognition.

In 1916 Liu went to Changsha for advanced education and enrolled in the same normal school that Mao Zedong attended. He was soon caught up in the radical currents that had influenced Mao, and on graduation he hoped to go to France on the work-study program in which Zhou Enlai had participated. Instead, he returned to the Hunan countryside and joined the program Mao had worked on. Then he went to Shanghai to learn more about socialism. In contrast to Mao, he became seriously committed to learning the Russian language in order to study Communism. The Comintern recognized his ambition and sent him to Moscow for two years just at the time the Chinese Communist Party was being formed.

By the time he returned to China to work with labor unions in Shanghai and Canton he was more knowledgeable about the day-to-day workings of the Communist Party than either Mao or Zhou. He had learned the Bolshevik tradition of party discipline and the need for organization if objectives were to be realized. He soon became one of the most skilled secret operators in the Party. Using a variety of aliases, he organized workers and students in the Kuomintang and, later, in the Japanese-occupied territories.

During the war with Japan, when Mao was devoting his attention to ideological writings in Yan'an, Liu was ceaselessly traveling about, organizing the administration of the guerrilla territories and building the structure of the Party. While Mao was concentrating on making philosophical contributions to Marxism-Leninism, Liu was dealing with the personalites who made up the Party, learning about the capabilities and limitations of each. Mao's attention was on abstract theories of warfare and revolution. Zhou's was on public relations with the outside world. Liu's was entirely on the internal problems of party-building and the practical problems of administration and personnel management.

Liu's contributions to ideological writings were in this same spirit. In July 1939, at the Institute of Marxism-Leninism at Yan'an he delivered a speech that was later published as *How to Be a Good Communist*. Much of this important book is devoted to nuts-and-bolts questions of Party membership and indoctrination, but it also included an important theoretical contribution: In an underdeveloped, agrarian society, such as China, with so few industrial workers, it is particularly important to use persuasion and seek to indoctrinate people of all class backgrounds in order to convert them into disciplined Party members. Liu emphasized the need for continuous propaganda and indoctrination to win over all kinds of people. In this sense Liu provided a theoretical basis for Mao's voluntarism.

At the time the Communist regime was established Liu made a second important theoretical contribution. He suggested that the Chinese Revolution was distinct and should serve as a model for the rest of Asia. In doing so, he advanced the idea that Mao had made creative additions to Marxism and should be recognized as coequal with Stalin. With Liu publicly praising Mao, it was easy for Mao to adopt a modest posture.

Liu's greatest verbal contribution to Chinese Communism was his praise of Mao as a theoretician; his chief pragmatic contribution, however, was his firm administration of the personnel of the Party. During the first decade of Communist rule his style of vocally glorifying the "Helmsman" while quietly administering the Party worked well. The result was the image of Chinese Communism in the 1950s as a harmonious balance of talents, consisting of the theoretical rhetoric of Mao, the public relations expertise of Zhou, and the administrative and disciplinary efficiency of Liu. But by the mid-1960s the strain between ideological aspirations and practical possibilities became great. The Cultural Revolution became, in effect, a struggle between the Mao and the Liu styles of Communism.

DENG XIAOPING: MASTERFUL TACTICIAN AND PRAGMATIC LEADER

No one other than Liu Shaoqi was vilified more than Deng Xiaoping (Teng Hsiao-p'ing) during the Cultural Revolution. But he proved to be the master tactician of them all, first by his swift advancement in the early years of the Party, and second by his astonishing success in being the only Politburo member in any Communist Party to have been purged — not just once, but twice — and to have regained that exalted position. Finally, he skillfully outmaneuvered all who would have been Mao's successors and became the supreme leader, diverting China's course from Mao's vision to a more pragmatic and technologically sound process of modernization.

Born in 1904 in Guang'an in Sichuan province into what Red Guards were later to call a "big feudal landlord family," Deng completed only part of high school before entering a year's work-study program in France at age fifteen. In 1920 Deng went to Lyons, but there is no record that he attended school there or that he learned any industrial skills. Instead he focused his considerable energies on the political life of the Chinese student community in France, joining the Chinese Socialist Youth League in 1922 and the Chinese Communist Party in 1924. In France he worked with Zhou Enlai and picked up the first of his many Party epithets, "doctor of mimeographing," because of his enthusiasm for publications. During the Cultural Revolution he was to be stigmatized by the Red Guards as a "capitalist roader," a "demon," and a "freak," but first he was to make his rapid move upward in the Party hierarchy.

On his way back from France in 1926 Deng made the first of his many visits to Moscow, where he spent nearly a year at the Sun Yat-sen University, at which revolutionaries were trained for work in the "colonies and semicolonies." While there he was apparently assigned to work with the warlord general Feng Yuxiang, who was also in Moscow at the time. On returning to China he worked as a political officer in Feng's Guominjun Army. In that capacity he was associated with Wei Gungzhi, who would become the wife of Ye Jianying. That fact may in part explain Deng's tolerance of the Old Marshall's determination to cling to power in his last years. When Feng broke with the Communists in 1927 and joined Chiang's Nationalist government, Deng moved to Shanghai to work for two years in the underground movement.

In 1929 Deng left the Party headquarters in Shanghai and sought unsuccessfully to establish a Seventh Red Army in Guangxi. The next year he joined Mao Zedong's forces and became the editor of the principal newspaper in the guerrilla base area. Deng participated in the Long March, and during the Japanese war he worked mainly as a political commissar, training propaganda workers.

The Communist victory over the Nationalists found Deng back in Sichuan as the secretary of the Southwest Military and Administrative Committee and a member of the Central Governmental Council and the Central Military Affairs Commission. In

1952 he was transferred to Peking to become Zhou Enlai's principal vice-premier, and in March 1955 he became the Secretary General of the Party, a post he was to hold for the next twelve years, until he was purged in the Cultural Revolution.

As Secretary General he became the key person involved in managing Party personnel and determining the careers of cadres. He drew up the reports that led to the purging of Gao Gang and Rao Shushi and to the Anti-Rightist Campaign (1957–1958) that sent several million intellectuals to the countryside or to labor camps. He did not, however, play a significant role in either the Great Leap or the subsequent purging of Peng Dehuai. Indeed, he had to depart early from the Lushan Conference, which decided Peng's fate, because, unlikely as it may seem, he broke his leg while playing ping-pong.[1]

Deng apparently had a complicated love-hate relationship with the Soviet Union. From 1949 to 1955 he served on the executive committee of the Sino-Soviet Friendship Association. In September 1954, however, he was involved in tough aid negotiations with Nikita Khrushchev, and in 1960, when he accompanied Mao to Moscow, he publicly called Khrushchev a liar. Deng was also the number two person in the Chinese delegation to the Soviet Twentieth Party Congress, at which Khrushchev denounced Stalin. This experience may have made him suspicious of the cult of personality as subsequently practiced by Mao Zedong, and inclined him more toward collective leadership practices. Deng was directly involved in the debates that led to the Sino-Soviet break, and in July 1963 he had two weeks of face-to-face exchanges with M. A. Suslov, the Soviet Union's leading ideologue. After returning from his second purging and gaining dominance over the Chinese political system, Deng took steps to lessen Sino-Soviet tensions. In 1979 he unexpectedly released a Soviet helicopter crew who had trespassed into Chinese territory, and in 1982 he sanctioned the thaw in relations. Just as Mao had an apparent love-hate feeling for the United States, and was obsessed with trying to get Washington to admit its mistreatment of China, Deng seems to have much the same feeling toward the Soviet Union.

[1] Roderick MacFarquhar, "Showdown at Lushan," in *The Origins of the Cultural Revolution*, vol. 2, in preparation.

THE VINTAGE YEARS OF CHINESE COMMUNISM

Nothing suggests the restless experimentation and the variety of perspectives within the Chinese leadership more vividly than the kaleidoscopic changes in posture and policies throughout the years. Specific years evoke quite different images of Chinese activities. 1951 — mass organizations are absorbed with the Three Antis Movement and the Resist America, Aid Korea Campaign. 1955 — Zhou Enlai advances the Bandung spirit abroad, while at home rational and vigorous programs are undertaken to socialize industry and agriculture. 1958 — the Great Leap begins, with the frantic efforts to "catch up with Great Britain" and create communes everywhere. 1961 — China is afflicted with famine but aggressively denounces the relative prosperity of the Soviet Union. 1966 — the Cultural Revolution and the madness of the Red Guards begin.

Each year since 1949 has been distinctive. Instead of following trends and counting on incremental developments, Chinese leaders have been striving for dramatic solutions. Or, we can hypothesize, instead of a unified leadership there has been a series of struggles.

The Chinese Communists speak of distinct stages in the history of their regime. The first, "Reconstruction," commenced with the founding of the government and the end of the civil war in 1949 and lasted until the end of 1952 when order was established. From 1953 to 1957, the "Period of Transition to Socialism," came the collectivization of agriculture, the start of the first five-year plan, and the beginning of state-supervised industrialization.

The third stage, "Socialist Construction," extended over the Great Leap years of 1958 to 1960 and involved the introduction of communes. The fourth stage is least discussed in Communist literature. It is referred to as the "Period of Readjustment," after the Great Leap, in which the country experienced an extremely severe depression and confronted the prospect of striving for economic development alone, without Soviet or any other foreign assistance. Finally, the Chinese talk of a stage of "Renewed Class Struggle and Socialist Education Campaigns," which began in 1962 and lasted throughout the Cultural Revolution. Thereafter the Chinese have not been able to classify their history because the changes began to come too quickly.

The amount of vacillation in Communist policies and practices was far greater than the number of stages and is best revealed in a year-by-year review of the Communist era.

1949: THE EXHILARATION OF CONQUEST

When, after years of struggle, the Communists finally came to power in October 1949, the Chinese still did not know what to expect. People were ready for change after years of turmoil, but were not sure whether they could trust their new rulers. In their search for legitimacy the Communists were paternalistic and constructive toward their supporters and ruthless and unforgiving toward those who defended the old order. During the first year the Party needed a drastic increase in membership, so it placed heavy emphasis on recruiting and welcoming new people, who were almost without exception young. Students and young people were identified as the natural supporters of the regime and were encouraged to assume leadership roles and to "correct" the thoughts and behavior of their elders. At the same time, in spite of the unquestioned victories of the People's Liberation Army, the regime was constantly uncovering "enemies" who had to be exterminated so that they might not destroy the new order. There was a blend of high expectation and fear throughout China.

The militant spirit of the new regime was heightened by the fact that administrative powers in the local areas were largely the responsibility of the political cadres in the People's Liberation Army who for years had been providing political guidance to the soldiers. These cadres strongly emphasized the importance of disciplined organizational behavior and saw the problem of ordering Chinese society as the same as maintaining morale and professional discipline within the army.

In the first year membership in mass organizations and united front groups was encouraged. In its search for legitimacy and acceptance the Party insisted that "minority" and "democratic" parties were supporting the new government, which they characterized as a coalition of Communists and non-Communists. But in less than two years most of the concern for "minority" parties disappeared, even though in 1949 the Communists had gone to great lengths to suggest that non-Communist elements would have a political future in China.

The most significant domestic issue was land reform. In the rural areas liberation involved the establishment of "people's courts." Landlords were brought before them and in highly emotional scenes were charged with all manner of private sin. The assembled crowd would decide if the landlord's land should be taken. Cadres indirectly manipulated these proceedings and usually claimed that in punishing the landlord they were only carrying out the passionate will of the people. In theory land redistribution was based on regulations that classified rural residents into five categories: landlord, rich peasant, middle peasant, poor peasant, and farm hand. Rich peasants worked part of their land and rented part; middle peasants owned all the land they worked; poor peasants rented some or all of the land they worked. People's tribunals were established to help in classifying people and to right previous wrongs.

By beginning with land redistribution and only later moving toward agricultural collectivization, the Chinese avoided the trauma that the Soviets experienced in eliminating the kulaks. The regime seemed to be promising that the tillers of the soil would indeed own their own land and that the Peking rulers were land reformers and not dedicated Communists. Between 1 million and 2 million landlords, few of whom could have owned more than a dozen or so acres, were executed during the land reform movement, which lasted into 1952.

1950: THE KOREAN WAR AND THE FOREIGN ENEMY

Only one year after the regime was established, Chinese troops were fighting in Korea in support of the Communist North Korean government. Chinese intervention against American troops marching toward the Yalu River did much to enhance the Communists' prestige, for this was the first time in modern history that Chinese armies were able to engage in a great-power conflict beyond Chinese soil. The war also marked the high point of Chinese dependence on the Soviet Union. The regime was seeking to emulate Soviet practices in nearly every phase of domestic life. At the universities Russian textbooks and Russian procedures replaced Western ones, and in government and industry Russian advisors were active. The Chinese army, resupplied with Russian equipment during the war, was transformed from an overgrown guerrilla force into a modern army.

During 1950 the Party instituted intensive programs of thought reform, particularly among the intellectuals. Professors at the major universities were required to write detailed autobiographical confessions in which they exposed their former antisocial and bourgeois thoughts and pledged to change their views. Indoctrination programs were established for all who were in any way identified with the Nationalist regime. Self-criticism and mutual criticism sessions were introduced into schools, neighborhoods, and places of employment.

Among domestic policies, the land reform program continued to dominate attention, but in addition to it were various bandit suppression campaigns against Kuomintang remnants and spy cases against individuals identified as inadequately loyal or found in suspicious circumstances. In the spring of 1950, before the Korean War, the regime had promulgated the marriage reform law, which provided equality for women, granting them the right to divorce and to consent to marriage. Marriage reform was accompanied by extensive programs involving women in all manner of public activities.

1951: THE MASS CAMPAIGNS

Although Peking maintained the posture that only Chinese "volunteers" were fighting in Korea, a sense of national mobilization for war existed throughout China. On every occasion Chinese leaders professed their complete dedication to the Communist bloc, under the leadership of the Soviet Union. Within China the number of Soviet technicians increased, and the Party pressed its cadres into every community. Probably at no time in modern history was China as united as it was during the years of the Korean conflict.

The Communist domestic innovations began to cause some internal problems, however. In March 1951 the leadership initiated the Party rectification campaign to tighten discipline over cadres, many of whom were being carried away with self-importance. By December 1951 the problem of maintaining standards of leadership had become so severe that it was necessary to expose all ranks of officialdom to vigorous self-examination. The result was the Three Antis Movement, directed against corruption, waste, and bureaucratization. The basis of the Three Antis Movement was the assumption that newly elevated officials were prone to act in selfish and antisocialist ways. The attack on Party and government officials was balanced with a continuing campaign against counterrevolutionaries who were presumably infiltrating the Party.

In the meantime the whole country was caught up in the Resist America, Aid Korea Campaign. Each day in every school, children were exposed to political instruction and dramas accentuating the themes of nationalism, world Communist solidarity, and anti-Americanism. In factories and offices, time was devoted to daily political sessions. At night sessions in the neighborhood or the city block people could manifest their feelings of solidarity with the government.

Near the end of 1951 the regime started the Five Antis Campaign, directed at individuals from whom money was extracted to help pay the costs of the Korean War. The attack was specifically directed against merchants and manufacturers who had been allowed to continue operations. Their capital was expropriated in the name of justice for one of five sins: bribery, tax evasion, theft of state assets, cheating in reporting labor or materials costs, and stealing state economic information. Company books were examined, and officials were publicly humiliated. Nearly 500,000 commercial and industrial establishments were attacked, and the businessmen found guilty lost their assets to the state. Nationalization and expropriation of businesses, particularly small firms, were justified not in ideological terms but by moral and ethical criticism and by appeals to nationalism at a time when the country was at war.

1952: THE BEGINNING OF PLANNING

Truce talks for the Korean War began in July 1951 and continued throughout 1952. Fighting also continued, but at a reduced level. The excitement of the war and the shrill propaganda campaigns, such as that of accusing the United States of germ warfare, died down by 1952. The Five Antis Campaign continued, however, and internal control in the form of indoctrination and self-criticism sessions became standardized. People were learning to use the vocabulary of Communist rhetoric.

The drive against intellectuals intensified, and reforms in education were designed to eliminate any remaining attraction to the liberal arts. Education was expected to be functionally relevant to the building of state power.

Above all, 1952 was notable for the new emphasis on economic policy. At the end of the year the first five-year plan was announced. All the Party's capabilities for propaganda and agitation were directed to increasing production. The earlier emphasis on social and economic equality and justice was replaced by the theme that everyone should sacrifice for the economic growth of the state and abjure a higher individual standard of living. The five-year plan was modeled on the Soviet pattern of giving primacy to heavy industry at the expense of agriculture and consumer interests.

Prior to 1952 the Chinese Communists were considered by their supporters to be dedicated primarily to eliminating the evils of traditional Chinese social life and promoting social equality. Their enemies believed them to be totalitarian rulers who were striving to remold Chinese society. After 1952 a new image began to emerge. Communist China became a "model" for rapid economic development to the rest of the underdeveloped world.

1953: PEACE AND STEPS TOWARD COLLECTIVIZATION

On July 27, 1953, the Korean truce was agreed upon, and Chinese troops began to return to their country. With peace came a dramatic rise in self-confidence. The process of bringing order and integration after so many years of internal division and warfare gave the Chinese economy the opportunity to benefit from the abilities and motivation of the Chinese people. Trade between the cities and the countryside was fully restored and factory production began to rise rapidly. The first part of the year was given over to the enthusiastic welcoming of the first five-year plan by the regime's public opinion mobilizing capabilities. By June, the new spirit of getting down to work and away from excessive propaganda demonstrations manifested itself in the Five Too Manys Campaign — against too many meetings, too many organizations, too many concurrent posts for cadres, too many documents, and too many forms to be filled out.

In 1953 advances toward the full collectivization of agriculture were substantial. At the end of 1951 the regime had initiated a three-part process for reversing the effects of land reform and removing the redistributed land from individual ownership. The first step involved the establishment of mutual aid teams consisting of from five to ten households that would pool their efforts on a seasonal basis. Membership was to be voluntary, but considerable social pressure was applied to ensure near-universal conformity. In practice the mutual aid teams gave legal form to patterns of cooperation that had traditionally existed in the rice-growing parts of China. The individual still owned his own land, tools, and animals.

The second step was the establishment of lower producers' cooperatives consisting of from twenty to twenty-five households that pooled their land, tools, and animals but were paid in proportion to their contribution of capital as well as of labor. The principle of ownership continued to exist, but state decisions governed production. During 1953 much of Chinese agriculture was transformed from mutual aid teams to lower producers' cooperatives.

Dissatisfaction among the peasants began to arise in 1953, especially over the decision that all surplus grain had to be sold to the state at fixed prices that did not favor the peasant. By the end of 1953 and during most of 1954 there were signs that the Party was becoming less enthusiastic about collectivization. Production declined and Party cadres in the rural areas lost much of their earlier enthusiasm. There might even have been a decision to delay further collectivization in 1955 had it not been for the personal intervention of Mao Zedong in July 1955. He ordered the cooperative movement to be pushed and the Party to prepare quickly for the next stage of collectivization. There was an economic basis for going ahead, because 1955 was a good crop year, the best since the Party had come to power.

The third step in the Chinese plan was the establishment of advanced or higher producers' cooperatives, in which all property was collectively owned and people were paid for their labor according to work points and work days. Advanced producers' cooperatives were like Russian collective farms. They were large units, involving whole villages or even counties. During 1956 nearly three-quarters of the countryside was brought into advanced cooperatives. Production was poor and peasant discontent again surfaced.

In 1953, as the momentum for collectivization was beginning to build, centralization of authority increased considerably. Although the administrative regions were not abolished until the next year, tension existed between Peking and some of them, particularly Manchuria, culminating in the first significant purge of senior Party officials. Gao Gang and Rao Shushi were accused of being involved in an anti-Party alliance against Peking. It appeared subsequently that part of the difficulty was that Gao Gang was engaged in autonomous relations with Soviet officials and was allowing Russian influence to rise in Manchuria. He had been a senior Party leader and was one of the six vice-chairmen of the Central People's Government Council. He was head of the northeast bureau of the Central Committee while Rao Shushi headed the east China bureau. They were charged with plotting to oust Liu Shaoqi. Gao Gang reacted to the charges against him by allegedly committing suicide. Rao was imprisoned and never heard from again. The case was handled with so little disruption and publicity that it reinforced the impression that Chinese leaders were united and free of the internal conflicts so characteristic of the Russian leaders.

1954: CONSOLIDATION

Domestically, 1954 was a year of increasing centralization and consolidation of political control. The leaders seemed to have a clear sense of direction, and the people showed they had learned what was expected of them. During the year a new constitution was adopted, and over 150 million people supposedly participated in discussion meetings about the draft that Mao Zedong had submitted. The Constitution reaffirmed the dual structure of Party and government. Foreign observers tended to agree with Peking's claims that the political revolution was complete and the regime in firm control.

In 1954 Peking became more actively engaged in foreign affairs. The Chinese were an important element at the Geneva Conference to arrange the French withdrawal from Indochina and the establishment of the governments of North and South Vietnam. After Stalin's death in 1953 relations between Peking and Moscow remained close for a time. They began to change when the Chinese started to assert the principle of equality, being no longer content with the position of "younger brother."

Then in 1954 came the Chinese military advances in Tibet and the first Quemoy-Matsu crisis. Tibet had been recognized as a part of modern China, but had always had considerable autonomy. The country was a Buddhist theocracy, and the Dalai Lama, secure in his remote capital at Lhasa, ruled in a feudal manner. In 1954 the Communists began to assert their political domination of Tibet and posted troops in the capital. They left the monks and the Dalai Lama free to perform their religious duties and some secular ones. The fact that the Chinese did not insist on an immediate social and political revolution encouraged the view that they were willing to accept a degree of Tibetan autonomy. During the next few years, however, tensions gradually increased, and in 1959, in the wake of the Great Leap, the Chinese finally demanded that the traditional Tibetan authorities be swept aside. The result was the tragic Tibetan revolt, which culminated in the flight of the Dalai Lama to India. The reception given to the Tibetans by the Indians, including Prime Minister Nehru, marked the beginning of Sino-Indian tensions, which led to the border clashes of 1962.

The Quemoy-Matsu crisis raised the question of the extent to which the United States would protect the Chinese Nationalists on Taiwan, and specifically whether the United States Seventh Fleet would defend the offshore islands. The Quemoy islands, located in the harbor of Xiamen, and the Matsu islands, in the harbor of Fuzhou, were held by Chiang Kai-shek's troops. In August 1954 the Peking leaders, including Zhou Enlai, intensified their public statements about liberating Taiwan. On September 3, Communist troops began shelling Quemoy heavily, and an attack appeared imminent.

The Chinese were uncertain about what the United States would do. In December the United States and Nationalist China signed a mutual defense treaty, which clarified the American commitment to defend Taiwan but still left uncertain what would be done to defend the offshore islands.

The first crisis passed when it became clear that the Nationalists were well entrenched and could not easily be removed. The situation eased without the United States revealing the extent to which the Seventh Fleet was prepared to assist in defending the offshore islands. Three years later the second Quemoy crisis also ended in Communist frustrations, but that setback was much more damaging to Peking's security because of the context in which it took place.

1955: THE SPIRIT OF BANDUNG AND THE SOFT LINE

From 1949 to 1955 the Peking regime maintained a high level of physical and psychological mobilization throughout Chinese society. The mood of the country was that of struggle and of vigilance in distinguishing friends from enemies. Early in 1955 the tone of government pronouncements changed, becoming more relaxed, more reasonable. In foreign policy China adopted a far softer and more accommodating position. The leaders appeared to be buoyed up by their accomplishments. By the end of the year, however, the domestic scene was once again tense as collectivization was accelerated, though the benign approach still dominated foreign relations.

By 1955 the new regime had achieved considerable success in transforming industry and commerce. The Five Antis Movement had cowed the remaining industrialists who had hoped to cooperate with the new government. It was clear that all industries would be transferred to state control and the old managers could aspire to be, at best, executives in state industries.

In the summer the weather was kind to the Chinese, and they

had the best crop since the Communists had come to power. Party leaders were prepared to rejoice over their good fortune and not enforce further collectivization that might only disrupt production. At this juncture, however, Mao abruptly intervened and challenged the entire leadership by insisting that the only correct policy was to press ahead immediately to the formation of advanced producers' cooperatives, regardless of peasant opposition or the dangers of a decline in production.

This was probably the first conspicuous demonstration of Mao Zedong's propensity for allowing the government to proceed under its own initiative until he felt he must intervene, whereupon he would interject his own ideas even at the cost of upsetting the entire process of government. Mao was prepared to be shrill, to insist that no alternative course of action was acceptable, and to make the issue one of ultimate values and loyalties. The Politburo and the Central Committee had to give in to Mao's wishes and press ahead with total collectivization.

The collectivization drive in the countryside was matched in urban areas by intensification of controls over intellectuals, publicized by the campaign against Hu Feng. Hu Feng and his associates were writers who professed support for the government but were inclined to question the excessive single-mindedness of the authorities. The attack on Hu Feng was intense and aggressive, and he and his associates were summarily purged.

These domestic developments did not in any way compromise Chinese efforts at projecting a benign face to the outside world. In the early years of the regime the Chinese Communists insisted that the Cold War was the absolute reality of international politics, that there could be only two opposing camps, and that the posture of neutrality adopted by India and other developing countries was merely a continuation of support for the imperialists. After Stalin's death, as the Communist bloc countries evolved toward more complex and flexible relationships, the Chinese saw that they could enhance their own position of leadership by identifying with the neutralists and turning neutralism into a broad united front in opposition to the United States and the principle of imperialism.

Accepting the sponsorship offered by Nehru of India, the Chinese, largely in the person of the skillful diplomat Zhou Enlai, took the initiative in courting the leaders of the newly emerging states.

Zhou Enlai vigorously stole the show at the Bandung Conference of Afro-Asian States in 1955. He attracted attention at the conference, partly because China had been feared as a dangerous and evil force only a few years before and the innocent presence of Chinese officials at an international gathering was novel. In addition, however, Zhou acted with his usual grace, suggesting to all that Peking was becoming a reasonable and constructive member of the international community, anxious only to eliminate the lingering evils of imperialism.

China, emerging as a leader of the underdeveloped world, seemed to have a new answer to the problem of speeding up change and progress. China also found it advantageous to appear to act somewhat independently of the Soviet Union. The Bandung Conference did not result in any substantive changes in international power relationships, but it did highlight the aspirations of the newly emerging states and provided China with an arena for leadership. Although India had been one of the principal forces behind the planned meeting of Afro-Asian states, Bandung resulted in the beginning of the decline of India's influence among the emerging nations and the rise of China as a competitor.

1956: CONFIDENCE AND DOUBTS AND ONE HUNDRED FLOWERS

The public relations successes of China at Bandung encouraged Mao to attempt a bolder role in foreign affairs. The Chinese initiated a major cultural campaign in 1956, inviting delegations from all developing countries to visit Peking and to view the new factories and farms that were the showpieces of the new government. The Chinese also became more active in Communist bloc affairs. Mao Zedong spoke out more and more as the senior Communist ruler in the world and offered advice, particularly urging the Soviet Union to be tolerant of the liberalizing tendencies in Poland.

In February 1956, at the Twentieth Congress of the Communist Party of the Soviet Union, Khrushchev made his secret speech attacking Stalin's memory. This was a shattering event for the Chinese, who still revered the memory of a great Stalin. The effects of the repudiation of Stalin were soon felt throughout the Communist world. Mao, showing his first sign of serious dissatisfaction with Khrushchev, began to champion liberalization within the bloc while still upholding the virtues of Stalin at home. A serious crisis developed in Poland, and in January 1957 Zhou Enlai interrupted his goodwill tour of Asian capitals, where he was seeking to build on the spirit of friendship he created at Bandung, and went to Moscow and Warsaw to mediate between Wladyslaw Gomulka, who was pushing for increased autonomy for Poland, and the Russian leaders, who sensed anti-Soviet aspirations in Polish developments. Zhou encouraged the Poles to try following their own road to socialism.

This posture of relative liberalism toward Polish developments had been matched in Chinese domestic policies by Mao's appeal in May for the intellectuals to express their criticisms of his government. Alluding to the late Zhou dynasty period when "one hundred schools" of philosophy, including the Confucianist, Daoist, and Legalist, had clashed with each other in seeking to give Chinese society direction, Mao proclaimed: "Let one hundred schools of thought contend; let one hundred flowers bloom." During the previous five years the intellectuals had been forced to undergo self-criticism sessions and to confess their antiproletariat sentiments, so they were extremely cautious in responding to Mao's invitation, suspecting that he was not sincere in his protestation of liberalization.

By the end of the year, however, more and more intellectuals began to work up their courage to express critical views, most of which were that the regime was not achieving its professed goals. It soon became apparent that there was widespread and deeply felt resentment against the regime. Mao was probably shocked at the intensity of the criticism. Instead of mentioning failings of the system that could be quickly put aright, the intellectuals began to raise fundamental questions about Communism.

In June 1957, Mao issued his essay *On the Correct Handling of Contradictions among the People,* in which he stated that some forms of conflict were healthy and could be expected even in a completely socialist and classless society, while others reflected class differences and had to be sharply repressed. He drew a line on criticism and initiated the Anti-Rightist Campaign, which brought all critical intellectuals under severe attack for being counterrevolutionaries. The Hundred Flowers period ended and repression of all forms of criticism was again the order of the day in China. Many Chinese and foreign observers, including Khrushchev, suspected that Mao might have called for open criticism to induce dissidents to reveal themselves so that he could identify and exterminate them. Another view is that Mao was genuinely surprised by the intensity of dissent.

During the fall of 1956, Mao was driven from his liberalizing approach by the shock of the Hungarian uprising, which became so extreme that Soviet troops were required to enter Budapest to crush the freedom fighters. In contrast to his earlier tolerance toward Polish liberalization, Mao strongly supported the Soviet move. He did, however, feel that the "counterrevolutionary" uprising had been encouraged by Khrushchev's faulty and inadequate leadership — faulty because he had turned on Stalin's memory and inadequate because his treatment of liberalization had only confused people about what constituted correct Communist behavior.

Thus 1956 saw a dramatic reversal of China's relatively liberal policies. Mao's conclusion was that greater effort would have to be devoted to the ideological training of the Chinese people. After 1956 he constantly worried over whether the revolutionary spirit of the Chinese, particularly the intellectuals and the young, was strong enough for China to achieve Communism.

1957: ADVANCING TO GREATER CONFLICTS

By mid-1957 the Anti-Rightist Campaign, initiated to overcome the weaknesses revealed by the Hundred Flowers disaster, had been absorbed into the larger Rectification Campaign, in which all organizations had to devote time every day to upgrading their ideological study and to weeding out all improper thoughts. The movement toward liberalization was thus absolutely reversed, and the spirit of the Hundred Flowers was dead. The intellectuals in particular became the targets of incessant attack through the Struggle between Two Roads Movement. Mao acknowledged that complaints against the bureaucracy were legitimate and that the government and the Party were in danger of becoming aloof from the people. Criticisms suggesting any rejection of the ideals of his revolution, however, had to be forcibly opposed.

Mao was beginning to seek alternatives, both to the rigid bureaucratic style that had been used by Stalin and was apparently not surviving his death, and to the liberalization that had caused such trouble in Hungary. His answer was to decentralize administrative controls, increase the activist role of cadres, and mobilize large numbers of people in collective enterprises that would call for little capital but much muscle. He was searching for methods that would replace scarce machinery and money with willpower and human energy, and that would ensure political continuity and control without relying on bureaucracy. Mao was unwilling to admit that the ultimate goal of his revolutionary efforts was merely to establish another bureaucracy while allowing economists and engineers to determine the most efficient policies for the country.

During 1957 various experiments in utilizing mass labor were tried. A major campaign, March to the Mountainous Areas, was carried out to expand water conservation by reclaiming wastelands and increasing the amount of arable land. These efforts directed attention to the problems of agriculture and the fact that it was the most likely source of exports to pay for the imported materials needed to expand industry.

In foreign affairs, 1957 marked a significant shift away from the themes of peaceful coexistence associated with the Bandung spirit toward a more militant and crusading line. When the Soviet Union startled the world by putting in orbit Sputnik, the first unmanned spacecraft, Mao reacted with elation and proclaimed, "East Wind now prevails over West Wind." He also made his second visit to Moscow, but by the end of the year it was apparent that Peking and Moscow saw the world in quite different ways.

According to Mao's reasoning, a major shift in world power had taken place and it was essential for Khrushchev to solidify and authenticate the gains for the socialist countries. Mao believed that a missile gap existed; he thought the Soviet Union had moved past the United States in strategic arms and that only the personal weakness and folly of Khrushchev prevented the Russians from realizing the political advantages of their technological successes. He was convinced that Stalin would have known what to do with superior power. Above all, Mao was maddened by Khrushchev's decision to seek a relaxation of tensions, a détente, with Washington, which reached its high point when Khrushchev visited the United States and met with President Eisenhower at Camp David, the presidential retreat in the Maryland hills.

The Russians, on the other hand, were more realistic. They understood, in spite of journalistic speculation, that there was no "missile gap," that Sputnik did not fundamentally alter the realities of power, and that the best they could accomplish was to bluff equality, not assert superiority. It was awkward for Moscow to inform Mao of these facts of international life, for in Moscow's relations with Peking it was helpful for Peking to believe that Moscow was indeed the world's preeminent superpower. The stage was being set for the profound clash that was to destroy the close bonds of the Sino-Soviet alliance, which had come into existence with the establishment of the People's Republic of China.

1958: THE FRANTIC YEAR

Events in 1958 were in many respects the most significant and dramatically far-ranging in the history of Chinese Communism. China attempted the most extreme domestic experiments and failed. In foreign affairs China put itself in the position of becoming the enemy of nearly all its neighbors. Both agriculture and industry were thrown into confusion and turmoil as reason gave way to revolutionary exhortation. In the midst of domestic upheaval, China again confronted the United States on the issue of the offshore islands and became embroiled in Tibet, setting the stage for conflict with India. In 1958 the split with the Soviet Union widened when Mao learned that he could not rely on Soviet nuclear protection.

The most dramatic domestic events of 1958 were the Great Leap Forward and the establishment of people's communes. Mao, in announcing the formation of the communes, suggested that the Chinese were moving ahead of Russia in becoming a truly Communist society and, according to the slogan that went with the Great Leap, would "catch up with Great Britain in fifteen years."

The Great Leap was a supreme attempt to ignore technological and physical constraints and build progress primarily on human willpower. Workers were called upon to work shift after shift with little rest; machines were driven without stopping for maintenance and repairs; and complex but efficient processes were pushed aside in favor of less efficient, more primitive ways that were less capital intensive. The Party line spoke of a policy of "walking on two feet" — that is, using both modern and traditional methods to exploit every way of making progress. Part of the problem was that this policy caused so much confusion that no methods were used effectively. The extreme folly of the Great Leap was the effort to decentralize heavy industry by establishing "backyard furnaces" in rural settings to produce steel.

Within a year it became obvious that the attempt was not working and that Chinese economic development was being severely set back. The damage of the Great Leap extended from the destruction of expensive machines because of lack of proper maintenance to the wasting of natural resources that could never be replenished. Miners, for example, frantically dug out rich veins of ore without shoring up tunnels, and did not extract the less rich veins at all. Consequently, mines had to be abandoned before they were fully worked, or the costly process of doing the job correctly had to be accomplished later, even though only ores of marginal quality remained.

The introduction of rural communes was most shocking to other Communist countries. Still-backward China was proclaiming that it was introducing a "free-supply system" in which people would receive what they needed and give only according to ability. In theory the communes were to be created by combining several advanced producers' cooperatives to form a production unit about the size of a county. Labor was to be mobilized on a large scale, and life was to be regimented along semimilitary lines. In the communes people were to be given free food, barbering, and some clothing. Very soon, however, the Chinese peasant shrewdly figured out how he could get the most with the least effort. The most economically disastrous feature of the communes was the decision that all land and animals would belong to the communes and that people could only earn work points, which would be collectively allocated according to the group's judgment of the appropriate rewards for different activities. It was soon apparent that peasants were not inclined to work hard on enterprises for which they got no personal reward.

To prevent disaster the regime finally had to retreat, even though failure was not publicly acknowledged. The leadership introduced the concept of private plots, which allowed peasants to manage for themselves from 5 to 10 percent of the collective land on their communes. Here they could grow vegetables and raise hogs and chickens. By 1959 private plots had become a vital element in Chinese agriculture. On them are now produced more than 90 percent of the country's meat and 85 percent of its vegetables. The rest of the land is still collectively worked to produce the country's grain. In 1960 severe famine was caused by a shortage of grain, and since then the largest import each year has been grain.

As a result of the attempt to establish an extreme commune system during the Great Leap, the Chinese Communist leaders learned that peasants would go only so far in working without personal incentives. Even during the height of the Cultural Revolution, when the country again experienced a swing to romantic revolutionary views, no major attempt was made to get rid of private plots.

Late in 1958 the leaders also retreated on the communes themselves. Instead of using them as the basic decision-making units of production and as the organizations that decided who got how much in return for what efforts, they shifted accounting down to the production brigade, and decision-making on work to the production team. In practice the brigade was really the old lower producers' cooperative and the team was the group that had made up the mutual aid team. In short, the communes continued to exist in form but in practice the older groups, with different names, again became critical, with the smallest unit deciding who would do what tasks at what time and the larger group marketing the produce and dividing up the returns.

While the country dealt with the problems caused by the Great Leap and the communes, Mao became more publicly involved in recriminations with Moscow. Khrushchev visited Peking and was not silent about his horror at what he saw. He rudely suggested that Mao had taken leave of his senses, for it was madness to suggest that a country so poor that not everyone had "even one pair of pants" could be entering the golden age of Communism.

In September the mood of crisis was heightened by the possibility of war. The regime had been goaded into trying to do something about the offshore islands in the harbor of Quemoy. The impetus behind the second Quemoy crisis was Peking's determination to force the Soviet Union into a hard-line position against the United States. The Chinese wanted Soviet backing during the crisis, and in particular they wanted the Russians to promise publicly that they would give China the protection of Soviet nuclear weapons. Moscow dragged its feet and indicated that if the Chinese got into war out of recklessness they should not count on Soviet assistance. The Soviets said that if they were to give the Chinese protection then greater coordination should exist between the two countries and that China should provide Russia with bases in Chinese territories. China was unwilling to strike such a bargain.

Many students of Sino-Soviet relations identify the tensions that arose over the second Quemoy crisis as a turning point in the alliance, and a harbinger of its eventual breakup. Mao had to face the fact that he disagreed with Khrushchev on more than matters of world Communism and that he could not trust the Soviet Union to help him in conflicts with the "imperialists."

Foreign and domestic crises thus combined to compel Peking to step up war preparation by emphasizing the militia and the guerrilla potential of the People's Liberation Army. The Everyone a Soldier Movement suggested that the leaders believed that a new war would require the type of mobile guerrilla warfare practiced during the Yan'an days in the war with Japan. The high command of the army clearly resisted this approach, and an effort was made to counter this resistance by the movement to "go down to the companies and soldier," under which army officers served periodically in the ranks as enlisted men. At this time Mao Zedong made his speech calling the United States a paper tiger, declaring that China was unafraid of nuclear warfare, for the country would be prepared to carry on, even without its urban centers.

Little attention was given to the announcement in 1958 that Mao was being replaced as chairman of the government by Liu Shaoqi. It was presumed that Mao was giving up these responsibilities in order to devote himself more completely to polemics with the Russians and ideological writing. Later, during the Cultural Revolution, it was revealed that Mao had not welcomed the change and that he was, in fact, ignored thereafter in matters of administrative policy. Indeed, at that time, the problems of 1958 severely disrupted the harmony of elite relations in the Chinese Communist party. The factions that were to become the bases for the power struggles of the Cultural Revolution were being formed, and the ideological divisions between the pragmatic leaders, who were opposed to much of the Great Leap, and the Maoists, committed to the spirit of revolution, also began to take shape during that critical year. Communist China was never to be quite as unified or as self-confident as it had been before the beginning of the Great Leap Forward.

1959–1961: SLOW RECOVERY

By early 1959 the Chinese were engaged in a basic policy retreat on all fronts, except for military preparations. Profound disagreement on precisely what should be done in the military area led in the fall of 1959 to the Peng Dehuai case. As chief of staff of the army, Peng had persisted in arguing that the country should maintain its ties with the Soviet Union, not only in order to gain nuclear protection but also because Russia was its only source of modern conventional arms. He believed that China had to advance technologically with the rest of the world and that a guerrilla army provided no real security. Mao won the argument, and Peng was removed from office for anti-Party activities and was never heard from again.

China's relations with its neighbors were strained by the harsh manner in which the Chinese put down the Tibetan revolt and drove the Dalai Lama into India. During the year there were border incidents with India, Nepal, Sikkim, and Burma.

China was forced to turn inward in 1959 and continued to concentrate on domestic affairs over the next two years. The country was in the grip of a major depression as a result of the Great Leap. Unemployment was widespread, production was down, and, most damaging of all, a series of agricultural disasters resulted in near famine and widespread malnutrition. The death rate rose as health conditions deteriorated. At the Ninth Plenum, in January 1961, the decision was made to shift the emphasis of government from industry to agriculture and to legitimize the concept of private plots and a free market for products raised on them.

The economic crises and China's isolation within the Communist world created a morale problem among Party cadres. The regime sent large numbers of cadres to the countryside in order to stimulate their ideological awareness. In the rural areas, however, they were not well received because the peasants resented what the Party had done. Control broke down, many thousands in Guangdong fled into Hong Kong, and throughout the country people began to move about, instinctively seeking the security of relatives. Lacking papers and work permits, they were called "black people" because they lived in a shadow world of illegality.

In 1960 the Sino-Soviet split became an open confrontation. The conflict had been carried out initially through veiled criticism. For example, the Soviets criticized and the Chinese praised the Albanian Communist party. At first the Chinese took a liberal position on the unity of the Communist world, encouraging, for example, the Polish experiments of 1956, but in time they moved toward a harder line, against relaxing Cold War tensions. The Moscow Conference of all Communist parties in 1957 resulted in a declaration, which China reluctantly signed, that called for the end of inter-Party feuding. The Soviets were determined to stop Chinese efforts to organize factions favoring their position in Communist parties throughout the world. After the Tibetan crisis and the first Sino-Indian border difficulties, however, when Russia showed sympathy for Indian sensitivities, and after the Soviet Union rejected the Chinese demand for nuclear protection during the 1958 Quemoy crisis, the polemics between the two parties became intense.

Finally in 1960 the Soviet Union withdrew its technicians and terminated its aid to China. The abrupt withdrawal of Soviet economic help, as well as the disasters of the Great Leap, severely damaged the Chinese economy. Never since that time has the Peking government displayed confidence in China's potential for rapid economic growth. Instead of suggesting that China might be a model of rapid industrial development for other African and Asian countries, Peking's propaganda began to emphasize themes of equality and revolutionary purity in describing Chinese developments.

It is possible to plot a steady year-by-year rise in the temperature of the Sino-Soviet conflict. In 1960, on Lenin's birthday, the Chinese published in the *People's Daily* an editorial called "Long Live Lenin," which implied that Khrushchev had abandoned the revolutionary ideals of the founder of Bolshevism. In 1961 at the Second Moscow Conference the Chinese appeared to be acting more temperately and finally agreed to sign the declaration against inter-Party criticism; but a few months later Zhou Enlai felt compelled to walk out of the Russian Party Congress when Khrushchev attacked Albania. In 1962 the Chinese openly criticized the Russians for backing down in the Cuban missile crisis and for being "adventurist" in the first place. From 1963 on, the Chinese ceaselessly charged the Russians with collusion with the United States, especially over discussions about nuclear controls and the test-ban treaty.

In 1961 economic difficulties in China increased, and during a brief period the authorities turned their backs and allowed a flood of refugees to leave the country and cross over into Hong Kong and Macao. Domestic difficulties were matched by increasingly bitter exchanges of polemics with the Russians, while China mounted an effective campaign among the Communist parties of the world in seeking support for its orthodox Marxist-Leninist position. The Chinese were largely successful in winning over Asian parties and dissident factions in some of the European parties. Peking also sought the support of Fidel Castro and the Cuban revolutionaries, but after a brief period of apparent solidarity the Cubans pulled back because of their economic dependence on Russian aid.

China's interest in Africa also dates from 1961, when, in competition with the Russians, Chinese leaders decided to expand their propaganda and trade fair efforts and began to provide modest amounts of economic aid and technical assistance. Peking's activities stimulated a rise in American interest in Africa as well as a substantial commitment by the Nationalist Chinese to provide assistance, in the hope of preventing the African states in the United Nations from shifting their votes from supporting Taipei's representation to that of Peking.

1962–1963: RECOVERY AND REEDUCATION

By 1962 the Chinese were recovering from the extreme disruptions of the Great Leap and were gradually returning to more orthodox economic practices. The disillusionment and exhaustion caused by the previous frantic years and the subsequent depression had left the Party seriously demoralized. Even within the army there was widespread discontent and loss of faith. It became apparent that while the inertia of routine daily processes was beginning to bring about improvement in living conditions, the necessity to sustain revolutionary commitment among the people would call for new efforts at political and ideological indoctrination.

At the Tenth Plenum of the Eighth Central Committee of the Chinese Communist Party, an appeal was made to revive the spirit of revolution. Mao Zedong called for the initiation of the Socialist Education Campaign, which led directly into the Cultural Revolution. The theme of the campaign was the need to attack all manifestations of revisionism and to learn from the People's Liberation Army. Propaganda cadres began to proclaim the power that came from "Learning from the Thoughts of Mao Zedong," which in the next few years would become an endlessly repeated slogan.

The Socialist Education Campaign was directed particularly toward rural cadres, who after the setback of the communes were especially disillusioned. The Four Clean-Ups Movement was designed to revive the revolutionary discipline of the lax and apathetic rural Party apparatus. In schools the slogan "from the communes, back to the communes" suggested that rural youths should first obtain an education and then return to help their rural communities progress, instead of remaining in the cities. This was all a part of what the Party called the need to eliminate the "three great differences," between town and country, between agriculture and industry, and between mental and manual labor. By August 1963 the effort to increase the flow of talent into the countryside in order to re-ignite the peasants' revolutionary ardor took the form of the Five into the Fields and the Five Fewers campaigns, which were also directed against excessive reliance on the bureaucracy. A major propaganda theme of the time was the need for all people to follow the example of the Dazhai farmers in Shanxi who, confronted with Mao's appeal for hard work, applied a form of guerrilla warfare to their collective farm. The workers supposedly worked and farmed simultaneously; managers and laborers cooperated in making decisions; and everyone sought to put into practice the Thoughts of Mao Zedong. Although these features of the Socialist Education Campaign suggested a return to some aspects of the Great Leap, the management of government was in the hands of pragmatic officials who appreciated the values of modern technology.

We know now that tensions building up within the leadership were soon to explode in the Cultural Revolution. Indeed, by 1964 domestic trends and foreign pressures from both the Sino-Soviet controversy and the prospect of an American military buildup in South Vietnam had set the stage for the massive convolutions of the Cultural Revolution, a dramatic series of events that we will discuss after first identifying the ideological trends and personal points of view that contributed to those amazing events.

EMERGING TRENDS AND PROBLEMS

The first decade of Communist rule was a remarkable period, during which the leaders accomplished a great deal and gave the impression that they would be able to achieve far more in the years ahead. Never before in Chinese history had the country been managed so completely, and certainly never in modern times was it as unified. Mistakes were made, but the leaders always gave the impression that they were ready to learn and to improve. China, allied with the Soviet Union and after an impressive performance in the Korean war, appeared to be an emerging regional, if not world, power. China now became a source of anxiety to its neighbors, for instead of being the power vacuum of Asia, it was seen as a potentially dynamic and possibly aggressive political force.

Yet by 1957 problems were beginning to surface. The country was heavily dependent on Soviet aid in the industrial sector. Its agriculture, while improving, had not shown that it could provide the surpluses necessary for it to serve as the catalyst to modernize the Chinese society and economy. China's population was growing at such a rate that progress was neutralized.

The central issue that slowly began to emerge by 1958 was whether China would be able to modernize effectively if it followed pragmatic and technically sound policies. The explosion of the Great Leap in 1958 and the Cultural Revolution in 1966 constituted Mao's answer. He had become convinced that China's weaknesses could only be overcome by changing the Chinese character and by tapping the strongest forces of human willpower. Ideological views about how to modernize the country had become the dominant issue of Chinese politics, just as ideological and intellectual perspectives had been substantively more important than economic and social changes in bringing down the imperial system. In the late 1950s the Chinese Communists ceased to cope with objective problems and instead plunged dramatically into profound ideological disputation.

In order to understand what happened we need to learn more about the policy problems that came to divide the Communist leaders and set the stage for the Cultural Revolution and the succession crisis after the death of Mao.

CHAPTER THIRTEEN

Policy Issues and Choices

Ideology, personality, and the instruments available for governing set much of the tone of the first years of the People's Republic. Inexorably, however, policy issues and the need to make hard choices about how to modernize China intensified the divisions within the leadership. Throughout the long period of struggling for power and during the excitement of the first years, it had been possible to submerge personal differences. Furthermore, enough needed to be done that everyone kept busy. But in time substantive policy problems became increasingly troublesome and turned the differences among the leaders into open conflicts.

The most acute disagreements involved questions about the economy, such as how much the Chinese should follow the Soviet pattern of stressing heavy industrial development, how centralized planning should be, how agriculture should be collectivized, and what weight should be given to material incentives as compared with spiritual exhortation. Disagreements over noneconomic policies included such questions as social organization, the ideological training of youth, the balance in education between "redness" and "expertness," and social policies touching on the role of women and the place of the family in the new order. Leaders also disagreed over such fundamental problems as the priorities of agreed-upon programs, particularly in the areas of national defense and military affairs.

OVERVIEW OF ECONOMIC PERFORMANCE

Most economists agree that during the first decade of the Communist regime the Chinese economy made significant strides, first in rehabilitation from wartime disruption and then in substantive growth, particularly in the industrial sector. After 1959, however, the economy suffered severely and generally stagnated. During the first decade China's industrial growth rate was third only to those of Japan and Pakistan in Asia, but it dropped nearly to the bottom of the list during the 1960s.

In part the achievements of the first decade reflected a natural pattern of Chinese history. The establishment of political order after a period of chaos was always accompanied by vigorous economic activity. During the war years millions of Chinese were learning new skills that would be invaluable when attention could be given to industrial and economic development. In Japanese-occupied territories the conquerors used Chinese labor for their war-related industries. This was particularly true in the industrial centers in Manchuria and also in Tianjin, Hankou, Shanghai, Canton, and even in such secondary centers as Taiyuan and Jinan.

China thus had a potential for development in its large and well-disciplined labor force, which had grown steadily during each decade since the 1911 Revolution. In contrast to many underdeveloped countries whose people have had little experience in factory life, China did not have to create a responsible and hard-working labor force. The new government did, however, play a critical role in moving quickly to counter the effects of inflation stimulated by the faltering Nationalists. By reuniting the urban and rural economies of China and introducing strict fiscal controls, the new Communist regime set the stage for sober economic activities.

Peking's initial commitment to emulate the Soviet model of economic development resulted in benefits and costs to China that are still difficult to appraise. An immediate consequence of the policy of "leaning to one side" and following the Soviet example was that China obtained a source of credit and technical assistance. During Stalin's lifetime it was common in the West to say that the Russians drove a hard bargain with the Chinese and that China was in some respects being exploited through Soviet "aid." It is now far less clear that this was the case. Alexander Eckstein made a detailed examination of this complex question and arrived at the cautious conclusion that, although Russian aid took different forms, it was on balance probably more generous toward China than toward the Eastern European socialist states.[1] The Russians bought commodities from the Chinese for which they had little need and sold to them items they could have used for the rehabilitation of their own economy. The Chinese got things their planners valued greatly and exported low-priority items to Russia. Negotiations for Russian aid were difficult and protracted, but the technical questions were exceedingly complex.

The importance of Soviet aid to China may be deduced from the fact that when it ceased and Soviet technicians were withdrawn in 1960, the Chinese economy began to falter. With the end of Soviet aid Chinese planners had to give up their dream of rapid industrialization and think instead of developing agriculture.

The extent of Russian technical assistance can be seen from the fact that between 1950 and 1960 at least 10,800 Soviet and 1,500 Eastern European specialists and technicians were sent to China.[2] Joint-venture firms were established in which Russian blueprints and factory plans were followed under Soviet guidance in order to establish new manufacturing industries quickly in China. Furthermore, various Soviet scientific and technological academies, institutes, and organizations made available to China great quantities of technical knowledge. Through such assistance the Soviets provided the atomic reactor and the diffusion plant that were critical in China's development of the atomic bomb.[3] When Soviet technicians were suddenly withdrawn under the heat of Sino-Soviet ideological polemics, they took with them the plans for many unfinished plants. The Chinese were able to finish some with great difficulty but had to abandon others. On the whole the Chinese unquestionably benefited greatly from Russian technical assistance.

[1] Alexander Eckstein, *Communist China's Economic Growth and Foreign Trade* (New York: McGraw-Hill, 1966), pp. 168–182.

[2] Ibid., p. 169.

[3] William L. Ryan and Sam Summerlin, *The China Cloud* (Boston: Little, Brown, 1967).

After the Korean War China had no other source of foreign assistance.

It is considerably more difficult to evaluate the relative costs and benefits of China's commitment to follow the Soviet planning model, which emphasized heavy industry at the expense of consumer goods. A strong case can be made that by 1950 China was on the threshold of the normal stage of industrial development, comparable to where Japan stood in the early 1920s, at which point Chinese industries could have produced light consumer goods and textiles for the world market. Even before the war with Japan, China was one of the three largest textile producers in the world, mainly supplying its huge domestic market but about ready to export. (Today China is the world's largest textile producer even though the regime has tended to favor heavy industries over light ones.) The industrial centers of mainland China thus had the skilled labor force and the technical competence to become a series of "Hong Kongs." According to this argument, if the Chinese had exploited their comparative advantages in international trade, they could have been turning out textiles, plastics, and light electrical goods for the rest of Asia and Africa, and they could have filled the gap created when Japan began to produce technically sophisticated commodities for the American and European markets.

Regardless of what might have been, the fact is that the Chinese missed this opportunity and focused on heavy industry until 1960. By 1971, however, China was showing more interest in exporting light consumer goods, but world conditions in the 1970s were quite different from what they had been in the 1950s. Seeking to enter world markets twenty years late, the Chinese encountered intense competition. Almost all the other underdeveloped countries now have their own textile industries and many aspire to become producers of light manufactured goods.

The social consequences of the Communists' economic policies may be more significant than the economic repercussions. The early stress on the development of heavy industries favored the urban labor force and in many respects made the Chinese worker an advantaged citizen in comparison with other groups in the society. Factory workers were given job security, and their wages were generally higher than rural laborers could hope to attain. The regime sought to universalize the prewar practice of the elite industries whereby workers were provided with housing near their jobs at nominal rents.

During the 1950s Chinese factory workers felt that they were relatively well off. Their consumption demands were quite limited. They had little information about conditions in other countries and could compare their lot only with the previous state of affairs — i.e., the hyperinflation of the civil war years, the disruptions of the Japanese war period, and the prewar world depression. The average worker and his family considered themselves fortunate to have a one-room apartment and a luxury item such as a radio. Some could look forward to saving enough to buy a bicycle.

These favorable conditions attracted people from the countryside to the cities, so that by the late 1950s the regime had to initiate several programs for moving populations back to the rural areas and discouraging the growth of the large industrial centers. By refusing to provide work permits and by insisting that young people prove their revolutionary dedication by going into the interior, the authorities hoped to diminish the number of unemployed urban people who were looking for a way to become a part of the favored industrial working class. The problem of a large unemployed urban population increased during the period of economic depression that followed the failure of the Great Leap. The need for administrative controls to prevent urban population expansion from completely outstripping employment opportunities still exists.

In the meantime, however, the regime continued to give the urban industrial worker economic rewards great enough to keep him satisfied. As a result Chinese workers became a conservative force, supporting the status quo, ready to employ the rhetoric of revolution and the routines of Communist indoctrination and not eager for any fundamental changes. The conservative character of the industrial workers was clearly demonstrated during the Cultural Revolution when they resisted the revolutionary demands of the Maoists and clashed with the Red Guards who sought to disrupt their factories.

The contentment of the industrial workers produced high morale in Chinese factories. Chinese managers maintained reasonably close contact with their laborers, and evidence indicates they paid more than lip service to the Communist ideal that those who engage in manual labor may contribute constructive ideas about improving production. The fact that all managers and executives spent one day a week engaging in physical labor also contributed to a sense of unity within the different factories.

Since the mid-1960s, when the focus of Chinese economic planning shifted from heavy industry to agriculture, public attention to labor has declined, but material advantages still remain. The shift, however, brought to light some fundamental problems that have plagued the Chinese ever since they sought to modernize.

CENTRALIZATION VERSUS LOCAL AUTONOMY

Possibly the most fundamental issue for Chinese development has been the question of how centralized China's economy and society can become without great reductions in efficiency. During the 1950s the Communist Party imposed totalitarian controls despite the great diversities of China and sought to influence decisions throughout the country. Yet every time the leaders tried to achieve total mobilization they seem to have weakened national unity.

During the first years of Communist government the need for national unity and acceptance of the regime's legitimacy became confused with the belief that centralized direction would accelerate Chinese economic and political development. Foreigners in particular were impressed with Chinese monolithic rule and assumed that centralized direction would cause China's economy to develop more rapidly than economies in the rest of the underdeveloped world. Yet during the 1960s the Chinese leaders, particularly Mao Zedong, indicated that efforts at strong centralization were creating problems. Most serious were the difficulties of excessive bureaucratization. Centralized control meant domination by officials in Peking who were generally out of touch with local problems and the attitudes of workers. Mao's attack on bureaucracy, which reached its shrillest note during the Cultural Revolution, was in fact an assault on what had once been considered China's optimal form of development — a highly centralized and rationalized model.

Yet bestowing real power on local authorities would have been tantamount to giving sovereignty to all the various regions of China. Some areas are rich, industrialized, urban, and sophisticated;

other are pathetically backward. To do away with the concept of uniformity and standardized growth would be to legitimize gross inequalities. If growth rates were allowed to become dramatically different from region to region, the result would be a challenge to national integration, and in time some parts of the country would probably be exploiting others.

Either freezing the country under a single set of standards, with Peking declaring uniform policies for the whole country, or decentralizing authority might set back national growth. The dilemma of where to concentrate power first appeared during the last days of the Qing dynasty when the Manchu rulers had to deal with the introduction of the railroad and telegraph. It remains a problem in the modernization of China. It has turned up in various guises, regardless of the type of regime, ever since the Chinese sought to alter the peculiar balance of the imperial bureaucratic system, in which the pretensions of centralized authority were combined with local accommodation. The dilemma, however, has become particularly acute under Communism because it exposes an ideological contradiction. Communism theoretically provides standardized and "scientific" policies for an entire society — that is, it supports centralization. But Communism is theoretically sensitive to the creative spirit of the working class and not dominated by officials — that is, it should support decentralization and local initiatives.

In coping with the question of centralization versus autonomy, the Chinese Communist regime vacillated. In the early years its propaganda stressed centralization, but regional authorities continued to function. With the Hundred Flowers and the Great Leap, although the appeal was for spontaneity, a move was made toward greater standardization. Early in the 1960s bureaucratization increased, but local officials had more autonomy. During the Cultural Revolution the ideological theme was strongly against centralization, but the destruction of the Party left the political and administrative scene to the mercies of the army, an institution with considerable central direction.

Of all the institutions that have emerged in modern China, the People's Liberation Army came the closest to balancing centralization and local autonomy. The army gave the appearance of being a standardized organization and it was capable of reacting in defense of the national interest, yet at the same time its regional field armies were remarkably autonomous. During the early decades, therefore, the People's Liberation Army increasingly became a model for national institutions.

The problem of centralization versus local autonomy was not just a matter of institutional arrangements but also a question of the application of policy to diverse regions. The problems involved in application can best be seen by looking at agriculture.

AGRICULTURE: FROM LAND REFORM TO COMMUNES

China has always been an agrarian country. Through the decades, regardless of industrial advances, about 85 percent of the Chinese people have lived in rural areas. Government agricultural policy, therefore, has been important to the well-being of the largest proportion of the population. Although not always appreciated by planners in Peking — especially during the years when Soviet assistance made possible concentration on urban industrial developments — the basic economic fact of China is that the modernization and growth of its economy depends on the success of its agricultural sector, which produces 70 percent of the country's exports and over half of its gross domestic product.

Even before Communism, Chinese farming was more sophisticated and more productive than agriculture in most underdeveloped countries. The Chinese farmer by the middle of the twentieth century had enough skill and knowledge to bring about quick increases in production by routine introductions of scientific information. During the last 300 years Chinese agricultural production improved its efficiency at a rate consistent with China's population growth. Farmers in the north, for example, long ago learned to rotate their crops and use fertilizer, usually in the form of human waste. In short, by the time the Communists came to power the Chinese had advanced about as far as they could without making radical changes in technology or in the structural organization of agriculture.

Improved modern technology calls for heavy capital investment for research, the development of better crops, and the use of more and better fertilizers. Altering the structure of Chinese agriculture — that is, making the units of land more efficient by combining small holdings with larger ones and by increasing the efficiency of the marketing and distribution system — can have only a marginal impact. The Communists have chosen to emphasize the second approach. Their record to date is very uneven. At times their policies have nearly produced disaster; at best they have been sufficient only to keep up with population growth, which the Chinese have always done with no help from national planning. In a few more years the Chinese will have to face the problem of greatly increasing the capitalization of agriculture. Until now most capitalization has gone to irrigation and terracing, a form of investment the Communists have also followed in seeking to reclaim land and expand the acreage under production. Since their break with the Soviet Union, the Chinese have begun to make significant investments in agriculture. At the time of the termination of Soviet aid, for example, China was importing less than 1 million tons of fertilizer a year, but by 1968 China was purchasing 6 million tons, and Zhou Enlai spoke of the need for 30 to 35 million tons of chemical fertilizer by 1975.

Basically, however, Chinese agricultural doctrine has been similar to the Soviet and Eastern European Communist policies of moving away from a "land to the tiller" phase toward collectivization. Chinese agricultural policies have been misinterpreted in several ways. There was a widely held view that the Chinese Communists, being closer to the peasants than other Communists, would not be inclined to move toward collectivization, but rather were agrarian reformers. Even when this turned out to be untrue, it was still widely believed that they had moved more slowly toward collectivization than other Communists and had used techniques unknown to the Russians. This view, however, overlooks the policies introduced by the Russians to the Eastern European countries after World War II. The Chinese Communists used precisely the same approach a few years later when they came to power. Thus, although the Chinese did not duplicate Stalin's policies of the late 1920s, they did follow his views of the late 1940s. In fact, a comparison of the number of years required for each stage of collectivization shows that the Chinese actually moved faster, and, with the communes, further than the Russians did (see box).

The initial stage of land reform was more political than economic, for during this period few changes in production level could

	IN RUSSIA	IN CHINA
Confiscation of landlord properties and redistribution among the peasants	1917–1920	1950–1953
"New Economic Policies" with greater liberties for peasants	1921–1928	No counterpart
Transitional stage with early forms of cooperation	No counterpart	1953–1955
Formation of the *kolkhozy* or advanced producers' cooperatives	1928–1935	1955–1957
Introduction of communes		1958

Source: From Klaus Mehner, *Peking and Moscow*, p. 149. Copyright © 1964 by G. P. Putnam's Sons and George Weidenfeld & Nicolson, Ltd. Reprinted by permission of the publishers.

be related in any way to changes in ownership. With the restoration of peace after World War II and the civil war there was an improvement in the distribution system, which brought more food to the country. Land reform was important, however, in building loyalty to the regime. Those who had been dispossessed were members of the new elite, and their interests lay in supporting the government, even as its policies changed.

Chinese peasants who had received land were quite willing to give it up a few years later to the requirements of collectivization — unlike Russian peasants, who, having benefited from confiscation, fought hard to hold on to what they had gotten. The Chinese peasant never developed a strong sense of the legitimacy of the title that came to him through land reform. Although he may have been awarded his land by decision of a people's court, he was somehow aware that he was on to a good thing that could not possibly last. Long-time residents of a village acknowledged the ancestral lands of their neighbors and, though willing to benefit from someone else's bad fortune, perhaps they did not really believe themselves to be the legitimate owners of their new property. They were prepared to follow meekly the Party dictates calling for the first steps of collectivization. Mao Zedong testified to the Chinese peasants' distrust of the confiscation and redistribution of land when he described how the farmers in his home district refused to recognize the legality of the Kuomintang's redistribution of his own family lands when in 1930 he was declared a "bandit."

During the summer of 1952 the Party began collectivization by introducing mutual aid teams, under which peasants were permitted to retain their land and the produce from it but cooperated with each other during busy periods. The operations of the mutual aid teams were practically identical with age-old traditions in the rice-growing areas of China; only in the northern regions were they novel. The important variation on tradition was the introduction of the Communist cadre who supervised "cooperation" and adjudicated disputes, which were apparently numerous and generally took the form of debates over whether particular individuals had "cooperated" as much as they should.

Even as the mutual aid teams were being set up, the cadres mounted pressure to move on to the next stage of collectivization — the lower producers' cooperatives. According to this arrangement, the equivalent of three or four mutual aid teams were brought together, labor was pooled, and all the land was managed according to government plans. The original owners were, however, paid rent for the use of their land, draught animals, and implements. About 5 percent of the land was left in private plots. In the summer of 1955 all mutual aid teams were brought into lower producers' cooperatives. By the following summer the whole country was caught up in the establishment of advanced producers' cooperatives, in which all distinctions with respect to previous ownership of land, animals, and tools were obliterated, and payment was made only on the basis of labor.

The advanced producers' cooperatives were considerably larger units, involving as many as 300 households at the level of the total collective. They were, however, subdivided into production brigades, which usually coincided roughly with the earlier lower cooperatives and consisted of twenty to forty households. These were further subdivided into production teams, which generally coincided with the original mutual aid teams and consisted of seven or eight households.

These changes reflect conflicting goals. The creation of larger and larger units was designed to achieve greater managing efficiency and consistency. It was easier for the Party leaders to ensure that centralized planning was being implemented if the farmlands could be brought together in huge holdings. Problems of marketing, storage, and distribution were also usually eased by using large units. On the other hand, efficiency in raising crops has generally been achieved in China only by moving the decision-making level closer to the group that could observe at first hand the right moment to start planting and harvesting. Control and planning have been facilitated by large units, while sensitive and correct decisions could be made only by those on the spot. In a strange way the basic problem of organizing agriculture has been a replica of the national dilemma between centralization and local autonomy.

In practice, emphasizing the creation of larger units gave the impression of rapid change, although development did not accelerate. Whenever production became the most critical consideration, the tendency was to stress the small, intimate group where specialized knowledge of conditions and a sense of solidarity among those who had to "cooperate" produced better results than management through the larger and more impersonal organization.

This difference was dramatically demonstrated at the next stage of collectivization when the people's communes were introduced in August 1958. These were massive organizations, covering whole counties and involving generally from 5,000 to 8,000 households. In the communes everything was to be planned from above, not just agriculture but also rural industries, schools, and even defense in the form of the commune militia. During the communes' first year or so the regime attempted to control all the means of production, which meant the elimination of the private pilots. At the same time, the planners hoped to compensate the peasants for their losses by offering free meals at commune mess halls and other free marginal services. The peasant's reaction was to take as much as he could for nothing while doing as little work as possible in return.

By the spring of 1959 the regime was in retreat. Private plots were restored, and the system of mess halls largely abandoned. The communes were gradually decentralized, so that by 1960 they were really little more than paper organizations. Instead, the production brigades became the accounting units. They kept records of how many work points each member had earned and "paid" him accordingly. Decentralization was carried even further by making the production team — a subdivision of the production brigade — the prime unit of decision-making in production matters.

The regime made a firm public commitment to respect the private plots, which, although consisting of only 5 percent of the land, were soon producing most of the country's meat, vegetables, and fruits. Despite the radicalism of the Cultural Revolution no centrally directed attacks were made on the private plots, and after the near famine that followed the extreme commune effort, Mao himself apparently became reconciled to the fact that collectivization in China would fall short of the elimination of private landholdings. During the period when the regime did seek to abolish them, the peasants reacted very much as the Russian kulaks had done and slaughtered their pigs and poultry rather than turn them over to the commune.

Kenneth R. Walker, after a detailed study of Chinese agriculture, concluded:

> In the current state of China's political and economic development, a private sector of agriculture, composed mainly of private plots, is a "necessary adjunct to the socialist economy." There are two reasons for this. The first is that the peasants have shown themselves unwilling to surrender all private ownership of land, presumably until they have enough confidence that the collective economy will supply their needs. . . . The second reason is that the Government found that a private sector was needed to make up the deficiencies in the public sector. . . . A division of responsibility was, therefore, needed, between the collective and private sectors, the former concentrating on the important food and industrial crops, while the latter produced vegetables and pigs.[4]

After the agricultural disaster that followed the effort to establish the communes in 1958 and 1959, the countryside was gradually brought back to normal when traditional institutions were reinstated and the peasants were encouraged to seek their own self-interest. By the early 1960s the regime was talking about "agriculture as the base" for economic development, but the government

[4] Kenneth R. Walker, *Planning in Chinese Agriculture: Socialization and the Private Sector, 1956–1962* (London: Frank Can, 1965), p. 93.

still had no clear idea about how to modernize farming. The effort to open up new lands, particularly in the northwest, was not really a new program and it offered little hope of making agricultural production keep up with population growth, to say nothing of providing the surpluses that are necessary for industrialization or raising living standards.

The near famine from 1960 to 1962 was a result of mismanagement and natural disasters and caused Peking to be much more concerned about its agricultural policies. Massive quantities of wheat were imported. Nearly half of China's foreign exchange earnings from 1962 to 1964 were used to purchase grain, mainly from Canada and Australia.

The population of China was growing at the alarming rate of between 2 percent and 2.5 percent a year. Calculations based on Chinese figures suggest that the amount of cultivated land per person declined from about 0.47 acres in 1952 to about 0.41 acres in 1956.[5] Peking's concern over the danger that China's urban population would grow faster than industrial development could provide jobs produced an official policy of enforced migration to the countryside.

THE ISSUE OF MATERIAL INCENTIVES

A basic issue that emerged from Chinese economic policies and has influenced most areas of Communist domestic policymaking has been how far the regime should go in offering material rewards in order to increase the efforts of the people. Chinese Communism is ambivalent toward material as opposed to moral incentives. The acceptability of material rewards is implicit in the goal of achieving national power and prestige, both of which can raise the standard of living. Chinese Communist propaganda dwells on the bitterness of life before liberation and holds out the confident hope of improved conditions under Communism. Whenever the Chinese can claim that they have advanced the material lot of their people, they do not hesitate to publicize the fact, thereby suggesting that people should properly desire to be better off.

[5] Pi-chao Chen, "The Political Economics of Population Growth," *World Politics* 23 (January 1971): 255.

But also basic to Maoist ideology is the value of equality in austerity and a belief that only people infected with the evils of bourgeois materialism could want an improved standard of living. According to Maoism, a true Communist is willing to work hard for the glory of Communism with no expectation of personal benefits. Traditionally in China the ultimate sin was selfishness, and therefore, long before Maoism, both Confucianists and Daoists insisted that spiritual incentives were more honorable than material ones.

These abstract issues of the right and wrong of material incentives have become concrete problems in several fields. In industry the policy of allowing modest material rewards resulted in the urban workers becoming an elite and conservative element of Communist China. Although their material rewards might seem to be modest when compared to what is expected in other societies, Chinese workers proved to be extraordinarily responsive to the benefits they received. Consequently Chinese planners had substantial evidence that material incentives could be extremely useful to the government. Political loyalty and economic performance directly followed the receiving of material rewards. Yet the country did not have enough resources to provide material rewards for all who worked hard for the national goals. People also had to be encouraged to expect self-sacrifice and to seek moral or spiritual rewards.

In agriculture the problem of incentives was more difficult than in industry. Should rewards for production gains be collective? If, for example, a unit (a commune, cooperative, brigade, county, province) increases production by 10 percent, should that unit be given a 10 percent increase in rewards? Doing so would mean that increases in production would benefit those who created them, and the regime would be unable to transfer surpluses from one area to another. If, on the other hand, those who increase their production are not proportionately rewarded, they may be less inclined to work harder the next year. The Chinese Communists have been perplexed by the question of where justice lies and what the most desirable policies for dividing the fruits of increased production are. Yet the early successes of the regime in countering food shortages lay precisely in taking from the more productive areas to supplement the less well-off ones.

The most acute problem of incentives goes beyond collective rewards to the question of justice in individual returns. The issue became particularly critical during the high point of the communes, when Peking briefly sought to enter a condition of true communism by providing many things, including meals and haircuts, to commune members at no expense and without keeping strict records of who did what work for how much pay. Very soon Chinese peasants enthusiastically sought to get all that they could for nothing and to do the least amount of work possible. The regime had to reestablish a system of work points, whereby individuals were rewarded in proportion to the significance of their contributions. The experience brought out into the open the question of how it is possible to justify differential rewards for different forms of labor. Without any basic market mechanism to demonstrate relative earning power, it proved to be exceedingly difficult to justify some people receiving more than others for a particular kind of work.

Above all the regime discovered that in agriculture the principle of material incentives had to be maintained in the form of the private plots of land on which families could raise vegetables, pigs, chickens, and ducks to sell in the open market for their own income. Even during the extreme radicalism of the Cultural Revolution the principle of private plots was not challenged.

With the introduction of the advanced producers' cooperatives and even more with the people's communes the peasants have confronted questions about the appropriate rewards for different tasks. Historically, peasants simply worked hard and did their best because hard work was their lot and suffering was the nature of life. With the introduction of work points and the principles of egalitarianism they began to ask why some people were paid more than others.

The Communists continue to seek to increase production without allowing an increase in consumption. Only in this way will they be able to gain the savings necessary for greater investments in a growing economy. They appeal constantly to people to be selfless and to accept nonmaterial rewards instead of improved material conditions. Up to a point nationalistic appeals have been effective, but basically the Chinese people are poor and, like peasants throughout the world, suspicious of those who would talk them out of their just rewards.

The Chinese will probably become impatient with the indefinite postponement of material rewards. During the first years of the revolution they were willing to make personal sacrifices for the collective goals of the revolution, but after three decades the appeal for further sacrifices can produce cynical reactions and a rising suspicion that they are being exploited by the regime. This problem, cast in ideological rhetoric, becomes the question of declining revolutionary spirit, a matter that haunted Mao Zedong in his last years.

THE SOCIALIZATION OF NEW GENERATIONS

Instilling ideological awareness and enthusiasm in new generations is another basic policy issue for the Chinese. Presumably the reason for indoctrinating people in Mao Zedong's Thought is to improve their effectiveness in all fields; yet concern over the erosion of revolutionary fervor also can make ideological indoctrination an end in itself rather than a means for improving performance. Leaders' concern for maintaining a revolutionary outlook can become counterproductive in the very things that the revolution is supposed to achieve.

A fundamental issue for Chinese Communism is the question of whether resources devoted to raising the level of ideological commitment might be more effectively devoted to pragmatic goals. Mobilizing the Chinese public in various campaigns and drives has required huge investments of talent and resources. The best organizational abilities in the country have gone into these mass efforts, but it has not been clear that they have benefited development as much as would the application of the same talent to actual problems. Some of the brightest and most energetically committed people in China have been the propaganda cadres who have directed all their efforts to influencing popular views rather than to carrying out substantial development projects. Yet if the spirit of the revolution were to disappear with the succeeding generations, history probably would judge the Communists to be failures.

The basic problem, of course, is that national policies in different fields have not been sufficiently successful to convince the leaders that their revolutionary achievements have earned public enthusiasm. Mao in particular continued to believe that a special effort had to be made to win people to the correct revolutionary outlook. Mao was especially concerned with the problems of the younger generation and with whether the country had a correct educational policy.

EDUCATION: RED AND EXPERT OR EQUALITY VERSUS QUALITY

One of Confucianism's most profound influences on Chinese culture was its emphasis on education, which encouraged a vulgarized but strong belief that schooling should be materially rewarding. Even with the lessening of Confucian influence and the introduction of Western knowledge, the Chinese continued to value education. Parents at all levels of society want their children to receive as much schooling as possible.

When the Communists first came to power, they immediately called for the elimination of Western educational practices and the introduction of Russian methods and textbooks. From the beginning the Communists distrusted "bourgeois" learning and wanted "proletarian" education. This meant that in the early 1950s students had to display correct political enthusiasm and study ideologically oriented subjects. By May 1957, when Mao Zedong initiated the Hundred Flowers Campaign, the leaders were assuming that the Chinese academic and intellectual community had been fully won over to proletarian thinking. Mao believed that if he gave intellectuals freedom to express their inner thoughts and to criticize the regime the results would be constructive. When the criticism turned out to be fundamental and divisive, Mao turned on the educational establishment and gave vent to deep-seated anti-intellectual sentiments. He stressed the need for educating only the proper "revolutionary classes" and rejecting bourgeois education.

The outcome of the Hundred Flowers Campaign shocked Mao and reinforced his distrust of intellectuals; it also signaled the emergence of dilemmas that have dominated educational policy in Communist China ever since. Their solution has nearly destroyed the Chinese educational system.

The three major issues in education are: first, a belief that an inherent conflict or tradeoff exists between political loyalty, in the form of ideological commitment, and technical competence and intellectual skills; second, an awareness that academic selection and competition tend to work against the lower classes, which are supposed to benefit from the revolution; third, a serious problem of inadequate opportunities for getting an education and finding appropriate employment after leaving school.

The intellectuals' challenge to the government, which surfaced during the Hundred Flowers Campaign, illuminated what the Communists call the "red and expert" problem. In China as in all other Communist countries, increasing intellectual sophistication has produced "revisionism," because the scientific mode of thinking is not consistent with ideological indoctrination. Students and researchers busy with their intellectual work find the Party study sessions in ideology tedious and a waste of time. Most Party officials have far less schooling than the intellectuals. Party cadres who are not intellectuals have felt that the students and university communities have lost touch with the workers and peasants, and are trying to become an isolated elite much as the Confucian mandarin class once was. The Party view has been that people should strive to be equally "red" (that is, ideologically committed) and "expert" (that is, technically skilled). It is hoped that intellectuals who strive to be both will not become vulnerable to anti-Party views.

Chinese professors at one point tried to argue that the more expert a person became the less time he had to give to "redness." Such an approach would concentrate ideological training in the early years and in the least specialized fields, while those working in complex areas, such as developing the atomic bomb and working in advanced physics and engineering, would not have to participate in endless meetings about the Thoughts of Mao Zedong.

The leaders in Peking could hardly sanction such a position because the colleges and universities were populated almost entirely by people without worker or peasant backgrounds. The Party bureaucrats were, however, willing to reduce the ideological demands on China's scientists because they appreciated these men's contributions to the development of weapon systems and industry. In terms of announced policies, however, the Party continued until 1978 to stress the primacy of politics and the need not only for extensive indoctrination programs but also for the education of students of the proper classes.

A frustrating irony for the Communists was that until 1966 the predominance of children from bourgeois backgrounds enrolled in colleges and universities increased with each year of Communist rule. The explanation for this odd fact is that competition for places in China's limited higher education establishments had become intense. Population growth had run far ahead of college expansion, and the children of culturally disadvantaged families, from rural and working-class families, lost out to those from families with a tradition of educational involvement. Leaders like Mao, with strong egalitarian feelings, were disturbed by the failure of the Communist educational system to help the children of peasants and workers get ahead.

The Communists are also beset by the choice between quality education for modernization and mass education for equality. Limited resources have ruled out expansion in both quality higher education and general education for all children. Early in the planning process the central government took over responsibilities for higher and technical education, leaving primary and secondary education to local authorities. This decision widened the gulf between the two, with the universities focusing on research and the advanced skills necessary for economic development, while the local authorities lacked the funds to provide effective primary schooling.

The central government was not unconcerned about primary education in the rural areas; it just lacked the resources to do much about it. In fact, in the realm of policy guidance, one of Peking's proudest formulations was the concept of the "part-work, part-study" schools, which were supposed to capture Mao's ideal of combining practical and academic work. In practice the concept allowed rural areas without professional teachers to believe that they were providing appropriate and even progressive education for their children by permitting them to attend part-time, informal, one-room schoolhouses and work in the fields during the busy periods.

The easy mobility that had always existed in China, making it possible for ambitious and bright rural children, such as Mao Zedong and numerous other Communist leaders, to leave home to attend inexpensive boarding schools, largely disappeared under Communist rule. Peasant children who received primary education in the new rural setting generally were not able to achieve examination scores which would qualify them to enter the urban secondary schools.

From 1955 to 1958 the expansion of primary schools in China

was considerable, but the quality of instruction did not keep up with it. More children were getting some education, but fewer rural children were getting schooling good enough to allow them to continue in the more competitive secondary schools. During the Great Leap, 22 million more students were "enrolled" in primary schools, but all these schools were supported by the local communes, and when agricultural disaster struck, most of them disappeared.

During the 1960s the trend was back in the direction of favoring quality education. For more than four years, from 1960 to 1964, almost no new schools were constructed in China, even though population growth was increasing the number of school-age children.

As a consequence of the vacillation between school expansion and school contraction and of the continuing and unrelenting population pressure, truly disturbing problems began to confront the Peking leaders. On the one side, growth in the number of potential students and the limited number of openings were creating deep disappointment and frustration among those not able to continue their schooling for as long as they wanted. Yet by 1962 the universities and secondary schools were beginning to produce more graduates than the sluggish Chinese economy could absorb. Students who had expected that they would be working in the historic reconstruction of their country discovered, after the Tenth Plenum of October 1962, that they were going to be caught up in the Go to the Countryside Campaign (*Shansan Xiaoxing Yundong*). This campaign was another effort of the regime to deurbanize China. By sending millions of energetic and ambitious young people into the countryside, the leaders hoped to revive the backward parts of China. The practice only increased students' restlessness.

All these problems created a feeling among authorities and students that little was right either with the educational system or with the employment prospects for intellectuals. The stage was thus set for the Cultural Revolution and for Mao's massive attack on the bourgeois character of the educational system. By 1965 Mao could argue that none of the major objectives of education that he had sought in 1949 had been realized. His goals had been to educate the masses, to combine practical and theoretical work, to eliminate bookish and abstract knowledge, and to put politics in command of knowledge.

SOCIAL POLICY: CHANGING VALUES AND IDENTITIES

Economic development, agriculture, and education present problems for any government. Social problems are in some respects more open to change, although in this area the Communists are so ambitious that many question whether their goals lie within the realm of the possible.

The Communists have been most successful as social revolutionaries. Peking's rulers would unquestionably have achieved greater success in other areas, particularly in their economic policies, if they had not placed the highest value on social and revolutionary change. Much of the reason for the costliness of the leaders' approach to other problems can be understood by recognizing their commitment to the creation of a socialistic and eventually a communistic society.

To a degree the Chinese Communists' drive for fundamental social and cultural change coincided with historical trends in the modernization of Chinese society. The decaying of the old institutions, the weakening of family bonds, and the declining vitality of religion and traditional morals had long been taking place in China. Change was accelerated by the war and Japanese occupation. Therefore the Communists up to a point could harness the momentum of history.

Social change must have a particular character, yet there was nothing inevitable about the specific forms, emphases, and policies that the Communists chose. Indeed, in most of their social and cultural policies the Communists were not merely responding to basic social change but were initiating their own preferred changes.

Appropriately, the Communist assault on the old social order began with the family, the primary social unit of traditional China. The marriage law was the first major edict announced when the Communists came to power. Even before land reform began, the Party initiated its campaign against the feudal status of women. The law itself was consistent with the trends in China. It abolished parent-planned marriages, set the age of consent at twenty for boys and eighteen for girls, decreed economic and political equality for women, and gave women the right of divorce.

In letter and spirit little was revolutionary in the law. Even the Chinese Nationalists had passed laws directed toward free choice in marriage and the abolition of concubinage. What was revolutionary was the Communist campaign to spread the word about the law and their efforts to implement it. During 1950 and 1951 cadres organized endless meetings calling for confrontation between wives and husbands. Wives were urged to denounce their spouses for their feudal attitudes. Divorce rates rose steeply. The number of suicides also rose as wives reacted to the humiliation of what they had done to their husbands in the emotionally charged atmosphere of the cadre-organized meetings.

Yet in spite of the overzealousness of the cadres, the marriage law and the campaign supporting it significantly changed the Chinese family. The subordination of women lessened, and the power of the family was greatly reduced. The authority of the father, which had once been almost absolute, was drastically weakened, and children gained greater independence. As part of the attack on the family tradition, children were urged to correct their parents' behavior and to report misdeeds to the authorities. The objective was the establishment of a new morality in which traditional family obligations would be replaced by Party loyalty. Young people were expected to help bring into being a society in which their basic identity would be determined by peer and political associations rather than by family.

In seeking to create a new society, the Party's assault on traditional sentiments soon reached beyond family relationships. The Chinese had always deeply valued personal friendships and the loyalty that goes with personal associations. The Communists attacked such sentiments as "feudal" and called for a new spirit of public obligation and impersonal comradeship. The spirit of the dedicated revolutionary, which was supposed to inspire the Party, was declared to be the ideal for all society.

The new social ethic was proclaimed to be especially binding for youth. Students were instructed to eschew individual fulfillment and dedicate themselves to selfless service to Party and country. In place of special friendships, everyone was expected to treat everyone else as a comrade. Romance and personal affection were declared to be vile bourgeois attitudes. Boys and girls were to work together without personal attachments. By the mid-1950s it was widely assumed abroad that the new ethic was taking hold, partly because drabness pervaded the country, with boys and girls dressing alike in blue cotton clothes.

During the first years of the regime the champions of the new ethic seemed to be Liu Shaoqi and the other Party organization leaders. They were tireless in their efforts to make both the Party and Chinese society models of revolutionary virtue. During these early years Mao appeared to be more relaxed and tolerant than the fanatically dedicated Party workers. It was Liu and the Party officials who urged the Chinese to admire most the activist Party cadre who humorlessly and unrelentingly strove to be a revolutionary hero. But after the Hundred Flowers Campaign Mao became increasingly concerned about whether the Chinese people were adequately committed to the new ethic. His concern was heightened by the Great Leap effort when he, more than the Party administrators, took up the belief that human commitment could triumph over all else. By the time the Cultural Revolution was beginning to take shape, Mao was the unqualified champion of the virtues of the new morality. Liu Shaoqi and the regular Party bureaucrats were less inspired by the spiritual aspects of the revolution.

The contrast between the new morality and the discredited feudal morality of traditional China is part of the larger problem of how a revolutionary Communist regime, seeking to revive Chinese national power, should come to terms with the cultural traditions of ancient China. Since the beginning of the twentieth century, Chinese intellectuals have been perplexed over how to reconcile their national traditions with their commitment to modern science and technology. During the Yan'an period Mao Zedong began to deal with the question of how a revolutionary movement striving to bring about the new world of socialism should respond to the history of a great civilization. The Communists' initial approach to the problem, which they called that of China's "cultural legacy," was to make a sharp but rather arbitrary distinction between the feudal aristocratic culture of the oppressive ruling classes and the popular democratic culture of the common people. By this formula the Party could denounce the higher culture of China, its art, literature, philosophy, and above all, its Confucian ideals of the amature gentleman, and stress folk culture. During the first years of the regime, peasant folk dancing and woodcuts were treated as the essence of traditional Chinese culture, and the major forms of landscape painting and classical opera were labeled "feudal."

By the mid-1950s more and more of the cultural legacy was gradually being accepted. Peking opera was again popularized, and new themes were presented in the old opera forms. Mao Zedong himself repeatedly revealed his personal liking for traditional poetry and produced numerous verses composed in the old forms. Since feudalism was presumed dead, it was possible to use old forms without fear that doing so would encourage the revival of old social views. The Hundred Flowers period was the high point of tolerance for the old, and Communist intellectuals freely talked about "developing the new out of the old" (*tuichen chuxin*).

With the Anti-Rightist Campaign that followed the Hundred Flowers, and particularly with the Great Leap, tolerance for the cultural legacy sharply declined. During the height of the Great Leap cultural purists had no place, and all who valued the old had to suppress their sentiments. During the bleak years of economic depression and slow revival in the early 1960s, cultural interests gradually reemerged, possibly as an escape from the intolerable present. In any case the Party, particularly Chairman Mao, became suspicious that the revival of features of the cultural legacy was working against revolutionary ideals.

The cultural legacy issue became one of the triggering elements of the Cultural Revolution. It is significant that this upheaval, which rocked the Communist system to its foundation, is called by the Communists a "cultural" revolution. Culture, for the Chinese Communists, provides the basic orientations of a society. Indeed, Mao was disturbed that the new revolutionary ethic was not taking hold.

At a more immediate level the Cultural Revolution was initiated by a clash over an apparently cultural matter. In November, 1965, a relatively obscure Shanghai critic, Yao Wenyuan, attacked the historian and playwright Wu Han for his new play, *The Dismissal of Hai Rui*. The charge was that it displayed feudal and bourgeois influences because it told of an official in the Suzhou area from 1569 to 1570 who was dismissed from office because he showed sympathy and understanding for the lot of the peasants. Wu Han was denounced for suggesting that class differences did not matter and for upholding bourgeois ideals of humanitarianism and "loving the people." The Party stated that such ideals have no place in a proletarian society in which the true class interests of the workers are respected and the illusion that class lines can be overcome by goodwill is rejected. Moreover, Wu Han's references to the past were considered a cover for criticism of the present. When he had the sympathetic figure of Hai Rui support the policy of returning land to the peasants, he was really suggesting the worth of private plots of land, thereby condemning Mao's communes and policies of total collectivization. Sophisticated Chinese audiences were expected to see Hai Rui as symbolizing Peng Dehuai, whom Mao had dismissed for criticizing his commune policies. Because Wu Han was a leading Communist writer, he presumably had the support of some powerful figures in the Party — he was seen as a protégé of Peng Zhen, the mayor of Peking and a Politburo member.

In the spring of 1966 China's cultural establishment was shaken by further exposés and charges that historical forms were being used to criticize Mao's revolutionary ideals. Deng Tuo, a secretary of the Party's Peking branch and close associate of Peng Zhen, was charged with veiling profoundly counterrevolutionary ideas in his newspaper column "Evening Talks at Yenshan," in which he had followed an almost Confucian style of relaxed and judicious observation about the human condition. Deng Tuo was also linked with Wu Han and a third literary figure, Liao Mosha, in vicious attacks in their "Three Family Village" essays, which had conveyed a greater sense of humanity and less devotion to class struggle than the dedicated Maoists would accept.

These were the events which directly set off the Cultural Revolution, but we must take note of one more fundamental issue before we look into the details of the Cultural Revolution.

MILITARY AFFAIRS: THE ARMY AS MODEL FOR SOCIETY

The Communists came to power out of a civil war, and in the first years of the regime administration was carried out by the army. The Korean War provided the People's Liberation Army not only with a major challenge but also with the opportunity to become fully modernized with Soviet assistance. During the Korean War the People's Liberation Army was transformed from a guerrilla force into a conventional force with modern equipment and firepower.

With this transformation came major issues that have in some ways continued to plague the Chinese leadership. The basic division was between military leaders who welcomed the modernization and technological transformation of the army and those who felt that guerrilla traditions were more appropriate in a poor country committed to a social revolution. Those favoring modernization wanted close association with the Soviet Union, the development of air power, and increased mechanization of all forces. Their views on organization and doctrine represented professionalism and sensitivity to international military trends. Other Chinese leaders continued to see the army in terms of its nonmilitary functions and wanted to increase its ability to help the country with the tasks of economic development. In the view of these officials the army was more important as a domestic institution than as a security force.

The clash was somewhat muted during much of the first decade of the regime, partly because of the existence of the Public Security Forces and the militia, which met many of the domestic objectives of the second group of leaders. With each year in power the Communists expanded the size of the militia, until in 1958, during the Great Leap and in conjunction with the establishment of the communes, the Party launched the Everyone a Soldier Movement. This drive was supposed to help prepare the country for any threat of international war — a danger heightened by the Quemoy and Matsu crisis of 1958. The drive was also apparently inspired, however, by the belief that the heroic ideals of soldiering and the experience of military drill are beneficial in creating the revolutionary ethic and inspiring enthusiasm.

The trend against professionalization of the People's Liberation Army was intensified in 1958 when Mao denounced an attempt to establish "bourgeois military thinking" in the Chinese army. The following year Defense Minister Peng Dehuai, who had been a hero in the war with Japan and the civil war, was purged from office, probably because his concern for maintaining the professional character of the army brought him into conflict with Mao Zedong. Peng apparently opposed Mao's policy of pursuing the ideological split with the Soviet Union. A military man, Peng argued that China needed modern supplies and equipment, which were obtainable only from the Soviet Union. In August 1959 the Military Affairs Commission "thoroughly settled accounts" with Peng Dehuai and Lin Biao replaced him.

Lin Biao's emphasis was on "giving prominence to politics" and raising the ideological level of the army. In this approach he was fully in accord with Mao's views that "men are more important than materials." In supporting Mao's slogan "human factor first," Lin Biao pushed indoctrination and created a set of model heroes for emulation not only by all the soldiers but by the entire Chinese population. Professional officers accepted parts of Lin Biao's program because they improved discipline and dedication, but they continued to worry about what China would be able to do if invaded. Some thought — as Peng Dehuai had — that security considerations called for greater caution in any ideological challenge to the Soviet Union.

During the period after the Great Leap, when the Chinese economy was in a state of severe depression and agriculture was experiencing three consecutive years of crop failure, morale in the army was also down. In part the problem reflected the fact that the Chinese army was still a peasant army, and the men were mirroring the attitudes and moods of the civilian population. But the problem was also one of continuing uncertainty about strategic doctrine. The idea of a people's army was not only repugnant to men just beginning to dream of China as at last having a modern military force, it also seemed to offer little hope for victory in case of a major war. Lin Biao and his associates, however, developed a counterargument that tried to add a military touch to Mao's requirements:

> In accordance with our situation, if there is a war within three to five years, we will have to rely on hand weapons. As to how to defeat the enemy with hand weapons, Chief Lin [Biao] has found a way, and it has to do with the question of distant war or close war. Distant war means to fight at a distance of several tens, several hundred, or even several thousand kilometres. Close war means to fight at a distance several metres and two hundred metres, or face to face. The enemy is stronger than we are in a distant war, but short

> distance fighting, and especially face-to-face fighting, is where our strength lies. We have to avoid the strengths and take advantage of the weaknesses of our enemy. In face-to-face fighting there can only be used hand grenades, bayonets, or flamethrowers. We have to use close fighting, night fighting, or trench warfare to defeat the enemy. . . . In the event of war within the next few years we can defeat the enemy by using close combat although we have no special weapons.[6]

Ironically, just as Chinese military doctrine was moving in the direction of discounting technology, Chinese scientists on October 16, 1964, detonated China's first nuclear device. China was in the strange position of being a nuclear power with an underequipped guerrilla force. Although the Chinese sought to gain whatever prestige they could from their nuclear success, they recognized that one bomb did not change basic power realities. Mao and Lin continued their pressure to use the army in its nonmilitary dimension and above all to hold it up as a model for other institutions in the society. They gave added weight to the Learn from the People's Liberation Army Movement. All organizations and individuals, especially Party cadres, were expected to regard the army as a means of solving all problems.

In the fall of 1965, Lo Ruiqing, army chief of staff, was purged, apparently because he continued to doubt the effectiveness of the old Yan'an guerrilla methods for the defense of China. The American escalation in Vietnam was the immediate issue of the purge. Lo Ruiqing favored a conventional buildup and the repairing of relations with the Soviet Union so that military assistance would be assured if the Americans invaded. Mao and Lin advocated a people's war strategy based on political mobilization, a withdrawal into a defensive and essentially guerrilla posture, and the avoidance of a massive military confrontation with any foreign enemies.

The elimination of Lo Ruiqing compromised the position of Party pragmatists and technicians who also wanted to restore better relations with the Soviet Union, not just in case of war but because they felt that Soviet aid was essential for any significant

[6] Ye Jianying, speech at Military Affairs Committee Conference on Training, January 1961, in *Gongzuo Tongxun* (February 20, 1961).

industrial and economic development. The issue within the army between technology and the human will, between technical and scientific competence, and political mobilization and dedication divided the entire Communist leadership and set the stage for the Cultural Revolution.

CONVERGING THEMES

By the middle of the 1960s, in one policy area after another, fundamental problems were beginning to arise. They had certain common dimensions, and the leaders, probably equally dedicated to rebuilding Chinese power and glory, became more and more consistent in their approaches to them. No single issue was enough to divide men who had gone through so much together, but cumulatively the differences were enough to create lines for deeper and more personal divisions.

Whether the problems were in agriculture, industrial development, education, social mobilization, or military policy, some men tended to stress rational and technical considerations, believed that skill and knowledge mattered and that power and efficiency were essential in strong, disciplined organizations. Others were inclined to believe that China's problems of development could be overcome only by political dedication, spiritual selflessness, and the initiative of all individuals working spontaneously together.

The leading spokesman for the latter view was, of course, Mao Zedong, who, not deeply enmeshed in administrative responsibilities, had been devoting himself to questions of history and ideology and to contemplating what had gone wrong in the Soviet Union. As his disagreements with Soviet policies under Khrushchev intensified, his statements about revolutionary spirit became more shrill. Domestically, Mao was irritated at the prospect of technicians and specialists dictating all policies. He felt obliged to speak out against the idea that a lifetime of revolutionary effort should be reduced to allowing economists and engineers to run affairs and to waiting for compound interest to bring about the accretions of power and wealth that would finally add up to China's destiny of renewed greatness. In his mind this would be no different from development under a nonrevolutionary system, for to Mao the sciences of the economist and of the engineer were bourgeois. His mood became one of impatiently wanting to assault all targets with massive outpourings of human effort and discarding the cautious advice of those who sought incremental development. The stage was set for the drama of the Cultural Revolution.

CHAPTER FOURTEEN

The Great Proletarian Cultural Revolution

One of the most extraordinary events in Chinese history, indeed in the history of any nation, was the Great Proletarian Cultural Revolution, which tore China apart between 1966 and 1969. The oddity of the Cultural Revolution lay not just in the bizarre conduct of an aging leader calling upon millions of young people to engage in a children's crusade, but also in the fact that Mao was seeking to destroy the Party, presumably the most valued object in his political life. The Cultural Revolution brought together madness and reason in a peculiar blend of idealism and sly calculation. It was the cause of great suffering, the Chinese now say, for over 100 million people.

UNCERTAIN TRENDS

The Chinese Communist craving for secrecy has meant that the facts of the Cultural Revolution are obscure, though the effects are dramatically obvious. All the world was able to see that the Chinese were in turmoil. The most central and vital institution of their political system, the Communist Party, was decimated, and the image of China as a model for developing countries was shattered by what seemed to be a fit of madness.

The Cultural Revolution unquestionably altered the history of Chinese Communism, for it compromised the mystique of authority of the Chinese leaders. Whether it accomplished any constructive objectives is still questionable. If Mao's interest was to urge a more rapid pace for domestic and economic development, he failed. The Cultural Revolution slowed Chinese progress, destroyed the education of a whole generation, and solidified factional divisions which for twenty years defined allegiances in Chinese politics. If Mao's objective was to raise the level of ideological commitment, he may also have failed. It is likely that instead of making the Chinese, particularly the younger generation, more radical and dedicated to the vision of a new society, the experience of the Cultural Revolution encouraged cynicism. Those who had been most enthusiastic found themselves in the most dismal situations; idealistic youths were called upon to follow the lot of the peasant and accept the isolation of rural China. Finally, the Cultural Revolution ended in military rule and a foreign policy that included an invitation to President Nixon to visit Peking and Chinese support for the military rulers of Pakistan in their suppression of the Bangladesh movement in East Pakistan — hardly idealistic or revolutionary policies.

The one immediate consequence of the Cultural Revolution was the elevation to power of the military. The People's Liberation Army was put in charge of managing China. In this respect the ultimate act of charismatic Mao Zedong differed little in its effects from those of most of the other charismatic leaders of Afro-Asian states, such as Sukarno and Nkrumah, who were succeeded by military rule. The only variation was that Mao remained at least formally in charge, while the others were pushed aside. Perhaps an iron law of political development holds that military predominance is a likely outcome of attempts by charismatic leaders to press revolution beyond the pace that the society is prepared to accept.

Why did the Cultural Revolution occur? No definitive answer can be given. The range of acceptable explanations reaches from the one extreme, that Mao was driven by his radical, revolutionary vision, to the other extreme, that Mao, desperately fighting elements that were about to push him aside, had to unleash all his political forces even if it meant he would achieve no more than a Pyrrhic victory.

The first interpretation suggests that Mao and his followers believed that the failure of the Hundred Flowers Campaign and Great Leap was caused by the ideological and spiritual weakness of those who represented Chinese Communism. They did not acknowledge that anything could be wrong with their policies, but rather insisted that those promulgating them lacked ideological commitment. The policy problem of the regime and the disappointing performance of the Party made these true believers feel that eventual success required simply renewed dedication and increased moral commitment.

Equally plausible, however, is the interpretation that Mao and his wife Jiang Qing sensed that they were being disregarded and that real power was gravitating to other hands. According to this view, the fact that Mao was following the traditional Chinese imperial pattern of confusing ruling and reigning meant that he had not been in full control of events and by trying to intervene had created great tensions. As a reigning figure he had allowed others to manage affairs, yet when Mao tried to rule again he seemed as arbitrary as any Chinese emperor. Communist ideology and Party discipline were not designed to cope with Mao's vacillations. Any shift from reigning to ruling was interpreted as a direct challenge to those who had been ruling while Mao reigned.

Although most of the world was horrified by the madness and the violence of the Cultural Revolution, some foreigners accepted Mao's purported logic and believed that the Chinese were finding a new and more egalitarian way to economic and political development, a way that would result in a total participatory society, unencumbered by bureaucracies or by any division of labor based on technical specialization. With hindsight we know that this was all empty rhetoric. What happened in fact was that tens of thousands were killed or committed suicide, and hundreds of thousands were sent into exile in rural communes or imprisoned in concentration camps and jails. Contentions that began as policy or ideological disputes degenerated into violent clashes as factions struggled against factions in deadly combat. Those who were seriously committed to using wisdom and knowledge to solve China's problems found themselves denounced as traitors by people possessed by passion, and more particularly, hatred for all who proclaimed the virtues of reasonableness.

THE CONVERGENCE OF POLICY ISSUES AND THE DIVERGENCE OF LEADERS

Foreign analysts of China generally agree that by 1963 the country was beginning to move ahead. The economy had recovered to a large extent from the disruptions of the Great Leap and from the subsequent years of depression. Orderly advances were being made on several fronts. Within the Chinese ruling circles these developments were the cause of tensions rather than satisfaction. Some of the leaders were pleased by progress achieved through disciplined action, guided by specialized and technical knowledge. Others, particularly Mao Zedong, were troubled by such progress. Mao's view was that the Communist revolutionary vision was debased and made irrelevant if the only result of the revolution was to allow technicians and economists to dictate national policy. If progress depended on rational economic policies, how did China differ from other developing countries that were also being guided by the logic of engineers and economists, by technocrats and scientific specialists? Mao felt that China had to return to the spirit that had inspired the Great Leap.

In Mao's opinion the Great Leap had failed not because it was poorly planned and did not make sense, but because those who directed it and participated in it lacked revolutionary ardor. What was needed was a higher degree of commitment. At the Lushan Conference of July 1959, when decisions were made that eased the commune movement and slowed the Great Leap, Mao passionately defended his policies against the charge of reckless impatience: "In regard to speed, Marx also committed many errors. He hoped every day for the advent of the European revolution, but it did not come. . . . It was only by the time of Lenin that it came finally. Wasn't this impetuousness? Wasn't this bourgeois fanaticism?"[1] Mao, in making his plea, which apparently failed to move the conference members, indicated his own frustration and helplessness by referring to the fact that he would have no posterity. (One son had been killed in battle and the other had been declared insane.) He

[1] "Speech at the Lushan Conference," *Chinese Law and Government* 1 (Winter 1968–1969): 42.

also indicated his determination to fight back, in the spirit of the guerrilla days, with the help of the People's Liberation Army. At Lushan, having made the point that only in bourgeois nations do newspapers act so foolishly as to publish bad news, he said:

> Suppose we do ten things, and nine of them are bad and are published in the newspapers. Then we are bound to perish, and should perish. In that event, I would go to the countryside to lead the peasants to overthrow the government. If the Liberation Army won't follow me, I will then find the Red Army. I think the Liberation Army will follow me.[2]

As a consequence of Mao's efforts at Lushan his influence increased and the Great Leap was revived briefly during the fall of 1959. Yet by the next year Mao's influence had again declined. The fluctuations in Mao's authority, apparent in 1958 and 1959, foreshadowed the Cultural Revolution and revealed the fact that tensions within the leadership extended beyond domestic issues to include military affairs and foreign policy. At the Lushan Conference Peng Dehuai criticized the commune policy. He charged that it was demoralizing the soldiers who had close peasant ties and went on to point out that the country was weakening itself through its isolation from the Soviet Union. The linkage of domestic and foreign policy helped to sharpen the lines of disagreement among the different factions of the Chinese leadership. Peng, however, was fighting against determined Maoist opposition, for Mao not only wanted to defend his commune policies but felt strongly about the folly and revolutionary evils of closer associations with the revisionist Soviet Union.

During the brief upsurge of Mao's influence at Lushan he was able to have Peng Dehuai purged from command of the army and replaced by Lin Biao; General Lo Ruiqing became the new chief of staff. The concepts of the "human wave assault" on the economy, the superiority of willpower to technical expertness, and nearly total collectivization of agriculture were thus joined with Lin's view that military policy should depend on people armed and prepared for guerrilla warfare, rather than on a modernized and professional force. The combination of these attitudes became the views of Mao and his immediate associates.

Early in the 1960s the tensions among the leaders seemed to

[2] Ibid., p. 35.

have lessened. After Mao had relinquished the ceremonial office of the chairman of the People's Republic, he disappeared for several months and the Party and state bureaucracies appeared to be managing domestic affairs with reasonable competence. During the Cultural Revolution it was revealed that Mao felt at the time that he had been pushed aside. He claimed that Liu Shaoqi and Deng Xiaoping had treated him after 1958 like "one of their parents whose funeral was taking place." During this period Mao was engaged in polemics with the Soviet Union. He probably devoted less attention to domestic matters because he was so absorbed with his almost personal conflict with Khrushchev.

The tempo of the Sino-Soviet controversy, which had begun slowly after the death of Stalin in 1953, picked up momentum with Khrushchev's dramatic attack on the memory of Stalin at the Twentieth Congress of the Soviet Communist party. The clash radically intensified in the spring of 1958 when the Soviets criticized the Great Leap, refused to support China in the offshore islands confrontation with the United States, and supported India in its border controversies with China. By 1959 the controversy had reached the point of no return, and Mao was convinced that Khrushchev was China's mortal enemy. Not only had he refused to give China aid, he also was undermining the very spirit of communism by seeking détente with the United States and encouraging revisionism at home.

In Mao's polemics, particularly in his Ninth Comment, entitled "On Khrushchev's Phony Communism and Its Historical Lessons for the World," he began to reveal clearly and coherently a set of attitudes on domestic and foreign affairs that may be characterized as the ideological basis of the Cultural Revolution. He showed his great concern with maintaining and transmitting to the next generation the spirit of true revolution:

> The question of training successors . . . is one of whether or not there will be people who can carry on the Marxist-Leninist revolutionary cause started by the older generation of proletarian revolutionaries . . . whether or not we can successfully prevent the emergence of Khrushchevite revisionism in China . . . a matter of life and death for our Party and our country.[3]

[3] "On Khrushchev's Phony Communism and Its Historical Lessons for the World," in William E. Griffith, *Sino-Soviet Relations, 1964–1965* (Cambridge, Mass.: MIT Press, 1967), p. 349.

The stage was set for the Cultural Revolution at the Tenth Plenum, in the fall of 1962, when Mao pointed out that a mass campaign had not been undertaken since 1958 and that a renewal of class struggle was needed. The result of the plenum was the Socialist Education Campaign of 1963, aimed at rural cadres, who were generally the best-educated members of village society and hence quite often the sons of "rich" rather than "poor" peasants.

Because the propaganda ministry found it difficult to reach the rural population, by 1964 they had to devise a new approach — the Learn from the People's Liberation Army Movement. The result of this effort was the introduction of political departments into most civilian agencies — and considerable confusion over the division of authority. Most civilian agencies already had a dual hierarchy of administrative-bureaucratic officials and the parallel Party arrangement. In addition to this structure they were now to bring in the equivalents of the army's political commissars.

Confusion between administrative controls and ideological education increased tension and a sense of the inadequacy of the intellectual leadership of all groups. The Maoist response was to declare that publicists and writers, who set the intellectual and ideological tone for the entire society, had been lax and had fallen into the misguided ways of revisionism. They were accused of being concerned more with technical questions than with ideological dedication.

As Mao became increasingly obsessed with revisionism, he saw more signs of it at home, and in foreign affairs even imperialism seemed less menacing. In 1964 the Vietnam War intensified, and China felt considerable concern about war with the United States. Some army leaders began to feel again the need to reduce tensions with the Soviet Union in order to gain material assistance if war broke out. The point at issue was whether the Communist states should prepare to unite in support of North Vietnam. The United States' decision to bomb North Vietnam and to commit major forces to the war forced the Chinese leaders into an intense debate in which foreign policy, particularly the balancing of American against Soviet dangers, merged with domestic issues. In taking a stand on these pivotal questions, the various factions tested their power, and the scene was set for the Cultural Revolution.

On the eve of the Cultural Revolution there were four major

groupings of Chinese leaders. First were Mao and the "court" that surrounded him and ceaselessly eulogized him, idolizing his every word and deed. The small inner group consisted mainly of ideologues and propagandists who stressed "uninterrupted revolution," "red over expert," and the need for a politically conscious "nation in arms." The key figures were Mao's wife Jiang Qing, who felt that she had been denied proper recognition and had a deep grudge against Liu Shaoqi's wife; Chen Boda, a long-time personal secretary of Mao and the drafter of many of his works; and Kang Sheng, a shadowy figure long close to Mao but never holding a separate command.

The second group consisted of the leaders of the Party apparatus who were strong Leninists and believed in hardheaded and pragmatic policies for national development. They accepted the cult of Mao's personality because it posed no threat to them and was useful in mobilizing the Chinese people, but they distrusted Mao's romantic style. The most important members of this group were Liu Shaoqi and Deng Xiaoping. (During the Cultural Revolution Liu would be called "the top Party person in authority taking the capitalist road" and "China's Khrushchev.")

The third group was made up of government officials, particularly Zhou Enlai, who were administratively oriented. This group seemed to have had much in common with the pragmatic Party apparatus men, but when the conflict became intense Zhou chose to support Mao. The decision may have been influenced by personal considerations and by Zhou's long-recognized propensity to side with the winner in any controversy. Zhou may have recognized that he and his administrators would be essential to the Maoists if they should win because the Maoists lacked managerial talent. The Liu-Deng faction would have less need for Zhou's talents because of the administrators supporting it.

The fourth group, which was divided into two factions, was the military. Lin Biao led those who accepted a national strategy based on a low level of technology and strong ideological motivation. During the course of the Cultural Revolution this group identified increasingly with the Maoists, but eventually, when the army was called in to actively help the Maoists, the military leaders tended to be concerned more with order than with revolutionary ardor. The other military faction was that of Lo Ruiqing, whose commitment to technology and better relations with the Soviet Union made him an ally of the civilian Liu-Deng faction.

In early 1965 Lo Ruiqing spoke out very sharply against the United States and by implication called for better relations with the Soviet Union. Deng Xiaoping also urged a limited rapprochement with the Soviet Union, for economic and political reasons. He went so far as to say that the rapid modernization of the Chinese economy, required aid from the advanced Communist countries. It was not the Maoists who responded first to these comments. Peng Zhen, mayor of Peking and a Politburo member, bitterly denounced any suggestion of unity of action with the Soviet Union to help North Vietnam. His thesis, later to be Lin Biao's, was that wars of national liberation call for self-reliance. In short, China should not cooperate with the evil forces of revisionism, even to oppose imperialism, and should allow others to fight their guerrilla wars without becoming directly involved. In September 1965, Lin Biao issued "Long Live the Victory of People's War," a pronouncement calling for people's wars to be fought throughout the underdeveloped areas in opposition to Western influences but insisting that the guerrillas should be self-reliant rather than depend on extensive Chinese aid.

Late in September 1965, Mao began to press his case for a cultural revolution at a meeting of the standing committee of the Politburo. The outcome of the debate was inconclusive, but a group of five was formed to supervise an intensification of ideological training. Peng Zhen was made chairman of the group, which also included Kang Sheng, Wu Lengxi (editor of the *People's Daily*), Lu Tingyi (head of the Party's propaganda bureau), and Zhou Yang (a Party specialist in dealing with intellectuals).

Hardly had the group of five been designated when Mao began to show his distrust of its members, apparently believing that they were not as loyal to or enthusiastic about his ideological commitment to uninterrupted revolution as they should be. This revealed the extent to which Mao's approach was subjective and somewhat fearful. He repeatedly suspected people who professed their loyalty to him.

At this juncture Mao began his move to attack all who he believed opposed him. In November 1965 Lo Ruiqing disappeared from public view, and in February 1966 it was announced that he had been arrested. Also in November, Mao left Peking for Shanghai, where he had the newspaper *Wen Hui Bao* publish "The Dismissal of Hai Rui," an attack on the play of the same name by Wu Han, a close supporter of Peng Zhen. Thus the direct attack on Wu Han for his presumed esoteric defense of the purged Peng Dehuai was also an attack on Peng Zhen and his "independent kingdom" in Peking. Peng Zhen was the member of the Politburo most directly responsible for cultural and ideological education, but Mao was increasingly disturbed that he was too permissive toward writers. Peng Zhen was also a quasi-military figure, in command of the Peking garrison. The combination of his strategic location and his blend of ideological and military roles made him a potential power in the Party.

Why Mao Zedong left Peking and went to Shanghai and Hangzhou to launch the opening diatribes of the Cultural Revolution is unclear. Presumably he knew he could command the support of the radical Shanghai branch of the Party, and there is evidence that he had trouble persuading the editor of Peking's *People's Daily* to publish his statements. Also a factor was the matter of military force. Apparently during the winter significant troop movements took place around Peking; it was later claimed in Red Guard publications that in February 1966, Peng Zhen had attempted a coup. Mao claimed afterwards that Peking was "already under Peng Zhen's complete control" and that he had no room even "to put in a needle."[4]

On the surface, the conflict was confined to questions of cultural and propaganda affairs, but behind the scenes fundamental struggles were taking place. In April 1966, Zhou Enlai associated himself with Mao's demands for a fierce and protracted struggle to wipe out "bourgeois ideology in the academic, educational, and journalistic field, in art, literature, and all other fields of culture." In May, Deng Tuo, a member of the Central Secretariat of the Party in Peking, was viciously denounced, and later so was Liao Mosha, another high official in Peking. It became clear that Peng Zhen could not defend his subordinates. By June the heads of most of the major universities and other academic institutions were purged. Peng was specifically charged with failing to carry forward with

[4] Quoted in Gene T. Hsiao, "The Background and Development of the Proletarian Cultural Revolution," *Asian Survey* 7 (June 1967): 397.

appropriate vigor the Socialist Education Campaign and for sympathizing with the prejudices of intellectuals.

On the campuses of the major universities students were divided into factions, each claiming to be more radical than the other, and each seeking out professors to be "struggled," that is, dragged into a public arena, physically tormented, and cursed by a howling mob. In government offices deviant behavior or merely private grudges were enough to trigger collective attacks, which at times were fatal. The seeds were thus planted for a generation of hatreds.

While these attacks in the cultural and educational fields were taking place and distinguished Chinese officials were being denounced for bourgeois leanings, Liu Shaoqi, who was soon to become the principal target of the Cultural Revolution, made a goodwill visit to Pakistan and Burma. China's prestige in Asia had seriously deteriorated since the failure of a Communist coup attempt in Indonesia and the removal of Sukarno from office late in 1965. A case might therefore have been made for a state visit by the chairman of the People's Republic to strengthen Chinese influence. The effect of Liu's absence from Peking for two weeks was to greatly weaken the anti-Maoist forces.

By May 1966, Mao felt confident enough to return to Peking and in the name of the Central Committee declare the official opening of the Great Proletarian Cultural Revolution. Peng Zhen was ousted, and on June 1 the Maoists took over the *People's Daily*. Although Zhou Enlai was out of the country on a trip to Albania, he threw his prestige behind the concept of the Cultural Revolution. Even Deng Xiaoping made a militant speech for Mao. (Deng was later to be charged, as were many other reluctant radicals, with "waving the red flag to oppose the red flag" — that is, with performing pro-Maoist acts without conviction while pretending revolutionary dedication.) Tao Zhu, secretary of the Central-South Region based at Canton, was moved to Peking to take charge of the propaganda apparatus, only to be purged later for being insufficiently radical.

On the surface the cult of Mao's personality seemed to be pervasive. Everywhere he was being extolled, and the power of his Thoughts was associated with all manner of achievements, from the raising of better watermelons to the winning of table tennis matches. Mao contributed to this frenzy by carrying out what was claimed to have been a spectacular nine-mile swim down the Yangtze River in world record time.

Yet in most of the country Mao had been unable to dislodge the forces of Liu and Deng from the Party bureaucracies. The removal of Peng Zhen had started the process of purges at the top level of the Party, but Mao also had to move against the great bulk of Party professionals. To do this he sought out extremely unlikely allies — the young people and the students of high school age. His theme had been initially that the propaganda ministry had to ensure that the next generation would be imbued with proletarian revolutionary ardor so that China could avoid revisionism. As the power struggle intensified, he saw youth as a source of power for attacking the entrenched Party officials.

THE RED GUARDS

No aspect of the Cultural Revolution was quite so colorful, chaotic, or bizarre as the Red Guards. Millions of high-school-age students poured over the land, shouting down distinguished leaders, destroying precious art objects, and extolling puritan virtues. The movement spanned two symbolic acts of Mao Zedong. On August 18, 1966, at a rally of nearly half a million ecstatic students in Peking he accepted a red armband from a Red Guard. Two years later, on August 5, 1968, he dramatized the end of his sympathy for youth by presenting a "treasured gift" of mangoes to a group of industrial workers who represented the first Worker-Peasant Mao Zedong Thought Propaganda Team and had been active in opposing all the conflicting Red Guard factions at Qinghua University. The first gesture demonstrated that Mao personally backed the Red Guards and that students throughout the country ought to emulate them. The second gesture showed that Mao's patience with the antics of the Red Guards was exhausted and that he believed that the working class must exercise leadership over all.

When the Cultural Revolution began with the attacks on Wu Han and his play, *The Dismissal of Hai Rui*, no indication was given that students might be particularly involved in the controversy. But a Central Committee circular issued on May 16, 1966, alerted the students that more than cultural matters might be dividing the nation's leadership:

> The present struggle centers around the issue of implementation or resistance to Comrade Mao Zedong's line on the Cultural Revolution. . . . It is necessary at the same time to criticize and repudiate those representatives of the bourgeoisie who have sneaked into the Party, the government, the army, and all spheres of culture, to clear them out or transfer them to other positions. Above all, we must not entrust these people with the work of leading the Cultural Revolution.

Soon afterward the masses were called upon to sweep out the "monsters and ghosts" in their organizations. In schools throughout the country, Party committees began to attack the "monsters and ghosts" among the teachers and administrators, and before long students were denouncing all in any position of authority, including the very Party committees that had mobilized them. The movement picked up momentum when the students at Peking National University turned on their officials and accused them of trying to limit criticism and preserve academic order.

Early in June 1966, the Party sent work teams into the schools with the mission to overthrow the school Party committees and to manage the election of preparatory Cultural Revolution small groups, one for each class and one for the whole school. A representative of each work team stayed behind to serve as liaison with the preparatory small groups. The process of organizing students at this stage was still orderly, and a hierarchy extended from the Provincial Party Committee to the Work Team liaison member to the All-School Preparatory Committee and then to the Class Preparatory Small Group. Later in the fall, however, the work teams were denounced as the work of Liu Shaoqi, the man who was to become the prime target of the entire Cultural Revolution. This was an early example of "waving the red flag to oppose the red flag."

The attack on the work teams created great confusion on the campuses, particularly at Peking National University. Government officials appeared at large meetings with the students but seemed unable to provide definite guidance until the Central Committee's Eleventh Plenum, which in its sixteen-point decision called for direct attacks on the Party hierarchy. The students were told to organize into Red Guard units and leave their campuses to confront their local Party headquarters and denounce the Party leaders in their communities.

Mao had called for the Eleventh Plenum of the Central Committee, but when it met on August 1, 1966, his forces seemed to be a minority, so he quickly mobilized supporters, including army representatives. Finally he packed the meeting so that he could get backing for his sixteen points for intensifying the Cultural Revolution and directing it against specific Party officials.

At this stage new confusion arose because many of the most activist students were sons and daughters of the cadres who had benefited most from Communist rule. Suddenly they were being called upon to attack the established Party people with whom they were associated either directly or through their families. Such students were reluctant to act and were quickly replaced by more aggressive students, who often turned out to be the sons and daughters of lower-level cadres who had not been able to advance in the Communist hierarchy because the middle and top ranks had been filled since 1949 by older cadres.

In schools throughout the country the Red Guard movement quickly picked up emotional momentum. Each day students were gathered together and harangued by their leaders on how Mao Zedong personally was counting on them to save the revolution. Mao worship became almost hysterical. The rallies throughout the country, but particularly in Peking, became great outbursts of emotion involving waving, singing, and often crying students.

The initial focus of the Red Guards was on "destroying the four olds" (old ideas, old culture, old customs, and old habits). This resulted in violent destruction of art objects in museums and irreplaceable religious artifacts in temples and shrines. Private homes were invaded, even that of Madam Sun Yat-sen in Shanghai, who was identified with traditional Chinese culture and a bourgeois lifestyle. To protect their homes, families owning anything of historic value painted on their doors slogans by Mao Zedong in the hope that this might save them from destructive visitations by the Red Guards.

"Destroying the four olds" soon merged into "great exchanges of revolutionary experiences," in which the Red Guards began to travel all over the country and converge on Peking to discuss "revolutionary experiences." In the beginning only "five kinds of red" students (poor peasants, middle peasants, workers, revolutionary soldiers, and revolutionary cadres) were permitted to travel, but by late fall of 1966 millions of students were moving about the country, taking over the railroads without paying for either their tickets or their accommodations.

With nearly 11 million Red Guards eventually visiting Peking, hoping to see Chairman Mao in person and proclaim to him their undying affection, a great deal of behind-the-scenes logistical support clearly must have been provided. In time it became apparent that the People's Liberation Army was making the "spontaneous" actions of the Red Guards possible. The army provided food, trucks, housing, medical care, and general guidance. On November 16, 1966, the Central Committee issued a circular calling for the end of travel by the Red Guards, but the students continued to move about throughout the winter. Transportation was seriously disrupted, and this affected industrial production. Factories could neither obtain raw materials nor ship out their products.

Meanwhile, in the schools and on the campuses, conflicts were developing among the various Red Guard factions. Competing Red Guard headquarters were set up, each insisting that it represented the true spirit of Maoism. The splits among students led to a decline in the role of high-school students, who had made up the bulk of the Red Guards, and gave greater initiative to college-age activists. Leadership thus shifted from the Red Guards to the Revolutionary Rebels. The Revolutionary Rebels were generally older students with a greater sense of political purpose and enough sophistication not to dissipate their energies by attacking the diffuse evils of bourgeois thought and culture. They focused on destroying the old cadres who had succumbed to "economism," and they were ready to take on the serious task of seizing power.

The Revolutionary Rebels quickly sought to establish alliances with the workers and peasants, but in light of the behavior of the Red Guards they were, not surprisingly, rebuffed. The working classes had seen enough of the follies of student activism and were suffering because of the disruptions of the economy by the Cultural Revolution. In December 1966 and January 1967, workers in Shanghai, Hankou, and elsewhere began to hit back by taking over the railroads (in order to visit Peking), initiating strikes, and spending the money in factory treasuries on personal consumer items. Anti-Maoist forces were probably behind these actions of the workers, especially the decision for factory managers to hand over large sums of money to their employees and encourage them to buy bicycles, watches, and radios. The workers remained loyal to the Liu-Deng professionals while the economy, which was the responsibility of the Maoists, was seriously threatened by inflation.

By the spring and summer of 1967 the activities of the Red Guards and the Revolutionary Rebels had brought China to the brink of anarchy. Dramatic scenes of hundreds of thousands of Red Guards parading before their revered Chairman Mao in Peking gave way to ugly scenes of angry mobs attacking teachers, civic leaders, and foreign diplomats. The violence of the Cultural Revolution was first systematically directed not only against symbols of authority but also all that was foreign and different and nonconformist. The assaults on authority were matched by attacks on all who in the slightest way deviated from the Guards' view of correct behavior. People whose hair was too long, who wore clothes that seemed strange, whose speech was not filled with the right clichés, were all violently attacked.

Things had gotten out of hand. Mao himself had little sympathy for "petty bourgeois romantic revolutionary fervor." He believed deeply in revolution, but he knew that it called for discipline and leadership. He had to look for a new vehicle to achieve his goal, and the obvious one was the People's Liberation Army, a force committed to revolution but not given to undisciplined behavior.

THE ARMY TAKES OVER

As early as 1958, during the Lushan Conference, Mao had indicated that if necessary he would call up the army to enforce his position. During the clash with Peng Zhen in the winter of 1965, Mao started to use the *Liberation Army Daily* to express his views, and even after his associates took over the *People's Daily* in 1966, the *Liberation Army Daily* continued to be the most authoritative source of Maoist opinion.

The importance of Lin Biao rose steadily. By August 1966, at the Eleventh Plenum of the Central Committee, he was officially designated Mao's "closest comrade in arms" and the heir-apparent. While the Red Guards dominated the central scene in China, the prestige of the army quietly rose; it had been remarkably successful in keeping the Cultural Revolution out of its own ranks. Of course behind the scenes the army provided essential logistical support for the Red Guards and even more unobtrusively provided cadres who were politically active among the Red Guards.[5]

At the beginning of 1967, during the "January revolution," the Red Guards reached their high point and began to carry out the slogan of "seize power." The People's Liberation Army experienced a near-crisis. The "January revolution" was a direct attack on the Party structure at the provincial and the Peking levels. The Red Guards demanded that all Party officials who could in any way be accused of being counterrevolutionary should be removed. Because most of the officials had been in office for nearly twenty years and many functionaries beneath them had been frustrated by lack of promotion and mobility, it was not hard to find people who were willing to prefer charges against officials.

Utter confusion resulted. All manner of leaders were suddenly under attack, and the Red Guards and the Revolutionary Rebels were engaged in "revealing" all kinds of secrets in their numerous newspapers and wall posters. Every day Red Guards at the various headquarters designed posters indicting specific leaders and explaining Party decisions. The explanations generally revealed that for many years intensive and extensive clashes had taken place between the factions of the Chinese Communist leaders. Many of the charges were false, but they did cause significant reverberations. People trying to defend themselves made countercharges and revealed other secrets. The exhilaration of public demonstrations gave way to the excitement of intense factional struggle and of character assassination. Leaders throughout the country as well as in Peking disappeared, and many suicides were reported.

In this atmosphere the army's Cultural Revolution group was reorganized, and Jiang Qing, Mao's wife, was made an advisor to it. It appeared that the army would have to support fully the

[5] Ellis Joffe, "The Chinese Army in the Cultural Revolution: The Politics of Intervention," *Current Scene* 8 (December 7, 1970): 8.

seizures of power by the Revolutionary Rebels. When the Red Guards ran into severe opposition from the workers, however, it was natural for the army to retreat and become the arbitrating force responsible for basic order. The Maoists in Peking realized that the momentum of the Cultural Revolution would decline if the Red Guards and the Revolutionary Rebels failed to get the backing of the army. On January 23, 1967, they ordered the army to intervene to support the "seizure of power." At this crucial juncture, however, the army refused to follow the revolutionary course and instead acted as a stabilizing force, seeking order rather than partisan support of the rebels.

Tension between the Maoists and the army was resolved by formalizing the balance among the key factions through triple alliances, which led to the formation of revolutionary committees. The triple alliance involved the Revolutionary Rebels, including the Red Guards, the Revolutionary Cadres (former Party members who had "remolded" themselves and were certified as loyal Maoists), and army representatives. In February 1967, the first Revolutionary Committee was established in Heilongjiang, and Peking declared that it was to be the model for the rest of the country, rather than the Paris Commune, which the Red Guards had been extolling. Many of the Red Guards complained that the triple alliance formula for establishing the revolutionary committees provided a mask behind which the old cadres and the pragmatic soldiers could reestablish themselves without any real change of heart. The charge that people were "waving the red flag to oppose the red flag" became more widespread because judgments about subjective commitments were to be decisive in determining who was to have power in China.

Although Jiang Qing and the other extreme radicals continued to call for revolution, Zhou Enlai and the moderate Maoists seemed to go along with the idea that the army should gradually restore order. The creation of revolutionary committees proceeded very slowly because of the difficulties in deciding who should represent the Revolutionary Rebels and the Revolutionary Cadres. Factions in the provinces contended with each other and refused to yield. They knew that exclusion from the revolutionary committees would mean political, and perhaps physical, death.

In mid-July the delicate balance in the army between its central command and its regional authorities was dramatically strained by the most significant event of the Cultural Revolution, the Wuhan incident.[6] A high-level delegation from Peking led by two Central Committee members, Xie Fuzhi, vice-premier and head of the Peking City Revolutionary Committee, and Wang Li, a member of Jiang Qing's Revolutionary group, went to Wuhan to try to settle the factional fighting between two huge rival Red Guard organizations. The local military commander, Chen Zaidao, had backed the more "conservative" faction, but Peking insisted that the other group be recognized and that Chen publicly withdraw his support. The two emissaries were physically attacked in their hotel and were finally saved by the dispatch of troops toward Wuhan. Chen was dismissed from his post, and Xie Fuzhi and Wang Li were welcomed back to Peking by a massive parade of more than 1 million people.

The immediate consequence of the Wuhan incident was a step-up of radical Red Guard actions under Jiang Qing's leadership. But more fundamentally the incident propelled the army into a more active role in controlling developments. The other regional commanders decided that they should be more rigorous in managing the formation of revolutionary committees and not permit the factional strife to get out of hand as it had in Wuhan. Jiang Qing in the meantime had demanded that the army be purged and that the Maoists should "drag out the handful of power holders in the army." By mid-August the military had counterattacked, and Wang Li, the hero of Wuhan, was purged for being excessively antiarmy. On September 5, 1967, Jiang Qing dramatically called for universal support of the army and denounced the Red Guards who had been attacking the military.

The army thus gradually came to the fore as the principal instrument of public rule. In September 1967, only six provinces had revolutionary committees, and in twenty-two provinces the army ruled directly. Thereafter, even when revolutionary commit-

[6] For a detailed discussion of the Wuhan incident see Thomas W. Robinson, "The Wuhan Incident: Local Strife and Provincial Rebellion during the Cultural Revolution," P-4511 (Santa Monica, Calif.: The Rand Corporation, December 1970).

tees were established they were clearly under the domination of the army. Indeed, the triple alliances were in many cases little more than facades for army control.

From April through July 1968, a last effort was made to revive the revolutionary processes. The Maoists were successful in obtaining the dismissal of the army's acting chief of staff, Yang Chengwu, as well as removing the commander of the Peking garrison and the political commissar of the air force. Apparently these men had moved too early in expressing their opposition to Jiang Qing and the radicals who could attack them without creating a general confrontation with the army.

By August, however, Mao had appointed envoys and organized the Worker-Peasant Mao Zedong Thought Propaganda Teams to disband Red Guards and had presented the first team with his famous mangoes. Mangoes were distributed throughout the country, and meetings were held to revere Mao's "gift" and to learn that the chairman no longer favored the Red Guards but honored the more conservative workers and peasants. By September the last revolutionary committees were established and the army was fully in control behind the scenes. Peking declared that the country was finally "all red." In the end China, like so many other newly developing countries, was dependent on its military to maintain order and to manage public affairs. The regional commanders set about breaking up Red Guard units and sending the youth to the countryside to take up the rural life of the peasant.

CHAPTER FIFTEEN

The Last Years of the Mao Era

The restoration of public order after the turmoil of the Cultural Revolution did not eliminate the deep divisions in Chinese politics. A chasm separated political language and action as the rhetoric of the country continued to adhere to the radical themes of the Cultural Revolution while substantive policies in most fields reverted to the more pragmatic practices of the pre–Cultural Revolution period. Antagonisms developed within the Party between the younger members who had benefited from the upheavals of the Cultural Revolution and the older cadres who had suffered. In the years that followed, these divisions provided the basis for the loose clustering of what were to be called the "radicals" and the "moderates." In general the "radicals," who were based in Shanghai, concentrated on ideological and cultural issues, dominated the mass media and the theater, and had as their leading patron Jiang Qing, Mao Zedong's wife. The "moderates," who managed the economy and administered the government, were generally the older cadres, many of whom had been humiliated and temporarily purged during the Cultural Revolution. The "moderates" held a variety of views, but in the main they were united in opposing the "radicals" on substantive policies and on their emotional ways.

THE NINTH PARTY CONGRESS AND THE RISE OF LIN BIAO

When Mao signaled the end of the Cultural Revolution in August 1968, the Chinese Communist Party was in a shambles. Power at the provincial and lower levels was in the hands of revolutionary committees in which People's Liberation Army officers played a dominant role. The concept of the Party, however, was never attacked and even the most revolutionary Maoists maintained the traditional view that the Party was the ultimate instrument for revolution. Their attack had been on those holding Party offices and on the bureaucratization of the Party.

Consequently it was relatively easy to reach agreement that the Central Committee should be reconstructed and another Party congress called. The "radicals" who had been forced out of power at the local levels hoped that they might still be able to recoup influence at the top, where Mao's preferences could be expected to carry weight. The military officers who had been brought into governmental roles through the revolutionary committees wanted a congress to legitimize their new powers. Finally, the old Party cadres who had been vilified and "dragged out" for public humiliation during the Cultural Revolution sensed that the process of their rehabilitation and restoration to high office might be accelerated by having the Party reestablished.

Thus there was broad agreement to convene the Ninth Party Congress in April 1969. The event served to dramatize the changes caused by the Cultural Revolution. The new importance of the army in government was vividly demonstrated by the fact that 40 percent of the representatives at the congress were army officers, and of the 279 members of the new Central Committee appointed by the congress, 123 were from the military.[1] At the Eighth Congress only 27 percent had been from the military. The effects of the purges could be seen by comparing Party officeholders of the Eighth Central Committee, appointed in March 1966, with those present when the Ninth Central Committee was formed: only fifty-four members of the full committee survived, and more critically, only three members of the nine-member Standing Committee of the Politburo remained.[2] Of the sixty-seven secretaries and alternate secretaries of the six regional bureaus, only thirteen survived.

[1] Richard Baum, "China: Year of the Mangoes," *Asian Survey* 9 (January 1969): 4.

[2] Gordon A. Bennett, "China's Continuing Revolution: Will It Be Permanent?" *Asian Survey* 10 (January 1970): 4.

Twenty of the twenty-eight provincial Party secretaries were purged, two were severely criticized, and one committed suicide.[3]

At its meeting the Ninth Party Congress produced a new Party constitution that contained an unusual article designating Lin Biao by name as Mao's successor. During the Cultural Revolution Lin Biao had been closely associated with Mao and he had written the introduction to the *Thoughts of Chairman Mao Tse-tung*, the "Little Red Book." Thus the Maoists approved him, as did the political commissar elements in the army.

The steady rise of Lin Biao in the Party hierarchy was not due to any outstanding ideological or administrative contributions. In April 1955 he was made a member of the Politburo; by May 1958 he was a vice-chairman of the Central Committee and the sixth-ranking leader. In September 1959 he replaced the purged Peng Dehuai as defense minister. In June 1966, with the fall of Chairman Liu Shaoqi, he officially became the second-ranking Chinese Communist. Much of his success came from his abiding commitment to the blend of political and military techniques he had learned at Whampoa and during the Long March. The simple guerrilla style of dealing with problems, which appealed increasingly to Mao as he grew older, was always Lin Biao's basic approach. When Peng Dehuai was purged because he felt that China needed a modernized military establishment to meet the challenge of the United States, Lin Biao naturally became the spokesman for a more militia and guerrilla oriented People's Liberation Army. The idea of a politically inspired army making do with primitive technologies was satisfying to Lin Biao and coincided with Mao's view of what China needed on the eve of the Cultural Revolution.

In September 1967, Lin Biao made a major statement on "people's wars" in which he advanced the view that Mao Zedong's strategy, which had brought the Communists to victory in China, was appropriate for advancing world revolution. He suggested that Mao's theory of building revolutionary base areas in the rural countryside in order to encircle the cities and eventually strangle them could be repeated, with the underdeveloped countries of Africa and

[3] Richard Hughes, "Mao Makes the Trials Run on Time," *New York Times Magazine* (August 23, 1970), p. 67.

Asia representing the "countryside" and America and Western Europe the "cities." Lin's doctrine was seen by some people as a declaration of Chinese support throughout underdeveloped areas for guerrilla or people's wars, such as the Vietnam War. Other analysts, however, noticed that he also called on the people to employ self-reliance.

The new constitution also called for a reconstituted Party that would combine the principles of the earlier triple alliance with a three-way alliance of old, middle-aged, and young people, along with the classic Maoist concept of the mass line and the principle "from the people, to the people."

Progress in Party consolidation and reconstruction was exceedingly slow. Six months after the Ninth Congress only thirty-seven county Party committees had been established in the more than 2,000 counties in China, and no provincial or autonomous region committees existed. The Struggle-Criticism-Transformation Campaign kept alive the tensions between the young Maoists who wanted power and the older cadres who could claim that they were purified and should retain office. In this process, the army had to decide how far it should go in making decisions or in allowing the contending factions to fight out their disagreements.

By late 1970 and early 1971 the army and the Maoists in Peking made a tacit agreement to side with the moderate elements in rebuilding the Party in return for maintaining the rhetoric of the Cultural Revolution. Thus "ultra-leftists" were purged, and "Party core groups" in the Revolutionary Committee — older cadres and army representatives — were placed in the new Party committees at various local levels. The chairmen of the revolutionary committees generally became the new secretaries of the Party committees. On December 13, 1970, the first provincial Party committee was established in Hunan, and in two weeks committees were set up in Jiangsu, Guangdong, and Jiangxi. Yet when the Hunan Party committee was established, only fifteen of the eighty-two counties in the province had Party committees, and in the country as a whole only 180 county Party committees existed. By April 1971, fourteen of twenty-eight provincial and special area committees had been formed, and all except the Shanghai committee were under moderate old cadres or military officers. The goal of reconstructing the Party for its fiftieth anniversary was not met. On July 1, 1971, there were still four provinces without committees — Sichuan, Tibet, Ningxia, and Heilongjiang. On August 26, 1971, these committees were finally organized. Yet at the county level fewer than 400 committees had been identified in the entire country.

REBUILDING THE MEANS OF GOVERNING

The effects of the Cultural Revolution on government institutions were somewhat uneven. The ministries responsible for nuclear development and advanced scientific research were almost untouched. Other ministries were brought to a complete standstill. For example, the Red Guards occupied the offices of the foreign ministry, destroyed the files, and brought China's diplomacy to a complete halt during most of 1966. All but one of Peking's ambassadors to other countries were recalled so that they could be put through the ordeal of the Cultural Revolution and "remolded." For nearly two years China had only one ambassador abroad, in Cairo. In this xenophobic spirit the Red Guards attacked various embassies in Peking, threatened the lives of French and British officials, and beat up Indian diplomats — with the result that Indian mobs attacked and caused the hospitalization of Chinese diplomatic personnel in New Delhi.

When Zhou Enlai assumed control of the remnants of administration after the shattering effects of the Cultural Revolution, accusations were made against groups who presumably had been excessively destructive. In particular, announcements were made that the destruction of the foreign office and the recalling of all but one of China's ambassadors had been the work of the ultra-leftist "five-one-six clique." (This group was inspired by the Central Committee circular of May 16, 1966 — hence 5/16.) The purge of this clique, and in particular the trial and execution of Yao Dienshao, signaled the return of bureaucratic order in government administration.

During the height of the Cultural Revolution the State Council had ceased to operate, and of the sixteen deputy premiers, eight were completely purged, five were criticized and demoted, and one died. Only two survived politically. After the Cultural Revolution the size of government was reduced by combining ministries. A feature of the continued use of radical rhetoric was the argument that fewer ministries were necessary because planning was being decentralized and popular participation increased. In practice, however, the reorganization rationalized administration and increased effective coordination among officials in Peking.

One of the consequences of the confusion that accompanied the reorganization of the government after the Cultural Revolution was a rise in the use of the concept of the "Center," a vague and nonspecified institution, as the top decision-making location. After the Cultural Revolution local officials would refer to the ultimate authority of an impersonal "center," which could be the ministry, the Central Committee, the Politburo, the Standing Committee of the Politburo, the prime minister, a deputy minister, or even Chairman Mao himself. Foreign visitors to China have often been told about how decisions are divided between the locality and the "Center," but generally they cannot learn precisely who the "Center" is because the briefing officers do not themselves know.

A second change, and possibly the most profound change to come out of the Cultural Revolution, was in the relationship between the Party and the government. Before the Cultural Revolution the Chinese followed the customary Communist practice of having parallel but separate structures of the Party hierarchy and the governmental bureaucracies, with Party officials at each level penetrating and providing additional control over the governmental bureaus and offices. Immediately after the Cultural Revolution the establishment of revolutionary committees at every level of government and in every institution and organization meant that there was only a single line of command. In time, the rebuilding of Party committees meant that there were both revolutionary committees and Party committees at every level.

This situation might have led to confusion and tension had it not been for the practice of having the membership of both committees directing an organization usually consisting of the same people, plus or minus only one or two individuals. In theory the revolutionary committees assumed responsibility for day-to-day administration while the Party committees dealt with longer range issues, but in practice this distinction had little meaning.

The consequence of this overlapping membership was to integrate the hierarchical structure of government in China to a degree unknown in any socialist state. In most institutions the practice was for the "leading figure" or "responsible official" of the revolutionary committee to be also the Party secretary, thus ensuring complete coordination and a direct line of authority.

The speed with which the Chinese economy recovered from the disruptions of the Cultural Revolution can be attributed in no small measure to the establishment of this system of authority and the alacrity with which the experienced cadres returned to their former offices and assumed responsibilities at every level of industry and commerce. Zhou Enlai in 1972 indicated to foreign visitors that less than 1 percent of the cadres had been removed by the Cultural Revolution.

The process of rehabilitation of officials customarily involved a period of service at a May Seventh School. These were institutions established in rural areas to which leading cadres might be assigned for a time of physical labor and ideological self-criticism. The rehabilitated cadres were also constantly reminded of the importance of ideological matters by the regular "struggle, criticize, and reform" sessions held in every institution and office. At these meetings all involved in an organization were brought together to confront each other to determine how operations might be improved and how they could better put into practice the Thoughts of Mao Zedong.

THE SOVIET THREAT AND THE AMERICAN OPENING

Both the initiation of the Cultural Revolution and the abruptness of its termination reflected Mao's changing views of the Soviet Union. In 1966 Mao was worried that the Soviet example of "revisionism" might eventually contaminate China and lead to a "restoration of capitalism." He saw the Soviet Union losing its commitment to Communism as the Russians became more interested in improving their material well-being. He therefore felt that it was even more urgent to elevate revolutionary fervor in China than to cooperate with the Soviet Union in opposing the United States in Vietnam. By 1969 Mao's fears of the Soviet Union had evolved into very concrete anxieties about a direct military threat to China.

In 1968 Russian troops occupied Czechoslovakia in support of the Brezhnev Doctrine, which held that the Soviet Union was justified in using force to prevent any socialist state from abandoning Communism. Then Chinese and Russian troops clashed several times on an island in the Ussuri River in March 1969. The Chinese were later to claim that the Soviets had "provoked" a total of 4,189 border incidents since the beginning of boundary negotiations between the two governments on October 15, 1964.[4] The situation in 1969 was much more tense because the Chinese were now aware that the Soviets might be less inhibited in using force, a conclusion drawn from the Czechoslovakian affair and Soviet propaganda, which was depicting China as recklessly irrational, as demonstrated by the excesses of the Cultural Revolution. At that time China was diplomatically isolated with no strong friends, and the Soviets were hinting in various capitals that it might be appropriate for Russia to destroy China's new nuclear capability before it became more significant.

Sino-Soviet relations had begun to deteriorate with Khrushchev's denunciation of Stalin at the Twentieth Soviet Party Congress in February 1956. We know now that the decisive event that created distrust between Moscow and Peking was the Quemoy-Matsu crisis of 1958. At that time the Chinese were concerned about the possibility of United States involvement, so they asked the Soviet Union for reassurances that their mutual defense treaty would apply in the event of an American nuclear attack. The Soviet response was that they would only commit themselves to support China in situations covered by prior consultations — a response the Chinese took to mean that Moscow wished to control Peking's foreign policy.[5] When the Chinese asked Russia to provide the same air force protection for Shanghai and the south China coast as it had during the Korean War, Russia responded by demanding naval facilities, which the Chinese interpreted as a revival of nineteenth-century imperialist ambitions for treaty concessions.

Thereafter distrust between the two governments rose so steadily that when the border incidents of 1969 occurred the two

[4] Thomas W. Robinson, "The Sino-Soviet Border Dispute," *American Political Science Review* 66 (December 1972): 1175–1202.

[5] A. Doak Barnett, "The 1958 Quemoy Crisis: The Sino-Soviet Dimension," *Problems of Communism*, July–August 1976, pp. 38–39.

countries were close to war. The threat of war was apparently made more explicit in the fall of 1969 when Prime Minister Kosygin, on returning from the funeral of Ho Chi Minh in Hanoi, met Premier Zhou Enlai at the Peking airport, at Kosygin's insistence.

The Soviet Union immediately began a massive military buildup in its far eastern and central Asian territories. By the spring of 1971 more Soviet forces were deployed against China than against NATO in Europe. The Soviet buildup ultimately reached the point of being the largest deployment of military forces capable of affecting the world balance of power ever to have occurred without a major war.

Mao Zedong and Zhou Enlai were then confronted with an urgent need to replan China's national security policies. For more than 150 years China had perceived its security problems as coming from the sea, for it had defended itself first against British and other European sea powers, then against Japan, and finally against the United States. During this period China had been able to allow its northern border to stand relatively unguarded, with armies deployed instead in the populated eastern and coastal areas. This fact explains in part the unique pattern of civil-military relations in modern China, as from the time of the warlords, through the Kuomintang period, and during the whole history of the People's Republic, Chinese armies were concentrated in the densely populated areas, and thus readily available to support the administrative tasks of government. By 1970, all that had changed, as the Chinese were again the prisoners of their ancient historic problem of having to guard the longest frontier in the world. To do so they had to extract resources from their rich agricultural areas to support standing armies in their unpopulated inner Asian reaches. This was the problem that long before had led to the construction of the Great Wall — a defense problem so costly that it contributed substantially to the fall of the great dynasties — the Han, the Tang, and the Ming.

Faced with this situation, and sensitive to the fact that they were surrounded by countries that distrusted their revolutionary intentions, Mao and Zhou decided to try again to ease tensions with the United States. Through ambassadorial talks in Warsaw, the United States in 1964 had assured the Chinese that it had no aggressive designs on North Vietnam or China. This American pledge had so convinced Mao that he felt free to initiate the Cultural

Revolution; and since the United States had continued to refrain from invading North Vietnam and was obviously anxious to extract itself from the war, the stage was set for a possible improvement in United States–China relations. In January 1970, Peking resumed the Warsaw talks with the United States; China stopped abusing the United Nations as a "tool of imperialism" and hinted that it wanted to join the world organization; and Peking returned most of its ambassadors to their posts with instructions to seek more cordial relations toward all countries, except the Soviet Union and its allies.

In the spring of 1971 Peking invited the American table tennis team, which was playing at the world championship tournament in Japan, to tour China. "Ping-pong diplomacy" was accompanied by China's admission of selected Western correspondents who could report to the world that order had been reestablished and economic growth was again under way. On July 9, Henry Kissinger, the president's national security advisor, followed up the Chinese initiative by secretly boarding a plane in Pakistan and flying to Peking for meetings with Zhou Enlai and Mao Zedong. These sessions laid the groundwork for the historic first visit of an American president to China, the announcement of which greatly surprised the world.

Aside from the great symbolic value of signaling a dramatic change in the state of Sino-American relations, President Richard Nixon's visit in February 1972, produced the Shanghai Communiqué. This striking document adopted the unique form of allowing each side to state its views on matters of disagreement but also contained the agreement that both governments would work to "normalize" relations. The United States stated that it agreed with "the Chinese on both sides of the Straits" that Taiwan was part of China, and that as "tension in the area diminishes," that is, once peace was arranged in Vietnam, "it would progressively withdraw its forces" from Taiwan. The Shanghai Communiqué also pledged both countries to support scientific and cultural exchanges.

Zhou Enlai hoped that this diplomatic opening to the United States would help to neutralize the Soviet threat, facilitate better relations with other countries, especially Japan, and help China gain admission to the United Nations. He expected such domestic benefits as increased Chinese access to the technology necessary for economic and military growth, and he hoped to strengthen the forces favoring order after the Cultural Revolution. With increasing numbers of foreign delegations visiting the country, all Chinese, especially the Cultural Revolution "radicals," would be put on their best behavior. President Nixon hoped the move would facilitate American disengagement from Vietnam, pressure the Soviets to pursue détente more assiduously, and strengthen his position in the forthcoming election.

During subsequent visits by Kissinger to China, agreement was reached for each government to establish in the other's capital a "liaison office" that would serve as an unofficial embassy until "normalization" was completed. Soon after the United States government lifted most restraints on trade with China and the American public was welcoming tours of Chinese performing arts troupes and athletic teams.

THE LIN BIAO AFFAIR

While progress was occurring on the international front China experienced a severe domestic crisis. On September 12, 1971, between the secret Kissinger visit and the state visit of President Nixon, the constitutionally designated successor to Mao Zedong, Lin Biao, was killed in an airplane crash in Mongolia, while apparently attempting to flee to the Soviet Union. The world learned that during the "September Crisis" other military leaders had also vanished, including Chief of the General Staff Huang Yongsheng, Air Force Commander Wu Faxian, and Navy Commissar Li Zuobeng. Yet for nearly two years the new Party hierarchy in China maintained a remarkably disciplined silence as cadres throughout the country were systematically told what the leadership claimed had happened. Finally, it was announced that heir apparent Lin Biao, the "closest comrade in arms of Mao" and a military defender of the "radicals," had attempted on three occasions to assassinate Chairman Mao Zedong and had plotted a coup d'etat.

It was subsequently charged that Lin Biao had been "left in form but right in essence," and while appearing to flatter Mao and extol his Thoughts, Lin's real motives were quite different. Cadres throughout China were told that Lin and his gang of "swindlers" had a plot to which they had given the code name "571 Plan" — a number which, when pronounced in Chinese, sounds like the words for "military uprising" or "coup." As a part of the systematic denunciation of Lin Biao, a document was circulated through the Party that purportedly was the actual plan of the plotters and achieved an aura of plausibility by stressing known criticisms of Mao's leadership style. In the document Mao was referred to as "Old B-52" — an allusion to the Chairman's practice of "flying" high above everyone else and while out of sight dropping his "bombs," or surprise directives, and then staying "out of reach" of any counterattacks. The document described Mao as unstable in his treatment of colleagues, which explained why an officially designated heir apparent would feel it necessary to assassinate him: "Today he woos *A* and strikes at *B*; tomorrow he will woo *B* and strike at *A*. . . . Viewed from several score of years of history, has there been anyone promoted by him and who has escaped a political death sentence later? . . . Has there been any political force which can cooperate with him from beginning to end?" [6]

Apparently Lin Biao's daughter revealed the plot to Zhou Enlai. When Lin discovered this, he, his wife, his oldest son, and six others boarded an Air Force Trident jet and attempted to escape to the Soviet Union.

THE DEATH OF ZHOU ENLAI

The Lin Biao affair had the effect of elevating Zhou Enlai to the second-rank position in the Party, as well as creating suspicions about the political loyalties within the army leadership, and discrediting further the "ultra-leftists" who, like Lin Biao, had profited by the Cultural Revolution. Zhou saw his task to be the improvement of economic and administrative management and preparing for the succession to Mao. His method was to accelerate the rehabilitation of old cadres purged and discredited by the Cultural Revolution.

Zhou's success in accomplishing his objectives can be seen from the membership of the new Central Committee that came out of the Tenth Party Congress, held in August 1973 to fill the leadership gaps created by the fall of Lin Biao and the purge of some 500

[6] Michael Y. M. Kau, *The Lin Piao Affair* (White Plains, N.Y.: International Arts and Sciences Press, 1975), pp. 78–96.

officers and cadres. The number of army officers was sharply cut back, down to only 30 percent, and the number of provincial level cadres greatly increased. At the congress Zhou also stressed the need "to strengthen the centralized leadership of the Party." [7]

Zhou accomplished this by dramatically bringing back, as deputy prime minister, Deng Xiaoping, the close ally of Liu Shaoqi who had been viciously vilified by the Red Guards and held for seven years under house arrest. Deng quickly sought to consolidate his position by assuming posts that made it possible for him to direct the Party, the government, and the army. Deng apparently had to move fast because in 1972 Zhou Enlai was diagnosed as having stomach cancer, although he was not hospitalized until the spring of 1974 and the world did not learn that he was seriously ill until that summer.

In the process of strengthening his political base, Deng contributed to the increasing polarization of Chinese politics into the camps observers tended to call the "moderates" and the "radicals." The former were largely the old cadres, who were primarily interested in the industrial and economic modernization of China, saw the value of material incentives, appreciated the importance of quality education and training in technical skills, and welcomed increased foreign trade and the importation of advanced technology. The "radicals" valued the traditions of the Cultural Revolution, stressed the need for ideological purity, the dangers of "revisionism," the merits of self-sufficiency, the need to emphasize "redness" over "expertness," and the evils of intellectual and spiritual contamination from abroad.

Under Deng's administration the Party apparatus was steadily strengthened by placing "moderates" in decision-making positions and leaving the "radicals" free only to control propaganda, the media, and education. Deng also challenged the political role of the army by forcing officers out of administrative positions, and he eventually even transferred some of the powerful regional military commanders who had held the same bases of power since 1949. Deng's problem was only partly political, for he also was concerned with how to meet the Soviet military buildup along the border. He

[7] A. Doak Barnett, *Uncertain Passage: China's Transition to the Post-Mao Era* (Washington, D.C.: The Brookings Institution, 1974), p. 56.

could not afford to increase defense expenditures without endangering the recovery of the civilian economy from the disruptions of the Cultural Revolution. He therefore sought to make the army more efficient and professional.

Opposition to Deng centered among the ideologically oriented members of the Party who could not forget that Deng had scorned ideology and favored pragmatic policies and orderly administration before the Cultural Revolution. With their control of the media the radicals sought to sweep the country into new propaganda campaigns, while Zhou Enlai from his hospital bed brilliantly deflected or reformulated the attacks in order to neutralize their impact.

The radicals, for example, pressed forward with a campaign denouncing Confucius as a "revisionist" who sought to preserve a "slave" society when China was on the verge of becoming a "feudal" society. The issue has some importance for theoretical Marxism and its stages of history, but in practice the anti-Confucius attacks could only be read as criticism of Zhou Enlai, because of his mandarin style, his welcoming of advice from foreigners, and his belief in learning. Zhou, however, reformulated the attacks into an "Anti-Confucius/Anti–Lin Biao Campaign" and this made it politically inoffensive. Similarly, when the radicals sought to discredit Zhou's policy of inviting foreigners to visit China by criticizing a film produced by Italian director Michelangelo Antonioni, Zhou's supporters initiated a campaign against Beethoven, which was clearly an attack on Jiang Qing, Mao's radical wife, who had insisted that the Philadelphia Orchestra play Beethoven's Seventh Symphony during its tour of China.

Zhou further strengthened the position of the moderates when he left his sickbed in February 1975 to preside over the Fourth National People's Congress, and to call for the creation of a "powerful, modern socialist country" in the next twenty-five years. At the time, it did not seem particularly significant that Mao had not personally endorsed Zhou's vision of the "comprehensive modernization of agriculture industry, national defense and science and technology" by the year 2000.

The radicals, possibly supported by Mao,[8] sought to attack

[8] Parris H. Chang, "Mao's Last Stand?" *Problems of Communism* (July–August 1976), p. 6.

Zhou's program by introducing a new campaign based on the "theory of proletarian dictatorship," which stressed the need for "proletarian views" (that is, the radical's views) to prevail over "bourgeois attitudes." In August 1975, the radicals introduced another exotic campaign against Deng and Zhou in the form of criticisms of the Chinese classical novel *Water Margin*. It was charged that the hero of the novel, Song Jiang, a Robin Hood–like leader, had in fact been a "capitulator," who ultimately sold out to the established authorities, and was thus at heart a "revisionist." During this campaign considerable comment was made about the existence within the Party of "right-deviationist wind," "capitalist-roaders," and in time, "those who would reverse correct decisions," which all were code words attacking Deng Xiaoping. Those doing the attacking used quotations from Mao's writing that could be explicitly applied as criticisms of Deng's policies. Thus they sought to make much over a statement by Mao that held that "class struggle" should not be sacrificed in emphasizing "stability" and "unity."

In spite of these attacks, Deng appeared secure until Zhou Enlai died on January 8, 1976. Deng gave the eulogy at the state funeral on January 15, but that was his last public act before his second purge from power. Under the control of the radicals, the Chinese press began to speak ominously about "an unrepenting capitalist-roader inside the Party." Apparently, in a Politburo meeting on the last night in January Mao failed to back Deng as the new prime minister. In a compromise, Hua Guofeng, the fifth-ranking member of the Politburo and the head of the secret police, was made the "acting prime minister." (Hua had served in Mao's home province of Hunan, and in the late 1950s, when Mao was having difficulty with Liu Shaoqi and Deng Xiaoping, Hua graciously built a special hall in honor of Mao in his family village of Shaoshan.)

At this juncture, the forces loyal to the memory of Zhou sought to reassert what had been the dominant policies of the last few years. In their efforts to relegitimize Zhou's domestic and foreign programs, they decided to stage a repeat of the Nixon visit. The Western press wondered whether the invitation to the discredited former president was a calculated insult to the new American president, Gerald Ford, for his excessive enthusiasm for détente with the Soviet Union and his foot-dragging on normalizing relations with the People's Republic. The Chinese press covered the visit at great length, stressing Mao's warm meeting with the Nixons. Apparently, the object was to convince the Party workers that the line initiated by Zhou Enlai was still correct.

Yet as soon as the visit ended, attacks on the "capitalist-roader in the Party" intensified. To make sure that no one misunderstood the meaning of the attacks, reference was made to the "false" doctrine that "it doesn't matter whether the cat is black or white as long as it catches mice." This was a widely recognized reference to a remark Deng Xiaoping had made shortly before the Cultural Revolution (when he was championing pragmatic solutions over doctrinal rigidity), which contributed to the earlier political disgrace from which Zhou had rehabilitated him. Although not yet attacked by name, it was clear to all that Deng was the target and that he was vulnerable without his patron. The Chinese press also spoke about the "scheming revisionist" doctrine of "falsely" equating "stability and order" and "economic growth" with class struggle, instead of making the class struggle the key to "studying the dictatorship of the proletariat."

In spite of the attacks on Deng, throughout March it still seemed that Zhou Enlai's arrangements would survive the polemical outbursts. The struggle was brought to a head, however, on April 4, the date of the Qing Ming Festival, when the Chinese traditionally go to cemeteries to refurbish ancestral graves. In Zhou Enlai's purported will — some charge that it was forged — he supposedly asked that his ashes be scattered throughout the length and breadth of China. Thus no grave, mausoleum, or special place honors his memory. On the Qing Ming Sunday in 1976, tens of thousands of people loyal to the memory of Zhou and undoubtedly eager to demonstrate their support for Deng, chose to go to the huge Tiananmen Square in the center of Peking to lay wreaths at the Monument of the Martyrs of the Revolution.

The wreaths were piled more than forty feet high and carried slogans attacking the radicals, most particularly Jiang Qing, Mao's wife: "Down with the Empress Dowager!" "Down With Indira Gandhi!" and "Let Us Remember Yang Kaihui" (Mao's first wife).

On the night of April 4, all the wreaths were removed. On April 5, a crowd of more than 100,000 gathered, chanting slogans, overturning at least one car, wrecking a fire engine, and tossing policemen's caps into the air. Later, the *People's Daily* was to claim that the trouble was caused by only "a few bad elements, sporting crew cuts, and taking turns at inciting the people by shouting themselves hoarse through a transistor megaphone." Yet Western observers noted that the crowd pressed toward the Great Hall of the People as though to "present a petition," and then it sprang to the other corner of the square and attacked a building belonging to the public security forces (Hua Guofeng's secret police).

The demonstration was, of course, organized and not spontaneous, but it did prove the strength of the Zhou-Deng forces. The crowd was finally dispersed by "tens of thousands of worker-militiamen, in coordination with PLA guards." Elsewhere in China, there were violent outbursts in sympathy with the events in Tiananmen Square. The Chinese power structure was splitting, and opposing elements were resorting to violence. On the night of April 7, the Politburo had an emergency meeting and announced that Deng Xiaoping had been stripped of all his offices but would be allowed to retain his Party membership "so he can be carefully observed." Hua Guofeng was made premier and first vice-chairman of the Party.

THE DEATH OF MAO ZEDONG AND THE FALL OF THE RADICALS

These events in the spring of 1976 suggested that the tide might be moving in favor of the radicals, yet those who held the key Party posts in both Peking and the provinces were solid moderates. Chinese politics seemed to be temporarily stalemated, with Premier Hua serving as a compromise leader.

This was the national picture on September 9, 1976, when the aged Mao Zedong died. The entire nation mourned the loss of their great national hero. Yet the funeral was barely over before it became apparent that without the ultimate, stabilizing authority of Mao, political conflict would intensify. At the memorial service Hua Guofeng left out of his oral speech a phrase in the written text that the Chinese press had claimed was a posthumous instruction from Mao: "Act according to the principles laid down." Later Hua charged that Mao's widow, Jiang Qing, had fabricated the quotation and that other radicals were altering the words of Mao. Apparently Jiang Qing told a Politburo meeting that Mao felt that Hua was incapable of managing the Party and that she should become the new chairman, but Hua asserted that the dying Mao had told him directly, "With you in charge I am at ease."

On the basis of accounts in wall posters it appears that Defense Minister Ye Jianying told Hua that he suspected that Jiang Qing and her three Shanghai "radical" colleagues were plotting a coup. The three were: Wang Hongwen, who had risen rapidly during the Cultural Revolution from textile worker to second-ranking member of the Politburo; Yao Wenyuan, the former Shanghai Party secretary, who ran the country's propaganda machinery; and Zhang Chunqiao, a vice-premier who also rose during the Cultural Revolution and had been a potential successor to Zhou and Mao. It seems that on the morning of October 6, a gunman shot into a procession of limousines in which Hua was riding, and when the alleged assassin was captured he confessed that he was acting on behalf of Jiang Qing and the three others. An augmented Politburo meeting was called that night in the Forbidden City, and during the meeting men from Mao's own bodyguard, Unit 8341 of the People's Liberation Army, arrested Jiang Qing, Wang, Yao, and Zhang.

The next day, when local leaders in Shanghai learned that Hua Guofeng had been appointed chairman of the Party but did not yet know of the arrest of the four, they decided to arm 30,000 members of the local militia to challenge Peking. The coup did not take place, however, because they learned of the arrests. Meanwhile, troops in Peking surrounded the Peking and Qinghua University campuses, and elsewhere more than thirty radicals were reportedly arrested, including Mao's nephew Mao Yuanxin, vice-chairman of the Liaoning Provincial Revolutionary Committee, and Yu Huiyong, minister of culture and a Jiang Qing protégé. In the weeks that followed there were more demonstrations in all the major cities, including Shanghai, which denounced the "gang of four." On October 24, Hua Guofeng was publicly proclaimed chairman of the Chinese Communist Party at a rally of 1 million people in Peking.

During the fall and winter of 1976 the Chinese press and radio attacked Jiang Qing daily and accused her of all manner of personal crimes, including love of luxury, secret viewings of such "immoral" Western films as *The Sound of Music,* and generally arrogant behavior. On December 25, 1976, Hua Guofeng told an agricultural conference that if the radicals had succeeded in their scheming for power it would have "touched off a civil war." Later reports indicated that there indeed had been sharp physical clashes in many cities and provinces, and that the army had to be sent into Fujian province to put down disorders.

After the arrest of the "gang of four," struggle sessions took place in nearly every organization, as individuals tried to explain away their associations with the radicals or face bleak career futures. In some cases leaders who were known to have been close to Zhou Enlai swung over to the radicals after their patron's death and the fall of Deng, but then when the radicals fell they were helpless. This apparently was what happened to the foreign minister, Qiao Guanhua.

Although the propaganda machinery sought to build something of a cult of personality around Hua Guofeng, the new chairman clearly lacked the authority of Mao. Hua had to depend very much upon the advice of a group of senior Party leaders. As of his first year in office this group consisted of Li Xiannian, a seventy-two-year-old economic manager; Marshall Ye Jianying, seventy-eight, the defense minister; General Chen Xilian, sixty-three, the Peking garrison commander; General Xu Shiyou, seventy, the Canton regional commander; and General Wang Dongxing, sixty, the chief bodyguard of China's chairman. It is noteworthy that all of these leaders were older than Hua Guofeng, and that they predominantly represented the military — indeed, of the eleven members of Hua's Politburo seven were members of the army.

The weakness of Hua's position came to light when three months after the arrest of the "gang of four" it became apparent that the elimination of the radicals had opened the way to divisions among the "moderates." The key issue was the question of the restoration of Deng Xiaoping; as Zhou's apparent successor Deng had been purged by the "radicals," but now that it was declared that the radicals had acted improperly during Mao's last days, it would seem proper to restore Deng once again. At the time of the first anniversary of Zhou Enlai's death, therefore, a major wall-poster campaign was initiated that called for the rehabilitation of Deng and denounced all those who had been involved in suppressing the Tiananmen incident of the previous spring.

Hua was then placed in an awkward position because as a compromise candidate he had implicitly, if not more directly, worked against Deng's becoming the prime minister and heir apparent to Mao. His dilemma could be seen in the wall posters that attacked Wu De, the mayor of Peking, for his role in restoring order and arresting the demonstrators who were honoring the memory of Zhou Enlai at Tiananmen. Yet Wu De was also the man who had publicly announced Hua's elevation to the post of chairman.

Deng's supporters made a major move to restore him to the post of deputy prime minister on the anniversary of Zhou's death, but they were not successful. Hua Guofeng, on the other hand, was not able to assert the same dominant leadership he had at the time of the earthquake in July 1976, even though he did call a series of conferences regarding agriculture, industry, and military affairs. In the spring of 1977 the balance of power lay with leading figures in the army, who apparently were divided over the question of restoring Deng Xiaoping. The issue was finally resolved in July 1977 when the Politburo restored Deng to all of his former posts, making him the most powerful figure after Chairman Hua.

Thus the immediate consequences of the death of Mao Zedong were the elimination of the leaders of the "radicals" and the emergence of a shaky coalition of "moderates." Chinese politics would continue to be influenced by intensely personal struggles, but the main outlines of policy appeared clear. The new chairman reiterated Zhou Enlai's vision of China becoming a modern, industrialized power by the end of the century. He also suggested that there should be more creativity in the arts and literature.

CHAPTER SIXTEEN

The New Leadership of Deng Xiaoping

During the year following Mao's death all surface signs indicated that the Chinese were ready to shoulder the tasks of modernizing their country with a blend of pragmatism and ideological dedication. In mid-July 1977, at the Third Plenum of the Tenth Central Committee, Hua Guofeng was officially confirmed as chairman of both the Party and the Military Affairs Commission; he thus became the established successor to Chairman Mao Zedong. At the same meeting, Deng Xiaoping was rehabilitated and restored as vice-chairman and a member of the all-powerful Standing Committee of the Politburo. A month later there was enough unity to convene the Eleventh Party Congress, which was composed of a new Central Committee that had been purged of all followers of the "gang of four." Chairman Hua in his opening address declared the Cultural Revolution ended, and Deng in the closing speech called for "less empty talk and more hard work."

Foreign observers spoke of a new Hua and Deng leadership team that could be expected to unite China after the turmoil of the Cultural Revolution. The Chinese media, however, spoke less of a team of leaders. Instead, articles would praise one or the other. This was because factional tensions were on the rise behind the scenes. Cadres throughout the Party busily sorted themselves out and identified their political futures with one or another of the leaders at the top. The basic division was between those who had suffered during the Cultural Revolution, and who saw the rehabilitated and pragmatic Deng Xiaoping as their champion, and those who had benefited from the Cultural Revolution and, respecting the memory of Mao Zedong, saw Hua Guofeng as their natural leader. A third major segment of the Party was composed of veteran cadres who had survived the Cultural Revolution and thus were suspected by the rehabilitated cadres, but who were also skilled bureaucrats, and were distrusted by those who felt closer to Hua and to Mao's traditions.

These divisions were reflected at the top in the divisions among the five members of the Standing Committee of the Politburo. Chairman Hua Guofeng had as his ally General Wang Dongxing, who had arrested the "gang of four." Marshall Ye Jianying and Li Xiannian upheld the interests of the People's Liberation Army and the veteran bureaucratic cadres. Deng Xiaoping had no ally at the top, but he was very active in organizing the State Council and staffing it with rehabilitated cadres. He also gained support among the intellectuals by calling for more help from scientists and engineers in carrying out the Four Modernizations.

Because of these divisions within the elite, many contradictory initiatives favoring either Hua or Deng were taken in the fall and winter of 1977–1978. In October there was a call for a third campaign against the followers of the "gang of four" and Lin Biao, a move widely interpreted as indicating that the rehabilitated cadres were determined to remove more Hua supporters. On the other hand, Hua Guofeng continued to denounce the "gang of four" publicly as "ultra-rightists," which suggested that it was still "safest to be leftist," and that Deng and his rehabilitated cadres should be careful not to go too far in their pragmatism. At the same time, in the economic field, Hu Qili called for wage incentives and other major economic reforms that broke with the Maoist tradition and appeared to be revisionist.

These contradictory tendencies were apparent at the Fifth National People's Congress (NPC) and the Second Plenum of the Eleventh Central Committee, which met in February 1978. At these meetings, Hua announced an extraordinarily ambitious ten-year plan. The plan, which had to be essentially abandoned in little over a year, called for 120 large-scale industrial projects, and set annual production targets of 60 million tons of steel and 400 million tons of grain by 1985. At the same time, Ye Jianying was made chairman of the NPC, and Deng pushed for a revised state constitution, which granted more freedom in an attempt to win the support of the more educated people. Specifically, the constitution included the "Great Four Freedoms" of "speaking out freely, airing views fully, holding great debates, and writing big-characters-wall-posters." These freedoms opened the door for the Democracy Wall movement in the fall of 1978. Western journalists stationed in Peking were impressed by the liberal views expressed by the small group of leaders of the Democracy Wall movement, who were writing daily statements questioning policies and asking for more changes. All of these were posted on a particular wall in the capital; hence the name Democracy Wall movement.[1] Deng, however, soon discovered — just as Mao had after his call for a Hundred Flowers movement in 1956 — that allowing even a modest degree of freedom opened the way to blunt criticisms of Communism and of his leadership. In April 1980, Deng had the Great Four Freedoms removed from the constitution, and Democracy Wall was closed by the police.

THE CLASH OF FACTIONS

Throughout 1977 and 1978 the supporters of Deng called for a continued campaign, not just against the demonstrable radicals, but also against all who had advanced themselves while others had suffered during the Cultural Revolution. They raised the cry that within the Party were three dangerous factions who were trying in their different ways to hide their political sins. The "swivel faction" was said to be composed of people with necks that allowed them to bow in all directions; the "wind faction" had people who would lean in whatever direction the political winds were blowing; and a "fade away faction" was made up of cadres who would drift away from meetings whenever it was time to criticize the excesses of the Cultural Revolution.

These attacks were clearly landing closer and closer to Hua

[1] For discussions of the dissidents, see John Fraser, *The Chinese: Portrait of a People* (New York: Summit, 1980), and Roger Garside, *Coming Alive* (New York: McGraw-Hill, 1981).

Guofeng and his associates. Although Hua fully supported the pragmatic policies identified with Vice-Premier Deng, he persisted in declaring that the "gang of four" had been "ultra-rightists." The continued factional infighting caused considerable confusion among the cadres who felt that it was still "safest to be leftist" even while carrying out pragmatic policies.

By the spring of 1978 it was generally recognized that Deng and Hua were heading toward a power struggle that would end with a single leader. The pro-Deng cadres began to speak of an "adverse current" in the Party that threatened the unity offered by the Four Modernizations. In particular, they said that the troubles came from a "whatever faction," which clung to "whatever Mao said," and an "opposition faction" of bureaucrats who wished only to hold on to their posts, who opposed all changes, and who refused to accept the need to "seek truth from facts."

The Deng forces were thus aligned not only against Hua's allies but also against the veteran cadres who looked to Ye Jianying and Li Xiannian as their leaders. The conflict came into the open with a campaign against cadres whose thinking, they said, was "ossified or semiossified." The struggle was contained, however, because important foreign policy developments dictated that the government present a united position toward the outside world.

DENG TAKES COMMAND OF FOREIGN AFFAIRS

Although the main outlines of the policies had been laid down by Mao Zedong and Zhou Enlai, Deng Xiaoping was able to dramatize his emerging superiority over Hua Guofeng in less than two years, in large part by taking command of China's foreign affairs. With considerable skill he continued the process of strengthening relations with the United States and opposing the Soviet Union and those who would tilt toward Moscow. In particular, in 1978 he found himself engaged in complex maneuvers with Vietnam, Moscow, the United States, and Japan.

When Mao Zedong welcomed Henry Kissinger and President Richard Nixon to China in 1971 while American forces were still fighting in South Vietnam, the Vietnamese Communists felt that Mao had stabbed them in the back. In spite of China's having provided North Vietnam with some $12 billion in aid and the help of 44,000 "technicians," the leaders in Hanoi now realized that China did not want an emerging power on its southern border, especially a Communist power that had warm relations with the Soviet Union. This became apparent after the conquest of South Vietnam in 1975, when Peking began to support the Pol Pot Communist regime in Kampuchea (Cambodia) vigorously in order to wean it away from Vietnam.

By early 1978 military clashes were beginning to take place between the Cambodians, backed by the Chinese, and the Vietnamese, backed by the Soviets. In the spring of 1978 Hanoi closed down all remaining private businesses — most of which were run by ethnic Chinese who had been in Vietnam for many generations — and forcibly moved large numbers of urban people, again disproportionately ethnic Chinese, to the countryside to engage in farming in the so-called New Economic Zones. These developments sent thousands of ethnic Chinese across the border into China and began the tragedy of the "boat people" who sought refuge by sea.

Even as tensions heightened with Vietnam, Deng responded to the initiatives of the Carter administration, welcoming a series of visits from the president's national security advisor and his science advisor. Hanoi at this juncture also sought to normalize relations with the United States, but it moved too slowly in dropping its unrealistic demands for American aid. On August 12, 1978, Peking and Tokyo announced agreement on a Treaty of Peace and Friendship, which had been stalled for several years by a Chinese demand for the inclusion of an "anti-hegemony" clause, their code word for an anti-Soviet declaration. To get agreement, Peking accepted the Japanese request for an additional clause stating that the treaty was directed against no particular state. This development — when combined with a flurry of Chinese diplomacy that sent Deng to visit the non-Communist states of Southeast Asia and Hua to Rumania, Yugoslavia, and Iran — quickened Moscow-Hanoi discussions, which culminated on November 3 in a mutual defense treaty that could be seen as directed against China.

Deng was now more than ever ready to seek full diplomatic relations with the United States, so he indicated that the issue of continued United States arms sales to Taiwan could be temporarily set aside. On December 15, Washington and Peking announced an agreement that would bring full normalization of relations on January 1, 1979. This created a mood of euphoria in the two countries which was not seriously dampened ten days later by Vietnam's full-scale invasion of Kampuchea. When Deng visited the United States immediately after the establishment of full formal diplomatic relations, he indicated that Peking would "teach a lesson" to Vietnam for its aggressive actions.

Confident that the normalization of relations with Washington had neutralized the Vietnam-USSR treaty, Deng ordered the PLA to attack Vietnam on February 17, 1979. In the brief war that followed the PLA did not achieve its objective of forcing the Vietnamese to withdraw from Kampuchea. Indeed, the battlefield problems of the PLA led to complaints that the political leadership had not been adequately generous in helping to modernize the Chinese military establishment.

In spite of these complaints, Deng's allies among the cadres were strengthened by his foreign policy moves. The expansion of foreign contacts heightened the importance of the moderates within the Party and left the more ideological and rural-oriented cadres with considerably less influence.

DENG CONSOLIDATES POWER

Simultaneously with his foreign policy moves Deng was active on the domestic front, consolidating his power by advancing new policies and promoting his associates. Three days after Peking and Washington announced plans for normalizing relations, the Eleventh Central Committee convened its Third Plenum, a meeting Deng's supporters were later to identify as the critical point in his ultimate triumph over Chairman Hua Guofeng. Although the Plenum decreed an end of the campaign against Lin Biao and the "gang of four," which was a concession to Hua and the remaining Maoists in the Party, the more telling decisions of the meeting included the verdict that the Tiananmen Incident of 1976 was a "revolutionary" event (and hence Deng's purge at the time a counterrevolutionary act), the adoption of "seek truth from facts" as the guiding slogan of the Party, and the promotion of Chen Yun, an economic authority and Deng's ally, to the Standing Committee. In sum, the

Third Plenum was seen as decreeing that ideology should be put aside in favor of a hard-headed approach to China's economic problems.

During the spring of 1979 Deng's leadership mounted attacks against a variety of domestic enemies, while also pulling in the reins on the economic modernization program. Within the Party Deng's supporters spoke of the need to continue fighting against an "adverse current," and outside the Party the authorities arrested the leading champions of the Democracy Wall and free speech movements, including Wei Jingsheng and Fu Yuehua. At the end of June, at the second session of the Fifth National People's Congress, it was announced that the ambitious goals of the ten-year plan had caused serious dislocations in the economy, including alarming signs of inflation, which would require three years of "readjusting, reforming, rectifying, and raising standards" — a change which continued in force long after the three years were up.

In the realm of personnel appointments, Deng's leadership was outstandingly successful at the Fifth Plenum in February 1980. His closest allies, Hu Yaobang and Zhao Ziyang, were appointed to the Standing Committee, while Hua's key allies, Wang Dongxing, Ji Dengkui, Wu De, and Chen Xilian, were all forced to "resign" from the Politburo. Furthermore, Liu Shaoqi was posthumously rehabilitated and Hu Yaobang was made secretary general of the newly reconstituted Party Secretariat.

As Deng's position became more secure, criticisms of Mao's leadership — especially the last years covering the Great Leap and the Cultural Revolution — became more official. Pictures of Mao were removed from most public places. Finally, in November 1980, the "gang of four" were "tried and convicted" on forty-eight counts, including causing the "deaths of 34,000 people." In the show trial, Jiang Qing and Zhang Chunqiao were sentenced to death, but they were given two years to repent. Many politically conscious Chinese felt that the unmentioned fifth person on trial was Mao Zedong.

The problems of the economy, which included two years of deficits of nearly 17 billion *yuan*, were used to justify the elevation of Deng's closest associates to even higher offices. In September 1980 Zhao Ziyang replaced Hua Guofeng as prime minister, and nine months later Hua "resigned" as Party chairman in favor of

Hu Yaobang. Finally, at the Twelfth Party Congress in September 1982, Hua was removed from the Politburo and became a mere member of the Central Committee. Aside from his misfortune in being cast as the personal rival of the more astute Deng Xiaoping, Hua was seen as too much the peasant simpleton to be trusted to manage the increasingly complex Chinese economy. Thus those personal qualities of a simple, dedicated man of China's rural interior which once worked to his advantage with Mao Zedong became liabilities. What had once been his good fortune — being blessed by Mao — became an albatross as China's search for modernization took radically new departures under Deng's leadership.

DENG'S ASSOCIATES: HU YAOBANG AND ZHAO ZIYANG

When he finally succeeded in removing Hua Guofeng from all his leadership responsibilities at the Twelfth Party Congress, Deng was seventy-eight years old. He was eager to see power transferred to younger men he could trust to keep China on the new course he had set. While ridding Chinese leadership of the comparatively young (sixty-one-year-old) Hua Guofeng, Deng still had to contend with a triumvirate of aged PLA marshalls who refused to step down — eighty-five-year-old Ye Jianying, eighty-three-year-old Nie Rongzhen, and eighty-year-old Xu Xiangqia — and with the seventy-seven-year-old veteran bureaucrat Li Xiannian. Deng's immediate hope was that sixty-seven-year-old Hu Yaobang, the new Party chairman, and sixty-three-year-old Zhao Ziyang, the new prime minister, would be able to combine to fill the role of his successor.

Both men had long associations with Deng Xiaoping. Hu Yaobang first met Deng in 1941 when they served as political commissars with the Red Army in northwest China's Taihang mountains. Hu was born in 1917 in Liuyang county, in Mao's home province of Hunan. He came from a poor peasant family, and at fourteen he ran away to join Mao's guerrilla forces in the Jingang mountains. He subsequently went on the Long March as a "little red devil," as child soldiers were affectionately called. He had no formal schooling and taught himself how to read and write.

It has been said that once Hu met Deng he became his "shadow," and the two men became inseparable. Like Deng, Hu is barely five feet tall, and they have strikingly similar physical appearances. They soldiered together for eight years, and the end of the civil war in 1949 found them both in Sichuan. Two years later they were both transferred to Peking, Deng as deputy prime minister and Hu as head of the Communist Youth League. During the 1950s and early in the 1960s, when Deng was the secretary general of the Party, Hu was gaining experience by serving on several committees. In 1965 Deng arranged for him to become the first secretary of Shanxi province. The next year, however, both men were to be victims of the Cultural Revolution. Hu was sent to the countryside, in his own words, "to sleep beside the cows." Nearly two years of "reeducation" by manual work at a May Seventh School was followed by five years of house arrest. When Deng made his brief comeback in 1975 as first vice-premier under Zhou Enlai, he freed Hu and appointed him to run the Academy of Sciences. When Deng was purged a second time after Zhou's death, Hu was again placed under house arrest and did not reemerge until the summer of 1977.

Aside from his long personal association with the sophisticated Deng, who came from a landlord family, had lived abroad for several years, and had long been in the centers of power, Hu's background as an uneducated peasant would have made him a more natural associate of the cadres loyal to Hua Guofeng. Yet as the head of the Academy of Sciences he showed sympathy for intellectuals. Hu displayed not only his loyalty to Deng but also his skills as a bureaucratic infighter in 1977 when, as deputy director of the general office of the Central Committee, he undermined the authority of Hua's ally Wang Dongxing. Deng subsequently made Hu, first head of the Organization Department, then chief of the Propaganda Department, and finally in 1980 secretary general, the post from which he moved on to become the Party chairman in 1981.

Zhao Ziyang's relationship with Deng had a shorter history. Born in 1919 in Huaxian county, Henan province, Zhao grew up in a wealthy landlord family that owned the area's main grain shop. While in high school he was attracted to the Communist Youth League. A more bookish person than either Deng or Hu,

Zhao early developed theoretical interest in how economies work. From 1950 he served in Guangdong province, becoming first secretary in 1965. During that period he wrote several articles on agriculture, calling for more liberal approaches. In 1967 he was denounced by the Red Guards and forcibly taken through the streets of Canton wearing a dunce cap. His next four years were spent in the countryside doing manual labor, but in 1971 he reappeared as a high Party official in Inner Mongolia before being reassigned to Guangdong the next year.

It was Zhao's five-year tenure as first secretary of Sichuan province, beginning in 1975, that brought him to Deng's attention. Taking over a province larger than France and Germany combined, with an economy in shambles, Zhao boldly introduced novel policies that gave both farmers and factory managers more material incentives. When private plots were expanded, agricultural production rose 25 percent in three years, and greater flexibility in industry produced an 81-percent increase in the same period. In making Zhao the prime minister in 1980, Deng hoped he would be able to bring about comparable improvements in the national economy.

As the two people most critical for the success of Deng's plan to change the direction of Chinese affairs, Hu and Zhao are surprisingly unprepossessing, colorless technicians without independent power bases. Zhao has had no experience in national politics at the capital — when he was in Guangdong he was the only first secretary not to have been a member of the Central Committee — and he never served in the army and so had no natural allies in the PLA. Hu has always operated under the protection of his patron, so it is difficult to judge how successful he might be after Deng's death.

Deng brought in other capable officials, including Wan Li, his leading troubleshooter; Hu Qili, former mayor of Tianjin; Hu Jiwei, director of the *People's Daily*; and Hu Qiaomu, head of the Academy of Social Sciences. (The various Hu's are unrelated, but factional opponents have talked of "Deng's gang of four Hu's.")

Taken as a group, Deng's associates lacked the qualities long identified with revolutionary leadership in China. None had charisma, and none had a record of heroic deeds or startling accomplishments. They were capable but uninspiring.

The appeal of Deng's leadership lay in the substance of his policies and the degree to which they represented changes from the Mao era.

DENG'S POLICY CHANGES

It is easier to contrast Deng Xiaoping's policies with Mao's than to give them precise definition. This is because Deng's so-called pragmatic approach has involved experimentation, frequent about-faces, and little consistent ideological orientation. Many of his initiatives were direct reactions to the extremes of the Cultural Revolution, and while he seemed to welcome ideas from abroad he also ruthlessly attacked "bourgeois values" as undermining the Chinese revolution.

In simple outline the contrasts between Mao Zedong's policies and Deng Xiaoping's are the following:

- Mao believed that ideological inspiration should be enough to motivate the Chinese people; Deng readily accepted the need for more concrete rewards.
- Mao wanted an egalitarian society, even at a poor level of development; Deng sought a more prosperous society at the expense of equality.
- Mao distrusted intellectuals and respected peasant values; Deng praised scientists and engineers, and wanted China to rise above its peasant culture.
- Mao accepted unquestioningly the socialist principle of centralized state planning and the ideal that the state should provide employment for everyone; Deng tolerated greater economic decentralization, a greater degree of autonomy for plant managers, more private plots for peasants, and greater inequalities of rural income — all in the hope of gaining increased production.
- Mao distrusted the outside world, was at home with the tales of ancient China, and suspected urban sophisticates; Deng felt less threatened by foreign ways, was more responsive to immediate events, had less sense of history, and was less inclined to idealize simple, rural ways.

- Mao wanted Chinese Communism to be a respected part of the Communist tradition that began with Marx and Lenin; Deng, while a dedicated Communist, wanted results for China's progress toward modernization and was impatient with ideological nuances.
- Mao believed that cadres could be "reformed" by being sent to the countryside and exposed to peasant living; Deng turned to more legalistic and bureaucratic means for dealing with deviance.
- Mao wanted ideological orthodoxy, was contemptuous of religion, and believed in conflict and struggle in order to arrive at a proper consensus; Deng accepted ideology as a political necessity, but was more tolerant of diversity, including religious believers, and believed that political faith could not replace competence.

These distinctions provide background for understanding the policy orientations favored by Deng and his associates following the Twelfth Party Conference. Although considerable experimentation continued to characterize Chinese policies in a number of areas after the conference and the five-year plan announcement at the National People's Congress in November 1982, the main features of the new era can be readily characterized.

THE RESPONSIBILITY SYSTEM IN AGRICULTURE

Although Mao had rural roots and praised the merits of farm work, his policies, paradoxically, were consistently tilted against the countryside and favored the cities. Under his rule the terms of trade between agriculture and industry benefited the latter, and the income of industrial workers rose more than twice as fast as that of the peasants. He also showed little confidence in the initiatives and skills of the individual Chinese peasant, for he stressed ever larger units of decision-making, such as the commune, rather than the household, which Deng chose to emphasize. Mao idealized the model brigade of Dazhai, whose members were supposed to have achieved near miracles by relying on their own efforts. Deng's administration revealed in 1980 that Dazhai was a fraud, its grain production figures were faked, a battalion of PLA soldiers had constantly helped out, the state had poured money into the model enterprise, and its leader, Chen Yonggui, had persecuted 141 people to death during the Cultural Revolution.

The post-Mao leadership's approach to agriculture has been based largely on policy experiments carried out by Zhao Ziyang in Sichuan from 1975 to 1979. Zhao's policy stressed material incentives and has been called the "responsibility system." This system is not based on a single national formula, but rather has evolved in somewhat different ways in different places. The key concept, however, is that individual households contract with either the brigade or the production team to work specific areas of the collective fields, promising to deliver to the collective a specified quota of grain. Anything above that contracted quota can be sold by the household, either to the state at about half again the base procurement price, or in many places at free market fairs at twice the procurement price. In addition, private plots are respected and in many places they have been expanded. Again the peasants can sell the produce of the private plots (largely vegetables, fruits, poultry, and meat) as they please.

For two years after the system was introduced in 1979, peasants were free to decide what crops they would plant on the land they had contracted to work; but because they were so responsive to the price differentials for the various crops, they produced too much of the more profitable items, such as peanuts and cotton, and not enough of the less profitable crops. Thereafter the contracts specified both the land to be worked and the crops to be raised, making the system essentially a form of sharecropping.

As a result of the responsibility system, collectivized land, especially in rice-growing south China, has again been divided into small plots that are worked individually. The effect has been a significant increase in production, a visible improvement in the standard of living of the peasants, and improved quality of food for city-dwellers. Between 1979 and 1982 total agricultural production increased 6.5 percent, with grains rising 3.7 percent, and among the industrial crops, cotton 10 percent, sugar 15 percent, and oil-bearing crops 26 percent. With nearly 90 percent of the peasants involved in the responsibility system, their per capita income rose in 1982 above the previous level of $130 a year, with some coming close to the urban per capita income of $296. In a few spectacular cases households reportedly made nearly $1,000.

At the same time, problems remain in agriculture. The central government is still buying grain at prices above what it is sold at in the state stores. A third of the state budget goes to various forms of subsidies, and nearly two-thirds of these subsidies are for grain purchases. Given continuing budget deficits (which in 1982 still amounted to over $3 billion), the government would like to reduce the food subsidies, but it fears the reactions of both peasants and urban workers. Although the responsibility system has inspired peasants to increased production, China still needs to import nearly a quarter of the grain it needs to feed its coastal urban population (about 15 million tons in 1982).

Administratively, the responsibility system has raised a few troublesome tensions. Rural cadres who once dominated the collective farming system, and whose income was based on work points which favored their leadership roles, now find that non-Party households can make more money than they do. Furthermore, the process of negotiating contracts at the production-team level can lead to intense conflicts among heads of households, who all appreciate the relative productivity of the different pieces of land and thus know who is being favored and who is being put at a disadvantage. Finally there is a problem because households can raise their incomes with more helping hands, thus the value of having more children has gone up, working against the regime's family planning goals.

In sum, Chinese agriculture is evolving toward a system that is more decentralized and based more on the household as the unit of accounting than either Mao wished or the Soviet Union has permitted, but less oriented to markets than either Hungary or Poland, the two Eastern European Communist systems most successful in agriculture.

INDUSTRY: CENTRAL PLANNING AND MARKET CONSIDERATIONS

Post-Mao policies in industry have been as experimental as those in agriculture, but the outcome remains more uncertain. Initially, largely under Hua Guofeng but encouraged by Deng, the ambition in industry was to expand the number of huge conglomerate enterprises based on heavy industry. Thus in 1978 Hua proclaimed that the targets for the new ten-year plan would be 120 large-scale industrial projects — including ten major iron and steel complexes, nine nonferrous metal facilities, ten new oil and natural gas fields, and thirty major hydropower stations. This approach of setting grand goals and calling for Herculean efforts was very much in the style of Mao Zedong. Mao's concept of experimentation and investigation was to plunge into grand endeavors and then figure out what needed to be done to carry them out; he was against careful planning and selective preliminary experimentation.

Such boastful planning worked no better for the Chairman's successors than for Mao himself. Barely a year after Hua had set these goals for industry, Chen Yun, Deng's ally and economic specialist, allowed that the goals were unrealistic and called for a three-year period of "readjustment" and retrenchment. The first basic difficulty was low labor productivity. Chinese workers failed to respond to greater material incentives because of a serious shortage of consumer goods. Workers might be paid more in bonuses, but as long as there were so few things to buy they were not inclined to work harder. Secondly, the emphasis on heavy industry revealed that China had severe bottlenecks in both energy and transportation. Factories were built but could only operate at 30 to 40 percent capacity because of inadequate power.

Deng and his associates therefore decided to shift the focus in industry from heavy to light, thereby not only producing more consumer goods for the workers but also raising export earnings. Further reforms involved providing more incentives for factory managers by allowing them to keep more of their profits and to have greater freedom in deciding what to produce. The economy responded to these directives with amazing speed, and by 1980 the total value of light industrial production had moved ahead of heavy industry.

In November 1982 the State Planning Commission, with the approval of the State Council, passed on to the National People's Congress a new five-year plan, which preserved the basic central planning process while allowing scope for some market forces. Specifically, the State Planning Commission identified three levels of the economy and three corresponding ways of directing it. First, there are the state enterprises, which by 1982 totaled over 900,000 and employed almost 8 million technical personnel. For most of these enterprises the state sets compulsory quotas, which control some one hundred key industrial products, such as steel, concrete, petroleum, and coal. The second level is involved in the production of major consumer goods, and also agricultural crops, for which the State Planning Commission establishes "guidance plans" — that is, suggested targets, often by province — but leaves the particular enterprises or regions to decide how much of which target they will strive for according to their judgments of profitability. Finally there are the thousands of small consumer items, too numerous for close central planning, which the state can still regulate by taxation and interest rate policies and by arbitrary price-setting.

Although the post-Mao leadership has been more tolerant of market activities, its bias is still in favor of planning. Thus the regime unquestionably continues to favor the state-run enterprises, and most Chinese workers prefer employment in such enterprises because they are the only ones that can provide security. The Chinese speak of them as providing the "iron rice bowl" because they give lifetime employment, bonuses, housing, retirement, and other benefits. These enterprises are unable to provide enough jobs for everyone, however, and in 1982 there were over 20 million young Chinese "awaiting assignment," i.e. unemployed. Thus the regime has had to encourage two other forms of enterprises. First are collectives, which can receive state loans for initial capitalization and tend to produce such simple items as washbasins, shoes, textiles, or to perform such simple tasks as assembling bicycles. Collectives tend to compete with each other and at times with state enterprises. Workers on collective enterprises may get bonuses in profitable years, but they do not have either job security or significant benefits.

Finally, in a very bold break from the socialist economy inherited from Mao, the Deng leadership has legitimized private enterprises, but severely limited their growth by allowing them to have, aside from family members, only three or four employees and enough apprentices to total a work force of only seven people. Such enterprises require the approval of the initiator's *danwei* (small group) and tend to be limited to such service activities as shoe repair, tailoring, knife sharpening, and repairing utensils. Although the authorities acknowledge the need for such enterprises to provide employment, they have not always been particularly cooperative in helping to establish them. A 1982 newspaper reported the case of a man who had to visit 32 bureaus and get 169 signatures to establish a repair stall in an undesirable location. On the other hand, the regime has announced that it wants 70 percent of all public eating places to be either collective or private enterprises.

In spite of its preference for state enterprises, the leadership discovered in 1980 that 65 percent of the growth in the economy was occurring outside the central planning process. None of the growth, however, was going into solving the basic problems of energy and transportation. There was also concern that the decline of nearly 17 percent in heavy industry might become the start of a downward cycle that would be hard to stop. Consequently, in 1981 there were further readjustments calling for strengthened central planning, less autonomy for plants, and more direction from the center in investments. The system of quotas and the identification of "responsibilities" were expected to keep incentives high even while central control became greater.

As a means of stimulating state enterprises, Deng's planners encouraged greater freedom for plant managers, and especially for allowing them to retain some of the profits. Under Mao taxes in industry were relatively modest, geared largely to the abilities of the least efficient producers; but profits, which could be exceedingly large, all went to the state until the planned quota was met, after which there was a 60-40 split between the center and the locality on over-quota profits — a form of revenue sharing. Under that system, capital was essentially free: The state, according to its planning, provided expansion capital in the form of grants. Under Deng, state enterprises were allowed to keep between 10 percent and 20 percent of their profits (the average was 12 percent) which could be divided in different proportions at the discretion of the plant managers among three established categories: bonuses, capital reinvestment, and the plant's welfare fund. Managers were also given some limited powers to dismiss truly incompetent workers, but in the main they were encouraged to reassign their unproductive employees to more menial tasks unrelated to actual production, such as janitorial work.

The problem of how to distribute bonuses in order to improve production has been a troublesome issue in most enterprises since 1977. The difficulties started because nearly every factory in China has redundant employees; people were hired not because jobs needed doing but because mouths needed to be fed. In short, Mao's rule combined industrial policy and welfare. In many plants it was acknowledged that nearly half the employees made no contribution to production and that if they were removed production would not decline; indeed, in some cases production might even go up, since the excess workers were in the way. If such workers were given bonuses the effect would be an increase in China's welfare bill rather than a stimulus to production. On the other hand, distributing bonuses according to individual productivity brought charges of favoritism and unjust treatment. If plant managers allocated too large a share of the bonus pool to themselves it also, understandably, caused discontent.

As a consequence of this problem, the institution of workers' congresses — a holdover from the Maoist egalitarian tradition — was, paradoxically, strengthened. Organized under the All-China Federation of Trade Unions, but not to be confused with Western trade unions, workers' congresses exist in every plant and seek to mobilize workers' support for greater production, better understanding of the quotas and the ambitions of the government, and participation in ratifying the draft plans and quotas passed down by the government and management. The elected leaders of the congresses strive to reduce tensions and to convince the workers to adhere to the "correct" decisions while opposing all "bureaucratic" work styles on the part of management.

WAGES AND CONSUMER COSTS

Because of inflationary pressures industrial workers were given an across-the-board supplement of five *yuan* a month in 1979. Wages in China do vary from industry to industry, and even from plant to plant, but a typical wage structure provides a spread between the new worker and the veteran, between common and skilled labor, and between manual and technical or managerial roles.

China is one of the few semi-industrialized countries that still requires a prolonged apprenticeship period. In almost every industry the Chinese have a three-year apprenticeship, during which workers are paid 18 to 22 *yuan* (that is, at an exchange rate of two *yuan* to the dollar, about $9.00 to $11.00) a month the first year, 19 to 23 *yuan* in the second, and 20 to 24 *yuan* in the third. After the apprenticeship period most industries have eight grades, with grade one getting from 28 to 36 *yuan* (about $14.00 to $18.00) a month, and grade eight from 104 to 120 *yuan* (about $52.00 to $60.00) a month. The average factory worker in grades four and five receives from 58 to 72 *yuan* ($29.00 to $36.00) a month. This would be the normal income of a married worker, with children, at midcareer. Most urban households have two or more wage earners.

The income spread among workers in China is comparable to that of workers in most industrial countries. The big difference is that Chinese managers and technicians earn considerably less than is the norm in industrial societies, even though they are ranked on a scale of eighteen grades. Technical personnel in the textile industry start at 80 *yuan* and go to more than 200 *yuan* a month; in the steel industry engineers begin at 120 *yuan* and may reach more than 300 *yuan*. At the major universities, where there are twelve ranks, there is an impressive spread between instructors, who get about 30 *yuan* a month, and senior professors who may receive over 360 yuan.

Although the Chinese have encouraged women to join the work force, and have built many neighborhood "factories" where housewives can congregate to knit or crochet gloves and sweaters and to make dresses and children's apparel for both domestic consumption and export, it is universally accepted that women should be paid less than men. In the textile industry the starting wage is about 23 *yuan* a month, and in the "neighborhood factories" the wage spread is from 20 to 32 *yuan*, with an average of 25 *yuan* a month. Primary-school teachers average about 40 *yuan* and middle-school (high school) instructors about 50 *yuan* a month.

The incomes of Party and state cadres vary considerably, particularly if all the perquisites of rank are added to the base salaries. The Chinese bureaucracy is divided into twenty-four regular grades. According to A. Doak Barnett, "Those in the lowest grades — from twenty-four to eighteen — receive somewhere between 40 and 90 *yuan* a month; the salaries of grades seventeen to thirteen range from roughly 100 to almost 160 *yuan;* the highest grades (a relatively small number of cadres from grade twelve up) obtain salaries that reportedly rise to about 400 *yuan* for grade six, and are higher above that."[2] The salary range of these officials, when combined with their access to special housing, cars, and staff assistants, means that Chinese executives are not far out of line with world standards in their income advantages over ordinary workers.

The Chinese reported in 1981 that 74.1 percent of all urban families had pooled incomes of between 300 and 600 *yuan* ($150 to $300) a year; 18.4 percent earned more than 600 *yuan;* and 7.5 percent earned less than 300 *yuan* a year.[3]

These income figures show that Chinese industrial workers earn above the per-capita national income. To appreciate their purchasing power, it is necessary to take into account the prices for consumer items in China. As we have already noted, rents and utilities are exceedingly low, only a few *yuan* a month. Food for a family of five costs about 60 to 75 *yuan* a month.[4] If both the husband and wife in a family of five receive average incomes, it would mean that they would have a little more than 30 *yuan* a month for clothing and consumer goods.

The most expensive item would be a new bicycle. In 1980, five models were available, ranging in price from 135 to 200 *yuan,* or about three months wages for a midcareer worker. (Of course, a buyer can turn to the large market in second-hand bicycles.) Men's leather shoes range from 8.70 to 15.60 *yuan,* and cloth and plastic shoes from 4.10 to 5.10 *yuan;* men's fur hats from 5.50 to 17.80 *yuan;* men's cotton pants from 6.20 to 12.40 *yuan,* cotton padded pants from 7.90 to 15.20 *yuan,* and cotton padded jackets from 9.50 to 21 *yuan.* Clocks cost from 13.30 to 27.20 *yuan;* flashlights from 1.74 to 2.84 *yuan;* and fountain pens from 2.15 to 14.08 *yuan.*[5]

The relationship between wages and prices reflects the relatively low productivity of Chinese labor, which is in turn affected by the level of China's technology and capital investment. Alex-

[2] A. Doak Barnett, *Uncertain Passage: China's Transition to the Post-Mao Era* (Washington, D.C.: The Brookings Institution, 1974), p. 133.

[3] *Beijing Review,* November 30, 1981, pp. 16–17; April 26, 1982, pp. 15–18.

[4] Barnett, p. 133.

[5] These department store prices were in Peking over the period from 1972 to 1982.

ander Eckstein calculated the time American and Chinese laborers would have had to work in 1972 to purchase comparable items. He discovered that for one hour's labor an American worker could buy 14.2 pounds of rice while a Chinese worker could buy 2 pounds, for a ratio of about seven to one. The comparable ratio for wheat flour was twelve to one; for carrots, twenty-five to one; for cucumbers, two to one; and for sugar, forty-six to one. The ratio for cotton prints was eighteen to one; for work pants, thirteen to one; and for tennis shoes, fourteen to one. With manufactured goods and durable consumer items, as one would expect, the Chinese wages would allow them to buy even fewer, so the ratios are greater: for drinking glasses, twenty-seven to one; for alarm clocks, twenty-seven to one; for transistor radios, fifty-three to one; and for watches, sixty to one.[6]

The Chinese wage-price structures have been remarkably constant; only a few modest adjustments in prices, and even fewer in wages, have been made since the 1950s. As a consequence, in every community or neighborhood, everyone knows exactly how much income everyone else has. (This has meant, incidentally, that even petty forms of corruption are difficult to accomplish; should anyone spend more than his income, he would immediately become suspect among his neighbors.)

RATIONING AND COUPONS

No other economy in the world uses administrative rationing as extensively as the Chinese. Although the carefully calculated relationship between wages and prices might seem adequate for controlling the way people balance outputs of effort and inputs of consumption, the Chinese government protects against any further uncertainties by an elaborate system of rationing. This system reinforces policing controls, since each person must go to different designated places every month or every six months to get the six to eight ration or coupon books required to buy both necessities and luxuries. The system of rationing strengthens the control of the *danwei* and makes geographical movements nearly impossible,

[6] Alexander Eckstein, *China's Economic Revolution* (New York: Cambridge University Press, 1977), pp. 306–307.

because the coupon books are locally issued. (Young people who slip back into the cities from the countryside are quite literally "gray people" because they cannot get ration coupons and must live off their parents' rations.)

Rationing covers such basic items as grain (rice, flour, and bean products), cooking oil, cotton cloth, soap, and various food items such as eggs, sweet potatoes, meats, fish, and sugar, as well as such industrial products as bicycles, sewing machines, shoes, blankets, and quilts. The amount rationed varies from place to place, and even more according to the individual. Among adults, unemployed females get the least, only a little over half what a male factory worker is allowed. Some items are rationed by the household, as, for example, one bar of soap a month.

The rations are not always severely limiting, but the need to obtain the ration books is absolute and usually extremely time-consuming. Shopping in the large cities can involve many hours of standing in line, and there are always the monthly queues to provide the evidence required for new coupon books. One of the reasons free markets or peasant markets can charge more is that they do not require ration coupons; only the state stores do.

A severe restriction on consumption is the rationing of industrial items. Each registered person gets only one such coupon every six months; but then, it takes, for example, five coupons to buy a pair of men's leather shoes, two for a pair of women's leather shoes, ten for a sewing machine, and between ten and fifteen — plus the special permission of one's *danwei* — to buy a bicycle.[7] Consequently, households and even extended families and friendship networks have to cooperate in making decisions and setting priorities for such purchases.

The concept of rationing according to the priorities of one's *danwei* is possibly carried to the extreme in the enforcement of the birth control policy. Not only is each couple expected to have only one child, but each small group, whether at the neighborhood or at the place of employment, has its quota, and is thus empowered to decide which couple can have a pregnancy in the next set period of time.

[7] Richard Bernstein, former *Time* correspondent in Peking, has collected the details of rationing in *From the Center of the Earth* (Boston: Little, Brown, 1982).

LABOR PRODUCTIVITY AND THE BOTTLENECKS OF ENERGY AND TRANSPORTATION

A distressing problem for China's planners is that even though the country has had one of the world's highest savings rates, the return on investment has not been proportionately high, and has been getting steadily lower. The government pushed for a savings rate of 24 percent of the country's gross national product for reinvestment during the first five-year plan; the rate reached 44 percent during one year of the second plan; and it averaged about 30 percent from 1949 to 1980. During the first five-year plan every 100 *yuan* of newly invested "accumulation," (the Chinese, like other Communists, reject the word *capital*) brought 35 *yuan* in increased production; but by 1982 the same 100 *yuan* of investment brought only a little over 10 *yuan* of expanded production. The *People's Daily* reported that in 1957 every $67.00 of assets produced $23.00 in profits and taxes for the state, but by 1976 the figure was only $13.00 from the same amount.[8]

The reasons for this decline in productivity go well beyond the problems of motivation. Planning has become more difficult as the economy has grown more complex, so unfortunate decisions are more frequent. At the beginning of central planning the country needed nearly everything and fine adjustments were not necessary, but by 1982 overproduction in certain areas was causing serious waste. In that year, for example, the country had inventories of more than a year's supply of steel, but the steel industry kept on producing. There was even expansion in the capacity for producing steel, as the planners concentrated on China's expected long-run needs rather than its current situation.

Aside from the questions of incentives and labor productivity, possibly the most troublesome problem for Chinese industry has been that of energy. The euphoria of 1977 and 1978 over what might be expected in industrial development was in no small part spurred by a belief that China would soon be exporting significant quantities of oil, which would pay for extensive purchases of plants

[8] Cited in Fox Butterfield, *China: Alive in a Bitter Sea* (New York: Times Books, 1982) p. 261.

and technologies. Unfortunately, 1979 was the peak of oil production. The huge oil fields at Daqing began to yield less, and no significant new onshore fields were discovered. China's domestic oil needs have also increased at a faster pace than anticipated, and by 1980, even after exports were reduced, the average factory was operating at 70 percent to 80 percent of capacity for lack of power. China's big hope is that the leasing of offshore drilling rights to Western and Japanese companies, which began in earnest in 1982, will in time result in extensive increases in production.

China has the world's third-largest reserves of coal, and once transportation has been improved this should become an increasingly important source of energy. Coal is the fuel for over half of China's power plants, and the government's objective is to double coal production by the year 2000. The extent to which the Chinese have been inefficient in their use of energy can be seen from the fact that China, with a much smaller GNP than Japan, uses almost exactly the same amount of commercial energy.

A further disturbing problem in energy is that China's huge rural population relies heavily on what are called "noncommercial" sources of energy, such as foraged branches, bark, twigs, and leaves from trees, and grasses, dried sod, animal dung, and other dried vegetation. The government has officially acknowledged that "500 million people suffer from a serious lack of fuel for at least three to five months a year and in the worst-off provinces 70 percent lack fuel for up to half of every year." [9] The goal of raising the standard of living for these people will mean that energy obtained from improved methods of production cannot go only for industrial uses.

SCIENCE, TECHNOLOGY, AND THE INTELLECTUALS

One of the greatest differences between Mao's rule and Deng's has been in the status of scientists and intellectuals with Western technical skills. Although Mao was initially trained as a teacher and thought of himself as a thinker, he deeply distrusted intellectuals and discounted the value of scientific and technological skills. During the Anti-Rightist Campaign of the late 1950s and even

[9] *New York Times*, October 3, 1982.

more during the Cultural Revolution intellectuals were under sustained attack, and many suffered severe physical torture. In contrast, Deng has declared that scientists are workers, essential for China's modernization, and not necessarily representatives of the bourgeoisie.

Under Deng the universities in China have been revived, admission is again based on competitive examinations, and education has been freed from the domination of political ideology and propaganda. Partly because of the near destruction of higher education during the last years of Mao's rule, there has been a shortage of qualified teachers with up-to-date knowledge. Consequently the Chinese authorities have rigorously pursued a policy of sending intellectuals abroad, particularly to the United States, to receive advanced training. In 1980 there were nearly 8,000 Chinese scholars in the United States alone, many of whom were supported by relatives abroad or by private arrangements. By 1982 there was rising concern that those who had been abroad, and those intellectuals in China who were in close contact with foreigners, were in danger of losing their revolutionary ideals and of becoming "contaminated" with bourgeois values. In China this meant a tightening of controls and warnings against associating with foreigners. Those sent abroad would now have to have one year's work experience after graduation from their Chinese university.

From 1977 to 1980 only 3 to 4 percent of middle-school graduates were admitted to institutions of higher learning.[10] During Mao's rule, success in getting into and getting ahead in schools and colleges depended on ideological standards and not academic excellence; thus Chinese education was striving to be, in the words of Susan Shirk, a "virtuocracy" rather than a "meritocracy."[11] Since then, academic standards have been steadily improved, and by 1982 China was producing the first graduates who were again receiving scholarly training. Chinese universities are still modeled along Soviet lines, in that they stress technical knowledge in rather narrow and specifically defined fields. The universities are not research institutions; research is centered instead in the various institutes of

[10] Yu Xiafu, "Open Up More Avenues for Education," *Beijing Review*, July 28, 1980, pp. 19–21.

[11] Susan Shirk, *Competitive Comrades* (Berkeley: University of California Press, 1982).

the Academy of Sciences and the Chinese Academy of the Social Sciences. The latter by 1982 had thirty-one institutes and over 3,000 researchers.

In 1982 the Chinese leaders were surprised to discover that, because of the need to slow the pace of industrial expansion it was not easy to assign jobs to all college graduates in the careers for which they were trained, to say nothing of the far larger numbers of graduates of middle schools (the equivalent of American high schools). In 1981 the regime indicated that nearly 20 million young people were "awaiting assignment." This problem compelled the planners to encourage more young people to start their own collective or cooperative enterprises. It also revived debates over the value of once again asking graduates to spend some time working in rural areas. By 1982 conflicting policies were at work: Many young people who had years earlier been assigned to indefinite work in the countryside were being allowed to return to their original urban homes, while new graduates were confronted with the prospect of being caught up in a revival of the earlier policy and being ordered to the countryside.

In spite of these difficulties, it remains true that the future of China's modernization depends heavily on raising standards of technical knowledge and improving the country's human resources through better education. In confronting this problem, Chinese planners in the late 1970s shifted from striving for universal schooling to improving the quality of education. Consequently, the numbers of both primary- and secondary-school students declined from 1977 to 1981 — from 146 million to 143 million elementary-school students and from 68.4 million to 49.6 million junior- and senior-high-school students.[12] In December 1982, the Chinese announced that as part of the 1981–1986 five-year plan they would, in the five years, be sending 15,000 students abroad to study science and technology, and that they would also spend $350 million to improve laboratory facilities at their colleges. Under the plan they intend to graduate 2.3 million students from secondary vocational schools, 1.5 million from colleges, and 45,000 from graduate schools.[13]

[12] Willy Kraus, *Economic Development and Social Change in the People's Republic of China,* (New York: Springer Verlag, 1982).

[13] Release from New China News Agency, Peking, December 12, 1982.

CHAPTER SEVENTEEN

China's Future Domestically and Internationally

The period of Deng Xiaoping's supremacy, following as it did the radical, revolutionary era of Mao Zedong, can be understood as one of technocratic experimentation in search of specific features of modernization. Science, technology, economics, management, and even to a limited degree the mechanism of the market became the new philosopher's stones, replacing Mao's slogans in praise of willpower, dedication, and revolutionary fervor.

Yet all was not to be sacrificed to pragmatism, for Deng and his associates remained steadfastly committed to what they called the "four fundamental principles": the mass line, the dictatorship of the proletariat, the leadership of the Communist Party, and Marxism-Leninism–Mao Zedong Thought. Indeed, the Chinese leadership was increasingly concerned after the Twelfth Party Congress over whether China could absorb Western technology without being contaminated by "bourgeois values." Could China open itself to the outside world and still protect its dedication to Communism, which it had nurtured during an era of virtual isolation?

Thus in a peculiar way Deng's rule revived the basic theme of all Chinese modernizers from as long ago as the reform movement of 1898: Can China preserve its values while adopting foreign techniques?[1] Originally it was, of course, Confucian values that were to be protected. Now under Deng the basic values to be guarded

[1] For documents reflecting these views see: Ssu-yu Teng and John K. Fairbank, *China's Response to the West* (Cambridge, Mass.: Harvard University Press, 1954).

as essential to China's national identity were, paradoxically, the imported values of Communism, modified by Chinese experience. Mao Zedong, particularly after the shock of the withdrawal of Soviet technicians at the time of the termination of Soviet aid in 1960, became obsessed with the ideal of self-reliance. He denied that China had any need for foreign ideas or practices. The post-Mao leadership, however, was quick to recognize that Mao's approach had failed and that China would, to some degree, have to turn to the outside world for help.

The issue, however, for Deng was harshly pragmatic: How big an opening should China make to the non-Communist world, and how candid should the government be about its need for foreign assistance? The questions were troublesome, for there were no easy answers. They created divisions among the cadres, some of whom still respected Mao's ideal of self-reliance. The issue also had ramifications for China's foreign relations because it sharpened a dilemma between form and substance. On the one hand, China had benefitted from successfully projecting the image of a powerful nation with a prospering economy; on the other hand, China's prospects for real development would be greatly enhanced if the country could obtain access to international developmental support and the loans at modest interest provided to underdeveloped countries by the World Bank and the International Monetary Fund.

As Deng's rule became more secure early in the 1980s, Chinese officials became more frank about admitting that China was indeed a developing country of the Third World in need of assistance. In foreign-policy forums, Chinese diplomats increasingly identified their country's interests with those of the Third World. Many leaders of Third World countries were, however, less than enthusiastic in welcoming China to their number, particularly since they could easily imagine China's needs absorbing all available international assistance and leaving little for them. In 1982 World Bank officials projected the prospect that by 1985 China's claims for assistance would equal those of India.

It is therefore appropriate in evaluating China's prospects for the future to raise fundamental questions about the state of Chinese society after more than three decades of Communist rule and the capabilities of the political system to achieve China's modernization.

THE VEIL OF SECRECY AND THE CRYPTIC COMMUNICATIONS PROCESS

Judging Chinese political capabilities is exceedingly difficult, if for no other reason than the extraordinarily high degree of secrecy that still surrounds all aspects of Chinese political life. Although the Chinese have become more open in discussing governmental affairs since the death of Mao, Party matters are still treated with almost absolute confidentiality. The Chinese public is rarely provided with information about the affairs of their leaders, and they usually receive little warning of impending decisions. Everyone is expected to conform to the current policy line and to act as though they expected no changes.

Complete secrecy is, however, impossible with 18 million government officials and nearly 40 million Party members. Moreover, even though the leaders act in support of the current consensus, they frequently have to engage in guarded policy debates. Consequently over the years the Chinese political elite has developed considerable skill in using cryptic forms of communication, often relying heavily on Aesopean language. A particular leader, for example, will advance a slogan and others will then pick it up and in repeating it show their support for that leader, while those who ignore the slogan, or employ a different one, in doing so indicate their opposition. At other times debate will take place by using historical allegories.[2]

Consequently, the Chinese people — to say nothing of outside observers — are often left to speculate about the significance of supposedly public events. Take, for example, the decision to send Foreign Minister Huang Hua to the funeral of Soviet leader Leonid Brezhnev. Huang was already rumored to be scheduled for retirement for reasons of poor health. In the summer of 1982 Brezhnev had initiated a move toward better Sino-Soviet relations, so much international significance was attached to Huang Hua's generous praise of the deceased Russian leader, especially since among the

[2] See, for example, Kenneth Lieberthal, "The Foreign Policy Debate in Peking As Seen Through Allegorical Articles, 1973–1976," *China Quarterly* 71 (September 1977): 528–554; and Merle Goldman, *China's Intellectuals: Advice and Dissent* (Cambridge, Mass.: Harvard University Press, 1981).

Chinese leaders Huang had been most vitriolic in attacking the Soviets. In Moscow, Huang Hua declared that "peace and friendship between the two countries completely conforms to the interests of the two countries and the two peoples, but also of peace in Asia and the world as a whole." But the day after Huang returned to Peking, while world capitals were still trying to evaluate the impact of his generous praise of the Soviet Union, he was declared to have stepped down as foreign minister. Were Washington and Moscow to conclude that Peking intended to slight Moscow by sending a lame-duck foreign minister? Or had Huang Hua gone too far in his warming up to Russia? Or had the Chinese only adhered in a routine manner to the established plan for his retirement? Since nobody knew the answers, all were left with their speculations about Chinese motives and calculations.

The trend under Deng's leadership, however, has been toward more orderly and rational procedures. Even though the tradition of secrecy remains strong, developments are more predictable than they were under Mao. New sources of uncertainty have, however, crept into the Chinese governmental processes. The most notable of these has been the practice, started in 1981, of trying to streamline state administration by reorganizing ministries. The process was inevitably prolonged because it involved complicated human and bureaucratic relations, so cadres were left uncertain as to what would be the emerging lines of authority. By 1982 the reorganization efforts had not produced the decisive decision-making Deng was after in all fields. Instead there was considerable timidity, as low-level officials held back, waiting to see how the top officials were working out their relationships.

The decline in the role of ideology, which was widely welcomed by the cadres in the governmental bureaucracy, also contributed a degree of uncertainty to policymaking and implementation. Deng and Hu Yaobang, for instance, called for a raising of the level of "spiritual civilization" to counter the trend toward consumer materialism and "bourgeois values"; but then, just before the meeting of the Twelfth Party Congress in 1982, the editors of the main organ of the PLA, the *Liberation Army Daily*, had to make a long self-criticism for having allowed the publication of an article that was too leftist in explaining a "spiritual civilization." Furthermore, the director of the PLA's political department was removed, demonstrating that questions of ideology could still destroy careers.

Yet in spite of these difficulties, the Chinese appear to be firmly committed to a rational, technologically based policy of modernization; and while the overblown enthusiasm of the Maoist propagandistic approach to development is gone, the fact remains that significant progress has been made under Deng Xiaoping's leadership. The Chinese, some with reluctance, are abandoning the wishful thought that progress for them should be the easy, rapid, magical product of sloganeering. They now appreciate the fact that they face in monumental form both the problems and the opportunities of the Third World. Precisely because these problems are great, they have learned to value their accomplishments, many of which are most impressive, in a sober spirit.

The new mood in China was accurately reflected in both the constitution and the five-year plan (1981–1986) adopted by the Fifth National People's Congress in November and December 1982. Both documents avoided the shrill rhetoric and exaggerated expectations so characteristic of the Mao era. They sought instead to provide quiet reassurance that the country had a responsible and realistic leadership.

The fourth constitution was in many respects a throwback to the first constitution of 1954 and contrasted sharply with the leftist constitution of 1965, which declared that Lin Biao (later to die a traitor) was to be Mao Zedong's successor, and the 1978 draft constitution, which extolled the "Thoughts of Mao Zedong." Like the 1954 constitution, the new one of 1982 provided for a president who would have more than just ceremonial responsibilities, but whose exact authority would depend largely on the personal prestige of the individual selected. The restoration of the office of president represented symbolically the total rehabilitation of the deceased Liu Shaoqi, who held that title when he was purged during the Cultural Revolution. In equal measure it was a blot on Mao's memory, for the Chinese widely understood that Mao had adamantly opposed having such a post.

The new constitution also tilted in favor of the State bureaucracy over the Party hierarchy in many respects. All previous constitutions, for example, had linked the PLA to the Party by specifying that the armed forces were "led by the Chinese Communist Party." In the new constitution the Central Military Commission is declared to be a State organization and not a Party office.

Possibly the most important expression of the new mood in

China was the acknowledgment in the new constitution that Chinese citizens had some rights and not just duties, that farmers would be guaranteed their private plots, that the communes should no longer have any governmental powers, and that all could complain or criticize state functionaries. With an eye to opening the economy to world trade, the constitution legitimized foreign enterprises and foreign investments that "accord with Chinese law," a dictum that is still vague in the commercial sphere.

The transition from Mao's style of rule to Deng's was even clearer in the new five-year plan, adopted in December 1982, one year after it had supposedly started. Instead of the grandiose targets of the past (including those of the Hua Guofeng years), the plan called for only a modest 4 percent growth rate, an actual cutback in such areas as steel production (1 million tons) and state capital construction (about 1.5 billion American dollars a year through 1983), and an increase in investments in consumer goods and light industry. Priority also went to coal production, oil exploration, and transportation.

In spite of the modest beginning it projected, the plan is supposed to lay the foundation for a quadrupling of the Chinese economy by the end of the century. The expectation is that by carefully restructuring the economy, giving more attention to consumer goods and light industry, and expanding foreign trade, the Chinese economy will in fact end up advancing more rapidly by the year 2000 than would be possible if another big push was made early in the 1980s. Much of the success of the plan will depend on the responses of the people to Deng's new priorities.

In looking at China's prospects in the last years of the twentieth century, therefore, we must go beyond the realm of governmental policy implementations and take note of more basic societal changes which will decisively shape the future.

NEW GENERATIONS AND CHANGING SOCIAL PATTERNS

One of the greatest paradoxes of the Chinese political system is that it was under Mao, and still is under Deng, a government of aged men ruling over an exceptionally young population. The average age of the members of the Twelfth Central Committee was over seventy, while the mean age of the Chinese population is estimated to be under twenty-four, and every two seconds another baby is born. China's gerontocracy still likes to use the political rhetoric of revolution, but China's younger generation prefers to dwell on more private matters.

Chinese politics has less of the tensions of fathers and sons than Western politics, and more of the tolerant acceptance of grandfathers and grandsons. The Cultural Revolution seemingly exhausted the Red Guard generation, even as it broke the spirit of the middle generation that was so much the object of its fury. Moreover, those who are passing through the post–Cultural Revolution school system have generally turned their backs on the politicized ways of their older brothers and sisters, and have contented themselves with more private concerns.

Thus the generational scene in China augurs change but not disruption. The general craving for order and for getting ahead suggests that governing may not be difficult, even though the problems confronting the government will not be easy to solve. Furthermore, social trends and government preferences are in many areas devoid of antagonism. The government's wishes for more trained specialists, for example, conform to the widespread ambition of most young Chinese to get a better education and to find a secure job in a modernizing industry. Even the government's drastic demand that couples limit themselves to a single child, a belated recognition that China has a severe population problem, has been generally well received, at least in urban areas, despite the Chinese tradition valuing large families (and especially many sons). The need for both parents to work if the couple is to earn enough money to buy more consumer goods makes it easier to accept the idea of having only one child. (But as we have noted, in rural areas the government's family planning objectives have been undermined by its "responsibility system," which favors larger families.) The long-run implications for the social character of China of having its urban society, and hence presumably its elite, composed largely of people who were only children is a matter for interesting speculation — especially given the evidence of the pleasure parents and grandparents get from doting on their offspring.

The improvements in living standards early in the 1980s has

reduced the uniformity of life, particularly in the larger cities. The legitimizing of material accumulation has stimulated interest in consumer goods, but also, according to the Chinese press, a rise in crime and corruption. Young Chinese in particular seem eager to learn more about the culture and practices of foreign youth, especially as a result of their exposure to large numbers of overseas Chinese tourists from Hong Kong and Southeast Asia.

Under Deng culture has been freed from stern limitations, particularly those imposed by Mao's wife, Jiang Qing. No longer limited to a few "revolutionary operas," the performing arts took on new life and gained greater audience interest. The regime, however, soon felt that experimentation, and particularly political free-thinking, was going too far. Writers were told that while they could criticize the malfeasance of corrupt officials, there could be no attacking socialism. Specifically, the Party decree held that while art no longer had to "serve politics," it would still have to "serve the people," a fine but not entirely meaningless distinction, since "politics" could include "incorrect" Party policies, while "the people" can only mean the righteous Party in its role as the "vanguard of the proletariat."

Although in the cultural realm, as elsewhere in Chinese society, discipline tends to come through one's small group or *danwei* and can thus be arbitrary, there was by 1982 some significant development of a more formalized legal system. Courtroom procedures were used to an increasing degree early in the 1980s to punish corrupt officials and to keep citizens in line; but severe constraints in applying legal forms still existed, if for no other reason than the lack of trained "legal workers," as judges, assessors, and lawyers are called. In January 1982, Chinese authorities announced that there were only 5,500 full-time and 1,300 part-time lawyers in the whole country. Lawyers in China usually earn from $30 to $40 a month.[3] The Chinese legal system, like its traditional predecessor, is not based on an adversary approach, as is Western law; rather, the prime responsibility of the defendant's lawyer is to safeguard the interests of the state and to help reform the wayward. Courtroom proceedings are dominated by the judge lecturing the accused,

[3] Christopher S. Wren, "China Moves to Resurrect a Credible Legal System," *New York Times*, December 5, 1982.

who as a result of prior interrogation pleads guilty and asks only for leniency in sentencing. At the December 1981 National People's Congress, Huang Huoqing, China's chief procurator, reported that during the first nine months of that year 99.97 percent of those prosecuted had been found guilty. Minor criminal cases and almost all civil actions are still handled by local mediation committees, which exist in every neighborhood and place of work. Such committees can sentence people to up to three years of labor reform in the countryside.[4]

The gradual Chinese movement toward a more formalized legal system is in no small measure a reflection of China's greater involvement with the outside world and the need to adapt Chinese practice to international standards. The Chinese have found that simply for the purpose of facilitating greater foreign trade and the smooth transfer of foreign technologies, it is essential to reassure foreign business people by promising that contracts will be protected by laws. In short, in the legal area as in many others, the demands of modernization have forced the Chinese to take greater heed of foreign ways. Thus the ultimate fate of China's modernization rests very much on the question of China's relations with the outside world. In order to get a better perspective on these prospects, it is necessary to review key aspects of China's foreign relations.

CHINA AND THE WORLD

Throughout Mao's rule, China's conduct toward the rest of the world vacillated between pragmatic calculation based on national interest and ideological dogmatism, between benign understanding and revolutionary ardor. The face China presented to the outside was generally influenced by the state of domestic developments; when the country was caught up in revolutionary campaigns its foreign policy became more hard-line, and when the emphasis was on economic development foreign relations stressed the businesslike advancement of foreign trade. The main thrust of Mao's policies, however, was to isolate China, so a major problem

[4] Ibid.

for his successor has been how to bring China back into the world without compromising Chinese values.

When Mao's rule began he committed China to a strong Cold War alliance with the Soviet Union, which was intensified during the Korean War. During the mid-1950s, however, China decided to court the neutrals and the newly emerging states of Africa and Asia by championing what was then called the "Bandung spirit," the spirit of the Conference of Afro-Asian States held in Indonesia in 1955. By the end of that decade, Chinese foreign policy was largely colored by its ideological competition with the Soviet Union over the issue of the organization and direction of Communist parties throughout the world. By the end of the 1960s the ideological rift between the Chinese Party and the Soviet Party had become a major state-to-state confrontation that escalated into military clashes and fundamental security considerations.

Mao's legacy in foreign affairs was his unalterable opposition to Soviet "revisionism" and "socialist imperialism." Immediately after assuming power, Chairman Hua Guofeng reiterated China's hostility to the Soviet Union and rebuffed Moscow's overtures for a reduction in tensions. Peking's concern over the Soviet threat set the stage for the improvement of relations with the other superpower, the United States.

IMPROVEMENTS IN UNITED STATES–CHINA RELATIONS

In the United States, the combination of frustration over the Vietnam War and the perception of China as severely weakened by its split with the Soviet Union and by its domestic upheavals made China seem less of a danger to world peace. During the period of the close alliance between the Soviet Union and China, and especially just after the Korean War, the view that China was a growing threat to world peace had considerable substance. The successes of the Communist leaders in establishing domestic order and providing economic growth during the 1950s made China seem increasingly formidable. Chinese revolutionary rhetoric contributed to the view that Peking was a danger to neighboring countries and to the stability of any country faced with revolutionary insurgency.

The Sino-Soviet split and the debilitating effects of the Great

Leap and the Cultural Revolution fundamentally changed Chinese power. Until Stalin's death the concept of a monolithic Communist world was accurate, but by 1969 Russian and Chinese soldiers were shooting at each other and Mao was preaching that Russian revisionism was a greater threat to China than American imperialism.

Hindsight reveals that although the inexorable trend throughout the 1960s was toward isolation and the weakening of China, events also seemed to support the earlier view of a dangerous China. The Quemoy-Matsu crisis of 1958 flushed out the fact that China could not count on the Soviet nuclear umbrella; but in 1959 the harsh suppression of Tibet kept alive the picture of an aggressive and dictatorial China. In 1960 the Soviets recalled their technicians and cancelled all industrial aid projects, a decision that nearly brought Chinese economic growth to a standstill; but the weakening caused by this development was soon obscured by the Sino-Indian border war of 1962. The fall of Khrushchev in October 1964 and the simultaneous detonation of China's first nuclear device increased anxieties that the Sino-Soviet conflict might be reversed and China might practice nuclear blackmail against its Asian neighbors — a consideration that apparently influenced the American decision to hold firm in Vietnam. Chinese revolutionary rhetoric reached new heights as the plans were formulated for a Second Afro-Asian Conference in Algiers in 1964 and for the establishment of the Djakarta-Peking axis in 1965. Above all else, Lin Biao's speech of September 1965, ambiguous as it was, suggested to many that China was about to take an active interest in "revolutionary wars" wherever they might occur. (Still, many careful analysts did interpret Lin's stress on "self-reliance" to mean that China would not be directly involved in supporting insurgencies.) Because Maoist enthusiasts throughout the world welcomed the speech as heralding an era of Chinese leadership in toppling existing governments, it was not surprising that Washington decision-makers also took Lin's words at face value.

China, coming out of the Cultural Revolution, faced far more than just the need to gain international respectability. After the border incidents of the summer of 1969 the Chinese were confronted with a dramatic Soviet military buildup along one of the longest borders in the world. Numerous public hints were given that elements in Moscow were weighing the desirability of a preemptive strike against the Chinese nuclear capability. The implied Soviet threat carried a particularly ominous note of credibility because the year before, Russian troops had occupied Czechoslovakia.

Moreover, after 1969 the Soviet Union engaged in a massive military buildup in its Far Eastern and Central Asian territories. The Russian deployment on their northern frontier meant that the Chinese lost the great good fortune of being able to leave that border relatively underguarded. As a consequence of allowing their ideological disagreements with the Russians to get out of hand and cause a rift in state-to-state relations, the Chinese were once again prisoners of their historical problem of having to mobilize massive forces along their northern frontiers.

Surrounded by enemies or countries that deeply distrusted Chinese intentions, Peking was ready to seek an easing of tension with the United States as early as 1964. Through the Warsaw talks, the Americans had made it clear that they had no aggressive designs on China or North Vietnam. This pledge set the stage in the post–Cultural Revolution environment for Peking to respond positively to President Nixon's statement in favor of better relations with "one quarter of mankind."

Under the leadership of Zhou Enlai, China in the summer of 1971 sought to break out of its isolation and to separate its various foes by blending diplomacy and propaganda to create distrust between the superpowers — the Soviet Union and the United States. Both Mao and Zhou warned Henry Kissinger that the American policy of seeking to reduce tensions with the Soviet Union, the policy of détente, was emboldening Moscow and making war inevitable. Presidents Nixon and Ford both sought to improve American relations with the two Communist powers while exploiting the conflict between them to the advantage of the United States.

From 1971 to 1974, trade between the two countries grew significantly, beginning with a total of $5 million and reaching $934 million. The Chinese imports grew most rapidly, as Peking purchased Boeing 707 airplanes, fertilizer plants, and wheat. China's exports to the United States were limited largely to raw materials and textiles.

The improvement of relations also brought a growth in cultural exchange. The Chinese discovered that Americans had a great curiosity about traveling to China and began to grant visas not only to official delegations, but to "friendship" groups and select individuals. Sports teams and performing arts groups from each country exchanged visits.

Immediately after the death of Mao Zedong the Chinese continued to show interest in improved relations with Washington, in part by rejecting overtures from Moscow. But the combination of Watergate and the change of administration with the victory of Jimmy Carter forced Washington to put China policy on a back burner.

The temporary halt in the progress of relations between the United States and China was broken by the combination of increased tensions between Peking and Hanoi, Deng's need for a foreign-policy success to help consolidate his position, and President Carter's desire to follow up his Camp David success in Middle East peacemaking with another foreign-policy achievement. The result was the decision of December 1978 to normalize relations between the United States and China.

At the time, just as in the Shanghai Communiqué of 1972, both Peking and Washington found it convenient to overlook their differences over the problem of the continued existence of the government calling itself the Republic of China, which controlled Taiwan.

THE PEKING-MOSCOW-WASHINGTON TRIANGLE AND THE PROBLEM OF TAIWAN

As President Nixon's envoy Henry Kissinger discovered, Mao Zedong and Zhou Enlai placed such primary concern on the perceived Soviet threat that they were ready to minimize the problem of Taiwan. This opened the way for Kissinger to advance the formula that the United States agreed with "the Chinese on both sides of the Taiwan Straits" that there is only one China. The Nationalist regime on Taiwan has persistently held that it is the only legitimate Chinese government, so it was in a weak position to object to the Shanghai Communiqué formula, even though it was profoundly shocked by Washington's sudden readiness to deal with the Peking regime.

As a consequence of the Shanghai Communiqué, the United

States and China opened "liaison offices" in each other's capitals, while Washington continued to have formal diplomatic relations with Taipei. This situation of semiofficial relations lasted from 1972 until 1978, and it saw United States trade grow not only with the People's Republic but also with Taiwan.

The next step in advancing United States–China relations was more difficult, since it called not only for a change in official diplomatic relations but also for a test of the alliance commitments of the United States. In the aftermath of the Vietnam War there was widespread international concern over how seriously Washington would take its treaty obligations. Fortunately for Washington, Deng's impatience for normalization in 1978 made it again seem possible to put off any final reckoning about Taiwan. Peking indicated that if relations were to be normalized, the formal mutual defense treaty between the United States and the Republic of China would have to be terminated — its terms allowed for a one-year notice of termination by either party — but at the same time, the Chinese suggested that they recognize that in light of a "problem left over from history" the United States might continue arms sales to Taiwan for a time. Congress, in accepting normalization with Peking and the termination of the treaty with the Republic of China, passed the Taiwan Relations Act, which provided not only for the establishment of an American Institute in Taiwan to oversee unofficial relations with Taiwan, but also for continued arms sales to Taiwan, the level and character to be determined by the United States government.

From 1978 to 1980 economic relations between the United States and the People's Republic of China (PRC) expanded; at the same time, American trade with and investment in Taiwan also rose sharply. The Carter administration's policy objective was to improve relations with the PRC while at the same time maintaining close but unofficial ties with Taiwan. Peking seemed prepared to cooperate in such an arrangement, since it did not make immediate public protest of the January 1980 sale of $280 million worth of military equipment.

It was widely assumed that China's continued anxiety over the Soviet threat and its need for technology in its modernization drive would be incentive enough for the Chinese to overlook the anomaly of uninterrupted American arms sales to Taiwan. In mid-

1980, however, Peking became publicly sensitive about United States relations with Taiwan after candidate Ronald Reagan called for more formal diplomatic relations with "our old friends and allies" in the Republic of China on Taiwan. After coming into office, the Reagan administration sought to reassure Peking of its desire for better relations with the People's Republic.

In May 1982, Vice-President George Bush went to Peking and delivered three letters from President Reagan to the Chinese leaders. These letters linked a pledge to reduce arms sales to Taiwan with a PRC commitment to work for a peaceful reunification of Taiwan with the mainland. Peking responded with a specific nine-point proposal to the leaders of the Nationalists on Taiwan, including a pledge that they would be treated as a special region and would be allowed to maintain their social and economic systems. Taiwan rejected the offer out of hand on the grounds that they had had enough experience with Communist pledges not to trust them. Washington, however, decided that the time was appropriate to try through quiet negotiations to work out a new understanding with Peking that might defuse the Taiwan issue. The result was a joint agreement, announced on August 17, 1982, which reaffirmed that Washington recognized only one China, with its government in Peking, and that it would limit sales of arms to Taipei so as not to exceed the quantity and quality of sales in "recent years."

It was hoped in Washington that the agreement would buy time to allow for improvements in relations with the People's Republic and a general relaxing of feelings over the Taiwan issue. In the meantime, however, the Soviet Union began a campaign to exploit the tensions between the United States and China over Taiwan. In particular, in the summer of 1982 Soviet leader Leonid Brezhnev, in speeches at Tashkent and Baku, called for a normalization of relations between Moscow and Peking, and the Chinese responded by agreeing to hold talks. Brezhnev's death in November 1982 was followed by strong Chinese statements in favor of better Sino-Soviet relations. These statements also indicated, however, that complete improvement was precluded by three major obstacles: the Soviet occupation of Afghanistan, Soviet support of the Vietnamese occupation of Kampuchea, and the massing of Soviet troops along the border with China.

The upshot of these developments was that the post-Mao

leadership seemed prepared to alter the triangular relations among Washington, Moscow, Peking so as no longer to be more antagonistic than the United States in opposing Moscow, and thus achieve more balanced relations with the two superpowers. At the same time, while they indicated annoyance with Washington over numerous issues involving more than just Taiwan, they showed that they also wanted to continue to obtain technology through both trade and cultural exchanges with the United States. On balance, the Chinese had more interests in common with the United States and with the West in general than with the Soviet Union, and their basic policies continued to reflect a tilt toward Washington and not Moscow.

At the same time, however, the context for relations between China and the United States had significantly changed from the early days of the Nixon-Mao opening. As geopolitical considerations lost their overriding sense of urgency, more mundane frustrations surfaced to cause, at the least, annoyances in the bilateral relationship. The Chinese, possibly expecting their newfound "friend" to provide grants of military items, showed little interest in accepting Washington's offer that they could purchase such equipment, but instead complained about some delays in licensing the export to China of sophisticated computers. The Chinese also complained that since the balance of trade favored the United States, Washington should allow a more rapid increase in Chinese exports of textiles and clothing — something which for both economic and political reasons the United States government felt it could not permit.

On the American side there was a steady growth in awareness that the popular image of Chinese society had been excessively idealized, especially as the first reporters stationed in Peking began to publish book-length accounts of daily life in socialist China. In the area of cultural exchange it seemed to many Americans that the Chinese were not reciprocating, since thousands of Chinese scholars were being given complete access to American universities and laboratories, while few American scholars were allowed to engage in substantive research in a China that was still secretive and suspicious of foreign penetration. Above all, American business people found that their initial hopes for selling in the China market were unrealistically high, and that trade negotiations with Chinese officials could be slow and complicated.

Many of these complaints on both sides reflected the growth of a more realistic and accurate understanding of each other; thus they constituted the normal irritants to be expected in relations between two different societies. These symptoms of aggravation suggested that the two countries were not likely to become as close as was once predicted. The problem of Taiwan has not disappeared, and the Chinese have displayed few signs that they will let the issue lose its saliency entirely. Indeed, the fact that Peking's initial response in the negotiations with Britain over the future of Hong Kong was strongly nationalistic and relatively insensitive to what outsiders perceived to be China's economic self-interest made it clear that Deng Xiaoping's leadership would probably forego the advantages of smoother relations with the United States rather than compromise Peking's claim to sovereignty over Taiwan. The surfacing of such irritations meant that relations between the United States and China had receded somewhat in the total foreign affairs concerns of both governments.

In describing their foreign policy position at the end of 1982, Chinese officials stressed that they would not ally themselves with either superpower and that they preferred to be thought of as a Third World country. Although Chinese influence among the developing countries was by then lower than in previous decades, and many poor countries were uneasy over the prospect of China becoming a competitor for international assistance, there was a basic accuracy in the Chinese description of themselves as a developing country.

Thus, in spite of periodic inconsistencies, largely in response to attacks on China's national pride, the fundamental foreign-policy approach of the Deng leadership has been to use foreign policy to facilitate modernization in ways that would open the country to advanced technologies without altering cultural values and eroding China's socialist identity. The great question mark for China, in both domestic and foreign policy, is whether it can succeed in modernizing its economy and society while protecting values identified with an ideology that no longer has the degree of popular appeal it once had.

The Chinese are determined to recapture the sense of greatness that was theirs when they saw themselves as the Middle Kingdom, the center of the world. The essence of the Chinese revolution has been precisely this striving to regain national power and greatness. Peking is determined to reverse the humiliations of the last 150 years. Central to its image of itself is its revolutionary heritage.

Chinese officials do recognize that tensions can exist between power or practical considerations and ideological principles. This dilemma was central to the change in the character of Communism in the Soviet Union.[5] The Chinese way of formulating the problem is to contrast "short-run considerations" with "long-range principles," which they deem unalterable. As long as Mao was alive, any policy was by definition "consistent" with the Thoughts of the Great Helmsman, but in the post-Mao era changes in policy are likely to be seen as more threatening to the ideological purity of the country.

CHANGING A CIVILIZATION

Viewed in a broader perspective, China today is a changing civilization with striking elements of continuity. In the post-Mao years China will become increasingly industrialized, and with its growing need for more advanced technology it will have to become more dependent on trade with other countries. Yet like Confucian China, the country will continue to be absorbed with itself and more comfortable in relative isolation. As in the past, China wants to be strong, and to be looked up to by other countries, but it also seeks to preserve the uniqueness and purity of its ideological principles.

In formal doctrine, Confucianism and Marxism stand poles apart. The traditions of reverence for the family, respect for hierarchy, and desire for harmony have been replaced by the doctrines of sacrifice of self and family for the state, egalitarianism, and struggle and class conflict. Mandarin values have been replaced by

[5] See Barrington Moore, *Soviet Practice: The Dilemma of Power* (Cambridge, Mass.: Harvard University Press, 1951).

cadre values; the quest to become a "superior man" through leisurely study, philosophical speculation, and the refinement of artistic sensitivities has given way to the ideals of purposeful action, political dedication, and ideological consciousness-raising.

Yet in spite of all these changes, many Chinese cultural habits persist. Chinese are still brought up to believe that they should emulate idealized standards and behave in highly conformist ways. As in old China, modern young people are taught the supreme importance of "correct" behavior. The traditional Chinese assumption persists that the perfection of society must begin with each individual seeking perfection in his own actions, and that this can only be done by first achieving perfection in one's thoughts. The character of the models for behavior has changed, but the emphasis on the importance of emulating models has not.

Daily life in China still reflects its Confucian heritage. The importance of family ties and personal relationships persist. Respect for the written word and for the wisdom of the official "philosopher" is unchanged. The habits of conformity and patience still hold.

China's response to the modern world remains ambivalent. The problems of changing one of the world's great civilizations has produced one of the longest revolutions in history. Several generations of Chinese leaders have grappled with the issues of how China should and should not be modernized. The struggles over the decades of this century have led to dramatic changes, and have in many ways brought China closer to world culture than before. Yet the Chinese continue to follow their own ways and to value their isolation. It is impossible to judge the pace at which China will change in the years to come, but what is certain is that the country will not lose its basic Chinese cultural characteristics. They will certainly reappear in modern guise.

Mao's revolution and Deng's have proved that China can change, but that it must also live on with its past.

Sources and Suggested Readings

In recent years there has been a great increase in the number of scholarly monographs on China. The writers of most of them presume that the reader is somewhat familiar with the subject. Probably the best guide to this literature is the bibliography in John K. Fairbank, *The United States and China*, 3d ed. (Cambridge, Mass.: Harvard University Press, 1971). A more detailed bibliography is in Charles O. Hucker, *China: A Critical Bibliography* (Tucson: University of Arizona Press, 1962). See also Michel Oksenberg, *A Bibliography of Secondary English Language Literature on Contemporary Chinese Politics* (New York: East Asian Institute, Columbia University, 1970).

In preparing this book, I consulted and relied on the following works. They can be profitably read by all who wish to explore Chinese history and culture further.

GENERAL INTRODUCTIONS

The most masterful overview of Chinese history and social evolution is the above-mentioned study by Fairbank. For a more detailed analysis see Edwin O. Reischauer and John K. Fairbank, *East Asia: The Great Tradition* (Boston: Houghton Mifflin, 1960); and John K. Fairbank, Edwin O. Reischauer, and Albert M. Craig, *East Asia: The Modern Transformation* (Boston: Houghton Mifflin, 1965). An introduction that balances political developments with cultural and artistic ones is Charles P. Fitzgerald, *China: A Short Cultural History*, 3d ed. (New York: Praeger, 1961). Political and diplomatic history from the beginning of the Western impact is well covered in Immanuel C. Y. Hsü, *The Rise of Modern China*, 2d ed. (London: Oxford University Press, 1975).

THE CONFUCIAN TRADITION

The richest single source of translations of traditional Chinese thought is William Theodore de Bary, Wing-tsit Chan, and Burton Watson, comps., *Sources of Chinese Tradition,* 2 vols. (New York: Columbia University Press, 1960). The standard translation of the Confucian classics is James Legge, *The Chinese Classics,* 5 vols. (1893–1895; reprinted Seattle: University of Washington Press, 1960). For a more sensitive and literary translation see Confucius, *The Analects of Confucius,* trans. Arthur Waley (1938; reprinted Atlantic Highlands, N.J.: Humanities Press, 1964). The standard textbook on Chinese philosophy is Fung Yulan, *A History of Chinese Philosophy,* trans. Derk Bodde, 2 vols. (Princeton, N.J.: Princeton University Press, 1952). The most detailed study of Confucius is H. G. Creel, *Confucius: The Man and the Myth* (1949; reprinted Westport, Conn.: Greenwood Press, 1973). The best introductions to Daoism are Arthur Waley, *The Way and Its Power: A Study of the Tao Te Ching and Its Place in Chinese Thought* (1938; reprinted New York: Random House, 1966); and Holmes Welch, *Taoism: The Parting of the Way* (Boston: Beacon Press, 1966).

THE CHINESE LIBRARY

The best general introduction to Chinese literature is Burton Watson, *Early Chinese Literature* (New York: Columbia University Press, 1962). For a technical review of Chinese historical scholarship see Charles S. Gardner, *Chinese Traditional Historiography* (Cambridge, Mass.: Harvard University Press, 1938). The character of the official dynastic histories is revealed in the following translations: Pan Ku (Bon Gu), *The History of the Former Han Dynasty,* trans. Homer Dubs, 3 vols. (1938, 1944, 1955; reprinted Ithaca, N.Y.: Spoken Language Services, 1971); Burton Watson, *Records of the Grand Historian of China,* 2 vols. (New York: Columbia University Press, 1961); and Ssu-Ma Kuang (Sima Guang), *The Chronicle of the Three Kingdoms,* 2 vols., trans. Achilles Fang (Cambridge, Mass.: Harvard University Press, 1952, 1965). For a detailed review of other aspects of Chinese classical literature see James Robert Hightower, *Topics in Chinese Literature: Outlines and Bibliographies* (Cambridge, Mass.: Harvard University Press, 1953). Introductions to Chinese poetry include James Y. Liu, *The Art of Chinese Poetry* (Chicago: University of Chicago Press, 1962); and Arthur Waley, *Ballads and Stories from Tunhuang: An Anthology* (London: Allen and Unwin, 1960).

THE TRADITIONAL CHINESE SYSTEM

Among the most informative and readable discussions of life and institutions in traditional China are Michael Loewe, *Imperial China: The Historical Background to the Modern Age* (New York: Praeger, 1966); Ray Huang, *1587: A Year of No Significance* (New Haven, Conn.: Yale University Press, 1981); Derk Bodde, *China's First Unifier: A Study of the Ch'in Dynasty as Seen in the Life of Li Ssu 280?–208 B.C.* (Leiden, Neth.: Brill, 1938); Arthur F. Wright, ed., *Studies in Chinese Thought* (Chicago: University of Chicago Press, 1953); John K. Fairbank, ed., *Chinese Thought and Institutions* (Chicago: University of Chicago Press, 1957); David S. Nivison and Arthur F. Wright, eds., *Confucianism in Action* (Stanford, Calif.: Stanford University Press, 1959); Arthur F. Wright and Denis C. Twitchett, eds., *Confucian Personalities* (Stanford, Calif.: Stanford University Press, 1962); Charles O. Hucker, *The Traditional Chinese State in Ming Times, 1368–1644* (Tucson: University of Arizona Press, 1961); E. A. Kracke, Jr., *Civil Service in Early Sung China, 960–1067* (Cambridge, Mass.: Harvard University Press, 1953); Derk Bodde and Clarence Morris, *Law in Imperial China: Exemplified by 190 Ch'ing Dynasty Cases* (Cambridge, Mass.: Harvard University Press, 1967); and T'ung-tsu Ch'ü, *Local Government in China Under the Ch'ing* (Stanford, Calif.: Stanford University Press, 1962).

CHINA'S FOREIGN RELATIONS

Classic studies of Chinese relations with nomadic "barbarians" are Franz Michael, *The Origin of Manchu Rule in China* (1942; reprinted New York: Octagon Books, 1965); Wolfram Eberhard, *Conquerors and Rulers: Social Forces in Medieval China,* 2d ed. (New York: Heinman, 1965); and John K. Fairbank, ed., *The Chinese World Order: Traditional China's Foreign Relations* (Cambridge, Mass.: Harvard University Press, 1968).

Early Western contacts are described in Hosea Ballou Morse, *The International Relations of the Chinese Empire,* 3 vols. (1910, 1918; reprinted New York: Paragon Book Reprint Corp., 1964); John K. Fairbank, *Trade and Diplomacy on the China Coast: The Opening of the Treaty Ports,* 2 vols. (Cambridge, Mass.: Harvard University Press, 1954); Immanuel C. Y. Hsü, *The Rise of Modern China* (New York: Oxford University Press, 1970).

A rich storehouse of documents that reveal Chinese attitudes is Ssu-yu Teng and John K. Fairbank, *China's Response to the West: A*

Documentary Survey, 1839–1923 (Cambridge, Mass.: Harvard University Press, 1954); and the most stimulating and subtle treatment of Chinese intellectual developments as a consequence of the Western impact is Joseph R. Levenson, *Confucian China and Its Modern Fate:* Vol. 1, *The Problem of Intellectual Continuity,* 1958; vol. 2, *The Problem of Monarchial Decay,* 1964; vol. 3, *The Problem of Historical Significance,* 1968 (Berkeley: University of California Press). The spirit of the Confucian mandarin in the face of the Western challenge is best conveyed by Mary C. Wright, *The Last Stand of Chinese Conservatism: The T'ung-Chih Restoration, 1862–1874* (Stanford, Calif.: Stanford University Press, 1957).

CHINESE SOCIETY

A lively general introduction to the Chinese rural society and economy is Fei Hsiao-t'ung, *China's Gentry: Essays on Rural-Urban Relations,* rev. ed., ed. Margaret Park Redfield (Chicago: University of Chicago Press, 1968). For studies of Chinese social structure and social mobility questions see Chung-li Chang, *The Chinese Gentry: Studies on Their Role in Nineteenth Century Chinese Society* (Seattle: University of Washington Press, 1967); for a masterful blending of sociological and historical analysis see Ping-ti Ho, *The Ladder of Success in Imperial China: Aspects of Social Mobility, 1368–1911* (New York: Columbia University Press, 1962). Also see Etienne Balazs, *Chinese Civilization and Bureaucracy: Variations on a Theme,* trans. H. M. Wright, ed. Arthur F. Wright (New Haven, Conn.: Yale University Press, 1964); Morton H. Fried, *Fabric of Chinese Society* (1953; reprinted New York: Octagon Books, 1969); E. A. Kracke, Jr., *Civil Service in Early Sung China, 960–1067* (Cambridge, Mass.: Harvard University Press, 1953); Max Weber, *The Religions of China: Confucianism and Taoism,* trans. Hans Gerth (Glencoe, Ill.: Free Press, 1951); and Arthur P. Wolf, ed., *Religion and Ritual in Chinese Society* (Stanford, Calif.: Stanford University Press, 1974).

RURAL ECONOMY AND VILLAGE LIFE

An exceptional economic history study that demonstrates that Chinese agricultural production kept pace with population growth is Dwight H. Perkins, assisted by Yeh-chien Wang, *Agricultural Development in China, 1368–1968* (Chicago: Aldine, 1969). A systematic review of both

Japanese and Chinese data on rural economics is Ramon H. Myers, *The Chinese Peasant Economy: Agricultural Development in Hopei and Shantung, 1890–1949* (Cambridge, Mass.: Harvard University Press, 1970). The classic anthropological study is Francis L. K. Hsu, *Under the Ancestors' Shadow: Personality and Social Mobility in China* (Stanford, Calif.: Stanford University Press, 1967). See also Martin Yang, *A Chinese Village: Taitou, Shangtung Province* (New York: Columbia University Press, 1945), and Lin Yao-hua, *The Golden Wing* (1948; reprinted Westport, Conn.: Greenwood Press, 1974). Studies that focus on changes with the Communist takeover include C. K. Yang, *Chinese Communist Society: The Family and the Village* (Cambridge, Mass.: MIT Press, 1965); William Hinton, *Fanshen: A Documentary of Revoution in a Chinese Village* (New York: Monthly Review Press, 1967); and Jan Myrdal, *Report from a Chinese Village,* trans. M. Michael (New York: Pantheon Books, 1965).

THE CHINESE FAMILY

A classic empirical study of the Chinese family is Olga Lang, *Chinese Family and Society* (1946; reprinted Hamden, Conn.: Shoe String Press, 1968); and the classic theoretical study is Marion J. Levy, Jr., *The Family Revolution in Modern China* (New York: Atheneum, 1968). More recent studies include Maurice Freedman, *Chinese Lineage and Society: Fukien and Kwangtung* (London: Athlone, 1971); Maurice Freedman, ed., *Family and Kinship in Chinese Society* (Stanford, Calif.: Stanford University Press, 1970); Margery Wolf, *The House of Lim: A Study of a Chinese Farm Family* (New York: Appleton-Century-Crofts, 1960); and Ida Pruitt, *A Daughter of Han: The Autobiography of a Chinese Working Woman* (Stanford, Calif.: Stanford University Press, 1945).

THE WARLORDS AND THE NATIONALIST PERIOD

The 1911 Revolution has most recently been analyzed in Mary C. Wright, ed., *China in Revolution: The First Phase, 1900–1913* (New Haven, Conn.: Yale University Press, 1968). The warlord period is covered in O. Edmund Clubb, *Twentieth Century China,* rev. ed. (New York: Columbia University Press, 1972); James E. Sheridan, *Chinese Warlord: The Career of Feng Yü-hsiang* (Stanford, Calif.: Stanford University Press, 1966); Donald Gillin, *Warlord: Yen Hsi-shan in Shansi Province 1911–1949* (Princeton, N.J.: Princeton University Press, 1967);

Lucian W. Pye, *Warlord Politics* (New York: Praeger, 1971); Ralph L. Powell, *The Rise of Chinese Military Power, 1895–1912* (Princeton, N.J.: Princeton University Press, 1955); Arthur N. Holcombe, *The Spirit of the Chinese Revolution* (New York: Knopf, 1930); Andrew J. Nathan, *Peking Politics, 1918–1923: Factionalism and the Failure of Constitutionalism* (Berkeley: University of California Press, 1975); and Ch'i Hsi-sheng, *Warlord Politics in China. 1916–1928* (Stanford, Calif.: Stanford University Press, 1976).

Little has been written on the Nationalist period. The formal system of Kuomintang rule is described in Ch'ien Tuan-sheng, *The Government and Politics of China, 1912–1949* (Stanford, Calif.: Stanford University Press, 1950); William L. Tung, *The Political Institutions of Modern China* (The Hague: Nijhoff, 1964); and Paul M. Linebarger, *The China of Chiang K'ai-shek: A Political Study* (1943; reprinted Westport, Conn.: Greenwood Press, 1973).

THE RISE OF COMMUNISM

In contrast to the Kuomintang, a great deal has been written on the early years of the Chinese Communist Party, the most important books being Edgar Snow, *Red Star over China* (1938; reprinted New York: Grove, 1971); Harold Isaacs, *The Tragedy of the Chinese Revolution*, 2d rev. ed. (Stanford, Calif.: Stanford University Press, 1961); Benjamin I. Schwartz, *Chinese Communism and the Rise of Mao Tse-tung* (Cambridge, Mass.: Harvard University Press, 1951); Shanti Swarup, *A Study of the Chinese Communist Movement* (Oxford, Eng.: Clarendon Press, 1966); Stuart Schram, *Mao Tse-tung* (Baltimore: Penguin, 1968); Jerome Ch'en, *Mao and the Chinese Revolution* (New York: Oxford University Press, 1967); and Richard C. Thornton, *The Comintern and the Chinese Communists, 1928–1931* (Seattle: University of Washington Press, 1969). The thesis that nationalism and reactions to the Japanese occupation were more important than landlord-peasant relations in explaining the rise of the Communist Party is impressively developed in Chalmers A. Johnson, *Peasant Nationalism and Communist Power: The Emergence of Revolutionary China, 1937–1945* (Stanford, Calif.: Stanford University Press, 1962). The most complete recent general history is James Pinckney Harrison, *The Long March to Power: A History of the Chinese Communist Party, 1921–1972* (New York: Praeger, 1972). On the final Communist victory, see Suzanne Pepper, *Civil War in China* (Berkeley: University of California Press, 1978).

THE COMMUNIST SYSTEM

Probably the most authoritative and illuminating single source for understanding the Chinese Communist system is the writings of A. Doak Barnett, in particular: *China on the Eve of Communist Takeover* (New York: Praeger, 1963); *Communist China and Asia: Challenge to American Policy* (Mystic, Conn.: Verry, 1960); *Cadres, Bureaucracy, and Political Power in Communist China* (New York: Columbia University Press, 1967); and *Communist China: The Early Years, 1949–1955* (New York: Praeger, 1964).

The early years of the regime are covered in W. W. Rostow, *The Prospects of Communist China* (New York: Wiley, 1954); Richard L. Walker, *China under Communism: The First Five Years* (New Haven, Conn.: Yale University Press, 1955).

The organizational discipline of the early Communist regime is stressed in Franz Schurmann, *Ideology and Organization in Communist China,* 2d enl. ed. (Berkeley: University of California Press, 1968). The best study of mass organizations is James R. Townsend, *Political Participation in Communist China* (Berkeley: University of California Press, 1967).

On the problems of administration, see Harry Harding, *Organizing China* (Stanford, Calif.: Stanford University Press, 1982). On the inner politics of cadres, see Lucian W. Pye, *The Dynamics of Chinese Politics* (Cambridge, Mass.: Oelgeschlager, Gunn & Hain, 1981).

On the politics of particular localities, see Ezra Vogel, *Canton under Communism* (Cambridge, Mass.: Harvard University Press, 1969); and Lynn T. White, *Careers in Shanghai* (Berkeley: University of California Press, 1974).

IDEOLOGY AND THOUGHT REFORM

The classic and rather grim study is Robert J. Lifton, *Thought Reform and the Psychology of Totalism: A Study of "Brainwashing" in China* (New York: Norton, 1961). Others that stress more the problems of intellectuals include Theodore H. F. Chen, *Thought Reform of the Chinese Intellectuals* (Hong Kong: Hong Kong University Press, 1960); Roderick MacFarquhar, *The Hundred Flowers Campaign and the Chinese Intellectuals* (1960; reprinted New York: Octagon, 1973); and Merle Goldman, *Literary Dissent in Communist China* (New York: Atheneum, 1971). On the role of the mass media see Frederick T. C. Yu, *Mass Persuasion in Communist China* (New York: Praeger, 1964); Franklin W.

Houn, *To Change a Nation: Propaganda and Indoctrination in Communist China* (Glencoe, Ill.: Free Press, 1961); and Alan P. Liu, *Communications and National Integration in Communist China* (Berkeley: University of California Press, 1971).

General treatment of Communist ideology and Mao's Thoughts include Stuart Schram, *The Political Thought of Mao Tse-tung*, rev. ed. (New York: Praeger, 1969); Arthur A. Cohen, *The Communism of Mao Tse-tung* (Chicago: University of Chicago Press, 1964); James Chieh Hsiung, *Ideology and Practice: The Evolution of Chinese Communism* (New York: Praeger, 1970); and Chester C. Tan, *Chinese Political Thought in the Twentieth Century* (New York: Doubleday, 1971).

An excellent analysis of cultural politics and literary dissent is Merle Goldman, *China's Intellectuals: Advice and Dissent* (Cambridge, Mass.: Harvard University Press, 1982). On the behavior of students, see Susan Shirk, *Competitive Comrades* (Berkeley: University of California Press, 1982).

POLICY AREAS

A good introduction to a wide range of Chinese Communist policies is to be found in Franklin W. Houn, *A Short History of Chinese Communism* (Englewood Cliffs, N.J.: Prentice-Hall, 1973). Agricultural policy is presented in Kenneth R. Walker, *Planning in Chinese Agriculture* (London: Cass, 1965); and Chao Kuo-chun, *Agrarian Policy of the Chinese Communist Party* (Bombay: Asia Publishing House, 1960). The most detailed treatment of the economy is Audrey Dannithorne, *China's Economic System* (London: Allen and Unwin, 1967). See an excellent general analysis in Alexander Eckstein, *Communist China's Economic Growth and Foreign Trade: Implications for U.S. Policy* (New York: McGraw-Hill, 1966). See also Barry M. Richman, *Industrial Society in Communist China* (New York: Random House, 1969); T. C. Liu and K. C. Yeh, *The Economy of the Chinese Mainland: National Income and Economic Development, 1933–1959* (Princeton, N.J.: Princeton University Press, 1965); Alexander Eckstein, Walter Galenson, and Ta-chung Liu, eds., *Economic Trends in Communist China* (Chicago: Aldine, 1968); Dwight H. Perkins, *Market Control and Planning in Communist China* (Cambridge, Mass.: Harvard University Press, 1966); and Alexander Eckstein, *China's Economic Development: The Interplay of Scarcity and Ideology* (Ann Arbor: University of Michigan Press, 1975).

The best sources of data on the Chinese economy are the *Almanac of China's Economy in 1981*, compiled by the Economic Research Center, the State Council of the People's Republic of China, and the State Statistical Bureau; Xue Muqiao, editor-in-chief (dist.: Cambridge, Mass.: Ballinger); and Willy Kraus, *Economic Development and Social Change in the People's Republic of China* (New York: Springer Verlag, 1982).

PERSONALITIES AND BIOGRAPHIES

For biographical information that covers Communist leaders as well as pre-Communist figures, see Howard L. Boorman and Richard C. Howard, eds., *Biographical Dictionary of Republican China,* 4 vols. (New York: Columbia University Press, 1967–1971). For Communist figures alone see Donald Klein and Anne B. Clark, *Biographical Dictionary of Chinese Communism, 1921–1965,* 2 vols. (Cambridge, Mass.: Harvard University Press, 1970). For more general treatment of the main leaders see Robert S. Elegant, *China's Red Masters: Political Biographies of the Chinese Communist Leaders* (1951; reprinted Westport, Conn.: Greenwood, 1971); Martin Eban, *Lin Piao* (New York: Stein and Day, 1970); Nym Wales, *Red Dust: Autobiographies of Chinese Communists* (Stanford, Calif.: Stanford University Press, 1952); Robert Payne, *Mao Tse-tung,* 3d rev. ed. (New York: Weybright, 1969); Stuart Schram, *The Political Thought of Mao Tse-tung,* rev. ed. (New York: Praeger, 1969); Lucian W. Pye, *Mao Tse-tung: The Man in the Leader* (New York: Basic Books, 1976); and Lowell Dittmer, *Liu Shao-ch'i and the Chinese Cultural Revolution* (Berkeley: University of California Press, 1974). An extraordinary history of modern China based on a series of biographies is Jonathan D. Spence, *The Gate of Heavenly Peace* (New York: The Viking Press, 1981).

PARTY POLITICS

See A. Doak Barnett, ed., *Chinese Communist Politics in Action: Studies in Chinese Government and Politics* (Seattle: University of Washington Press, 1969); John M. Lindbeck, ed., *China: Management of a Revolutionary Society* (Seattle: University of Washington Press, 1971); and Parris H. Chang, *Power and Policy in China* (University Park: Pennsylvania State University Press, 1975). For policies and politics as reflected at the local level, see Ezra F. Vogel, *Canton under Communism* (New York: Harper & Row, 1971). See also John W. Lewis, *Leadership in Communist China* (Ithaca, N.Y.: Cornell University Press,

1963); Roderick MacFarquhar, ed., *China under Mao* (Cambridge, Mass.: MIT Press, 1966); and William T. Liu, ed., *Chinese Society under Communism: A Reader* (New York: Wiley, 1966).

FOREIGN POLICY

The classic study is still A. Doak Barnett, *Communist China and Asia: Challenge to American Policy* (Mystic, Conn.: Verry, 1960). For a detailed analysis see Harold C. Hinton, *Communist China in World Politics* (Boston: Houghton Mifflin, 1966); and the same author's *China's Turbulent Quest: An Analysis of China's Foreign Policy Since 1945*, rev. ed. (New York: MacMillan, 1973). On Chinese military policy see John Gittings, *The Role of the Chinese Army* (London: Oxford University Press, 1967); Alice Langley Hsieh, *Communist China's Strategy in the Nuclear Era* (Englewood Cliffs, N.J.: Prentice-Hall, 1962); and Samuel B. Griffith II, *The Chinese People's Liberation Army* (New York: McGraw-Hill, 1967). On the Sino-Soviet dispute see two studies by William E. Griffith, *The Sino-Soviet Rift* (Cambridge, Mass.: MIT Press, 1964); and *Sino-Soviet Relations, 1964–1965* (Cambridge, Mass.: MIT Press, 1967); and Robert S. Elegant, *Mao's Great Revolution* (New York: World Publishing, 1971).

THE CULTURAL REVOLUTION

Numerous books have been written either about or climaxing with the Cultural Revolution. The best include: Edward E. Rice, *Mao's Way* (Berkeley: University of California Press, 1972); Stanley Karnow, *Mao and China: From Revolution to Revolution* (New York: Viking Press, 1972); Thomas W. Robinson, ed., *The Cultural Revolution in China* (Berkeley: University of California Press, 1971); and Alan P. Liu, *Political Culture and Group Conflicts in Communist China* (Santa Barbara, Calif.: Clio Press, 1976).

There have also been some excellent eyewitness accounts, including those of participants. Liang Heng and Judith Shapiro, *Son of the Revolution* (New York: Alfred A. Knopf, 1983); Ken Ling, *The Revenge of Heaven* (New York: Ballantine, 1972); Gordon A. Bennett and Ronald N. Monteparto, *Red Guard: The Political Biography of Dai Hsiao-ai* (Garden City, N.Y.: Doubleday, 1972); and Neale Hunter, *Shanghai*

Journal: An Eyewitness Account of the Cultural Revolution (Boston: Beacon Press, 1971).

Specialized studies include Philip Bridgham, "Mao's 'Cultural Revolution': Origin and Development," *China Quarterly* 29 (January 1967); Philip Bridgham, "Mao's Cultural Revolution in 1967: The Struggle to Seize Power," *China Quarterly* 34 (April 1968); Harold Hinton, "The Beginning of the Cultural Revolution," in Lucian W. Pye, ed., *Cases in Comparative Politics: Asia* (Boston: Little, Brown, 1970); Richard Baum, "China: Year of the Mangoes," *Asian Survey* 9 (January 1969); Chalmers Johnson, "Lin Piao's Army and Its Role in Chinese Society," *Current Scene* 4 (July 1 and 15, 1966); Charles Neuhauser, "The Chinese Communist Party in the 1960s: Prelude to the Cultural Revolution," *China Quarterly* 32 (October 1967); Michel Oksenberg, "China: Forcing the Revolution to a New Stage," *Asian Survey* 7 (June 1967); Thomas W. Robinson, *The Wuhan Incident: Local Strife and Provincial Rebellion During the Cultural Revolution,* P-4511 (Santa Monica, Calif.: The Rand Corporation, 1970); and Hong Yung Lee, *The Politics of the Chinese Cultural Revolution* (Berkeley: University of California Press, 1978).

SUMMARY INTERPRETATIONS OF MODERN CHINA

A provocative comparative interpretation of China and Russia is Klaus Mehnert, *Peking and Moscow* (London: Weidenfeld and Nicolson, 1963). A very imaginative and solid interpretation of Maoism and Chinese culture is Richard H. Solomon, *Mao's Revolution and the Chinese Political Culture* (Berkeley: University of California Press, 1971). See also Lucian W. Pye, *The Spirit of Chinese Politics: A Psychocultural Study of the Crisis in Political Development* (Cambridge, Mass.: MIT Press, 1968).

The opening of China to more visitors had produced both travel accounts and pictorial presentations that combine the present scene and China's artistic treasures. For reports of trips, see Norma Lundholm Djerassi, *Glimpses of China from a Galloping Horse: A Woman's Journal* (New York: Pergamon Press, 1974); and Jerome Alan Cohen and Joan Lebold Cohen, *China Today and Her Ancient Treasures* (New York: Abrams, 1974). For a combination of a thoughtful evaluation of the current scene and a consideration of future prospects, see A. Doak Barnett, *Uncertain Passage: China's Transition to the Post-Mao Era* (Washington, D.C.: Brookings, 1974).

Western reporters stationed in China have begun to provide realistic accounts of daily life there. In particular, see David Bonavia, *The Chinese* (New York: Lippincott and Crowell, 1980); Richard Bernstein, *From the Center of the Earth* (Boston: Little, Brown, 1982); and Fox Butterfield, *China: Alive in the Bitter Sea* (New York: Times Books, 1982).

Index